ALGORITHMS FOR THE PEOPLE

Algorithms for the People

DEMOCRACY IN THE AGE OF AI

JOSH SIMONS

PRINCETON UNIVERSITY PRESS

PRINCETON & OXFORD

Published by Princeton University Press
41 William Street, Princeton, New Jersey 08540
99 Banbury Road, Oxford OX2 6JX

press.princeton.edu

All Rights Reserved

ISBN 978-0-691-24400-6
ISBN (e-book) 978-0-691-24491-4

British Library Cataloging-in-Publication Data is available

Editorial: Matt Rohal
Production Editorial: Jill Harris
Jacket Design: Chris Ferrante
Production: Erin Suydam
Publicity: Kate Hensley and Charlotte Coyne
Copyeditor: Cynthia Buck

Jacket images: Shutterstock / VectorStock / Suzy Bennett (Alamy Stock Photo)

This book has been composed in Arno

Printed on acid-free paper. ∞

Printed in the United States of America

10 9 8 7 6 5 4 3 2 1

For Leah

CONTENTS

ALGORITHMS FOR THE PEOPLE

Introduction

"WE DEFINITELY oversample the poor," explains Erin Dalton, deputy director of the Data Analysis Department in Allegheny County, Pennsylvania. "All of the data systems we have are biased. We still think this data can be helpful in protecting kids."[1] Erin is describing the Children, Youth, and Families (CYF) office's Allegheny Family Screening Tool (AFST). This machine learning algorithm mines a database to predict the risk of a child suffering abuse or neglect, producing a score from 1 (lowest risk) to 20 (highest risk). When CYF receives a call reporting possible abuse, a caseworker notes down the details and performs a screening on AFST. If the risk is deemed high enough, a social worker is sent to the child's home. The stakes are high. One in four children experience some form of abuse or neglect in their lifetime. Almost two thousand die across the country every year.[2]

Allegheny County wanted to use its impressive, integrated database to reduce the number of cases of violent maltreatment that were reported but mistakenly ignored and to tackle stubborn racial disparities in child welfare provision. Over several years, with exemplary care and consideration, the county engaged some of the world's best computer scientists, brought in local stakeholders and community leaders, and commissioned regular technical and ethical reviews. And yet AFST still seemed to replicate patterns of racial and economic inequality, disproportionately subjecting poorer, African American families to unwanted and often unnecessary supervision. In Allegheny County, 38 percent of all calls to the maltreatment hotline concern Black children, double the expected rate based on their population. Eight in every 1,000 Black children have been placed outside their home, compared to 1.7 in every 1,000 white children. As one mother explains, frequent visits from investigating authorities can be frustrating: "'Why are you so angry?'" they ask me, 'Because I am tired of you being here! Leave me alone. I'm trying to get you to go away. We want you to go away.'"[3]

As more of our physical world is converted into numerical data, and more of our behavior is measured, recorded, and predicted, institutions will have strong incentives to widen the range of decisions supported or supplanted by predictive tools, imperceptibly narrowing the spheres in which judgment, empathy, and creativity are exercised and encouraged. As AFST has been fed more data, the "accuracy" with which it predicts "bad outcomes" has steadily increased. "Getting them to trust," explains Erin Dalton, "that a computer screen is telling them something real is a process." Caseworkers are now given less scope to exercise professional judgment and ignore AFST's risk predictions.[4]

In the real world, the design and use of predictive tools like AFST is often messier, more confused, and much less glamorous than the utopian or dystopian visions of AI in movies or novels. Officials find themselves frustrated by poor-quality data and the need to direct technical choices they do not fully understand. Computer scientists feel confused by vague rules and laws and are acutely aware that building predictive tools involves moral and political choices they are not equipped to make. Citizens subject to their predictions feel disempowered by predictive tools, unable to understand or influence their inner logic. Although you cannot always "teach people how you want to be treated," as Pamela Simmons explains of child welfare services, "sometimes you can change their opinion." As she points out, "there's the opportunity to fix it with a person," whereas with AFST, you "can't fix that number."[5]

Three important gaps often fuel these feelings of frustration, confusion, and disempowerment. There is an experience gap between those who build predictive tools and those who use them to make decisions: computer scientists rarely know what it is like to make decisions as a social worker or police officer, as a judge or parole board, as a content moderator or campaign manager. The accountability gap between those in positions of responsibility and those who actually design predictive tools leaves those with responsibility unable or unwilling to justify design choices to the citizens whose lives they shape. Finally, a language gap makes it harder to bridge the experience and accountability gaps: those in positions of responsibility, whether a CEO who wants to make hiring more efficient or a local government leader who wants to further the cause of racial justice, rarely understand the language of computer science in which choices that implicate values and interests are articulated.

These gaps matter because our lives are increasingly structured by the moments in which people in institutions make choices about how to design and use predictive tools. The lives of families in Allegheny County have been shaped by the moment when computer scientists responded to the county's request for proposals, and then by the moment when they sat with county leaders and CYF staff to make choices about AFST's design. The lives of criminal defendants across the country have been shaped by the moments when local officials decided whether to purchase tools that predict the likelihood that they will reoffend, then by the moment when those officials decided how those tools should be used to inform decisions. The lives of citizens who communicate on Facebook and access information on Google have been shaped by the moments when engineers and policy teams sat down to translate the requirements of the First Amendment or civil rights law into choices about the design of the machine learning systems used in ranking and content moderation. As predictive tools become ever more ubiquitous, the pursuit of justice and democracy will depend in part on how we bridge these gaps of experience, accountability, and language.

I have spent my career bridging these gaps, translating between computer scientists and those in positions of responsibility in technology companies, governments, and academia. Too often, choices about the design of predictive tools are driven by common misunderstandings about the fundamental terms of computer science, as well as by only a vague understanding of what existing laws and values mean for data analytics that often obscures deeper and more intractable political disagreements that ought to be surfaced and debated. If the effects of the widespread use of predictive tools on our society, economy, and democracy depend on how we design and deploy them, we must pursue a vision for technology regulation that goes beyond theorizing the "ethics of AI" and wrestles with fundamental moral and political questions about how technology regulation supports the flourishing of democracy. That is what this book aims to do.

The starting point is establishing a clearer understanding of predictive tools themselves. We need to get under the hood of prediction. I do this by exploring one kind of predictive tool: machine learning. Machine learning is a collection of techniques and methods for using patterns in data to make predictions: for instance, what kinds of allegations of child abuse turn out to be serious, what kinds of people tend to reoffend, or what kinds of advertisements people tend to click on. Wherever institutions can use predictions to inform decisions, or reframe decisions as exercises in prediction, machine learning can be a powerful tool. But the effects of machine learning depend on choices about the design of machine learning models and the uses of their predictions to make decisions. Child welfare agencies can use machine learning in ways that unintentionally reinforce poverty and racial injustice, or they can use it to empower experienced staff and promote social equality. Internet platforms can use machine learning either to drive short-term engagement and fragment public debate or to encourage shared understanding and experiment with innovative forms of collective decision-making.

Unlike other works on the subject, this book does not assume that the challenges posed by machine learning are new just because the technology is. It articulates a different starting point, a fundamental truth buried in the language of statistics and computer science: machine learning is political. Choices about how to use data to generate predictions and how to use predictions to make decisions involve trade-offs that prioritize some interests and values over others. And because machine learning increases the scale and speed at which decisions can be made, the stakes of these choices are often immense, shaping the lives of millions and even billions of people at breakneck speed.[6]

Machine learning shifts the point at which humans control decisions. It enables people to make not just individual decisions but choices about how decision procedures are structured. When machine learning is used to rank applicants for a job and invite the top 50 percent for interviews, humans exercise control not in deciding which individual candidates to interview, but in designing the model—selecting the criteria it will use to rank candidates and the proportion it will invite to be interviewed. It is not call screeners' decisions about individual allegations of abuse and neglect that shape the lives of millions of families across Allegheny County, but choices about how AFST is designed and how call screeners are instructed to use it to make decisions.[7]

By forcing institutions to make intentional choices about how they design decision procedures, machine learning often surfaces disagreements about previously implicit or ignored values, goals, and priorities. In Allegheny County, the process of building and integrating AFST encouraged a debate about how call screeners should make decisions. Caseworkers felt that decisions should be based on the severity of the allegation, whether it was that a child had been left to play in the street unwatched or had been physically abused, whereas supervisors tended to think that one-off incidents could be misleading and were often misunderstood by those who made referral calls. They preferred to focus on patterns in administrative data that could be used to generate predictions of individual risk. CYF's managers realized that they wanted call screeners to approach their decisions differently, to focus less on the severity of the allegation in the referral and more on the risk to the people involved. As Erin Dalton explains: "It's hard to change the mind-set of the screeners. . . . It's a very strong, dug-in culture. They want to focus on the immediate allegation, not the child's future risk a year or two down the line. They call it clinical decision-making. I call it someone's opinion."[8]

Similar debates revolve around many of the cases we explore. Whether in the provision of child welfare services, the criminal justice system, or policing, or in the ranking of content on Facebook and Google, designing and integrating machine learning models forces institutions to reflect on the goals of their decision-making systems and the role that prediction should play in them. As more and more decisions are made using prediction, we must engage in public arguments about what different institutions are for, what responsibilities they have, and how decision-making systems should reflect those purposes and responsibilities. This book offers a framework to guide that endeavor. I use the tools of political theory to sharpen our reasoning about what makes machine learning political and what its political character means for regulating the institutions that use it.

By starting with the political character of machine learning, I hope to sketch a systematic political theory of machine learning and to move debates about AI and technology regulation beyond theorizing the ethics of AI toward asking questions about the flourishing of democracy itself. Approaching machine learning through the lens of political theory casts new light on the question of how democracies should govern political choices made outside the sphere of representative politics. Who should decide if statistical tools that replicate racial inequalities in child welfare provision or gender inequalities in online advertising can be justified? According to what criteria? As part of what process? How should Google justify ranking systems that control access to information? Who should determine whether that justification is satisfactory? Should Facebook unilaterally decide how to use machine learning to moderate public debate? If not, who should, and how? By following the threads of machine learning models used in different kinds of organizations, we wrestle with fundamental questions about the pursuit of a flourishing democracy in diverse societies that have yet to be satisfactorily answered.

Above all, my aim is to explore how to make democracy work in the coming age of machine learning. Our future will be determined not by the nature of machine learning itself—machine learning models simply do what we tell them to do—but by our commitment to regulation that ensures that machine learning strengthens the foundations of democracy. Our societies have become too unequal and lack an appreciation of the political goals of laws and regulations designed to confront entrenched divisions of race, gender, class, and geography. Fear of the uncertainties involved in empowering citizens in processes of participatory decision-making has drained public institutions and public spaces of power and agency. How we govern machine learning could exacerbate these ills, but it could also start to address them. By making visible how and why machine learning concentrates power in courts, police departments, child welfare services, and internet platforms, I want to open our imaginations to alternative futures in which we govern institutions that design and use machine learning to support, rather than undermine, the flourishing of democracy.

The Structure of the Argument

This book is structured in two halves. Each half follows a similar structure but explores machine learning systems used in two different contexts: I examine the political character of machine learning, critique existing proposals for governing institutions that design and use it, and outline my own constructive alternative. In both halves, I argue that existing proposals restrict our capacity to wrestle with the connections between political values and choices in machine learning, and that to govern machine learning to support the flourishing of democracy we must establish structures of political oversight that deliberately keep alive the possibility of revision and experimentation.

The first half of the book explores the machine learning systems used to distribute social benefits and burdens, such as in decisions about child protection, loan applications, bail and parole, policing, and digital advertising. In chapter 1, I describe the specific choices involved in designing and integrating machine learning models into decision-making systems, focusing on how AFST is designed and used in CYF's decisions about investigating allegations of abuse and neglect. I show that the choices involved in machine learning require trade-offs about who wins and who loses, and about which values are respected and which are not. When patterns of social inequality are encoded in data, machine learning can amplify and compound inequalities of power across races, genders, geographies, and socioeconomic classes. Because predictions are cloaked in a veneer of scientific authority, these inequalities can come to seem inexorable, even natural, the result of structures we cannot control rather than social processes we can change. We must develop structures of governance that ensure the design and use of machine learning by institutions to advance equality rather than entrench inequality.

Common responses to this problem are to impose mathematical formalizations of fairness, which I explore in chapter 2, or to apply the law and concept of discrimination, the subject of chapter 3. Underpinning both responses is the idea that if characteristics like race and gender are not morally relevant to the distribution of benefits and burdens, decision-making systems should be blind to those characteristics. Despite its superficial appeal, this idea can lead us to avoid political arguments about when and why people should be treated differently to address structural disadvantages that are corrosive of equal citizenship. In chapter 4, I propose a structure for governing decision-making that, animated by the ideal of political equality, invites us to confront rather than ignore questions about the moral relevance of difference and disadvantage.

The second half of the book explores the machine learning systems used to distribute ideas and information. In chapter 5, I look at the design of ranking systems that use machine learning to order the vast quantities of content or websites that show each time you load Facebook or searches on Google. Because people are more likely to engage with content ranked higher in their newsfeed or search results, ranking systems influence the outcomes they are meant to predict: you engage with content that Facebook predicts you are likely to engage with because that content is displayed at the top of your newsfeed, and you read websites that Google predicts you are likely to read because those websites are displayed at the top of your search results. Building these ranking systems involves choices about the goals that should guide the design of the public sphere and the civic information architecture.

In chapter 6, I argue that Facebook's and Google's machine learning systems have become part of the infrastructure of the digital public sphere, shaping how citizens engage with one another, access information, organize to drive change, and make collective decisions. Their unilateral control over these ranking systems involves a distinctive kind of infrastructural power. Unlike railroads or electricity cables, Facebook's newsfeed and Google's search results not only enable people to do what they want to do but shape what people want to do. Ranking systems mold people in their image, commandeering people's attention and shaping their capacity to exercise collective self-government. We must develop structures of governance within which corporations design infrastructural ranking systems that create a healthy public sphere and civic information architecture.

The common response to the infrastructural power of Facebook and Google is to invoke competition and privacy law. I argue that the goals of protecting competition and privacy are of instrumental, not intrinsic, importance: they matter because and insofar as they support the flourishing of democracy. We should instead begin by analyzing the distinctive kind of power that Facebook and Google exercise when they build ranking systems powered by machine learning. I propose that structures of participatory decision-making should be built into every stage of Facebook's and Google's design of machine learning systems, allowing for deliberate experimentation and social learning about how best to support the flourishing of democracy in the design of infrastructural ranking systems. I call this the democratic utilities approach.

The two halves of the book connect two debates in political philosophy, law, and computer science that are too often considered separately: fairness and discrimination in machine learning and competition policy and privacy law in the regulation of Facebook and Google. Those interested only in debates about fairness and discrimination in machine learning can read chapters 1 through 4, and those interested only in debates about regulating Facebook and Google can read chapters 5 through 8, but anyone interested in how democracy can flourish in the age of AI should read both.

My motivating question connects these two debates: If our aim is to secure the flourishing of democracy, how should we govern the power to predict? Because machine learning is political, the pursuit of superficially neutral, technocratic goals will embed particular values and interests in the decision-making systems of some of our most fundamental institutions. The regulatory structures that we build must enable deliberate experimentation and revision that encourage us to wrestle with the connections between fundamental political values and choices in machine learning, rather than prevent us from doing so, for it is those connections that will determine the kind of future we build using machine learning. As the legal scholar Salomé Viljoen argues, machine learning raises "core questions [of] democratic governance: how to grant people a say in the social processes of their own formation, how to balance fair recognition with special concern for certain minority interests, what level of civic life achieves the appropriate level of pooled interest, how to not only recognise that data production produces winners and losers, but also develop institutional responses to these effects."[9]

A book about the politics of machine learning therefore becomes an argument about making democracy work in a society of immense complexity. To ensure that we pay unwavering attention to the political choices buried in technical systems, we must avoid forms of political oversight that constrict our capacity to discuss and make decisions together about value-laden choices and instead embed forms of participatory decision-making every step of the way: in designing machine learning models, in setting standards and goals, and in governing the institutions that set those standards and goals. My proposals for reforming civil rights and equality law and for regulating Facebook and Google are not meant to be definitive statements about regulatory policy, but rather prior arguments about how to structure the institutions and processes we develop to regulate machine learning *given* its unavoidably political character. My goal is to show how democracies should regulate the power to predict if the overarching aim is to secure and promote the flourishing of democracy itself.

A political theory of machine learning illuminates how to think about uses and abuses of prediction from the standpoint of democracy. Attempts to govern the power to predict through technocratic regulations that aspire to exercise state power with neutrality, such as by conceiving of the state as the arbiter of fair decision-making, or by conceiving of the state as the protector of economic competition and personal privacy, will make the governance of prediction a matter not for public argument but for expert decree.

Only by wrestling with the political character of machine learning can we engage with the political and morally contestable character of debates about how to use prediction to advance equality and create a healthy public sphere and civic information architecture. There is no way to design predictive tools that can get around these moral and political debates; in other words, there is no technological solution to how we should govern the power of prediction. Instead of asking questions about the implications of technology for democracy, as if we were passive agents who need protection from the inexorable forces of technology and the institutions that build it, this book asks what a flourishing democracy demands of technology regulation.

My Approach

When I started reading philosophy and political theory, I often wished that scholars would explain how their experience has shaped their arguments. It seemed obvious that political theory was shaped by experience and emotion as well as by analytic rigor, so why not be reflective and open about it? My work in an unusual combination of spheres is central to the argument and approach of this book, so I want to explain, briefly, where I am coming from.

I started thinking about how to regulate data mining while working in the UK Parliament. In 2016, Parliament was scrutinizing the Investigatory Powers

(IP) Bill, the United Kingdom's legislative framework for governing how the intelligence agencies collect and process personal data. Alongside Sir Keir Starmer MP, Tom Watson MP, and Andy Burnham MP, I was working to ensure that judges as well as politicians signed off on requests by intelligence agencies for data collection and analysis. The more I spoke to people in intelligence agencies the more I saw the enormous gulf between what was happening in practice—mass data collection and processing, with limited oversight or evidence about how effective it was—and the public debate about the legislation. It became clear that identifying and articulating political questions about how data are used to make decisions required understanding predictive tools themselves.[10]

After I moved to the United States for my PhD, I quickly enrolled in an introductory machine learning class. Much of what I read went over my head, but a basic training in statistics was enough to help me appreciate the moral and political stakes of debates in computer science about the design of machine learning models. And yet, when I looked around, almost everyone writing about it was either a computer scientist or a lawyer. Few political theorists were seriously engaging with questions about what prediction is, how predictive tools should be designed, or how institutions that build and use them should be governed. So I set about reading all the computer science I could.

Soon after, I began working at Facebook. There I was a founding member of what became the Responsible AI (RAI) team, which needed people with multidisciplinary backgrounds that included ethics and political theory. Over four years at Facebook, I worked with the teams that built many of Facebook's major machine learning systems, including the newsfeed ranking system and the advertising delivery system. The second half of the book uses this experience to explore what makes Facebook's and Google's machine learning systems political and the concrete choices that Facebook and Google make in designing them.[11]

These experiences convinced me of three things. First, the salient moral and political questions about prediction depend on choices made by computer scientists in designing predictive tools. Second, those choices are shaped by the institutional context in which they are made: the policies and culture of a company or public body, the temperament of those who lead it, and the processes established to run it. Third, this institutional context is itself shaped by law and regulation. Any compelling and principled account of how to regulate institutions that use predictive tools must start by reckoning with how they work in practice and are built.

This combination of experience in politics and policy, AI teams in big technology companies, and scholarly training in political theory motivates the argument of this book. If I had lacked any one of these experiences, I doubt I would have thought in quite the same way about the connections between the design of predictive tools, institutional context, and law. To the extent that my approach is illuminating, it is because I have been fortunate enough to see through the eyes of those who build predictive tools, those who lead the companies that build them, and those who are responsible for regulating them.

By using these experiences to imagine what things would look like if political theorists were steering debates about technology regulation, I hope to generate new questions for political theorists, computer scientists, and lawyers. For political theorists and philosophers, my goal is to offer a clear sense of the central moral and political questions about prediction and a strong argument about how to answer them. For computer scientists, my goal is to pose new questions for technical research based on a sharp sense of how technical concepts connect to familiar political ideals. And because my goal is to reframe concepts that underpin current legal approaches to the governance of technology, I should acknowledge to lawyers that many of the legal and policy implications of my argument are often orthogonal to, and sometimes at odds with, existing fields of discrimination, competition, and privacy law. Future work will develop more finely tuned policy interventions.[12]

My approach to this subject is also the result of my background. Although this book is a work of political theory and philosophy, it is also intended as a work of political strategy. My life is devoted to the practice and study of politics, and proposals for political reform succeed when the right coalitions can be built around them. At several junctures, my goal is not to advance a definitive argument about a particular law or concept, but to clarify the stakes and pitfalls of particular strategies for reform by interrogating the concepts and arguments that underpin them. I hope to show what the world might look like if we pursue this or that path, and how each path might affect the flourishing of democracy.

Technology regulation is an opportunity, but one we could easily miss. Grasping that opportunity will require computer scientists, political theorists, and lawyers to collaborate to ensure that powerful institutions are explicit about the values and interests they build into their decision-making processes. That will require that politicians and policymakers confront the ambiguities and limits of some fundamental concepts, laws, and institutions that govern public bodies and private companies. By showing how technology regulation and democratic reform are connected, my aim is to offer a compelling approach to one of the great challenges of our time: governing organizations that use data to make decisions—whether police forces or child welfare services, Facebook or Google—in a way that responds to some of the challenges our democracies are facing. Regulating technology and reenergizing democracy are entirely connected. Thinking hard about how we regulate technology sharpens some of what feels anemic and constricted about our democracies. And conversely, technology regulation is an opportunity to reimagine and reanimate democracy in the twenty-first century. Above all, I hope this book offers some compelling ideas about how we might grasp that opportunity with both hands.

1

The Politics of Machine Learning I

No idea is more provocative in controversies about technology and society than the notion that technical things have political qualities. At issue is the claim that the machines . . . can embody specific forms of authority.[1]

—LANGDON WINNER, "DO ARTIFACTS HAVE POLITICS?" (1980)

ALLEGHENY IS A MEDIUM-SIZED Pennsylvania county of about 1.2 million people; Pittsburgh is the county seat. The county has a history of working-class revolt, beginning with the Whiskey Rebellion of 1791, and it was home to the world's first billion-dollar corporation, J. P. Morgan and Andrew Carnegie's U.S. Steel. In 1997, Marc Cherna was hired to run Allegheny County's Children, Youth, and Families (CYF) office, which, as he put it, was "a national disgrace": CYF was processing just 60 adoptions a year, leaving 1,600 children waiting for adoption. Cherna recommended creating a single Department of Human Services (DHS) that would merge several services and house a centralized administrative database. Built in 1999, the database now holds more than a billion records, an average of 800 for each person in the county.[2]

CYF wanted to use these data to improve its decision-making. Too many dangerous cases were being missed, and the stark racial disparities found in cases were deemed worthy of further investigation. When officers receive a call reporting possible abuse, the "callers [often] don't know that much" about the people involved in the allegation, explains Erin Dalton, leaving call screeners with limited information to assess the risk to the child. Prejudice and bias can creep in as callers make unsupported assumptions about Black parents or the neighborhoods in which they live. CYF hoped that, by using data about each person's "history" from the administrative database, call screeners could make "more informed recommendation[s]" to better protect vulnerable children.[3]

After it decided to build a predictive tool, CYF did everything it could to structure a fair and transparent process for designing and adopting this tool, offering an exemplary lesson in bridging the gaps of experience, accountability, and language. The office empowered call screeners to explain to computer scientists designing the tool how they weighed different factors when making decisions. CYF also commissioned academics to develop transparent explanations of the tool, completed an ethical review of the entire decision-making system, and worked closely with community stakeholders.

None of these measures could address underlying racial inequalities in child welfare provision. Across the United States, child protection authorities are disproportionately likely to investigate Black families and disproportionately likely to remove Black children from their homes. When Cherna joined DHS in 1997, Black children and youths made up 70 percent of those in foster care, but only 11 percent of the county's children and youth population. These disparities remain stubbornly high. In 2016 Black children and youths made up 48 percent of those in foster care, but 18 percent of the county's population. CYF found that its predictive tool simply reproduces these disparities and, when it is used to make real-world decisions, compounds them.[4]

This finding prompted CYF to reflect on how decisions were made to investigate allegations of abuse and neglect and on the goals of child protection itself. Caseworkers felt that decisions should be based on the severity of the allegations, whereas supervisors felt that, because one-off incidents are often misunderstood by those who observe them, it would be better to estimate the risk of individuals involved in allegations using past administrative data. Although they appear purely technical, choices involved in machine learning, by prioritizing the interests of some social groups over others and protecting some fundamental values while violating others, raise fundamental questions about the purpose of decision-making. Machine learning is political.[5]

This chapter uses the Allegheny Family Screening Tool (AFST) to explore what machine learning is and why it matters. I begin by examining the appeal of machine learning's two promises of fairness and efficiency, which incentivize institutions to use prediction in decision-making. I then explore what machine learning is and describe the discrete choices involved in designing and using machine learning models. I then argue that machine learning is irreducibly and unavoidably political. Machine learning is a process embedded within institutions that involves the exercise of power in ways that benefit some interests over others and prioritize some values over others. Data mining can map, and machine learning can reflect, the multiple dimensions of inequality with unmatched precision. This exploration of the political character of machine learning sets the foundations for the rest of the book.

The Promise of Machine Learning

Decisions are hinges that connect the past to the future, a point of indeterminacy where, for a brief moment, the future hangs in the balance. We especially experience that indeterminacy when we make big decisions: the stomach flutter when deciding whether to marry someone, or the pang of anxiety when deciding whether to quit a job and move to a different town. Even minor decisions—deciding to fix that persistent warning light in the car, or deciding not to have that extra beer—shape the connection between the past and the future. The capacity to make unexpected decisions in full knowledge of the past, without allowing those decisions to be determined by it, is part of what makes us human.[6]

Machine learning holds two fundamental promises for decision-making: the promise of efficiency and the promise of fairness. The consulting company McKinsey & Company estimates the global value of the efficiency gains offered by machine learning to be worth as much as $6 trillion. McKinsey explores using machine learning for "predictive maintenance, where deep learning's ability to analyze large amounts of high-dimensional data from audio and images can effectively detect anomalies in factory assembly lines or aircraft engines"; or in logistics, to "optimize routing of delivery traffic, improving fuel efficiency and reducing delivery times"; or in retail, where "combining customer demographic and past transaction data with social media monitoring can help generate individualized product recommendations."[7]

Machine learning offers efficiency gains in the public sector too. Machine learning can help government bodies be "more efficient" in "terms of public sector resources and shaping how services [are] delivered," and it can even "play a role in addressing large-scale societal challenges, such as climate change or the pressures of an aging population," which often require the processing of large volumes of information. Machine learning could also "improv[e] how services work, sav[e] time, and offer meaningful choice in an environment of 'information overload.'"[8]

The great obstacle to these efficiency gains is the slow and uneven pace at which machine learning is adopted in practice. Just 21 percent of the businesses that McKinsey surveyed had embedded machine learning in "several parts of the business," and just 3 percent had integrated it "across their full enterprise workflows." There is a growing gap between companies that build their own predictive tools, often large firms in financial services or the technology sector, and the typically smaller firms in education, construction, and professional services that purchase off-the-shelf tools. This gap is fast becoming a significant driver of economic inequality.[9]

The second promise of machine learning is fairer decision-making. In a town hall debate in Boston, Massachusetts, Andrew McAfee, a professor at the Massachusetts Institute of Technology (MIT), argued that an app that uses machine learning to grade students' exams is a fairer way to assign grades than a teacher grading individual exams. "If you think teachers are grading the one-hundredth exam with the same attention as they graded the first," argued McAfee, "I have hard news for you. . . . And if you think that if you gave teachers the exact same exam five years in a row and they would give you the same grade on it, I have really hard news for you." He argued that, instead of having teachers assign grades, subject to irrelevant factors like tiredness, the kind of day they have had, or how much they like a student, machine learning would remove human biases and make decisions with perfect consistency. "Let me assure the students in this room," he concluded, "if you want to be evaluated fairly and objectively, you desperately want that app."[10]

Consistency connects the efficiency and fairness promises of machine learning. Whereas people treat cases differently for all kinds of irrelevant reasons, machine learning models generate predictions with complete consistency, treating cases differently only if they are in fact statistically different for some prediction task. And according to one common view, consistency is what makes decision-making fair. The United Kingdom's Royal Society, for instance, argues that, as well as being "more accurate," machine learning can "be more objective than human[s]," helping to "avoid cases of human error," like issues that "arise where decision-makers are tired or emotional."[11] Or as Erin Dalton explains about AFST, "Humans just aren't good at this. They have their own biases. And so having a tool like this that can help to provide that kind of information to really talented staff really does just change everything."[12] Machine learning promises decision-making that is not only more efficient, but fairer too.

What Is Machine Learning?

Many decisions we make are based on regularities or patterns. I wear my rain-coat because there are dark and ominous clouds (it will probably rain). The United States has just declared war on Iran, so I head to the store to stock up on gas (the price of oil will probably go up). Most of those who make decisions about a child's safety, releasing a defendant on bail, issuing a mortgage, or hiring someone—or even about whether to call an election or go to war—do so in one way or another based on an assessment of probabilities, regularities, and patterns.

Machine learning automates the process of discovering patterns and regularities by training a model to make predictions about an outcome of interest based on structures and patterns in data sets. An algorithm learns from data in which combinations of statistically related attributes serve as reliable predictors of an outcome of interest. Where people are concerned, the aim "is to provide a rational basis upon which to distinguish between individuals and to reliably confer to the individual the qualities possessed by those who seem statistically similar."[13]

I use the term "machine learning" in this book deliberately in order to distinguish my focus on predictive tools from the somewhat slippery, mythical term "artificial intelligence." AI is better thought of as a scientific field rather than as a single technology that aims to build smart machines to achieve particular goals. Machine learning is better thought of, not as a single technology, but as a set of techniques and methods for prediction.[14] Thinking in terms of techniques and methods draws attention to the human choices involved in designing and using predictive tools. As the computer scientist Cynthia Dwork explains, while many "foster an illusion" that algorithmic "decisions" are "neutral, organic, and even automatically rendered without human intervention—reality is a far messier mix of technical and human curating" because data and algorithms reflect choices: "about data, connections, inferences, interpretations, and thresholds."[15]

How predictive tools work depends on how we design and use them. Machine learning is a set of techniques developed by humans that address problems defined by humans, and training is done on data sets that are assembled by humans and reflect the structures, opportunities, and disadvantages of a very human world. This way of thinking about predictive tools helps make visible discrete human choices that shape how machine learning models work.

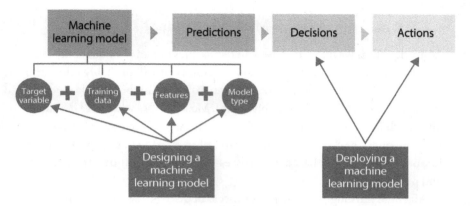

FIGURE 1.1. Building a decision-making procedure that uses machine learning

As Janine, one mother in Allegheny County, put it: "A computer is only what a person puts into it." Our moral, legal, and political analysis should focus on these human choices—which are the focus of much of this book.[16]

We can separate two kinds of choices involved in machine learning. First is a set of choices about the design of a machine learning model, or how data will be used to make predictions: the outcome the model will learn to predict, the data the model will learn from, the features the model will use to predict the outcome, and the training algorithm that will be used to generate the model. The second is a set of choices about the deployment of a machine learning model, or how predictions will be used to make decisions: whether the model will be used to support or supplant human decisions and what actions will result from those decisions.

Predictions

TARGET VARIABLE

The first choice in machine learning is the outcome that a model will learn to predict. An analyst (the person who builds a model) usually has something they want to know about, called the "outcome of interest." This can be simple, such as which emails are spam, or more complex, such as whether candidates for a job would be good employees. The analyst must define a precise proxy for that outcome of interest that can be quantified, measured, and predicted—the "target variable." The art of machine learning lies in turning vague problems in the real world into specific questions about the value of a target variable.[17]

Consider an easy case: building a model to detect spam. Suppose we define "spam," the outcome of interest, as "unwanted email." We need a target variable that serves as a reasonable proxy for unwanted email, something measurable that a model can be trained to predict. The easiest approach would be to use emails labeled as spam to train a model to predict whether new emails have features similar to those already labeled as spam. This is a proxy for the true outcome of interest, which is whether new emails are in fact spam. As definitions of unwanted email change or advertisers develop crafty new ways to make spammy emails look like regular emails, the proxy too must be changed and updated.[18]

Translating a vague problem into a target variable is often complex. Banks must decide whether an individual is sufficiently creditworthy to be offered a loan and what interest rate to attach to that loan. Creditworthiness is not an objective concept that captures something out there in the world, but a concept defined by banks, regulators, and the credit industry that changes with financial conditions and varying appetites for risk. As such, financial institutions exercise considerable discretion in defining the target variable used to predict creditworthiness. The choice of exactly what target variable is predicted by credit default models, and how those predictions are used in loan decisions, will shape who gets what loans.

Defining target variables always involves judgment. Consider how employers might use machine learning in hiring. An employer might define a good employee as someone who makes the most sales, produces the most in the least amount of time, stays in their job the longest, or contributes most to a team's work ethic. Predicting each of these outcomes implies a view about questions of value: the qualities of a good employee, and whether the purpose of employment is to generate revenue, increase production, decrease staff turnover, or boost a firm's morale. All are plausible candidates. Also implied is a prioritization among different interests. If an employer defines the target variable as the predicted length of time a candidate will be in the position, this could produce a model that tends to rank men above women, because, on average, men tend to stay in a position longer than women do.[19] An employer's use of the Myers-Briggs (MBTI) test to predict personality types could also impact genders unequally, since MBTI personality types are distributed unevenly across genders.[20]

Defining the target variable is often the most significant choice in machine learning. It can have profound effects on those subject to a model's predictions. Consider the AFST. The Child Abuse Prevention and Treatment Act, signed into law by President Richard Nixon in 1974, gives states the authority to define abuse and neglect, above a certain minimum definition. There is no way to directly measure abuse and neglect, so AFST uses several proxies.[21]

The original version of AFST used two models that predicted different target variables. The first predicted the likelihood that an allegation of abuse and neglect deemed not to require further investigation (screened out) would be re-referred within two years—the probability of re-referral being conditional on being screened out. The second predicted the likelihood that an allegation of abuse and neglect deemed to require further investigation (screened in) would lead to a child being removed from their home and placed in foster care within two years—the probability of placement being conditional on being screened in. The original AFST system displayed the highest of the two risk scores.[22]

The problem with the first target variable is that it built in discrimination. CYF's own research, in finding that Black families are disproportionately likely to be called in by other residents, identified referral calls as the major source of racial discrimination in the county's child protection system. The model defined "maltreatment" in terms of an activity that CYF knew to be racially biased. As Erin Dalton explains, "We don't have a perfect target variable. We don't think there are perfect proxies for harm."[23]

It is worth dwelling on why the risk of a child being placed in foster care is a better target variable than the risk of re-referral. Placement is an event that CYF directly observes: CYF always knows when a child has been placed in care. Placement is also a better proxy for abuse and neglect, because CYF removes children from their homes only in the most serious cases. Moreover, decisions about placement are made by different people than those making decisions about call screening. As Alexandra Chouldechova, the computer scientist who helped evaluate AFST, explains: "By predicting an outcome that cannot be directly determined by the staff, we reduce the risk of getting trapped in a feedback loop" in which workers "effect the outcome predicted by the model"—for instance, by gathering incriminating evidence about cases the model labels as high-risk. Allegheny County eventually removed the re-referral prediction model from AFST.[24]

TRAINING DATA

Since machine learning is about using data to make predictions, how we understand machine learning depends on how we understand data. Data are often assumed to represent something objective, as if each data point represents a fact: where someone lives, how much they earn, or which welfare pro-grams they use.[25]

Yet data reflect not fixed representations of reality, but human choices about what to measure and how. Data are provisional information whose provenance, presentation, and context require further scrutiny. As the philosopher of statistics Ian Hacking writes, "Society became statistical [through] the enumeration of people and their habits. . . . The systematic collection of data about people has affected not only the ways in which we conceive of a society, but also the ways in which we describe our neighbour. It has profoundly transformed what we choose to do, who we try to be, and what we think of ourselves."[26]

Data reveal patterns about populations. States and corporations measure people not primarily because they want to know about each individual, but because they want to understand the behavior of social groups, societies, and countries. The more data an institution has, the more sophisticated the patterns they can detect and the more effectively they can use those patterns to predict, mold, and control. The power of the world's largest tech companies depends not on more sophisticated machine learning techniques, but on the volume of data they have and the speed and efficiency with which they can gather more. Google is good at detecting spam because it can assemble a data set of billions of labeled examples. The power of machine learning often depends on the volume of training data.[27]

The second step in machine learning is to assemble these training data. Choices about the target variable determine what a model learns to predict, and choices about training data determine what a model learns from. As with defining a target variable, assembling and interpreting data sets requires the exercise of judgment.

Consider the use of predictive tools in the Covid-19 crisis. As soon as the virus hit, scientists began to build models to predict how many could die. The range of predictions was enormous, from 200,000 to 2.2 million in the United States, and from 20,000 to 510,000 in the United Kingdom. Despite the often misleading reporting of these numbers, the range reflected an openness about the limits of what scientists understood about the disease and its spread. Imagine a simple version of a model predicting how many could die from Covid-19 in a country in which deaths are treated as a function of the number of those vulnerable multiplied by the infection rate multiplied by the fatality rate. Each of these variables incorporates a dizzying range of uncertainties.[28]

Take the fatality rate, calculated by dividing the total number of cases by the total number of deaths. Gathering data on these numbers is far from simple. At the start of the pandemic, most countries were vastly underestimating their total number of cases. In the United States and the United Kingdom, where testing was constrained, the number of reported cases was anywhere from three to sixty times fewer than the number of actual cases. Then there were the false positives and false negatives produced by Covid-19 tests. A false positive rate of 4 percent might sound low, but for every one million tests, that could be forty thousand mistakes. Estimating the number of deaths is even more complex. Again, the problem was not just about partial data but about inherent uncertainties in the data-gathering processes. What it meant for a death to be "caused" by Covid-19 was not clear: Should the death of someone in a hospital who had been dying from terminal cancer and tested positive count? Because hospitals were among the first places to get tests, such deaths were among the first cases counted as Covid-19 deaths. But what about my grandma? She died in a care home in Bury, United Kingdom, in April 2020 aged ninety-four. She had a cough and difficulty breathing, yet because there were no tests available at the time, hers was not recorded as a Covid-19 death.[29]

Data represent not facts but judgments. The more you explore data sets, the clearer the judgments involved in constructing them become. One simple input, the death rate, requires countless choices about measuring the infection rate and deciding whose deaths count as Covid-19 deaths. Predictions can obscure the choices involved in assembling data.

Choices about what to measure—and what not to measure—are inextricably bound up with structures of power. Those least likely to produce data trails are often those most excluded by society, as institutions have less interest in gathering data about those who cannot engage in the formal economy. This results in "the non-random, systemic omission of people who live on big data's margins."[30] For instance, Street Bump is an ingenious app built in Boston that uses the accelerometers in smartphones to detect potholes. This can help cut the costs of keeping roads safe. Potholes are most effectively reported, however, in areas where most people have smartphones, that is, in generally wealthier neighborhoods that already have fewer potholes. Relying on the app would cause authorities to reduce services to already underserved, poorer communities. The widespread assumption that data accurately represent a population is more often wrong than right.[31]

AFST is also an example of partial data. In its original form, one-quarter of the variables in AFST's training data set were measures of poverty, while another quarter tracked the juvenile justice system. As a result, AFST was trained on data that disproportionately represented low-income, African American households and excluded the kind of data produced by wealthier, white families, such as private health insurance. "We really hope to get private insurance data. We'd love to have it," explains Erin Dalton. The over- or underrepresentation of a social group in data distorts the predictions of a model trained on that data.[32]

As well as being unrepresentative or biased, data can also capture historic or current prejudice. Three decades ago, St George's Hospital in London developed an algorithm that sorted applicants to its medical school using historic admissions decisions. Those admissions decisions had systematically disfavored women and minorities with equally impressive credentials. The editors of the *British Medical Journal* observed that "the program was not introducing new bias but merely reflecting that already in the system."[33] This is an important point. Machine learning systems reflect historic inequalities. If "prior decisions affected by some form of prejudice serve as examples of correctly rendered determinations, data mining will necessarily infer rules that exhibit the same prejudice."[34] The issue here is not about inaccurate data, but about data that accurately reflect an unjust world. Outcomes produced by machine learning models often reveal underlying social inequalities.

Latanya Sweeney discovered an illustration of data reflecting not historic but current prejudice. Google was more likely to show ads that looked like arrest records when a user searched for a Black-sounding name. This happened not because the companies paying for these ads intended to target Black people, but because Google's "quality score," which it used to rank advertisers' bids, had learned which ads got the most clicks from viewers. Because people searching for Black-sounding names more often clicked on arrest records ads than those searching for white-sounding names, Google was more likely to return arrest records ads in searches for Black-sounding names. Google's results reflected users' prejudices, but in doing so it unintentionally solidified them.[35]

FEATURES

The third choice involved in machine learning is selecting the features to include in a model, sometimes called "attributes."[36] Data never wholly reflect the complexity of a single person, as it "is often impossible to collect all the attributes of a subject or take all the environmental factors into account within a model."[37] Businesses and governments often rely on crude and imperfect proxies. For instance, the car insurance rates of Black families often drop significantly when they move from inner-city neighborhoods to the suburbs, not because anything has necessarily changed about their objective risk (the car might even have been parked in a valet garage), but because insurance companies use reductive features like zip code as proxies for risk. Car insurance rates are also determined as much by the risk of others like you as by your own individual risk. If you happen to be a safer driver than the average young man, or have better eyesight than the average old-age pensioner, then tough luck. Even vast numbers of attributes produce a reductive representation of each person.[38]

Machine learning can avoid some of the worst effects of using coarse, reductive features. Compare the features that a human and a machine learning model might use in hiring. When looking at a person's educational background, humans often focus on the reputation of colleges, even though a college's reputation may say little about the applicant. Applicants from low-income or ethnic minority backgrounds are systematically disfavored if these groups graduate from prestigious colleges at disproportionately low rates. Machine learning can distinguish more granular features that might better predict the target variable—for instance, applicants' grades in courses relevant to the job, regardless of where they went to college. Similarly, in a display of so-called rational racism, humans often use protected attributes because the information they want is hard to obtain. Given racial disparities in conviction rates, employers may consider race where they do not have access to criminal records, even though race is a poor predictor of an individual's criminal record. By learning more sophisticated statistical relationships between features, machine learning can help address rational racism.[39]

Whether or not protected attributes like race are included in a model often makes little difference in machine learning.[40] The features that a model uses to sort people in relation to a target variable—to predict whether a child is at risk of abuse or whether a job applicant will be a good employee—often also sort individuals according to membership in a particular class. Cynthia Dwork calls this "redundant encoding"—when other variables encode information about the members of protected classes.[41] Many criteria "genuinely relevant [to] making rational and well-informed decisions" also "serve as reliable proxies for class membership."[42] For this reason, machine learning can often "discover patterns of lower performances, skills, or capacities protected-by-law groups."[43] Correlations between protected attributes and features like income or conviction rates often reflect patterns of systemic inequality.

These are not examples of machine learning gone wrong because of biased or unrepresentative data, but cases in which data accurately reflected social inequalities and patterns of disadvantage. Organizations may use legitimate criteria—referral calls for Allegheny County or job tenure for employers—but find that those criteria are distributed unevenly between advantaged and disadvantaged groups. If a particular attribute is distributed unevenly across a population, more precise machine learning will simply reflect that distribution more accurately. Data mining can map, and machine learning can reflect, the multiple dimensions of inequality with unmatched precision. Powerful predictive tools illustrate the multiple ways in which our chances in life are shaped by the structure of our social world.

MODEL

The final choice in machine learning is the selection of the model, which involves what may be unfamiliar terms like "logistic regression models," "decision trees," "K nearest neighbour (kNN) classifiers," "random forest models," and "gradient boosting algorithms," like XGBoost. To decide which model to select, an analyst will often randomly split a data set into three components: a training set used to fit the models; a validation set used to decide which model to deploy; and a test set to assess the capacity of the trained model to generalize.[44]

In applied machine learning, model selection often involves trade-offs between complexity, accuracy, and error rates. The original versions of both AFST models used logistic regression fitted to weighted features. The computer scientists who updated the system decided to change the AFST's model, however, because, while more complex random forest and XGBoost algorithms produced slightly more accurate models, simpler LASSOO and logistic regression approaches were easier to implement and easier to debug. In high-stakes settings such as child protection, models that are easier to manage, maintain, and interpret may often be preferable.[45]

Decisions

The effects of predictions depend on how they are used to make decisions. The effects of decisions depend on what kind of actions they produce.[46]

PREDICTIONS TO DECISIONS

The first choice in deploying a model is deciding how to use predictions to make decisions. A model can be used to supplant human decisions, such as when a model ranks job applicants and automatically invites the top half for interviews. Or a model can be used to support human decisions, such as when a model's ranking of applicants is presented to a person who decides whom to invite to interview. Delegating a decision to a model, often called "automation," is itself a choice for which an institution can be held accountable.

Clarity about the goals of decision-making must be achieved before making choices about using predictions in decisions. The DHS in Allegheny County had three goals in introducing AFST. First, DHS wanted to use its administrative database to improve the accuracy of decisions. Before AFST, 52 percent of call-in reports from 2010 to 2016 were judged not to require further investigation (screened out). Of those, 52 percent were re-referred for a new allegation within two years, suggesting that those cases might have benefited from further investigation. Machine learning models often perform much better than people at narrow prediction tasks.[47]

Second, DHS wanted to make decision-making more consistent. Call screeners weighed different information in different ways: some focused on the history of a mother's interaction with the welfare system, while others placed more weight on a father's criminal record. When the county analyzed cases that resulted in significant harm to the child—known as "critical incidents"—it found that multiple referrals had been made in cases that were not deemed to require further investigation. While some of these decisions were defensible in isolation, had call screeners looked at the broader pattern, they would have seen a clear picture of risk. As Chouldechova explains: "The primary aim of introducing a prediction model is to supplement the often limited information received during the call with a risk assessment that takes into account a broader set of information available in the integrated system."[48]

Third, DHS aimed to promote equity. People can be unreliable and unfair in how they make decisions—for instance, by placing disproportionate emphasis on recent cases in which a child was seriously harmed, or by treating a family's address in a high-crime neighborhood as a proxy for parental risk. It can be hard to evaluate what drives particular human decisions, as people impose a retrospective rationality on decisions that involved memory, stories, and emotion.

Because of the stakes of the decision, CYF decided not to use AFST to "replace human decision-making" but to "inform, train, and improve the decisions made by . . . staff." To do so, CYF had to decide how to present AFST's predictions to caseworkers. The agency decided to present AFST's predictions as discrete risk scores ranging from 1 to 20, using a color coding system that begins with green for a score of 1, then gets warmer through shades of yellow and finally red, like a thermometer. These colors convey as much information as the numbers: green means "nothing to see here," while red means "WARNING!" After AFST was deployed, the number of screened-in calls that were investigated increased by 22 percent.[49]

Even the choice to present AFST's predictions as discrete risk scores involved judgments about how call screeners should understand risk. Each number on the AFST scale represents a ventile of the estimated probability distribution, that is, there is a 5 percent chance a case will fall within this category. Because the probability distribution is logistic, risk scores presented to call screeners do not represent linear increases in the underlying risk of placement. The difference between placement risk for scores of 18 and 20 might be significantly greater than the difference in placement risk for scores of 2 and 4, or 12 and 14. The difference between placement risk might be greater for two scores of 19 than for scores of 6 and 10. AFST's scores should not be treated as linear estimates of underlying risk, and yet it is not clear if this has been clearly conveyed to call screeners.[50]

Prediction can change how humans make decisions, subtly displacing the exercise of judgment, empathy, and contextual knowledge. As the writer and antipoverty campaigner Virginia Eubanks, who first explored the AFST case, writes, AFST "is supposed to support human decision-making," and yet, in practice, the algorithm seems to be "training the intake workers."[51] CYF used to require calls with a risk score of 18 or higher (the riskiest 15 percent) to be automatically flagged for further investigation, subject to manager override. Now CYF requires that calls with a score of 16 or higher (the riskiest 25 percent) be automatically flagged, and managers must provide a clear justification for any override. What's more, call screeners are now shown only the requirements for automatic screen-in or screen-out for cases with the lowest and highest risk scores, not their underlying scores. Once a machine learning model has been deployed, there are strong incentives to widen the scope of prediction and narrow the scope for the exercise of human judgment.[52]

DECISIONS TO ACTIONS

Machine learning invites reflection on the connection between decisions and actions. Whereas the link between human decisions and actions is obvious— you fix the warning light after you decide to fix the warning light, and you stop drinking beer after you decide to stop drinking beer—the actions that result from decisions informed by prediction are often less obvious and more contestable. In AFST, a call screener uses risk predictions to decide whether to screen in a call, unless the predicted risk is above 16, when caseworkers are automatically sent to investigate. If the call screener decides that further investigation is required, caseworkers are sent to the child's home to investigate. Depending on what the investigation reveals, families might be required to accept regular visits from child protection services, or a child might be placed in foster care.

The Politics of Machine Learning

It is now commonplace to assert that technologies are never neutral. But rarely do scholars or policymakers explore what that means, or more precisely, why choices about the design of technology involve moral and political judgment. Two notable exceptions that have profoundly influenced this book are Cathy O'Neil's *Weapons of Math Destruction* and Safiya Noble's *Algorithms of Oppression*. Both of these books recognize that choices about the design and use of predictive tools benefit some people but harm others, that they bake in some values but foreclose others. As O'Neil puts it, "Models, despite their reputation for impartiality, reflect goals and ideology. . . . Our own values and desires influence our choices, from the data we choose to collect to the questions we ask. Models are opinions embedded in mathematics."[53]

Interests and Values

There are two senses in which choices in machine learning are political. First, they almost always prioritize the interests of some social groups over others. Consider AFST's choices that reproduced racial disparities in child welfare provision. First was the choice of target variable. Because Black families are disproportionately likely to be referred for reasons not relevant to the underlying risk of abuse and neglect, AFST built in racial bias when it chose to predict the risk of re-referral. Second was the choice of data to include in the training set. Using solely DHS's administrative data, poorer Black families were disproportionately likely to be flagged for investigation, whereas including data that captured information about wealthier families, such as private insurance, or excluding data from the juvenile justice system might have reduced racial disparities. As long as race conditions the opportunities that people are afforded and data sets reflect the outcomes of systemic racism, choosing how to assemble and use training data in machine learning will be unavoidably political.[54]

Second, choices about the design of machine learning models are political because they build in some values but foreclose others. In AFST, designing and integrating the predictive tool prompted CYF to reflect on how decisions about investigating allegations of abuse and neglect should be made. Two competing theories were unearthed. Caseworkers felt that decisions should be based on the severity of the allegation, whether a child was left unattended for a while or was physically abused. Supervisors felt that one-off incidents could be misleading and were often misunderstood by those who made referral calls, preferring to use administrative data to estimate the risk to children of the people involved in an allegation. By focusing on rare but egregious cases that may not be captured by averages, the first approach prioritizes the prevention of the worst kinds of harm. Whereas by focusing on statistical patterns, the second kind focuses on preventing harm to the maximum number of children. Although both approaches are defensible, they imply different views of the purposes of child protection and the values that should guide decisions to investigate allegations of abuse and neglect.[55]

In an unequal and unjust world, there is no way to avoid prioritizing some interests and values over others in the design of machine learning models. CYF hoped AFST would enable better measurement and understanding of racial disparities. "I see a lot of variability," notes Erin Dalton, speaking of call screeners' decisions. "I would not go so far as to say that [AFST] can correct disproportionality, but we can at least observe it more clearly." Yet even with the best of intentions, predictive tools replicate patterns of inequality encoded in data, subjecting disadvantaged groups to the unalterable judgment of predictive systems. The costs can be all too human. As one father described the experience of being investigated: "I didn't think it was fair, but I wasn't going to fight it. I thought maybe if I fought it they would actually come and take her. . . . That's the first thing you think: CYF takes your kids away. It's a very sick feeling in the stomach, especially with the police there. I'll never forget it."[56]

Raising the Stakes

As Cathy O'Neil and Safiya Noble argue, machine learning also increases the scale and speed at which predictions can be used to make decisions. Machine learning raises the stakes of how we structure decision-making; at the same time, because machine learning is a technical process executed by computer scientists, it can obscure underlying moral and political choices. Machine learning both amplifies and obscures the power of the institutions that design and use it. The danger is that the predictions generated by machine learning models all too quickly come to feel inevitable, natural, beyond our power to control.

CONTROL AT SCALE

Because machine learning models make predictions in the same way across time, space, and cases, choices about the design of models fix a certain way of making predictions on an enormous scale. Machine learning models leave no room for discretion or chance or variation; they make predictions in the same way on a much, much bigger scale than has ever previously been possible. Even models used in relatively small geographic areas impose consistency on a much bigger scale than human decision-makers could, raising the stakes of choices about how they are designed.

How individual call screeners make decisions can change over time. Imagine that a call screener goes home over the weekend and reads a series of books about the history of racism in the US welfare system that change her mind about how to weight the factors involved in screening decisions. After returning to work on Monday, she vows to make decisions differently and encourages colleagues to do the same. Such a change cannot happen with predictive tools. The way AFST generates risk predictions is fixed until humans retrain the model with new data or change the target variable it predicts. Whatever prejudice the model embeds is frozen in place, affecting the lives of the 1.2 million residents of Allegheny County. Choices about the design of machine learning models are best compared not to individual human decisions, but to choices about the rules, policies, and even the laws that shape how institutions make decisions on a significant scale.

Many of the examples we explore operate on a much bigger scale than AFST. We examine the models used to predict the risk that someone will reoffend across the United States and the models used by Facebook and Google to moderate content and distribute information that shapes what billions of people across the globe read, see, and hear. By changing the design of Facebook's machine learning models, Mark Zuckerberg can change, with the stroke of a pen, the content that people across the globe see every day. Machine learning makes that scale possible. If the choices involved in machine learning are political, the scale at which machine learning enables decisions to be made raises the stakes of those choices.

CONTROL AT SPEED

Machine learning also enables decisions to be made at immense speed. When Facebook's content moderation or advertising system benefits some social groups over others, or prioritizes some values over others, the speed at which the system operates enables it to make millions of decisions every second, further raising the stakes of how those systems are designed and deployed. The same is true of AFST. A call screener can evaluate a limited set of information about a limited number of cases, but AFST can perform hundreds or thousands of screenings every minute, limited only by the power of Allegheny County's computers.

In many examples we explore, the speed of machine learning becomes even more problematic because predictions influence the outcomes they are meant to predict, creating a kind of feedback loop between predictions, decisions, and actions. Consider AFST. Training AFST on data that disproportionately capture information about poorer, African American families makes it more likely that AFST will flag these families as high risk and subject them to more frequent investigation by authorities. As a result, children from poorer, African American families are placed in foster care at disproportionately high rates, which further increase racial disparities in the measured risk of placement. These data are then fed back into AFST, and the loop begins again. Taking actions based on predictions that reflect patterns of inequality can produce self-reinforcing loops of injustice.[57]

THE OBFUSCATION OF CONTROL

The predictions of machine learning models can quickly come to feel natural or inevitable, obscuring the political character of the human choices that went into their design. As O'Neil puts it, the result of algorithms like AFST is "that we criminalize poverty, believing all the while that our tools are not only scientific but fair."[58]

The politics of machine learning is often buried in the technical details of the choices made in the process of machine learning: deciding what the model will predict, assembling the training data, deciding which features to include, and selecting the model. While machine learning encourages more explicit reasoning about trade-offs in the design of decision procedures, it forces that reasoning to be articulated in technical, quantitative terms. To those not trained in translation between the quantitative and the qualitative, recognizing the implications of technical choices for interests and values can be extremely difficult. Machine learning "is political in the sense that [it helps] to make the world appear in certain ways rather than others. . . . Realities are never given but brought into being and actualised in and through" the design and deployment of machine learning models.[59] How machine learning models are designed and used not only "produces winners and losers," but "define[s] who wins and who loses" and "determine[s] the stakes of winning and losing."[60]

Data reflect the structure of our social world. How we choose to use data to make predictions—the design of machine learning models—and to use predictions to make decisions—the deployment of machine learning models—has an unavoidably political character. By appearing inexorable and immutable, predictions can obscure the uncertainties, as well as the moral and political judgments, involved in generating data. By enabling an institution to exert greater control over how predictions are generated and used on a bigger scale and more quickly than ever before, while hiding that control behind a veil of scientific authority, machine learning both amplifies the power of the institutions that use it and obscures in whose favor that power is exercised and the values on which it is based. Because it may be the most powerful predictive tool humanity has yet invented, machine learning is an excellent case study for interrogating the power of prediction, which it takes to a clarifying extreme. Machine learning has become sufficiently powerful that questions about how we should govern predictive tools have become central to the flourishing of democracy itself.

The fundamental starting point of this book is that predictive tools are political. Unearthing the politics of particular predictive tools requires considerable patience and a willingness to traverse disciplinary and institutional boundaries. The rest of this book explores questions about how democracies should govern the political choices involved in designing and using predictive tools. If predictions could be made from data produced in a world free from injustice, then perhaps we could avoid those questions. But that is not our world.[61]

Performative Prediction

The concept of performative prediction is a useful case study in the political character of machine learning because it illustrates the connections between predictions, decisions, and actions. Moritz Hardt, a computer scientist at Cornell, defines "performative prediction" as what happens when predictions "influence" or "trigger actions that influence the outcome" they aim to predict, such that a model's "prediction causes a change in the distribution of the target variable."[62] Although this idea has been well studied in other contexts, it is relatively new to computer science. We return to it often here.

Imagine a bank using machine learning to predict the probability that loan applicants will default on their loan. The actions the bank takes on the basis of these predictions shape the effects of those actions. Suppose the bank finds that African Americans have higher average rates of loan default. If the interest rate that the bank attaches to loans depends on loan default predictions, such that it assigns higher interest rates to individuals with a higher probability of default, this higher rate could increase the proportion of those individuals who do in fact default. This effect would produce another self-reinforcing loop, because it would increase racial disparities in default rates, further increasing the average interest rate assigned to African Americans; that higher rate, in turn, would increase the proportion who do in fact default. As Hardt writes: "In a self-fulfilling prophecy, the high interest rate further increases the customer's default risk."[63] Actions taken based on a model's predictions (the interest rates attached to loans) can cause outcomes that confirm those predictions (an increasing rate of loan default and default risk).

Understanding performative prediction depends on information that is often hard to obtain, reminding us of the importance of the judgments and uncertainties that underpin data. For instance, in a bid to advance racial justice, suppose the bank pledges to grant an equal proportion of loans to African Americans and white Americans. If a lower proportion of African Americans are in fact unable to repay their loans, this approach would grant loans more generously to African Americans than an unconstrained, optimally accurate model would, effectively offering loans to people who cannot afford to repay them and thus increasing racial disparities in the average default rate. Whereas if the bank's data systematically underestimate the ability of African Americans to repay, granting them an equal proportion of loans makes the bank more generous in granting loans to African Americans who can in fact repay, improving their long-run welfare. The moral and political implications of using predictions to make decisions depend on a fine-grained understanding of the institutional realities in which predictive tools are built and used.[64]

Performative prediction is extremely common in the real world, and one of the most powerful mechanisms by which machine learning can entrench existing social inequalities. When predictions are used to make decisions and actions are taken on the basis of those decisions, predictions themselves can affect the distribution of the outcome being predicted in the population. If predictions are generated from data that reflect patterns of disadvantage, predictions can shape the world in their image, projecting the injustices of the past into the future. As O'Neil argues, "Big Data processes codify the past. They do not invent the future. Doing that requires moral imagination, and that's something only humans can provide. We have to explicitly embed better values into our algorithms, creating Big Data models that follow our ethical lead."[65]

As we explore many cases of performative prediction, let me end with an example that has nothing to do with machine learning. In situations of uncertainty, people tend to use stereotypes to make decisions. In structuring people's incentives, these stereotypes can encourage behavior that confirms the stereotype, fueling a process similar to performative prediction. In robbery, when offenders use visual clues to decide which victims are likely to resist, offenders have an incentive to select victims who hold negative stereotypes about them: "[Whites] got this stereotype, this myth that a black person with a gun or knife is like Idi Amin or Hussein. And [a] person [who believes] that will do anything [you say]."[66]

As a graduate student in Chicago in the 1960s, Brent Staples, later an editor at the *New York Times*, noticed that white stereotypes created an incentive for him to behave in ways that confirmed that stereotype. "I became an expert in the language of fear," he explains. "Couples locked arms and reached for each other's hand when they saw me. Some crossed to the other side of the street." Initially, he would reassure them by whistling Vivaldi's "Four Seasons" and watch "the tension drain from people's bodies. . . . A few even smiled as they passed me in the dark."[67]

"One night," however, Staples "stooped beneath the branches and came up on the other side, just as a couple was stepping from their car into their town house. The woman pulled her purse close with one hand and reached for her husband with the other. The two of them stood frozen. . . . I felt a surge of power. . . . If I'd been younger, I'd have robbed them, and it would have been easy. All I'd have to do was stand silently before them until they surrendered their money."[68] Stereotypes about Black male violence function as performative predictors, shaping the incentives and self-understandings of Black men themselves in ways that encourage them to engage in behavior that confirms the stereotype. Blacks are twenty times more likely to rob whites than whites are

Blacks, and because arrest rates are higher for robbery than for other crimes of theft, a disproportionate number of Black men end up in prison.[69]

There is nothing determinative about performative prediction. It depends on the actions taken on the basis of predictions. After all, Brent Staples chose not to rob that couple. But "by conflating forecasting the future with replicating the past," the risk is that predictive tools make it easy to rationalize "continuing structural inequality."[70]

2

Fairness

A good laboratory, like a good bank or a corporation or government, has to run like a computer. Almost everything is done flawlessly, by the book, and all the numbers add up to the predicted sums. The days go by. And then, if it is a lucky day, and a lucky laboratory, somebody makes a mistake . . . then the action can begin . . . [1]

—LEWIS THOMAS, *THE MEDUSA AND THE SNAIL* (1979)

AN ARTICLE IN 2016 made predictive tools central to debates about race and criminal justice reform. ProPublica, the investigative newsroom, found persistent racial disparities in the error rates of a risk prediction tool used in the criminal justice system across the United States. The piece began with two stories. Brisha Borden was on her way to pick up her god-sister from school in Fort Lauderdale, Florida, when she saw a blue bicycle and a silver scooter. She and her friend tried to ride them down the street, but as they realized the bike and scooter were too small, a woman ran out yelling, "Hey, that's my kid's stuff." They dropped the stuff and walked away, but a neighbor had already called the police. Borden was arrested and charged with petty theft. She was eighteen.

Vernon Prater, who was forty-one, was arrested and charged with shoplifting tools from a Home Depot store. Prater had already been convicted of armed robbery and attempted armed robbery and had served five years in prison, whereas Borden had a much less serious record of juvenile misdemeanors. When the two were admitted to jail, the risk prediction tool labeled Borden as high risk and Prater as low risk. Both predictions turned out to be wrong. Two years later, Borden had not been charged with any new crimes, while Prater was serving an eight-year prison sentence for stealing thousands of dollars of electronics from a warehouse. Borden's prediction was what computer scientists call a false positive: an incorrect prediction of high risk. Prater's was a false negative: an incorrect prediction of low risk. Borden was Black. Prater was white.[2]

Computer scientists have taken different views about the risk prediction tool, fueling a subfield of computer science that explores different mathematical definitions of fairness. This chapter describes four of these definitions of mathematical fairness across social groups, each of which aspires to embody Aristotle's principle of equal treatment: that similarly situated people should be treated similarly and differently situated people differently. I show that the mathematical impossibility of simultaneously achieving fairness according to more than one of these definitions makes the trade-offs involved in using data to make predictions in an unequal world inevitable. Given these inescapable trade-offs, I argue that mathematical definitions of group fairness make two mistakes.

First, mathematical definitions apply equal treatment to the wrong thing. The imperative to treat people as equals applies to human decisions, not machine predictions. Our decision-making goals often do not translate straightforwardly into the design of predictive tools. The moral irrelevance of some characteristics to human decisions does not require forcing those characteristics to be statistically irrelevant to machine predictions; in fact, imposing mathematical definitions of group fairness may sometimes fail to treat people as equals. Group fairness in machine learning is generally orthogonal to, and sometimes actively undermines, equal treatment in human decision-making.

Second, mathematical definitions of group fairness bake a particular interpretation of equal treatment into machine learning models, placing that interpretation beyond the reach of public scrutiny and political contest. Aristotle believed that the meaning of equal treatment cannot be deduced from first principles and that disagreements about similarity and difference are central to debates about justice and equality. Living together in political societies requires us to justify our judgments about who is similar and to whom in particular cases. By building into machine learning models the assumption that protected characteristics are not justifiable bases on which to treat people differently, group fairness definitions can block public discussion about the moral relevance of difference. Debates about group fairness definitions should not distract from the more important question of what responsibilities institutions should have to address structural inequalities by using protected characteristics to treat differently those who are differently situated.[3]

The regulatory strategy for which this chapter argues is simple. If regulators insist on imposing constraints on predictive tools, they should institutionalize Cynthia Dwork's individual fairness approach. Instead of attempting to impose a universal definition of equal treatment, Dwork's approach forces institutions to define precisely who a predictive tool treats similarly to whom, isolating political judgments about the interpretation and application of equal treatment. Because the critical virtue of Dwork's approach is that it addresses how computer science is institutionalized in the real world, it has been widely overlooked in debates about fair machine learning. Its strength is not that it has the right fairness definition, but that it does not attempt to find one.

Generally, however, law and policy should focus on how predictions are used to make decisions, not on how data are used to make predictions. If we wish to advance social equality, we should be wary of reaching for mathematical definitions of group fairness because they embed contestable interpretations of ethical principles into the design of predictive tools, often harming the groups they are meant to help. Instead, we should generally build unconstrained, well-calibrated machine learning models but use their predictions to make decisions in ways that resemble affirmative action—for instance, by applying different decision thresholds across social groups. Machine learning models are predictive tools; humans are decision-makers. When machine learning models unearth social inequalities, fair machine learning is not a solution to the underlying problem—it is a tool to help us diagnose it.[4]

Defining Fairness

The risk prediction tool that ProPublica analyzed is called COMPAS (Correctional Offender Management Profiling for Alternative Sanctions). When defendants are booked into jail in Broward County, Florida, where Brisha Borden and Vernon Prater were arrested, they are asked to respond to a COMPAS questionnaire with 137 questions, including "Was one of your parents ever sent to jail or prison?," "How many of your friends/acquaintances are taking drugs illegally?," and "How often did you get into fights at school?" Arrestees are also asked to agree or disagree with the statements "A hungry person has the right to steal" and "If people make me angry or I lose my temper, I can be dangerous." Answers are fed into the COMPAS model, which generates an individual risk score that is reported in three buckets: "low risk" (1 to 4), "medium risk" (5 to 7), and "high risk" (8 to 10).

COMPAS combines information about past crimes with respondents' answers to predict individual risk across multiple categories of "criminogenic needs," including substance abuse, stability of residence, social isolation, and criminal personality. This chapter focuses on one target variable: recidivism risk, which is the risk that someone will commit a crime—"a finger printable arrest involving a charge and a filing for any uniform crime reporting code"— within two years of release.[5] COMPAS predicts the risk of both general recidivism, which refers to all crimes, and violent recidivism, which refers only to violent crimes. Judges use these recidivism prediction models to decide whether to release a defendant on bail, and parole boards use them to decide whether to release a prisoner on parole.[6]

ProPublica accused COMPAS of racism: "There's software used across the country to predict future criminals. And it's biased against blacks," read the subheading on the article. ProPublica found that COMPAS's error rates—the rate at which the model got it wrong—were unequal across racial groups. COMPAS's predictions were more likely to incorrectly label African Americans as high risk and more likely to incorrectly label white Americans as low risk. "In the criminal justice context," said Julia Angwin, coauthor of the ProPublica article, "false findings can have far-reaching effects on the lives of the people charged with crimes."[7]

Understanding this claim, and the research it prompted, requires exploring the mathematical definitions of fairness that computer scientists have developed. I describe four definitions of what it means for a predictive tool to be fair across social groups. Each aspires to apply the ancient principle of equal treatment to machine learning: to treat those who are similar similarly and those who are different differently.[8]

Four Fairness Definitions

False Positives and False Negatives

Let me introduce some simple notation. Let Y denote the target variable to be predicted; let A denote a protected attribute which can take on two values, 0 or 1, female or male, black or white; let X denote other observed individual attributes like income, zip code, or height, or more complex derived variables like the films people tend to watch or advertisements they tend to click on; and let U denote unobserved individual attributes, such as weight or marriage status, intelligence or communication skills. A model is trained using the

TABLE 2.1.

Predictor $\hat{Y}$	Target Variable Y	Term
$\hat{Y} = 1$	$Y = 1$	True positive
$\hat{Y} = 0$	$Y = 0$	True negative
$\hat{Y} = 1$	$Y = 0$	False positive
$\hat{Y} = 0$	$Y = 1$	False negative

observed variables (A and X) to predict the target variable (Y). The predicted target variable, the outcome of the model, is $\hat{Y}$, whereas the actual variable would be Y.[9]

When computer scientists examine a machine learning model, the first thing they look for is accuracy, that is, the probability of correctly predicting the target variable, or $P(Y = \hat{Y})$. There are other ways of evaluating a machine learning model. Assume that the model is designed to classify each case as either 1 (positive) or 0 (negative), often called a "binary classifier." This classifier would predict, in recidivism, whether or not an individual will commit a crime within two years of release; in placement, whether or not a child for whom a referral call is made will be placed in foster care within two years; in default, whether or not someone will default on their loan within ten years; or in job tenure, whether or not a candidate will remain in the position for five years. There are four possible relationships between the predictor $\hat{Y}$ (the prediction about whether the individual will recidivate, the child will be placed in foster care, the person will default, or the candidate will remain in the position) and the target variable Y (whether the individual does in fact recidivate, the child is in fact placed in foster care, the person does default on their loan, or the candidate does remain in the position).[10]

What each of these terms means in the real world depends on the target variable that a model predicts. Let's use loan default prediction as an example. A model's true positive rate is the frequency with which a classifier correctly predicts a positive outcome, such as someone predicted to default actually defaulting. Its true negative rate is the opposite: someone predicted to not default actually not defaulting. Whereas the "true" rates (positive and negative) are about how often the model gets it right—how often $\hat{Y} = Y$—the "false" rates (positive and negative) are about how often a model gets it wrong. The false positive rate is the frequency with which a classifier incorrectly predicts a positive outcome, such as predicting that someone will default when they do not in fact default. The false negative rate is the frequency with which a classifier incorrectly predicts a negative outcome, such as predicting that someone will default when they do not in fact default. For COMPAS, a false positive is an incorrect prediction that someone will recidivate within two years of release and a false negative is an incorrect prediction that someone will not recidivate within two years of release.

These measures can be used to evaluate the fairness of a machine learning model in different ways. One is to require equality in the true positive rate (TPR):

$$TPR: P(\hat{Y}=1|Y=1, A=0) = P(\hat{Y}=1|Y=1, A=1)$$

Under this requirement in hiring, we would have to hire an equal proportion of well-qualified individuals from protected and nonprotected groups. Often called "equality of opportunity," this measure of fairness is thought to respect the principle of equal treatment because it acknowledges that knowing whether a person is a member of a protected group provides no information about their probability of getting the job.[11] We could also focus on the rate at which a classifier makes mistakes by requiring equality in the false positive rate (FPR) and the false negative rate (FNR):[12]

$$FPR: P(\hat{Y}=1|Y=0, A=0) = P(\hat{Y}=1|Y=0, A=1)$$
$$FNR: P(\hat{Y}=0|Y=1, A=0) = P(\hat{Y}=1|Y=1, A=1)$$

This is the first definition of group fairness that computer scientists developed: equal FPR and FNR. This definition is thought to respect the principle of equal treatment because protected traits cannot be used to predict the probability that the model will get it wrong (that $\hat{Y}=1$ when $Y=0$, or that $Y=0$ when $\hat{Y}=1$). Knowing someone's race or gender provides no information about the probability that the model will make a mistake about them.

The effects of equalizing error rates depend on what a model predicts. Often when using machine learning to assess individual risk, the positive label denotes a prediction of high risk—for instance, that someone will recidivate or default on their loan, or in AFST, that a child will be placed in care within two years of an allegation of abuse and neglect.[13]

At first glance, FPR and FNR appear to capture a straightforward intuition. In criminal law, because a positive classification entails the severe consequence of conviction, wrote the jurist William Blackstone, "it is better that ten guilty persons escape, than that one innocent suffers." Because false positives are much (ten times) worse than false negatives, an extremely high "beyond reasonable doubt" standard should be set for juries to convict defendants. FPR simply holds that rates of false conviction should be the same for everyone, including members of different racial groups. The requirement is violated when Black people are disproportionately likely to be incorrectly convicted, as if a lower evidentiary standard were applied to Black people than to white people.[14]

This was similar to the accusation that ProPublica leveled at COMPAS. ProPublica found that COMPAS's false positive rate was 45 percent for black defendants and 23 percent for white defendants and that its false negative rate was 48 percent for white defendants and 28 percent for black defendants. In other words, COMPAS was three times more likely to classify as high risk Black defendants who did not go on to commit crimes than white defendants, and three times more likely to classify as low risk white defendants who did go on to commit crimes than Black defendants. Because the model got it wrong in harmful ways more often for Black people than for white people and got it wrong in beneficial ways more often for white people than for Black people, ProPublica argued, COMPAS was racist.[15]

CALIBRATION

The company that designed COMPAS, Northpointe, issued a robust rebuttal. Northpointe accepted ProPublica's finding that COMPAS produced uneven false positive and false negative rates, but argued that ProPublica had the wrong definition of a machine learning model's fairness. Northpointe maintained that it was more important for a model's risk predictions to mean the same thing for Black and white people, otherwise known as "subgroup calibration."[16]

Subgroup calibration is the second definition of fairness I explore. It is arguably the most fundamental concept for evaluating fairness in machine learning because it guarantees that a model's predictions will mean the same thing for different social groups. Northpointe's argument was that judges and parole boards could treat people equally only if the predictions they used to make decisions meant the same thing for different races.

Subgroup calibration is best understood via a simpler idea called positive (and negative) predictive values, which hold that the likelihood of someone having a characteristic when a classifier predicts they will have it (or not having it when it predicts they will not) should be equal across protected groups. In subgroup calibration, this idea is applied to probability estimates. In loan default predictions, subgroup calibration requires that, among those predicted to have a 10 percent chance of default on a loan, white and Black people will in fact default at similar rates. In hiring predictions, among candidates predicted to have a 50 percent chance of remaining in a position for five years, it requires that women and men will in fact remain in the position for five years at similar rates. Put more technically, conditional on the risk estimates produced by a predictor, outcomes should be independent of protected attributes. Written formally, subgroup calibration in the positive and negative rate requires:[17]

$$P(Y=1|\hat{Y}=1, A=0) = P(Y=1|\hat{Y}=1, A=1)$$
$$P(Y=0|\hat{Y}=0, A=0) = P(Y=0|\hat{Y}=0, A=1)$$

A well-calibrated model is generally a good thing in machine learning, but it is especially important when people use predictions to make high-stakes decisions. Subgroup calibration ensures that a decision-maker can be confident about treating risk scores in the same way for different social groups. AFST is a good illustration of this. If call screeners are presented with scores that mean different things for different racial groups, it is hard to see how they can treat people as equals when using AFST to make decisions. In fact, AFST was found to be unevenly calibrated around the top two scores of 19 and 20. Screened-in referrals that received a score of 20 led to placement in 50 percent of cases involving Black children and only 30 percent of cases involving white children. Because scores above 16 are automatically screened in, the uneven calibration across race of scores of 19 and 20 makes call-ins involving children from one racial group disproportionately likely to be automatically flagged for further investigation. Northpointe made a similar point. To treat Black and white people as equals requires that those who use COMPAS's predictions are confident that risk scores mean the same thing for Black and white people.[18]

ANTICLASSIFICATION

The third fairness definition is anticlassification, which holds that a classifier must not explicitly consider the protected attribute A. Just as people should not offer someone a job or grant an applicant a bank loan on the basis of race or gender, because those characteristics are morally irrelevant to decisions about employment or loan applications, machine learning models should not use protected attributes like race or gender to make predictions. Formally, any mapping $\hat{Y}\colon XY$ that excludes A will satisfy this definition of fairness. Some have suggested extending the definition to require the exclusion of variables closely correlated with A as well as the protected attribute itself. For instance, zip codes might be excluded from a model that predicts loan default probability, because zip codes closely correlate with race and ethnicity.[19]

Anticlassification is ineffective because, in machine learning, excluding protected attributes often does not remove information about the individual members of sensitive groups. As Cynthia Dwork's concept of redundant encodings illustrates, the set of attributes X, variables other than the members of a protected group, almost always contains information that correlates with information about A, the protected attribute. Most variables correlate with the members of protected groups, not because of statistical bias or unrepresentative data, but because patterns of inequality and disadvantage ensure that an individual's race or gender correlates with all kinds of features statistically relevant to prediction. The predictions of machine learning models generally reflect the uneven distribution of the outcomes they predict or the variables they use, even when protected attributes are removed from the training data and the model. Machine learning models reproduce social inequalities even when protected variables are removed.[20]

Anticlassification may also be counterproductive. The exclusion of protected attributes removes information relevant to accurate prediction, which can harm groups whose welfare it is supposed to promote. Suppose gender is excluded from a model that predicts the risk of violent recidivism. As women are less likely to commit violent crimes, the exclusion of gender removes information relevant to predicting violent crime—that is, models that exclude gender will generally overstate women's risk of violent recidivism.[21]

DEMOGRAPHIC PARITY

The fourth fairness definition, demographic parity, also captures the intuition that protected traits are morally irrelevant to the distribution of benefits and burdens. Demographic parity requires that the demographics of those receiving positive (or negative) classifications be equal across protected groups: an equal proportion of women and men should be hired, or an equal proportion of Black and white people should receive a loan.[22]

Demographic parity has obvious appeal. By equalizing outcomes across protected and nonprotected groups, it captures the intuition that a person's capabilities or talents are independent of their race or gender, and so people should have the same probability of qualifying for a benefit or avoiding a penalty regardless of their race, gender, or other protected attribute. Whereas anticlassification translates this into the crude requirement to exclude protected traits from decision-making, demographic parity holds that if protected attributes are irrelevant to whether individuals deserve benefits or burdens, then benefits or burdens should be distributed evenly across protected groups.[23]

More formally, demographic parity is the requirement that a predictor $\hat{Y}$ be statistically independent from the protected attribute A:

$$P(\hat{Y} \mid A = 0) = P(\hat{Y} \mid A = 1)$$

This formulation can be relaxed slightly to capture the four-fifths rule in US discrimination law, which holds that if a protected group receives positive classifications at less than 80 percent of the rate of the nonprotected group, there is a rebuttable presumption of disparate impact.[24]

Like anticlassification, imposing demographic parity can do more harm than good. For instance, classifiers that satisfy demographic parity might have significant disparities in accuracy across groups. An employer could deliberately hire men and women at the same rate, but hire men with excellent qualifications and women with poor qualifications, making it appear as if men are better at the job when, in fact, the employer has simply chosen a better-qualified subset of men than women. This outcome could be unintentional. If a company has historically hired more men than women, it will have more data about men than about women, and thus a classifier trained on data about past performance might predict performance more accurately for men than for women.[25]

Demographic parity can also be unfair to individuals. Consider a bank that imposes demographic parity on a loan default prediction model by ensuring that the gap between the rates at which loans are granted to Black and white people is no more than 10 percent. Imagine two people applying for loans: a Black woman with a credit score of 65, a history of several loan defaults, and a significant mortgage, and a white woman with a credit score of 81, no history of loan defaults, and no mortgage. Under the demographic parity requirement, the Black woman might be granted a loan and the white woman refused one despite the white woman being more qualified. Imposing demographic parity requires that she be rejected because of her race, violating the principle that motivated demographic parity in the first place—that protected traits are morally irrelevant to the distribution of benefits and burdens. There are myriad such examples, writes Dwork, "in which [demographic] parity is maintained, but from the point of view of an individual, the outcome is blatantly unfair."[26]

Is Fairness Impossible?

With these four definitions of group fairness in machine learning, we are now in a better position to understand the debate between ProPublica and Northpointe. Northpointe argued that if COMPAS were to respect ProPublica's definition of fairness and equalize error rates, the model would have to sacrifice a more important definition of fairness, subgroup calibration. But why can't a model respect both fairness definitions? Why can't a machine learning model be well calibrated and have equal error rates across subgroups?

Computer scientists derived a mathematical answer to the question. They found that when a target variable is unevenly distributed across two social groups, a model that predicts that target variable cannot have equal error rates and equal rates of successful prediction across those groups. A model can respect ProPublica's definition of fairness and have equal error rates, but only if the model sacrifices equal calibration across groups. Or a model can respect Northpointe's definition of fairness and be equally well calibrated, but only if the model has unequal error rates across groups. In technical terms, when the base rates of a target variable differ across social groups, a model that predicts that target variable cannot have equal error rates (be wrong equally often) and be equally well calibrated (have its predictions mean the same thing) across those social groups. It is impossible to simultaneously achieve both ProPublica's and Northpointe's definitions of fairness.[27]

Because this impossibility result is derived mathematically, it appears to reveal an unfortunate but inexorable fact about our world: we must choose between two intuitively appealing ways to understand fairness in machine learning. Many scholars have done just that, defending either ProPublica's or Northpointe's definitions against what they see as the misguided alternative. Nathan Srebro, a computer scientist at the University of Chicago, proposed a version of ProPublica's definition of fairness, the "equal opportunity" definition outlined earlier, and described Northpointe's definition as "optimal discrimination" because it results in a higher proportion of Black defendants being wrongly labeled as high risk.[28] ProPublica dismissed Northpointe's definition as "the characteristic that criminologists have used as the cornerstone for creating fair algorithms, which is that the formula must generate equally accurate forecasts for all racial groups."[29]

Because this mathematical result has the veneer of inevitability, the assumption underpinning it has received far too little attention, especially from social scientists. Mathematical assumptions often denote features of our world. In this case, a model cannot have equal error rates and be equally well calibrated across subgroups if—and this is the important "if"—that model predicts an outcome that is unevenly distributed across subgroups, or in technical terms, if base rates of a target variable differ across subgroups. The uneven distribution of an outcome across social groups has nothing to do with mathematics but is a social fact that reflects social patterns and processes encoded in data.

COMPAS offers a clear example. The outcome that COMPAS is trained to predict, recidivism, the risk that someone will commit a crime within two years of release, is distributed unevenly across Black and white Americans. Black Americans are more likely to be stopped and searched, more likely to be arrested when stopped, more likely to be charged and convicted, and then more likely to be given disproportionately harsher sentences. In Broward County, Florida, where Brisha Borden and Vernon Prater were arrested, 21 percent of Black defendants are rearrested for violent offenses, compared to 12 percent of white defendants. In this case, because group membership (race) is correlated with the target variable (recidivism), the assumption of the impossibility theorem holds. This isn't merely a coincidence. Because Blackness makes someone a target for unjustified differential treatment in the US criminal justice system, race influences the target variable. The impossibility result affirms that when membership in a protected group and the target variable are not independent, there are unavoidable trade-offs in the design of predictive tools.[30]

The impossibility result is about much more than math. Northpointe's and ProPublica's definitions of fairness cannot both be achieved because the underlying outcome that COMPAS sought to predict is distributed unevenly across Black and white people. This is a fact about society, not mathematics, and it requires engaging with a complex and checkered history of systemic racism in the US criminal justice system. Predicting an outcome whose distribution is shaped by this history requires trade-offs because the inequalities and injustices of our world are encoded in data—in this case, because America has criminalized Blackness for as long as America has existed. The result reveals not inexorable facts of mathematics or nature, but something about the trade-offs involved in prediction in the context of social inequality.[31]

Most of the cases we explore in this book involve outcomes that are distributed unevenly across protected social groups: placements of children in foster care, rates of loan default, how long people stay in their jobs, click rates on different kinds of Facebook and Google content. Because the base rates of these outcomes systematically differ across race and gender, it is not possible for a model that predicts these outcomes both to have equal error rates and to be equally well calibrated across race and gender. As Safiya Noble argues, we must be alert to the ways in which data record the consequences of inequality and injustice, and we must ask ourselves how decision-making systems that use data should be structured, what goals they should have, and how they should achieve them when patterns of concentrated disadvantage are encoded in data.[32]

Equal Treatment in Machine Learning

Mathematical definitions of group fairness make two mistakes in interpreting and applying the principle of equal treatment. First, they apply it to the wrong thing. Equal treatment is an ethical principle of human decision-making, not of machine predictions. Making decisions that treat people as equals may not require that predictive tools respect mathematical definitions of group fairness, and predictive tools that respect those definitions may fail to treat people as equals. Second, because mathematical definitions of group fairness embed a particular interpretation of equal treatment in the design of predictive tools, group fairness definitions can block discussion about the moral relevance of difference and disadvantage.

Decisions, Not Predictions

Aristotle was the first to write down the principle that like cases should be treated similarly and unlike cases dissimilarly, and also to argue, more ambitiously, that unlike cases should be treated "in proportion to their unlikeness." A few hundred years earlier, Aesop's fable told of a fox who invites a crane for dinner, then serves soup in a shallow dish. The fox overlooks a relevant difference that requires differential treatment: the crane has a long beak and needs a different vessel to drink from. The crane makes the point by inviting the fox for dinner and serving soup in a long, narrow jar.[33]

Aristotle's principle of equal treatment is an axiom of ethical behavior, a principle meant to guide humans' decision-making. The first problem with mathematical formalizations of group fairness is that they apply Aristotle's principle to machine predictions rather than to humans decisions. This may prove not just ineffective but harmful.

Suppose COMPAS were required to respect equal error rates. An enterprising police department might come up with a plan to ensure that it equalized error rates without sacrificing the accuracy of the model by increasing arrests and prosecutions for low-level drug crimes, knowing that most of those arrested and charged for minor drug crimes were at low risk of violent recidivism and would be released to await trial. This plan would reduce racial disparities in false positive rates of the COMPAS violent recidivism prediction model because it would alter the risk distribution of Black people. And yet it would also inflict real harm on Black communities, increasing rates of arrest and prosecution for minor charges. Satisfying narrow statistical constraints provides no guarantees about how data will be generated in the real world. In this case, reductions in racial disparities in error rates would not indicate a more racially just system.[34]

This is why Northpointe was right. The purpose of machine learning is to accurately predict a target variable, not to make decisions. ProPublica's definition of fairness, equalized error rates, applies an intuition about human decisions to machine predictions. When humans use predictions to make decisions, it is more important that those predictions mean the same thing for different social groups than that they respect some mathematical definition of group fairness. This is true of both COMPAS, which generates risk predictions about recidivism that humans use to make decisions about bail and parole, and AFST, which generates risk predictions about abuse and neglect that humans use to make decisions about further investigation. As Jon Kleinberg explains: "A preference for fairness should not change the choice of estimator. Equity preferences can change how the estimated prediction function is used . . . but the estimated prediction function itself should not change."[35] The principle of equal treatment does not require that machine predictions not respect mathematical definitions of fairness, but that when machine predictions are used by humans to make decisions, those predictions should be well calibrated across different social groups.

Consider how COMPAS is used to make different kinds of decisions in the criminal justice system. After being convicted of stealing a push lawnmower and some tools, Paul Zilly was sentenced on February 15, 2014, in Barron County,

Wisconsin. The prosecutor recommended a year in county jail and follow-up supervision, and Zilly's lawyer agreed. But Judge James Babler overturned the deal. Babler had seen Zilly's COMPAS scores, which predicted that he was at high risk of violent recidivism. Zilly protested that the score did not consider changes he had made to his life—"not that I am innocent, but I just believe people do change." But it didn't matter. "When I look at the risk assessment," explained Judge Babler, "it is about as bad as it could be." Judge Babler imposed a sentence of two years in state prison and three years of supervision.

Judges in Wisconsin are supposed to use risk scores only to decide whether defendants are eligible for probation, not to make sentencing decisions. Zilly's lawyers decided to call as a witness the man who designed COMPAS, Michael Brennan Jr., who explained that he had not wanted COMPAS to be used in courts at all. "I wanted to stay away from the courts. But as time went on, I started realizing that so many decisions are made, you know, in the courts. So I gradually softened on whether [COMPAS] could be used in the courts." Still, Brennan explained, "I don't like the idea myself of COMPAS being the sole evidence a decision would be based upon." After Brennan's testimony, Judge Babler reduced Zilly's sentence: "Had I not had the COMPAS, I believe it would have been likely that I would have given one year, six months." In Florida's Broward County, where Brisha Borden and Vernon Prater were arrested, David Scharft, director of community programs in the county sheriff's office, maintained, "We don't think the [COMPAS] factors have any bearing on a sentence."[36]

By applying the principle of equal treatment to machine predictions rather than human decisions, group fairness definitions can do more harm than good. And yet their seductive promise of mathematically guaranteeing fairness makes humans' incentives to defer to machine predictions even more potent. This is what happened to Paul Zilly. Even COMPAS's designer did not want judges to use his tool to assign sentences. And yet they did.

Awareness of Difference

There is a second problem with group fairness definitions: they embed in machine learning models the idea that traits like race and gender are morally irrelevant to decision-making and so decision-making systems should be blind to these traits. This assumption can foreclose the very reflection that machine learning invites: how to interpret and apply the principle of equal treatment, and how to think about the moral relevance of difference and disadvantage.

Aristotle understood that interpreting and applying the principle of equal treatment is part of what it means to live together in political society. In itself, the principle of equal treatment is abstract, a formal relationship that lacks substantive content. The principle must be given content by defining which cases are similar and which are different, and by considering what kinds of differences justify differential treatment. Deciding what differences are relevant, and what kinds of differential treatment are justified by particular differences, requires wrestling with moral and political debates about the responsibilities of different institutions to address persistent injustice. Instead of embracing the practice of citizens justifying judgments about similarity and difference to one another, group fairness definitions attempt to find a single, universal definition of who is similar to whom and then build that definition into the design of machine learning models.[37]

Consider the bank that uses default predictions to make decisions about loan applications, which we explored at the end of the last chapter. In a bid to reduce racial disparities, suppose the bank decides to grant loans at equal rates to Black and white people, knowing that doing so will result in rejections of some qualified white loan applicants and a temporary drop in profit. Because disparities in loan default risk are driven by unjust social processes like segregation, redlining, and discrimination, the bank feels that race is morally relevant to making decisions about who should receive a loan, and that, as an important social and economic institution, it has a responsibility to address those unjust social processes. A short-term intervention, in this view, will achieve long-run justice.[38]

In this case, instead of imposing any mathematical definition of fairness on its loan default prediction model, the bank should simply apply different risk thresholds for granting loans to Black and white people. By offering the seductive promise of a technological guarantee of fair decisions, imposing group fairness on the risk prediction model will foreclose public debate about whether race is morally relevant to the bank's decisions about loan applications. Building assumptions about the moral irrelevance of protected traits into machine learning models avoids the need to debate how to interpret and apply the principle of equal treatment with sensitivity to social and institutional context, which is exactly the debate that machine learning invites us to reckon with.[39]

Mathematical definitions of group fairness hinder, rather than support, debates among citizens about how to interpret and apply the principle of equal treatment. They make it all too easy for institutions to promise that the fairness of their decision-making systems is guaranteed by mathematics, while in practice those systems compound social inequality. By applying a principle meant for human decision-making to machine predictions, they mischaracterize the role it should play in political society as a question to which there is a correct answer, rather than as an ideal for citizens to debate. We need to design machine learning models to invite, rather than foreclose, the asking and answering of the fundamental question: How should institutions use data that encode patterns of inequality to make decisions that shape the future? Fair machine learning is a tool for identifying patterns of social inequality, not a solution to addressing them.

Individual Fairness and Bridging the Gaps

There is one final definition of fairness that addresses these critiques: Cynthia Dwork's individual fairness approach. Individual fairness recognizes the need to interpret and apply equal treatment in a contextual way and to think institutionally about how to achieve this in practice. Individual fairness forces institutions to articulate how they define who is similar to whom in particular cases. This critical strength has been widely overlooked because it sits between the disciplines of computer science, law, and political theory, and between the spheres of academia, government, and business.

Group fairness definitions require that machine learning models respect certain statistical requirements across social groups. As we have seen, Dwork and her colleagues have demonstrated that these group fairness conditions provide no guarantees that machine learning models will be fair to individuals. In response, Dwork has proposed a different approach that guarantees fairness for individuals with respect to a particular classification task. For each classifier, a distance metric defines who should be considered similar to whom, and the distance metric is imposed as a constraint on the classifier. In technical terms, the distance metric defines any two individuals as alike if their combinations of relevant attributes are close to one another in the space defined by the metric. If the distance between two individuals in the task-specific distance metric is sufficiently small, individual fairness holds that they should receive the same classification. The distance metric guarantees that any two individuals who are similar with respect to a particular task will be classified similarly.[40]

Dwork's formalization respects how Aristotle meant the principle of equal treatment to be applied. Precisely because Aristotle did not believe there was any universal way to interpret and apply the principle of equal treatment, disagreements about similarity and difference are central to debates about justice and the best political regime. We must justify judgments about who is similar to whom and who is different from whom in particular cases and debate the meaning we give to the principle of equal treatment.[41]

This formalization illuminates how to think about individual fairness. Individual fairness encapsulates and applies the formal structure of Aristotle's principle without trying to impose a particular interpretation across all cases. Because individual fairness, as an approach to fairness, is, in a sense, empty, practitioners have often dismissed it as too hard to implement in practice, since defining a distance metric requires interpreting and applying the principle of equal treatment. Yet this is a mistake. Just as Aristotle's principle was supposed to draw attention to the need to justify how similarity is defined in particular contexts, so the emptiness of individual fairness highlights the need for clear definitions of who is similar to whom in particular classification tasks.[42]

If we think institutionally about fair machine learning, we see that the emptiness of individual fairness is its greatest strength. Individual fairness makes it easier to hold institutions to account for how they interpret Aristotle's principle in particular cases. By isolating judgments about who is similar to whom, individual fairness isolates the moral and political judgments required to reason about fairness in machine learning. Defining a distance metric forces those who design and deploy machine learning models to specify who is similar to whom, preventing organizations from burying value-laden judgments in the model itself. Individual fairness thus makes it easier to hold organizations to account by requiring them to publish and justify their distance metric.

Individual fairness offers interesting possibilities for institutional innovation. Several recent papers have described practical procedures for defining and training a distance metric. Christina Ilvento, a computer scientist and student of Dwork's, has developed an approach that consults human fairness arbiters, who are assumed to be free from explicit biases and to possess domain knowledge, to train an appropriate distance metric. This is like learning a distance function from the judgments of a panel of ethical experts who examine the similarity of different pairs of individuals with respect to a particular classification task. Computer scientists and those experienced in making decisions are invited to collaborate to define and apply equal treatment, applying the experience of those who understand the decision-making context in which a machine learning model will be used to the definition of equal treatment that is imposed on it.[43]

Individual fairness may incentivize institutions to develop ways to explain and visually represent the judgments about similarity and difference embedded in distance metrics. Imagine if Northpointe were required to impose a distance metric on COMPAS and explain exactly how and why they defined similarity and difference in their model. Or imagine if advertising companies were required to impose distance metrics on advertising delivery systems powered by machine learning and publish how and why those metrics define similarity and difference in particular contexts.

Individual fairness is too often dismissed for being empty, for requiring a further answer to the question of who is similar to whom. That criticism misses the importance of institutionalizing the process of making and debating moral and political judgments about similarity and difference. Individual fairness is replete with institutional possibilities: companies could be required to assemble panels of domain experts, document the process by which they arrive at judgments to train a distance metric, and submit this information to a regulator and to the public. Or regulators in particular industries could themselves define distance metrics and require companies and government agencies to impose them on their classifiers.

Individual fairness requires that judgments about how similarity is defined be made explicit, inviting an intentionality to interpreting and applying the principle of equal treatment. And that is a good thing. After all, we cannot define away the politics of machine learning and the questions it raises about the pursuit of justice in diverse democracies.

3

Discrimination

Our Constitution is color-blind, and neither knows nor tolerates classes among citizens. In respect of civil rights, all citizens are equal before the law.[1]

—JUSTICE JOHN MARSHALL HARLAN (1896)

I have a dream that my four little children will one day live in a nation where they will not be judged by the color of their skin, but by the content of their character.[2]

—MARTIN LUTHER KING JR. (1963)

In order to get beyond racism, we must first take account of race. There is no other way. And in order to treat some persons equally, we must treat them differently. We cannot—we dare not—let the Equal Protection Clause perpetuate racial superiority.[3]

—JUSTICE HARRY BLACKMUN (1986)

The war between disparate impact and equal protection will be waged sooner or later, and it behooves us to begin thinking about how—and on what terms—to make peace between them.[4]

—JUSTICE ANTONIN SCALIA (2009)

SPEAKING OF PREDICTIVE POLICING, one resident of Crenshaw in Los Angeles explained that, "being African American Black, you . . . hear growing up, knowing this is happening . . . even if you don't really know the term that they're using."[5] The problem is that predictive policing makes the police "over-patrol certain areas." "If you're only looking on Crenshaw and you only pulling

Black people over then it's only gonna make it look like, you know, whoever you pulled over or whoever you searched or whoever you criminalized—that's gonna be where you found something." As another Los Angeles resident explained, predictive policing works "off stereotypes . . . past experiences . . . the history of a community's crimes."[6]

Predictive policing can easily become a case of performative prediction, the concept I described in chapter 1. Around the world, police forces like the Los Angeles Police Department (LAPD) use models trained on past crime data to predict the risk of future crime in different neighborhoods.[7] Because law enforcement detects a small fraction of total crime, when these predictions are used to allocate police resources, crime is disproportionately recorded in neighborhoods labeled as high risk. When these new data are fed back into the models, a giant, destructive feedback loop sets in. The police begin to treat residents of high-risk neighborhoods as more prone to crime, and those residents detect this unwarranted suspicion and begin to feel hostile toward the police. As Cathy O'Neil argues, in this "pernicious feedback loop . . . the policing itself spawns new data, which justifies more policing. And our prisons fill up with hundreds of thousands of people found guilty of victimless crimes. Most of them come from impoverished neighborhoods, and most are black or Hispanic." Predictive tools project the imprint of injustice into the future.[8]

Laws that regulate decision-making are supposed to prevent such injustice. In areas like employment, housing, education, and criminal justice, antidiscrimination and equality laws constrain how institutions are permitted to make decisions, prohibiting them from discriminating against protected groups and enabling individuals to bring claims if they have been discriminated against. How these laws are interpreted and applied over the coming decades will influence how organizations across our society design and deploy machine learning models.

"Discrimination" is just another word for "judgment." The word comes from the Latin *discriminare*, to distinguish between or to separate. Machine learning is itself a kind of discrimination, a set of statistical techniques for learning reliable bases for discriminating between outcomes of interest. By reminding us that discrimination is not in itself bad, machine learning invites us to reflect on what discrimination is, when and why it is wrong, and how we should address it. As with mathematical definitions of fairness, I argue that uncritical reliance on the concept of discrimination may prevent institutions from using categories of disadvantage to empower disadvantaged groups. To distinguish unfair discrimination from statistical discrimination, we must reach beyond prohibitions against discrimination and consider when and why to treat people differently to secure equal citizenship.[9]

By embracing the ambition to eliminate discrimination, we have caught ourselves in a bind. The logic of discrimination contains an appealing but destructive myth of blindness and neutrality that treats ignorance of difference as the engine of moral progress. This eliminates the need for history and context—for politics—in decision-making, stifling debates about what kinds of differences should justify differential treatment in institutional decision-making. Too often, invocations of discrimination support a crude, universal imperative for blindness that enables those with power to avoid hard questions about the interpretation and significance of difference. We are in danger of losing the habit of deciding which values beyond efficiency should be respected by institutions, whether private companies or government agencies, as they design decision procedures. Discrimination law risks becoming—and may already have become—a tool for entrenching injustice.

I focus on the United States because that is where the meaning of discrimination is most fiercely contested. (Interested readers can follow the footnotes for a similar argument about the United Kingdom, where the problems I consider are often incorrectly dismissed as uniquely American.[10]) I argue that, as currently interpreted and applied, US discrimination law often fails to ensure that machine learning models are built to advance equality and may even block the kinds of design choices required to use machine learning to address patterns of inequality. The idea of discrimination may not support the legal obligations needed to prevent machine learning from compounding injustice and corroding relations of equality among citizens.[11]

I offer two responses, one in the domain of law, the other in the domain of politics. In law, the meaning and grounding of discrimination must be deliberately broadened to support awareness and sensitivity to difference, including by offering sharper tools with which to reason about when and why we should use protected traits to ensure that decision-making systems do not compound patterns of injustice. I sketch a few possible reforms to discrimination law that might further this goal.

But in politics, discrimination must be put back in its place. Because discrimination has become—and perhaps always was—so imbued with the mythology of neutrality and blindness, I suspect that the idea of discrimination cannot be wholly untethered from formalistic conceptions of equal treatment. If we continue to place so much weight on the idea of discrimination, these formalistic conceptions will spill over into the political domain, undermining the acknowledgment of difference and suffocating the politics and policies of empowerment and antisubordination. This is not a philosophical argument about the inherent meaning of discrimination; it is a political argument about the practical limits of what ordinary citizens take it to mean. In politics, we must escape the straitjacket of discrimination, shake off the fictions of blindness and neutrality, and articulate other ideals to guide the collective goals needed to ensure that the governance of decision-making protects and secures relations of equality among citizens in a flourishing democracy.

P(click)

Let me introduce a new example: Facebook. We will explore several dimensions of how Facebook uses machine learning, but for the next few chapters we focus on a stylized example of a model used in Facebook's advertising system.

Machine learning makes Facebook's scale possible. Facebook uses machine learning to power the advertising system that distributes ads to its 2.9 billion users. In societies across the world, this system shapes which citizens see which kinds of ads, affecting the distribution of economic opportunities on a mind-boggling scale. The system uses hundreds of machine learning models, each trained to predict something quite specific. Some are classifiers that predict a binary outcome, such as whether an ad contains nudity. Most assign some probability to a particular action, such as the probability that a user will click on an ad or reaction—such as the probability that a user will find the ad distasteful. How these different models interact is extraordinarily complex; even Facebook doesn't know exactly how they fit together. In this chapter, we explore the simple model that Facebook's machine learning systems use: p(click).[12]

P(click) predicts the probability that a user will click on a particular advertisement. It is trained on Facebook's vast trove of data about which kinds of users tend to click on which kinds of ads. The model learns which patterns and regularities about user behavior are statistically useful for predicting click probability. When presented with a particular ad, p(click) uses these patterns to make an inference about the probability that someone will click on it. These statistical patterns connect the features of past ads—whether they were about housing or employment opportunities, what kinds of companies posted them, what they looked like, and so on—to the features of the users who tended to click on them—their shopping or reading behavior, their interests and communications. P(click) uses past patterns (such as users' click behavior patterns) to make predictions that shape the future (determining who sees which ads).

Suppose there are gendered patterns in the kinds of job ads that men and women tend to click on. Women are more likely to click on ads for shorter-term service-sector and administrative jobs, while men are more likely to click on ads for longer-term blue-collar jobs. These patterns of click behavior feed into the data on which p(click) is trained, and as p(click) is an accurate and well-calibrated machine learning model, it results in women being shown more ads for shorter-term service-sector and administrative jobs and men being shown more ads for longer-term blue-collar jobs. Suppose also that the average income attached to the job ads that men tend to click on is considerably higher than the average income attached to the job ads that women tend to click on. In this case, p(click) will consistently show job ads with higher average incomes to men than women. Men will tend to click on job ads with higher average incomes than women, feeding more click data that reflect gender disparities into p(click), which then reflects these disparities in the ads it displays, and so on.[13]

P(click) is a challenging case because it is not clear what the right response is. As we have seen, imposing mathematical definitions of group fairness may have counterproductive effects. Forcing p(click) to show women ads with the same average income as those it shows men may simply increase the number of ads shown to women in which they are not in fact interested, not only reducing Facebook's revenue but also harming women who might have otherwise seen ads for welfare-enhancing jobs. P(click) invites further exploration of how we should use data that encode patterns of inequality to make decisions that shape the future.[14]

Machine learning is the most powerful tool for statistical discrimination humanity has yet invented. P(click) learns what statistical patterns are useful to predict who is likely to click on which ads. When p(click) predicts that you are likely to click on an ad, it is reporting something about the patterns and regularities it has learned—for instance, that people like you who like Barack Obama's page, have many cat photos, are in their fifties, and tend to use Facebook after 8:00 PM have a high probability of clicking on ads like this one. In predicting click probability, the model is using patterns of behavior to discriminate between people who are and are not like you.

Machine learning models have no preconceptions about what those characteristics are. A model uses variables to make predictions because it has learned those variables are statistically useful to accurately predict some outcome. Unlike in racial profiling, where it can be hard to verify whether actions are driven by racial animus, we know that machine learning models cannot feel hatred or distrust. They simply reflect how features of our social world—some unjust, others innocuous—produce statistically useful relationships among variables. Machine learning models like p(click) do not go looking for race or gender, but precisely because race and gender condition the opportunities we are afforded, patterns correlated with race and gender predict all kinds of outcomes, including users' click behavior on Facebook. Machine learning models are racist or sexist only if we are.

Because all machine learning is in a sense discrimination, p(click) illustrates both the opportunity and the challenge presented by machine learning. Machine learning offers a world in which important institutions articulate the consideration they have given to collective ambitions as they design their decision-making systems. And yet to attain that world, we must give institutions the right incentives by articulating what those collective ambitions are and who is responsible for achieving them. Machine learning can be a powerful tool for advancing equality among citizens, but unless we are clear about the duties of different institutions to advance equality, machine learning will propel networks of decision-making systems that entrench some of the most pervasive social inequalities. This is what makes machine learning an interesting but difficult case for discrimination law.

Discrimination Law

Discrimination is one of the most successful ideas of the twentieth century. In democracies around the world, discrimination laws regulate and restrict decision-making in a diverse range of activities, from housing and employment to credit and welfare, in both private and public institutions. Decisions judged to be discriminatory provoke near-universal condemnation. The ambition to eliminate wrongful discrimination has become part of what it means to live in a democracy.[15]

President John F. Kennedy bound the promise of American democracy to the aspiration to eliminate discrimination in 1963, when he described to Congress "the democratic principle that no man should be denied employment commensurate with his abilities because of his race or creed or ancestry." A year later, after the Birmingham civil rights campaign, Kennedy proposed legislation that would give "all Americans the right to be served in facilities which are open to the public—hotels, restaurants, theatres, retail stores, and similar establishments." This became the Civil Rights Act, signed into law by President Lyndon B. Johnson on July 2, 1964. The act's most important provision was Title VII, which prohibited employers with more than fifteen employees from discriminating on the grounds of race, color, religion, sex, or national origin. It included hiring and firing, promotion and demotion, and almost all other decisions made by an employer about their employees. It was soon followed by the Civil Rights Act of 1968, known as the Fair Housing Act, which was signed into law during the riots following the assassination of Martin Luther King Jr.[16]

In this section, I argue that discrimination law may fail to prohibit the design of machine learning models that reproduce persistent patterns of social inequality and explore what this suggests about the underlying goals of discrimination law.

The Logic of Discrimination Law

Let's begin by exploring the logic of discrimination law. Discrimination law prohibits decision-making systems from discriminating against certain social groups; in the language of law, policies or practices cannot discriminate against members of protected classes, such as race or gender.

For much of human history, discrimination was overt and obvious: public signs said NO BLACKS ALLOWED or jobs ads said "men only." After civil rights legislation barred government agencies and private companies from distinguishing between people on the basis of race or gender (or any protected class), those who sought to discriminate were forced to use criteria that appeared neutral but which they knew were distributed unevenly among different races and genders. This made discovering discrimination a question of discovering intent. Was there a defensible reason for choosing a criterion, or was it deliberately chosen to discriminate among protected classes? The terrain of the moral argument shifted, but the moral argument itself seemed clear enough: it is wrong to make decisions about people based on morally irrelevant characteristics. In 1981, the Republican strategist Lee Atwater offered a chilling illustration of how this shift affected presidential campaigning:

> You start out in 1954 by saying, "Nigger, nigger, nigger." By 1968 you can't say "nigger"—that hurts you, backfires. So you say stuff like, uh, forced busing, states' rights, and all that stuff, and you're getting so abstract. Now, you're

talking about cutting taxes, and all these things you're talking about are totally economic things and a by-product of them is, Blacks get hurt worse than whites. . . . "We want to cut this," is much more abstract than even the busing thing, uh, and a hell of a lot more abstract than "Nigger, nigger."[17]

The structure of discrimination law is a legacy of this pivot from overt to covert racial discrimination. Most laws prohibit overt discrimination on the basis of protected characteristics—called "disparate treatment" in the United States and "direct discrimination" in the United Kingdom—and they also prohibit apparently neutral decision-making systems that have an unjustified adverse impact on members of protected groups, called "disparate impact" in the United States and "indirect discrimination" in the United Kingdom. Machine learning invites reflection on the meaning of both kinds of discrimination, but especially the second. Is the purpose of prohibiting disparate impact to ferret out cases of hidden discriminatory intent? Or to ensure that institutions do not compound inequality among protected and nonprotected groups?

DISPARATE TREATMENT

We start with disparate treatment. Disparate treatment occurs when a policy or procedure uses membership in a protected class, such as race or gender, to make decisions.[18] In practice, disparate treatment is usually equated with intent, in part because judges historically confronted cases like the shop signs that said NO BLACKS ALLOWED or the job ads that said "men only." Simple statistical models are a little more complex, but easy enough. If one of three input variables in a linear model is race, it seems reasonable to describe the model's outputs as having been produced "because of" membership in a protected class. Similar logic has recently been applied to machine learning.[19]

In 2019, the US Department of Housing and Urban Development (HUD) filed a discrimination suit against Facebook. HUD argued that Facebook's advertising delivery system, powered by machine learning, violates nondiscrimination requirements in the Fair Housing Act. Because Facebook's system shows different housing ads to different groups of users, including different races and genders, HUD argued, the system delivers ads to users "because of" their race or gender. Facebook was not sure how to respond. The phrase "because of" is deceptively simple, encompassing a range of possible meanings, each of which had different implications for actions Facebook should take. Facebook's first response was a perfect illustration of the most obvious way to think about how disparate treatment applies to machine learning: it decided to exclude protected traits from the machine learning models that powered its advertising delivery system, fearing that unless they excluded protected traits, they would be found liable for disparate treatment.[20]

This is the anticlassification definition of fairness we encountered in the last chapter. As we saw, excluding protected traits makes little difference in machine learning and can even be harmful, because membership in a protected class tends to be correlated with a host of variables that are statistically useful to predict some outcome. Facebook's engineers knew this. They understood that Facebook's advertising delivery system does not need race or gender to make accurate predictions about which ads different users will click on. Because race and gender shape the opportunities we are afforded in life—in education, income, and access to justice—the kinds of ads people tend to click on are correlated with race and gender. It was easy for Facebook to remove race and gender because it made no difference to the accuracy of its system. But neither did it make any difference to the impact of the system on the pursuit of equality across races and genders.

A few months later, in August 2019, HUD proposed a rule for applying discrimination law to machine learning models. The rule stated that, provided a machine learning model did not use inputs that were "substitutes or close proxies" for protected characteristics, such as a person's race or gender, organizations using the model would be immune from discrimination charges. A defendant could rebut a discrimination claim by showing that "none of the factors used in the algorithm rely in any material part on factors which are substitutes or close proxies for protected classes under the Fair Housing Act." HUD's rule would make it almost impossible to bring discrimination suits against organizations using machine learning, provided they removed protected traits and close proxies as inputs. This rule extended the anticlassification fairness definition to prohibit the use of proxies (variables closely correlated with protected traits) as well as protected traits themselves.[21]

The logic of the whole anticlassification approach is misguided. Protected traits correlate and interact with a host of other variables in a data set because membership in protected classes shapes who we are and how we behave. Deciding which variables to include or exclude on the basis of individual correlations simply misses many of the complex ways in which inputs are correlated both to one another and to membership in a protected class. This was exactly what Facebook found. Facebook went through a painful process of exploring what might count as a "proxy" for a protected trait. Should a variable that records the likelihood that someone will shop for baby clothes count as a proxy for gender? Should variables about what kinds of music people listen to count as a proxy for race? What about zip code? Every engineer and data scientist understood the futility of this process. In a world of complex and ubiquitous correlations, excluding variables on the basis of individual correlations with protected traits does not hide information about protected characteristics from a machine learning model. As Dwork argues, when individual membership in protected groups is redundantly encoded in other variables, removing the trait makes little difference. And yet, HUD affirmed, this is what the law requires.[22]

The appeal of HUD's approach is easy to understand. Whereas in human decision-making it is hard to prove that a decision wasn't made because of race or gender, removing gender and race from a machine learning model seems to guarantee that decisions are not made because of race or gender. Even in human decision-making, this was never a plausible approach to interpreting and applying equal treatment, because it confuses the means of advancing equality with the goal itself. When most forms of discrimination were shop signs that barred Blacks or job ads that sought men, prohibiting the use of protected traits was a powerful way to advance equality. But when those prohibitions are applied to human minds, the relationship between the means and the goal of advancing equality becomes strained. Not only is it hard to gather evidence about a person's state of mind, but it is not clear what it means, at a fundamental conceptual level, to say that someone made a decision because of race or gender. The problem is not just that the human mind cannot be seen by others; the whole enterprise of basing the governance of decision-making on fuzzy models of mental processes is morally unilluminating. It depends on a narrow idea of what makes discrimination bad, namely, that it is wrong to make a decision on the basis of morally irrelevant traits.[23]

We return to this point, but for now the point is simply practical: provided a machine learning model uses neither protected traits nor extremely obvious proxies, it will be extremely difficult to demonstrate that it commits a disparate treatment violation. HUD's proposed rule would undermine its own discrimination suit. Facebook's engineers felt that there must be something wrong with the law if they would be immunized from discrimination simply by removing protected traits from advertising delivery models.

DISPARATE IMPACT

The second kind of violation of US discrimination law is disparate impact, which is similar, though not identical, to indirect discrimination in UK law. A disparate impact case involves three stages, each of which answers a particular question.[24]

At the first stage, the question asked is whether there has been a disparate impact of the policy on members of a protected class. The plaintiff must demonstrate that the policy or procedure, such as the use of p(click) to distribute ads, causes adverse effects on a protected class. There are important practical questions about the threshold for disparate impact and how to demonstrate that a policy or practice causes the adverse effect, but these are not difficult to resolve in principle or unique to machine learning. In fact, machine learning may make it easier for organizations to gather statistical evidence of disparate impact even before models are deployed. This could be a good thing. It could make scrutiny of decision-making easier, including scrutiny by companies themselves using machine learning to continuously detect policies or practices that produce outcomes that are statistically worse for one group than another.[25]

The second-stage question probes whether there is some business justification for the disparate impact. This stage is often the most important part of the disparate impact case. A defendant has the opportunity to defend the policy or procedure on the grounds that it is justified by "business necessity." The meaning of business necessity can be conceptualized in terms of a spectrum with two extremes, neither of which, in practice, is enforced by courts. A strict view of business necessity requires that a policy or practice that produces disparate outcomes across a protected group is essential for the business to turn a profit, such that a big business would have to sacrifice billions of dollars to hire a few more minority workers. By contrast, a weak view of business necessity, sometimes described as the "job-related" standard, simply requires that the policy or practice be demonstrably related to the requirements of a job, such that a business could justify a policy or practice of hiring several thousand fewer minority workers on the grounds that otherwise productivity would be reduced by a few dollars per employee.[26]

Courts have continuously expanded the scope of the business necessity justification since it was established in *Griggs v. Duke Power Co.* in 1971. In Title VII, the defense now simply requires a business to demonstrate, in line with the guidance of the Equal Employment Opportunity Commission (EEOC), that a practice is strongly predictive of, or significantly correlated with, job performance. Much of the scholarship about discrimination law, and about Title VII disparate impact law specifically, focuses on the content, scope, and purpose of this business justification defense.[27]

In machine learning, satisfying this second requirement might involve two important steps: showing that the target variable predicted by a model is sufficiently related to a legitimate business interest and showing that the model accurately predicts that target variable. Courts have generally been reluctant to dispute plausible explanations by businesses of whether a predicted trait is useful or, in employment cases, job related, citing limited domain expertise.[28] If the court accepts a defendant's justification of the target variable, proving that the model accurately predicts that target variable will be even easier. Machine learning models are often much more accurate than comparable alternatives. For instance, machine learning models used in hiring have been shown to predict job performance much more accurately than a range of traditional metrics.[29]

Machine learning may make it easier to proceed through the first two stages of the disparate impact process—easier for the plaintiff to offer prima facie evidence of disparate impact, and easier for defendants to offer rational justifications of why an outcome was chosen and the accuracy with which a model predicts it. This makes sense. Companies find machine learning useful because it accurately predicts something genuinely useful for making a profit. It is not surprising, therefore, that under a broad interpretation of the business justification, disparate outcomes produced by machine learning models are both more obvious and more defensible.[30]

The third and final stage of the disparate impact process thus becomes increasingly important. The question here is: Could a less discriminatory means achieve the same ends? If a defendant passes the business justification test, the third stage gives the plaintiff the opportunity to demonstrate that another policy or practice could have been used that would result in less disparate impact. This third stage has received much less attention from scholars, in part because few cases have proceeded beyond the first two requirements.[31]

How might a plaintiff demonstrate that an alternative machine learning model that serves the employer's legitimate interests but produces less disparate impact is available? Reasonable alternative ways of designing a machine learning model could be to predict a different outcome, assemble an alternative training data set, or use different features, as well as to find different ways to use a model's predictions to make decisions. The future of discrimination law will be shaped by the standards developed by courts and regulators to compare reasonable alternative data-driven decision-making systems.

There are easy cases. In Facebook's case, a plaintiff could show that adding additional features into p(click) would have produced an alternative model that was just as accurate but produced less disparate impact. Or in the case of COMPAS, a plaintiff could show that Northpointe could have trained COMPAS on a data set free from error-strewn and biased arrest data without sacrificing accuracy. In these cases, if Facebook or Northpointe refused to adopt the alternative procedure, they would be found liable for discrimination. Notice what is going on here. Facebook or Northpointe may have been lazy, not bothering to explore alternative models that were comparably accurate but less discriminatory, in which case the disparate impact process serves as a tool for enforcing best practice in machine learning. This might be practically important, as sloppy machine learning often produces disparate outcomes, but discrimination law aims to achieve more than simply enforcing best practice. Alternatively, if Facebook or Northpointe knowingly chose a model that produced more disparate impact but no more accuracy, the third stage of the disparate impact process effectively serves as a tool for detecting hidden discriminatory intent.[32]

Most cases will not be so straightforward. Suppose HUD's discrimination suit against Facebook has gone to court, hinging on the p(click) model we have examined. I want to imagine how the judge presiding over the suit might reason through the case. She has listened to oral arguments and is sitting down to consider her verdict, drawing on the evidence and briefs before her. Following her reasoning brings out the limits of the third stage of the disparate impact process and the whole logic of discrimination law. If I am right that machine learning makes it easier to satisfy the first two stages of the disparate impact process, it is critical to probe the logic of this third stage. Focusing squarely on it, I believe, draws attention to the contested meanings of discrimination that underpin discrimination law, taking us to the question of what discrimination law is for.[33]

The judge first considers the disparate treatment argument. Facebook's brief explains the process the company went through to ensure compliance with prohibitions against disparate treatment. They began by removing protected traits and close proxies from p(click). They then conducted a statistical analysis of the training data set, which contained hundreds of variables about user behavior. Facebook found that even when gender and close proxies were excluded, users' gender could accurately be predicted from the remaining training data. The judge wonders: *How should I think about what the model is doing in this case?*[34]

She considers HUD's argument that Facebook's analysis demonstrates that p(click) violates equal treatment. The model was effectively "recovering" gender from other variables in the training data set and using it to predict the probability that different users would click on a particular job ad. As such, the model was using an immutable but irrelevant individual trait to make determinations, violating equal treatment. HUD's brief compares the model to a person who hides their intent to discriminate by choosing facially neutral criteria. They may not put up a shop sign or post a job ad that explicitly refers to a protected class, but decision-making procedures that bury information about the membership of protected classes in machine learning models should be understood as cases of disparate treatment.[35]

She then considers Facebook's response. Pointing out that most variables in its training data correlated in some way with gender, Facebook (surprisingly) has decided to take on the broader issue, arguing that accurate machine learning models almost always reproduce group-based statistical patterns. Because women tend to click on job ads with lower average incomes than are offered in ads clicked on by men, p(click) was showing job ads with lower average incomes to women relative to what it showed men. This difference was driven not primarily by the use of gender or close proxies, but by the way gender conditions who we are and how we behave. Facebook argues that forcing machine learning models into a false form of blindness, by deliberately hiding the complex correlations between gender and user behavior, will not change this underlying fact about our society. Our judge feels inclined to agree. She does not believe that when protected traits can be accurately predicted from training data, even after protected traits and close proxies have been excluded, equal treatment has been violated. She accepts Facebook's argument and rejects HUD's disparate treatment case.[36]

The judge then examines the disparate impact arguments. The first two requirements are straightforward. HUD demonstrates that p(click) consistently showed ads for jobs with higher average incomes to men than to women. This is persuasive evidence of prima facie disparate impact. Facebook then justifies this disparate impact by arguing that delivering ads to users on the basis of predicted click probabilities falls within its legitimate business interest. Since this is effectively Facebook's business model, and the judge has no grounds within discrimination law for disputing that business model, she feels compelled to accept this justification. The judge therefore turns to the third stage of the disparate impact process: examining whether an alternative machine learning model would achieve the same legitimate interest with less disparate impact. Knowing that HUD, the plaintiff, has no way of proposing such a model without access to Facebook's training data, model, and features, she requires Facebook to submit a report summarizing its own process of comparing alternatives.[37]

The judge decides to keep three considerations in mind as she reads the report: the disparity in outcomes across men and women produced by the different models, how accurately they predict the legitimate target variable, and the comparative costs involved in designing and deploying the models. She uses easy cases to think about a spectrum. At one end, if Facebook could easily develop an alternative model, and the model would be equally accurate but produce less disparity in outcomes, Facebook should be required to adopt it. The costs would be minimal, and the procedure would be equally effective at achieving the same legitimate interest, but with less disparate impact. At the other end, if attaining this alternative would consume Facebook's entire profit and the model would be much less accurate, with only slightly less disparate impact, Facebook should not be required to adopt it. The costs would be significant, and the procedure would be less effective, with only marginally less disparate impact.

The judge then applies these criteria to the case before her. Facebook reports that the best way to significantly reduce outcome disparities would be to impose a version of demographic parity on $p(\text{click})$ that sets a maximum gap between the average income of job ads shown to men and those shown to women. The costs of this approach could be significant, because it would make $p(\text{click})$ less accurate, thereby showing more ads that people are not interested in. This approach would reduce gender disparities in the average incomes of job ads, but result in a lower proportion of the ads Facebook displays being clicked on.

Our judge wrestles with the implications of her decision. On the one hand, she does not want to set a precedent in which machine learning models that entrench patterns of inequality are off the hook because they are statistical and complex and courts lack the technical expertise to evaluate comparisons of reasonable alternatives submitted by companies like Facebook. On the other hand, she does not think there are adequate grounds to conclude that Facebook's decision not to adopt the alternative was unreasonable; moreover, neither she nor the claimants have the resources to determine whether there are alternatives other than the one Facebook has presented.

In the end, she concludes that she lacks the expertise to impose judgments about the trade-offs that Facebook can reasonably be expected to make in designing p(click). There are legitimate arguments for both p(click) and the alternative in Facebook's report. Since p(click) furthers Facebook's core business purpose, in which it has considerable expertise and experience, she feels that she cannot meddle in the complex question of whether the alternative would in practice produce long-term social gains for women, and if it would, whether those gains would be sufficient to justify the likely costs to Facebook. It is up to Facebook and consumers to make a judgment about that. She therefore finds Facebook's p(click) not liable for discrimination under disparate impact, as well as under disparate treatment.

After returning home, she reflects on what she learned from the case. The whole disparate impact process asks courts to make a judgment about the trade-offs that businesses can reasonably be expected to make between the impact of the procedure on a protected class and the utility of the procedure for the business. The disparate impact process approaches this trade-off by asking an overarching question: Is the disparity in outcomes produced by the policy or procedure justified? The first stage requires a plaintiff to show that justification is required, because the procedure results in disparate outcomes that have an adverse effect on a protected class. The second offers the defendant the opportunity to justify the procedure on the basis of some more or less expansive notion of business utility. The plaintiff can then show that the whole trade-off is unnecessary because there is a way of achieving comparable business utility with a smaller disparity in outcomes.

The problem with the third stage is that the real world is not clear-cut. Machine learning illustrates that a Pareto-improving alternative decision-making procedure can rarely be demonstrated. For Facebook to be required to adopt the alternative to p(click), empirical research would need to show that doing so would actually benefit women, because, as we saw in the last chapter, whether imposing demographic parity benefits disadvantaged groups depends on real-world facts about the uncertainties and measurement error in the data on which machine learning models are trained. In the last chapter, the bank's imposition of demographic parity benefited African Americans when its data systematically underestimated the ability of African Americans to repay loans, but it harmed African Americans when it led to more loans being granted to people who could not in fact repay. Similarly, whether imposing demographic parity on p(click) would benefit women depends on how it changes people's click behavior and how the advertising model interacts with the real labor market. The problem with the third stage of disparate impact, our judge concludes, is that discrimination law does not provide grounds for judges to reason about the burdens it is reasonable to impose on particular institutions because it does not make the purpose of imposing those burdens clear.

As machine learning becomes an ever more common component of decision-making systems, discrimination suits that follow this logic will also become increasingly common. And they may all too often produce the same result. I now want to consider why. Why does the logic of discrimination law seem limited in its capacity to find institutions liable for discrimination when they use decision-making systems that do not use protected traits but that nonetheless reproduce patterns of injustice? The answer has to do with the common understanding of what discrimination law is for.[38]

The Purpose of Discrimination Law

Complex and contested laws tend to be enacted precisely because they embody the aspirations of multiple actors, binding several political purposes together in support of one piece of legislation. Often, however, the structure and application of the law turns out to favor one set of political purposes. That is what has happened with discrimination law. Discrimination law risks becoming indelibly bound to formalistic interpretations of the principle of equal treatment.[39]

Two principles capture competing visions of what discrimination law is for. The first is the anticlassification principle, which embodies a formalistic approach to equal treatment similar to mathematical definitions of group fairness. On the anticlassification view, discrimination law aims to prohibit the use of protected traits in decision-making because membership in a protected group is morally irrelevant to decisions about the allocation of benefits and burdens: the terms of a mortgage, the success of a job application, whether someone is granted bail or receives an ad.[40]

The second is the antisubordination principle. On the antisubordination view, discrimination law aims to eliminate the systematic exercise of the power of one group over another that is embedded within and entrenched by important decision-making systems in order to confront and eradicate relations of subordination and domination between social groups. This exercise of power need not be intentional or conscious, though sometimes it will be. Social groups are granted the status of protected classes not because membership in these groups is always morally irrelevant to decision-making, but because they have historically been subject to unjust structures of discrimination and subordination, perpetuated and reinforced by decision-making procedures.

Whether anticlassification and antisubordination are in tension depends on the case. Let's explore three kinds of cases: in the first, the principles support the same conclusion; in the second, the principles can be stretched to support the same conclusion, but they are often in tension; in the third, the principles are in flat-out contradiction. The progression through these cases tracks the development of the kinds of cases that discrimination law has confronted, providing a stylized history of discrimination.[41]

The first kind of case is straightforward: shop signs that ban Blacks or job ads that ban women. These cases violate both anticlassification and antisubordination. Signs that ban African Americans from the use of public facilities not only use a morally irrelevant trait in the distribution of benefits and burdens but also entrench racial domination. Although today we have consigned such cases to the dustbins of history, it is easy to forget that the deliberate exclusion of some groups from public social, economic, and political activities is the form that discrimination has taken for most of human history.

The second kind of case begins to bring out the tension between the principles of anticlassification and antisubordination. This kind of case historically involved assessing whether factors like education or literacy were legitimate criteria for distinguishing between citizens, or whether they were simply a new face on the same public signs and job ads.

Consider the *HUD v. Facebook* discrimination suit. HUD's proposed rule, firmly rooted in the principle of anticlassification, holds that the removal of protected traits and close proxies should immunize Facebook from discrimination charges because it guarantees that predictions are not made because of individual membership in protected groups. On the antisubordination view, whether or not protected traits should be removed depends on an empirical analysis of how best to reduce disparities across protected and nonprotected groups. On this view, we should focus our moral evaluation, not on whether Facebook uses gender in its prediction models, but on how Facebook can best ensure that inequality is not reproduced. If Facebook discovers that including protected traits reduces disparities across protected and nonprotected groups, anticlassification demands exactly the opposite course of action demanded by antisubordination.[42]

This sharpens the tensions between basing our moral evaluation of decision-making procedures on the legitimacy of the criteria they use and basing it on the effects they have on relations of power between citizens. On the antisubordination view, gender can be accurately predicted from Facebook's training data even when it is formally excluded because gender conditions who we are, how we behave, and the opportunities we are afforded. That is why gender constitutes a protected class in the first place: decision-making structures have excluded women from important opportunities and imposed undue burdens on them for much of human history. By asking organizations to hide the complex correlations that characterize our social world, anticlassification requires decision-making procedures to be designed as if we lived in a color-blind, gender-blind society, whereas antisubordination requires that decision-making procedures be designed in full knowledge of the society in which we actually live.

The third kind of case is even clearer. These are cases in which the principle of antisubordination supports a design choice that violates the principle of anticlassification. The most obvious example is affirmative action. In machine learning, narrowing outcome disparities across protected groups often requires the explicit use of protected characteristics, an action prohibited by anticlassification. The next chapter explores these cases in more detail.[43]

For the past half-century, there has been an uneasy truce between anticlassification and antisubordination. Slowly but surely, courts have narrowed the conditions under which affirmative action is permitted and widened the range of permissible facially neutral procedures that produce disparate outcomes.[44] This widening of permissible actions that entrench subordination, along with the failure to comprehensively justify affirmative action, suggests that unless we draw attention to the conflict between these principles, anticlassification may slowly suffocate antisubordination. Unless the idea of discrimination can be extended beyond the principle of anticlassification, disparate impact may become an increasingly blunt tool for the pursuit of social justice.[45]

Machine learning brings this struggle to a head. Machine learning makes it difficult and even counterproductive to distinguish statistical from unfair discrimination by distinguishing legitimate from illegitimate criteria. Machine learning forces us ask: How far does the idea of discrimination capture what is wrong with using decision-making systems that use only legitimate criteria but nonetheless replicate and entrench patterns of social inequality? This question compels us to examine the underlying purpose of disparate impact: whether it extends the logic of disparate treatment by ferreting out cases of hidden discriminatory intent or engages in a justified kind of social engineering to empower disadvantaged groups and advance social, economic, and political equality.[46]

The ever more widespread use of machine learning may force a confrontation between the idea that discrimination is wrong because it uses morally irrelevant criteria in decision-making and the idea that discrimination is wrong because it compounds unjust structures of power. In human decision-making, the tension between these ideas can be overlooked, buried within the opacity of the human mind. We have never had to work out what it means to say that a person made a decision because of race or gender because we can never peer into another person's mind. The practical constraints on detecting discrimination have shielded us from having to work out what makes discrimination wrong.[47]

That is the strange thing about machine learning. It would seem that, because this book is about machine learning, it should also be about the future. And in a sense it is. But what makes machine learning interesting, to me at least, is that it constantly reminds us how much history matters. What machine learning models do depends on history. The ideas and laws that democracies draw on to govern machine learning depend on history. That is why machine learning requires that we decide how we wish to use the past to make decisions that shape the future.

We may need to choose between these two understandings of what discrimination is for. If Facebook's advertising system delivers job ads with lower incomes to women than men, then Facebook, without intending to, will entrench inequality and injustice on an enormous scale. And yet, if the purpose of discrimination law is understood to be anticlassification rather than antisubordination, Facebook's advertising delivery system will be immune from the reach of discrimination law. US discrimination law may fail to prevent organizations from building machine learning systems that entrench the most pervasive structures of power in American society.

Putting Discrimination in Its Place

There are two ways we should respond to this problem. In the realm of law, we should broaden the idea of discrimination to more firmly root antidiscrimination in antisubordination. This would ensure that discrimination prohibits decision procedures that have a justifiable objective and do not use protected traits but nonetheless reinforce patterns of inequality and injustice. By retelling the history of discrimination law to focus on how it has been shaped by social movements and the politics of antisubordination, we can leverage the power of an idea that already has broad rhetorical purchase. I suggest a few practical reforms that might advance this goal.[48]

In the realm of politics, however, we should put discrimination back in its place. Because discrimination has become—and perhaps always was—so imbued with the mythology of neutrality and blindness, it can stifle and block more substantive conceptions of political equality. That process is most dramatic and obvious in the United States, where constitutional law always spills over into politics and public debate, but it has also occurred in other countries. The United States is not alone in reducing the concept of discrimination to formalistic interpretations of equal treatment and in finding political arguments about what we owe to each other on account of differences produced by unjust social structures constrained by the rhetoric of discrimination. In politics, we should draw on other ideals to guide the collective ambition to confront entrenched structures of power and develop new regulatory structures to embody them.

By pressing the urgency of this political response, machine learning makes clear that all kinds of characteristics that institutions might justifiably use in prediction are distributed unevenly across protected classes. This is true of clicks, as we saw with Facebook's p(click) model; of recidivism, as we saw with Northpointe's COMPAS model; of crime rates, as we saw with predictive policing; and of the risk that a child will be placed in foster care, as we saw with AFST. As Ellen Kurtz, director of research for Philadelphia's Adult Probation and Parole Department, explains: "If you wanted to remove everything correlated with race, you couldn't use anything. That's the reality of life in America."[49] In an unjust world, we must move beyond formalistic conceptions of equal treatment and debate the moral significance of difference and disadvantage.

Law

For discrimination law to prevent the use of machine learning from entrenching injustice, it must be more firmly rooted in the principle of antisubordination.

Several legal scholars have begun this intellectual work. It starts with renaming these laws antidiscrimination, not nondiscrimination. Then we must retell the history of antidiscrimination law. From the 1970s, reactionary social and political forces pushed back against the gains made by civil rights movements in the 1960s, encouraging courts to narrow and redefine doctrines in discrimination law devised to dismantle segregation. Over time the effect was to constrain the scope of antisubordination, hollowing out and emptying discrimination law of its substantive content and the ambitious ends sought by its original proponents. Discrimination law needs to rediscover its animating moral and political purposes in America's civil rights tradition, which go far beyond the principle of anticlassification.[50]

Reva Siegel persuasively articulates this approach. She argues that "both anti-subordination and anti-classification might be understood as possible ways of fleshing out the meaning of the anti-discrimination principle, and thus as candidates for the 'true' principle underlying discrimination law."[51]

> To claim that struggle for equality in this country has not been about subordinated groups seeking to dismantle social structures that have kept them down makes a travesty of American history. The moral insistence that the low be raised up—that the forces of subordination be named, accused, disestablished, and dissolved—is our story, our civil rights tradition. It is what has made that tradition anything that anyone ever had reason to be proud of. The anti-subordination principle is not some alien, discredited Other, some reckless theoretical sally wisely avoided and marginalized by cooler heads. It is the expression of the American revolutionary tradition in our own time, the living source of our commitment to the Declaration and its promises of equality, the warm lifeblood of the American spirit. It points, sometimes proudly, sometimes defiantly, but always honestly, to what we have done, to what we should have done, and to what we have yet to do.[52]

The erasure of antisubordination from the history and politics of civil rights should be fiercely resisted, as that erasure is driven by "political contestation" as much as by any "moral or philosophical principle inherent in anticlassification."[53] The doctrine of disparate impact aims to enshrine this expanded meaning of discrimination in law, "increasing the scope of what may be prohibited while, at the same time, trading on the emotive appeal of the traditional use of [discrimination]."[54]

The problem with this approach is that it underplays what machine learning makes clear: that the principle of antisubordination is often in tension with, and sometimes flatly contradicts, the principle of anticlassification. Seeking to invoke discrimination to capture the injustice of group disadvantage may distort our thinking about structural injustice and political equality, "weakening or diluting the current level of feeling opposed to racial prejudice."[55] As the legal scholar Benjamin Eidelson argues, "Equating group inequality with wrongful discrimination may distort our thinking about the distinct wrong of *oppression* by shoehorning it into the paradigm defined by characteristic cases of discrimination."[56]

What's more, in the minds of ordinary citizens, the idea of discrimination may always be tilted in favor of anticlassification. Owen Fiss made this point in the 1970s when he observed that the idea of discrimination pulls against the politics and policies of antisubordination. Fiss named the anticlassification principle the "anti-discrimination" principle, a "choice of words" that, in Siegel's view, was "quite unfortunate, because there is no particular reason to think that anti-discrimination law or the principle of anti-discrimination is primarily concerned with classification or differentiation as opposed to subordination and the denial of equal citizenship."[57] Yet it may be that Fiss chose his terms carefully because he believed that antidiscrimination cannot in fact be untethered from anticlassification and that, as a result, "the nation's civil rights heritage" compels "a stark choice" between anticlassification and antisubordination— exactly the choice that machine learning may force us to make.[58]

Discrimination's rhetorical appeal lay in its ability to encompass the antisubordination goals of the civil rights movement while also enabling the white majority to express their qualified support for civil rights by embracing the anticlassification view. The common understanding of the idea of discrimination that underpins discrimination law may shape whose aspirations are likely to be achieved. The history of US discrimination law suggests that it may be extremely difficult to untether the idea of discrimination from its roots in the principle of anticlassification.[59]

Two practical reforms might more firmly root discrimination law in the principle of antisubordination. First, the burden of proof in the third stage of the disparate impact process should shift from plaintiffs to defendants. Instead of requiring plaintiffs to show that an alternative procedure exists that would achieve a business's legitimate purposes but with less disparate impact, defendants should be required to show that they undertook reasonable measures to ensure the unavailability of any such alternative. It has always been extremely difficult for a plaintiff to demonstrate the existence of reasonable alternatives, and machine learning will make it even harder, especially without access to the defendant's training data, features, and models. Knowing that courts will expect reasonable alternatives to be explored before a machine learning model is deployed, and clear justifications of design choices to be documented, institutions would have incentives to proactively explore how best to ensure that machine learning does not exacerbate underlying inequalities.[60]

Second, courts could abandon the three-stage disparate impact process altogether, replacing it with a straightforward balancing judgment. Instead of proceeding through a series of discrete stages, courts should simply ask: Are the disparities in outcomes produced by this policy or procedure justified? This change would enable courts to analyze the evidence holistically, without artificial separation into three stages. Not only might better decisions be made, but courts, plaintiffs, and, most importantly, citizens, would be forced to recognize discrimination suits for what they are—difficult and contextual judgments about the allocation of burdens in pursuit of a collective political goal. Changing the disparate impact process from a structured to a balancing process would, in my view, be a good idea for that reason alone. If we start to recognize what is really going on in discrimination law, we might just start to be intentional about acknowledging what our collective ambitions really are, and what burdens we are willing to impose on different actors to achieve them.[61]

Politics

In the sphere of politics, we should put discrimination back in its place. In the next chapter, I argue that we should articulate a positive ideal of political equality that goes beyond discrimination to establish laws and regulatory structures to govern decision-making. Here I want to lay the ground for that argument.

The story about HUD's discrimination suit against Facebook illustrates how anticlassification understandings of discrimination spill over from law into politics and public debate. Facebook responded to HUD's charge by removing protected traits from machine learning models, knowing that it would make little difference to its effects on racial and gender equality. The very fact that Facebook chose to remove those traits suggests something about how Facebook thought most people understand discrimination. Facebook felt that for many people—whether citizens who use the platform, judges who rule on discrimination suits, or regulators who enforce the law—using protected traits in decision-making systems violates the all-powerful principle of anticlassification. Facebook's strategy was a cheap and easy way to guarantee immunity from the charge of discrimination in the court of public opinion. HUD's proposed rule did the same thing, immunizing institutions from discrimination suits provided they remove protected traits and close proxies. Because the rule would have broad popular support, HUD reasoned, it did not matter that it would make it harder to use disparate impact law to hold companies like Facebook to account. Facebook and HUD understood the rhetorical purchase of anticlassification and formalistic interpretations of equal treatment.

The lessons from this story go beyond the current state of discrimination law. They are about how the idea of discrimination comes to encapsulate the entirety of our ambitions for governing decision-making. Anticlassification encourages a futile and confused quest to eliminate the role of irrelevant traits in decision-making, hindering our capacity to articulate and impose obligations that would ensure that decision-making does not entrench existing structures of power across social groups. As Anna Lauren Hoffman, a legal scholar at the University of Washington, argues: "Certain well documented tendencies in the way courts have interpreted ideals like fairness and antidiscrimination have arguably hindered its effectiveness. These tendencies point toward (perhaps fatal) limits of antidiscrimination discourse for realizing social justice in any broad or meaningful way—limits that extant work on data and discrimination risk inheriting." If discrimination cannot escape the straitjacket of anticlassification, civil rights must escape the straitjacket of discrimination.[62]

My point is not about the inherent philosophical meaning of discrimination—if there is such a thing—but about its political purchase. Too often, the stories told in public about what discrimination is and why it is wrong are indelibly bound to the principle of anticlassification. The actions taken by Facebook and HUD illustrate the power of the idea that discrimination is wrong because it involves the use of morally irrelevant characteristics in decision-making. No matter how elaborate the philosophical theories scholars develop to move discrimination beyond the principle of anticlassification, they continue to run up against the deep liberal instincts that support it. Liberalism offers the powerful but mythical promise of neutrality, of blind decision-making that respects the principle of anticlassification. Lady Justice must be blind, but the politics and policies of antisubordination cannot be blind. We need a political language and imagination that articulates the ambition to confront entrenched structures of power and that extends beyond the idea of discrimination.[63]

As a matter of political strategy, we should not expect the concept of discrimination to single-handedly guide laws and regulations that address the systematic exclusion of disadvantaged groups. Already, commissions and committees are being scrambled to work out how to extend discrimination law to the design and use of predictive tools, but without stopping to confront the tensions simmering beneath the surface of discrimination law itself. If discrimination proves incapable of supporting the antisubordination principle because, as the historian Michael Selmi argues, "we have never been committed to eradicating racial or gender inequality beyond immediate issues of intentional discrimination," we must shift the terms of the debate.[64]

Predictive tools require institutions to be intentional about the goals they impose on decision-making systems. The process of designing and integrating those tools invites us to consider how and to what ends the power to consciously shape our social world based on unprecedented knowledge about the multiple dimensions of inequality should be exercised. Fighting inequality requires that we understand outliers, the groups our society has oppressed and subordinated, and build our collective ambitions around their experiences. But to achieve this, it may be necessary to confront deep questions about the extent of our collective ambition to overturn entrenched structures of power. To support a flourishing democracy, we need an ideal that invites—requires—institutions to see the injustices of the past and to justify how they use difference and disadvantage to make decisions in light of that knowledge. In the age of machine learning, we must move beyond discrimination as the sole ideal that animates the governance of decision-making.

4

Political Equality

Whether originally a distinct race, or made distinct by time and circumstances, [the blacks] are inferior to the whites in the endowments of body and mind.[1]

—THOMAS JEFFERSON, "NOTES ON THE STATE OF
VIRGINIA" (1785)

We wish to plead our own cause. Too long have others spoke for us. Too long has the publick been deceived by misrepresentations in things which concern us dearly.[2]

—SAMUEL CORNISH AND JOHN BROWN RUSSWURM,
"TO OUR PATRONS" (1827)

The power of the ballot we need in sheer self-defence—else what shall save us from a second slavery?[3]

—W.E.B. DU BOIS, THE SOULS OF BLACK FOLK (1903)

never trust anyone who says they do not see color. this means to them, you are invisible.[4]

—NAYYIRAH WAHEED, SALT (2013)

RECALL THE IMAGINARY *HUD vs. Facebook* lawsuit. Despite her ruling in Facebook's favor, suppose that our judge issues a scathing judgment that holds Facebook responsible for compounding social inequality. Citing compelling evidence that Facebook's ad delivery system was displaying ads for lower-paid, lower-quality jobs and for mortgages with poorer terms to African Americans than in ads displayed to white Americans, she points out the pernicious self-reinforcing effects of this system: more African Americans were clicking on ads for poorer-quality jobs and mortgages, further exacerbating racial disparities in the labor market and in access to finance. Suppose that Facebook's executives decide to address this criticism by asking its engineers to redesign the advertising system to intentionally advance racial equality and that they start by experimenting with p(click).[5]

Facebook explores two changes to p(click). First, it adds race as a variable in the training data and the model itself. Facebook finds that including race enables p(click) to make more fine-grained predictions in full knowledge of underlying inequalities, helping to narrow, although not eliminate, racial disparities in the quality of mortgage and job ads. Second, it decides to impose a version of demographic parity, requiring there to be no more than a 5 percent gap between the average interest rate of mortgage ads and the average income of job ads shown to Black and white users. Facebook investigates the effects of imposing demographic parity and finds that, while it would reduce p(click)'s accuracy, the reduction is only temporary because the intervention actually changes people's behavior. Over time racial inequalities in the mortgage and job ads that Facebook displays could be narrowed without sacrificing accuracy. Facebook decides that this is a reasonable intervention, one that trades short-term costs for long-term benefits to African Americans and to society as a whole.[6]

The catch is that these two interventions are probably illegal. As deliberate uses of race to determine who sees which advertisements, they violate the formalistic interpretations of equal treatment that underpin disparate treatment (or direct discrimination) and equal protection law. As we have seen, the grip of anticlassification on discrimination law generally prevents institutions from discriminating on the basis of race, even when doing so promotes racial equality. Not only do companies like Facebook have no incentive to ensure that their machine learning models advance racial equality, but even if they wanted to, the law may prevent them from doing so. This chapter sketches an alternative approach to governing decision-making. Guided by the ideal of political equality, it would allow, and in some cases require, institutions to experiment with using machine learning to reduce entrenched social inequalities.

The flourishing of democracy motivates the argument. If citizens are to collectively govern themselves as political equals, important institutions must ensure that decision-making systems do not compound entrenched inequalities of power and that they sometimes actively address those inequalities. The ideal of political equality captures the antisubordination concern that institutions in sectors like housing, education, employment, and criminal justice may unwittingly structure their decision-making in ways that entrench the subordination of social groups historically barred from participating as equals. By focusing our gaze on concrete structures of power, political equality offers an animating aspiration to guide the governance of decision-making and the use of predictive tools.[7]

Political equality helps diagnose the problem with the formalistic interpretations of equal treatment that characterized both the mathematical definitions of group fairness in chapter 2 and the anticlassification view of discrimination law in chapter 3. If our underlying goal is to ensure that the governance of machine learning establishes and secures the conditions of political equality, we should question the moral premise that protected traits are morally irrelevant to, and should not be used in, decision-making. We should instead embrace the need to constantly debate when and why categories of disadvantage justify differential treatment to advance equality among citizens.

Political equality enables us to be more granular about the responsibilities of different actors with respect to different social groups in designing decision procedures. First, political equality supports principled distinctions between responsibilities with respect to different social groups, distinguishing race from gender, and both from categories like socioeconomic class, geography, and sexual identity. Second, political equality supports principled distinctions between the responsibilities of different institutions, based on how institutions affect the capacity of citizens to live and function as political equals. By inviting us to identify and remove obstacles to relations of equality, the ideal of political equality guides our reasoning about the responsibilities of different actors with respect to different social groups to actively address, or to not compound, structural social inequalities.

This alternative approach suggests a fundamental rethinking of the obligations and institutional structure of how we govern the decision-making of private companies and public bodies. First, I argue for a shift from negative prohibitions to positive duties. Prohibitions against discrimination may not in practice prevent institutions like Facebook, banks, child protection agencies, parole boards, and the police from unwittingly using machine learning to compound structural social inequality. We should develop nuanced positive duties to advance equality that differ across institutions and social groups. Second, I argue that these positive duties should be enforced not simply ex post by courts that impose individual remedies, but by empowered and well-resourced equality and civil rights regulators who consider whether an institution has undertaken reasonable efforts to discharge its positive duties in the design of decision-making systems. I describe an iterative and dynamic process of administrative regulation, underpinned by a new AI Equality Act. This would amount to a wholesale transformation in civil rights and equality law and the institutional structure through which it is enforced.

Goals

The Ideal of Political Equality

Societies are characterized by difference and diversity. People have different incomes and educations, tastes in music and literature, different opinions, moral beliefs, and plans of life, and they live in neighborhoods with different levels of wealth or crime. Political equality holds that in the realm of public life and collective decision-making, regardless of how much each citizen earns or what they know or where they live, all citizens count for the same. People who are unequal and unlike have equal standing as citizens.[8]

As one of the foundational ideals of democracy, political equality is rooted in the idea that citizens co-create a common life and live together through the consequences of what they decide. Constitutional democracies aspire to a kind of coauthorship in which citizens relate to each other and govern themselves as free and equal members of a common enterprise. Political equality motivates democratic habits and norms: looking your fellow citizen in the eye regardless of relative status or wealth or race, opening yourself to others' experiences regardless of how they differ from your own.[9] Political equality also lies behind the feeling of anticipation and collective power when we vote on polling day and see images from across the country of millions of others doing the same.[10]

As Aristotle argued, democracy is not a static political system, but a continuous project of co-creating the institutional structures that best approximate a set of foundational ideals. Because the citizens who govern themselves change—as relations among social groups evolve, the balance between rich and poor shifts, and the structure of an economy develops—democracy must also change. Different kinds of institutions best embody the ideals of democracy in different societies at different times. In Aristotle's time, political equality was embodied in the selection of officeholders by lottery: because all citizens—excluding women, foreigners, tradespeople, slaves, and children—were considered capable of rule, so rulers were chosen at random from the entire citizenry. In modern democracy, political equality underpins the principle that each citizen's vote counts for the same, no matter how educated or wealthy they are. For much of the history of democracy, the ideal of political equality has motivated reform and revolution, inviting us to constantly reimagine social, economic, and political institutions to better approximate the promise of that ideal.[11]

Exploring the ideal of political equality illuminates much about the structure of democracy, both as it is and as we might wish it to be. For instance, as the political theorist Danielle Allen argues, political equality clarifies that negative rights are not prior to, or more fundamental than, positive rights, but that each supports the other. A right to association is not merely a negative right to associate without government interference, but a positive right to gather with fellow citizens to protect your collective political power and hold your government to account. Today "the Chinese government" imposes "great restrictions on the freedom of association," not just "to limit freedom of conscience but also to minimize the likelihood that political solidarities will form capable of challenging its authority." In the US Bill of Rights, by contrast, "the right to assemble was closely conjoined to the right to petition political authorities for changes in policies."[12]

Political equality is an ideal that can guide how we structure the governance of decision-making to support the flourishing of democracy. We can decompose political equality into two component ideas: nondomination, which is similar to the principle of antisubordination examined in the last chapter, and reciprocity.

Nondomination requires the removal of a particular kind of threat to political equality. Structures of domination prevent some citizens from participating in their community in fundamental ways, whether in work, education, criminal justice, or elections. Securing freedom from domination requires that citizens have an "equal share of control over the institutions—the laws, policies, procedures—that necessarily interfere with [their lives] . . . to protect each individual from domination by another, and any group from domination by other groups."[13] Like the principle of antisubordination, this requirement recognizes that freedom from domination is essential to protect the "legitimacy, stability, and quality of democratic regimes."[14] For private companies and government agencies, nondomination requires not only that decision-making systems avoid entrenching inequalities of power across social groups, but that citizens themselves are empowered to participate in judgments about the goals of decision-making systems that affect their capacity to function as equals.[15]

Reciprocity requires a certain kind of attitude toward the exercise of power by some over others. All political choices benefit some people more than others, including, as I have argued, choices in machine learning. Reciprocity requires that those who benefit from political choices recognize that others have lost and that they commit to ensuring that those loses are not permanent. Reciprocity is fundamental to political equality because, "when settled patterns emerge in who is bearing the losses that result from political decision-making, political equality has come undone. The goal . . . is to establish practices that result in political losses circulating through the citizenry over time." Reciprocity places *everyone* on the hook: Facebook for entrenching inequalities of race and gender, Allegheny County for reproducing racial disparities in child welfare provision, and Northpointe and the Los Angeles Police Department for cementing racial domination in America's criminal justice system. For private companies and government agencies, whether welfare agencies, police forces, banks, or social media companies, reciprocity requires reflection on how their decision-making systems can create concrete barriers to the capacity of citizens to function as equals in their common life.[16]

The ideal of political equality holds that every institution in a democracy has a responsibility to protect against domination and to support the conditions of reciprocity over time. That responsibility varies in scope and content across institutions and social groups, requiring further moral and political argument informed by an understanding of the concrete threats to the capacity of some citizens to function as equals and the role of particular institutions in reinforcing or removing those threats. Because political equality depends on that further moral and political argument, political equality is political all the way down. It must be continuously interpreted and applied by citizens in particular societies at particular times.[17]

Rethinking Equal Treatment

The ideal of political equality helps us diagnose what is wrong with the formalistic conceptions of equal treatment that motivated the mathematical definitions of group fairness we explored in chapter 2 and the anticlassification view of discrimination law we explored in chapter 3.

In countries where liberalism exerts a powerful grip over politics and law, formalistic interpretations of equal treatment have come to dominate ethical reasoning about decision-making. The basic liberal response to racial injustice has been to insist that since race is morally irrelevant to the distribution of benefits and burdens, decisions should not be made because of, and should be blind to, race. As John Roberts, the chief justice of the US Supreme Court, famously put it, "The way to stop discrimination on the basis of race is to stop discriminating on the basis of race."[18] Call this the "treatment-as-blindness" view.

The appeal of this view stems from the power of the idea that a person's race, gender, religion, caste, or creed is irrelevant to their moral worth. In *The Merchant of Venice*, Shylock, promising to seek revenge for the seduction of his daughter, tells two mocking Christians:

> I am a Jew. Hath not a Jew eyes? Hath not a Jew hands, organs, dimensions, senses, affections, passions; fed with the same food, hurt with the same weapons, subject to the same diseases. . . . If you prick us, do we not bleed? If we tickle us, do we not laugh? If you poison us, do we not die? And if you wrong us, do we not revenge? If we are like you in the rest, we will resemble you in that.[19]

This definition of equal treatment is increasingly being challenged. "The opposite of 'racist' isn't 'not racist,'" argues the activist Ibram X. Kendi, "it is 'antiracist.'"[20] Or as Beverly Tatum put it, "Visualize the ongoing cycle of racism as a moving walkway at the airport." Treatment-as-blindness is like "standing still on the walkway. No overt effort is being made, but the conveyor belt moves the bystanders along to the same destination." The only way to change your destination is to "turn around" and walk "actively in the opposite direction at a speed faster than the conveyor belt."[21] On this view, people of different races and genders are unlike in precisely the sense that justifies differential treatment—that is why those characteristics are protected. "The way to stop discrimination on the basis of race," rebuffed US Supreme Court justice Sonia Sotomayor, "is to speak openly and candidly on the subject of race, and to apply the Constitution with eyes open to the unfortunate effects of centuries of racial discrimination."[22] Call this the "treatment-as-awareness" view.

Political equality helps us identify the flaws in the treatment-as-blindness view. As Owen Fiss argued, treatment-as-blindness "does not formally acknowledge social groups, such as Blacks; nor does it offer any special dispensation for conduct that benefits a disadvantaged group. It only knows criteria or classifications; and the color black is as much a racial criterion as the color white." This view treats positive action as "a form of discrimination" that "is equally arbitrary since it is based on race"; as such, it provides no "basis or standards for determining what is 'reform' and what is 'regression.'"[23] Treatment-as-blindness has "traditionally been" defended "and legitimated on the grounds that [it] further[s] the liberal goals of state neutrality, individualism, and the promotion of autonomy . . . formal equality before the law," but such "neutrality [can] re-inforce dominant values or existing distributions of power."[24]

Treatment-as-blindness fails to "address the historical disadvantage suffered by those subject to discrimination."[25] It makes an unsupported jump from im-perative to respect the equal moral worth of persons to the moral irrelevance of protected characteristics in making decisions about the distribution of benefits and burdens. Structures of domination constitute exactly the kind of difference that justify the differential treatment of advantaged and disadvantaged groups. When things that appear alike are not in fact alike, treating them similarly can do both an injustice. As Supreme Court justice Harry Blackmun put it in 1978: "In order to get beyond racism, we must first take account of race."[26]

The philosopher Elizabeth Anderson extends this idea, arguing that the treatment-as-blindness and treatment-as-awareness views actually invoke differ-ent concepts of race: "Not all discrimination on the basis of race is discrimina-tion on the same basis." A white couple who fear a Black man for no good reason are subjecting him to an essentializing and stereotyped judgment, whereas an institution using race to advance racial equality uses race as a proxy for subjec-tion to unjust structures of domination. Using race as a proxy for unjust disad-vantage is not the same as using race to make prejudiced judgments.[27]

We should reject the treatment-as-blindness view in favor of the treatment-as-awareness view. In the United States and the United Kingdom, such a re-definition of equal treatment may be long overdue. As US Supreme Court justice Antonin Scalia wrote: "The war between disparate impact and equal protection will be waged sooner or later. . . . It behooves us to begin thinking about how—and on what terms—to make peace between them."[28] We should make that peace by holding the ideal of political equality at the front of our minds. To treat unlike cases "in proportion to their unlikeness," as Aristotle emphasized, our empirical investigations and moral evaluations should focus on how treating differently situated people differently may best support the conditions of political equality over time.[29]

ACROSS SOCIAL GROUPS

The ideal of political equality supports principled distinctions between the goals that decision-making systems should have with respect to different social groups. Because different groups have been prevented from relating as political equals in different ways, political equality may require that different obligations be imposed on decisions that affect different races and genders, sexual identities, socioeconomic classes, or people who live in different places.

Consider the category of race. Race is a cultural construction whose origins lie five hundred years ago in the justification of the slave trade. Race denotes a clumsy, bureaucratic effort to classify and control that elides as many variations in culture and history as it illuminates—for instance, the distinct histories and experiences of Black Americans and Black Britons. I use the term "race" not because it is an objective category, but because it is a category on the basis of which people are and have been routinely treated differently, and one that shapes the daily experience of both racial majorities and racial minorities in institutional settings we have explored, such as access to finance, child protection, policing, and the criminal justice system.[30]

The ideal of political equality aspires to having citizens bridge racial boundaries to encounter one another and participate in public life as equals. The sociologist W.E.B. Du Bois, the first African American to earn a PhD from Harvard University, is worth quoting at length:

> The Negro is a sort of seventh son, born with a veil, and gifted with second-sight in this American world,—a world which yields him no true self-consciousness, but only lets him see himself through the revelation of the other world. It is a peculiar sensation, this double-consciousness, this sense of always looking at one's self through the eyes of others, of measuring one's soul by the tape of a world that looks on in amused contempt and pity. One ever feels his twoness,—an American, a Negro; two souls, two thoughts, two unreconciled strivings; two warring ideals in one dark body, whose dogged strength alone keeps it from being torn asunder.
>
> The history of the American Negro is the history of this strife,—this longing to attain self-conscious manhood, to merge his double self into a better and truer self. In this merging he wishes neither of the older selves to be lost. He would not Africanize America, for America has too much to teach the world and Africa. He would not bleach his Negro soul in a flood of white Americanism, for he knows that Negro blood has a message for the world. He simply wishes to make it possible for a man to be both a Negro and an American, without being cursed and spit upon by his fellows, without having the doors of Opportunity closed roughly in his face.
>
> This, then, is the end of his striving: to be a co-worker in the kingdom of culture, to escape both death and isolation, to husband and use his best powers and his latent genius.[31]

Political equality requires that civic identities sit alongside Black racial identities, neither subsuming nor dominating the other. As the philosopher Meira Levinson argues, this requires a set of civic "skills and habits," such as "the skill and habit of viewing the world from multiple perspectives," of recognizing that "there's not just one way to be American or patriotic." It may also require a certain way of reasoning about and governing decision-making.[32]

Race is a legitimate basis for differential treatment because race is a proxy for centuries of domination and exclusion from practices of reciprocity, which is itself differentially experienced. Race is a crude proxy for disadvantage because the relationship between race and disadvantage is contingent, not inexorable, and yet it is also a pervasive proxy for disadvantage because race has been among the most persistent categories for treating people differently in American history. If the goal is to organize power in social, economic, and political institutions to establish and secure the political equality of Americans, we must reason about the decision contexts in which using race to treat Black and white people differently would help to equalize participation.

This view clarifies that justifications of differential treatment do not flow the same in both directions. The fact that race is a category of persistent disadvantage justifies positive action on behalf of those who are disadvantaged, not those who are advantaged. The fact that gender is a category of disadvantage justifies positive action, not on the grounds of gender, but on behalf of women, because women are subject to the myriad consequences of that disadvantage. Political equality rejects the moral equivalence of decision-making systems that cause disparate impact to advantaged and disadvantaged groups, affirming the shared responsibility to remove obstacles to political equality and recognizing that categories of disadvantage are morally relevant to executing that responsibility.[33]

Contrast race with another barrier to political equality: geography. Geography is a particularly neglected category of disadvantage. People born in places with lower average incomes, less access to capital and investment, and poorer education and health-care systems are subject to a range of connected decision systems that make it systematically more difficult for them to function as political equals. Insofar as geography is a practical barrier to political equality in relevant decision contexts, it may be a legitimate basis for treating people differently. For instance, if geography is driving exclusion, polarization, and stratification in higher education, geography may be a legitimate criterion to use in making decisions in higher education.[34]

Consider Danielle Allen's proposal that, above a threshold for measuring educational potential, such as GPA and SAT scores, colleges should admit students to maximize geographic diversity within that cohort and over time. Within any given zip code, the highest-performing applicants would be chosen first. Instead of treating SAT and GPA scores as true measures of talent, a geographic lottery recognizes that, "in order to spot the talent that is everywhere, one needs to identify those who, above all others, have made the most of the resources available to them in their immediate surroundings." As Allen argues,

> socioeconomic groups are not among the categories protected by equal access to jurisprudence, but that jurisprudence nonetheless establishes a useful framework for a moral consideration of what it would take to establish that we had achieved equal access. Admissions procedures that maximize geographic diversity by selecting for such diversity from a pool of applicants above the entrance threshold would be far stronger contenders for meeting an equal access bar than current practice.[35]

Different goals may be relevant to decision-making systems that affect different categories of disadvantage. Consider the category of gender identity. People face barriers to participation on the basis of gender identity that they do not face on the basis of socioeconomic class and geography, such as access to public toilets and other gendered public spaces. Political equality might require an obligation to ensure equal access to public spaces for people of different gender identities that may not apply on the basis of socioeconomic class or geography. But since race has consistently been a basis on which some people have been barred from accessing public spaces, such an obligation may apply to people of different races.

Political equality invites us to be cognizant of the frequent intersections of categories of disadvantage, as identified by concepts of intersectionality or concentrated disadvantage. Decision-making systems can stitch together patterns of inequality, subjecting some social groups to a series of interrelated obstacles in the basic activities of citizenship.[36] For instance, low-income Black mothers who seek welfare services are subject to systems of supervision and decision-making that weave together different spheres of impoverishment and disadvantage.[37] Political equality may support especially stringent responsibilities in these cases.

Political equality may also enable us to leverage the possibilities offered by machine learning for using more direct proxies for disadvantage. Although there may be compelling expressive reasons to use categories like race and gender to treat people differently, those categories may not always be the most effective proxies. Machine learning can enable institutions to construct nuanced definitions of disadvantage targeted to particular kinds of decisions—for instance, by including the intersection between geography and school attendance with race in admissions decisions to elite universities, or the intersection between gender and socioeconomic class in hiring decisions. Applying political equality to machine learning unlocks fertile moral debates about what differences should count in what contexts to support relations of equality among citizens over time.

ACROSS INSTITUTIONS

Political equality also supports principled distinctions between the goals of decision-making in different institutions, depending on how institutions affect the capacity of citizens to function as equals. When institutions use machine learning to control access to something fundamental to citizenship, such as freedom from arbitrary treatment by law enforcement, this poses a greater threat to political equality than when intuitions use machine learning to do something trivial, such as to recommend films.

The concept of basic interests is helpful. People have "basic interests in the security, nutrition, health, and education needed to develop into, and live as, a normal adult. This includes developing the capacities needed to function effectively in the prevailing economic, technological, and institutional system, governed as a democracy, over the course of their lives."[38] The more critical a good or service is to securing a basic interest, the greater the risk the institution that controls that good will cement domination and corrode reciprocity. The greater the threat an institution poses to political equality, the more stringent the obligations imposed on it should be.[39]

Political equality invites us to focus on an institution's role in securing citizens' basic interests instead of whether it is a public body or a private company. The Children, Youth, and Families Office was unusual in being a public body that built AFST in-house, collaborating with a team of academics to execute an exemplary process of public consultation and feedback. But many goods and services necessary for citizens to function as equals are provided by private companies. The obligations imposed on institutions should depend not on their legal status, but on their role in securing the conditions of political equality over time.[40]

Or consider another example. Compare two predictive tools that are both cases of performative prediction. One we have encountered already, PredPol, the predictive policing system used by the LAPD: as more police officers are sent to higher-risk neighborhoods, more crime is recorded in those neighborhoods, driving up their measured risk and ensuring that more police are sent there in the future. The other is an imaginary machine learning model designed by Uber to predict the risk of prospective passengers to drivers in Los Angeles: as the model predicts higher average risk scores for Black passengers, average wait times increase for Black passengers, pushing many toward other means of transport. Because those who intend to commit crimes continue, of course, to use Uber, the proportion of Black passengers who do in fact pose a risk increases, further driving racial disparities in average wait times. Both systems exacerbate racial inequalities, but they have different effects on the capacity of Black people in LA to function as political equals.

Multiple considerations should factor into judgments about how these cases bear on political equality. If citizens can obtain the good or service from another source, the threat to political equality is reduced. Black Uber passengers have alternatives, like LA's public transport system, whereas the state is the only institution that can imprison citizens and deprive them of the vote. There is no recourse and no alternative for those subject to predictive tools used in criminal justice. While Uber's system deepens racial inequalities in access to transport, PredPol makes Black residents disproportionately likely to end up in prison, deprived of their liberty and subject to the disadvantages associated with having a criminal record. My point is not to defend a judgment about which is worse, but to illustrate the kind of situations that political equality invites us to consider in evaluating the role of institutions in securing citizens' basic interests.[41]

These examples are meant to illustrate a form of reasoning, not to offer a definitive account of the duties that political equality might entail with respect to different institutions across different social groups. Political equality supports open public argument about the moral relevance of particular categories of disadvantage and the responsibilities of different institutions to address it. Machine learning may help inform this reasoning by enabling us to identify more direct proxies for disadvantage than categories traditionally protected by law. It may also illuminate the connections between different forms of disadvantage, supporting a more articulate and discerning account of who is different from whom in ways that justify differential treatment in different institutional contexts. Machine learning may force us to recognize "the tendency

for equal treatment of the unequally situated to exacerbate, rather than challenge, inequality," perhaps helping to "diffuse the unease which character-
ises . . . discussions of 'positive discrimination' and affirmative action."[42]

Practice

The ideal of political equality can open up our institutional imaginations about
the governance of decision-making. Let's explore two kinds of reform to the
governance of decision-making that the ideal of political equality might
support.

Positive Equality Duties

In 1996, California passed a ballot measure, Proposition 209, known as the
California Civil Rights Initiative, which prohibited the use of race to advance
racial equality. Prop 209 exemplified the formalistic approach to equal treatment that equates race-conscious efforts to advance political equality with the
racism of banning Black people from public spaces: "The state shall not discriminate against, or grant preferential treatment to, any individual or group
on the basis of race, sex, color, ethnicity, or national origin in the operation of
public employment, public education, or public contracting."

California State Assembly speaker Willie L. Brown Jr. argued that support
for Prop 209 would not "be on the basis of anything except pure, unadulterated
exploitation of racism." His opponent and friend, Democrat-turned-
Republican California assemblyman Bernie Richter, argued that "making
policy decisions based on a person's ethnicity—on the way they were born—
is wrong." "Those of us who advance Prop 209," he continued, "stand in the
shoes of Jefferson, and Lincoln, and King." In 1996, Prop 209 passed with
55 percent in favor and 45 percent opposed. In November 2020, almost fifteen
years later, Californians rejected a ballot measure to repeal Prop 209, despite
a summer of racial justice activism and polls suggesting that white citizens
supported measures to combat racial disparities. The margin had increased:
57 percent voted not to repeal Prop 209 and 43 percent voted to keep it. Public
bodies in California still cannot use race to advance racial justice.[43]

The ideal of political equality supports what I call positive equality duties
(PEDs). PEDs permit the use of protected characteristics in a defined set of
decision contexts provided there is a strong basis in evidence that doing so
advances equality among protected and nonprotected groups. PEDs would

permit organizations to treat different people differently for the purpose of addressing concentrated disadvantage, "based on the recognition that equal treatment . . . may lead to an unequal outcome, and that therefore preferential treatment is needed." PEDs are not exceptions to the principle of equal treatment, but rather a recognition that equal treatment requires the differential treatment of those who are differentially situated. Like the Constitution of South Africa, deliberately written to confront the country's violent history of racial oppression, we should understand PEDs not as "a deviation from, or invasive of, the right to equality," nor as "'reverse discrimination' or 'positive discrimination,'" but rather as "integral to the reach of . . . equality protection."[44]

PEDs would require institutions to demonstrate in designing decision-making systems that they took reasonable measures to explore how best to advance equality among protected and nonprotected groups. Institutions would have to take preemptive measures to evaluate the impact of decision-making procedures, compare alternative ways of designing those decision-making procedures, and take reasonable steps to understand and address observed disparities across protected and nonprotected groups. There would be a legal presumption that when protected characteristics are used as part of reasonable efforts to discharge a PED, and when there is a strong basis in evidence that doing so will reduce inequalities across protected groups, the use of protected traits will not constitute a violation of disparate treatment (or direct discrimination).

PEDs would transform the governance of decision-making. They would require institutions to directly confront the disadvantages that follow from membership in protected groups and, more broadly, to undertake measures to encourage participation in public life by those groups. As the Clinton administration's "Affirmative Action Review" put it, PEDs would require intuitions "to expand opportunity for women or racial, ethnic, and national origin minorities by using membership in those groups that have been subject to discrimination."[45] As Virginia Eubanks argues, predictive "tools . . . left on their own, will produce towering inequalities." If they are not "built to explicitly dismantle structural inequalities, their increased speed and vast scale [will] intensify them dramatically."[46] Given this, positive duties may be "the most appropriate way to advance equality and to fight discrimination, including indirect discrimination."[47]

Determining the scope and content of PEDs should be motivated by the underlying idea of political equality, with sensitivity to how different institutions can empower different social groups to participate in a community of political equals. The legislature should define the content and scope of PEDs, using the ideal of political equality to support principled distinctions between PEDs imposed across different sectors, institutions, and social groups. This process will compel regulators to confront the difficult question of when PEDs merely permit institutions to use categories of disadvantage to address disadvantage and when they actually require doing so. Regulators should develop clear guidance about how different institutions should evaluate the trade-offs involved in comparing alternative decision-making systems before they are deployed. Because political equality embraces ceaseless moral and political debate, PEDs would be the subject of fierce contestation. That is part of what makes them attractive.

In the United States, the biggest obstacle to PEDs would be the Supreme Court. "The Court has limited the scope of constitutionally permissible programs to a narrowly defined concept of intentional discrimination, and has excluded affirmative action addressed to mere racially disparate impact." In equal protection doctrine, when the Court evaluates whether a race-conscious decision advances a compelling governmental interest, structural inequalities that motivate the need for race-conscious action in the first place are irrelevant to justifying that action. "The racially disparate maldistribution of societal benefits and burdens has become constitutionally irrelevant. Only intentional discrimination matters. And because most contemporary discrimination results from implicit bias or structural forces, most contemporary discrimination simply does not exist." This argument "smother[s] racial equality beneath a tacit baseline assumption that the current allocation of resources is itself fair and equitable—despite the long history of overt, implicit, and structural racism on which it rests." Only social movements and legislative action will force the court to shift that position.[48]

RETHINKING AFFIRMATIVE ACTION

Political equality suggests a different approach to justifying affirmative action. Consider three justifications generally offered for affirmative action. The first holds that resources—jobs, college places, seats in legislatures—should be allocated in proportion to the demographic distribution of different social groups. Where there are significant deviations from those distributions, affirmative action policies should be instituted to ensure that the distribution more closely mirrors distributions in the population. The second justification focuses on compensation, arguing that affirmative action repairs past wrongs. The final justification argues that affirmative action promotes the diversity that institutions require to function best, for instance, by ensuring that a broad range of perspectives and backgrounds are brought to educational institutions.[49]

Political equality supports a justification of affirmative action that differs from these in three important respects. First, the political equality justification orients affirmative action forward rather than backward in time. Affirmative action is carried out as one of a suite of policies required to support a substantive vision of political equality, not an isolated compensation for past wrongs, thus avoiding holding citizens from one social group responsible for wrongs perpetrated against another, pitting citizens against one another in a ceaseless ledger of injustice. The political equality justification focuses on the responsibilities of all citizens to support the conditions of each other's political equality over time. Each citizen has reason to support affirmative actions that dismantle systems of domination because each has a duty to support the conditions for all to relate and govern as political equals.[50]

Second, the political equality justification of affirmative action is instrumental rather than intrinsic. Decision-making systems, particularly those that use machine learning, matter because they affect distributions of resources that can "crystalize [into] durable power differentials (domination) and hierarchical status orders"; distributions of resources matter because they affect relations of power among citizens; and relations of power among citizens are objectionable when they prevent some citizens from participating as equals. The purpose of affirmative action is not to achieve a just distribution of resources, but to remove barriers to political equality. When that instrumental purpose is achieved, the justification falls away, building into the justification of affirmative action a definition of the relevant time horizon. Affirmative action policies are required until the obstacles faced by some citizens to participation as equals have been removed.[51]

Third, the political equality justification leaves open the question of who should be targeted by affirmative action policies and how. The aim is to dismantle the mechanisms that cement structures of domination and corrode practices of reciprocity over time. The political equality justification grounds the analysis of which social groups are included in affirmative policies and which institutions are subject to them in a concrete analysis of the structural barriers to political equality that different institutions impose on different social groups. There is no principled reason why affirmative action policies should exclude socioeconomic class or geography, for instance, if there is compelling evidence that these are categories on the basis of which political equality has been denied and that affirmative action policies could address these disparities.[52]

Political equality calls "for reframing the affirmative-action debate within a broader institutional effort to address structural inequality," as the legal scholar Susan Sturm argues. Political equality, she continues,

> is an affirmative value focused on creating institutions that enable people, whatever their identity, background, or institutional position, to thrive, realize their capabilities, engage meaningfully in institutional life, and contribute to the flourishing of others. It covers the continuum of decisions and practices affecting who joins institutions, how people receive support for their activities, whether they feel respected and valued, how work is conducted, and what kinds of activities count as important work. . . . Integration and innovation requires an orientation toward understanding how practices and programs relate to a larger system. This orientation engages a wide range of stakeholders in an ongoing practice of institutional design . . . [an] ongoing reflection about outcomes in relation to values and strategies that enable people in many different positions to understand the patterns and practices and to use that knowledge to develop contexts enabling people to enter, flourish, and contribute. . . . This . . . invites a both/and approach to framing race, one that both considers race and insists that race be connected and justified in relation to more general values. . . . This move is not the same as color blindness. Instead, it nests race—and other social categories that operate to shape levels of participation and engagement—within a broader set of . . . goals and values. It legitimates the specification of affirmative goals and strategies and invites inquiry about the relationship of race (and other categories of difference) to the realization of those goals and values . . . employ[ing] various forms of race-consciousness to take account of the ways that institutions and policies erect barriers to full participation by people of color, and to forge long-term partnerships with the communities and institutions invested in the success of people of color. These strategies . . . reflect long-term institutional commitments to antiracist culture change.[53]

Political equality places affirmative action on firmer ground, focusing tortured debates on the argument that really matters: political equality is foundational to a flourishing democracy, and it requires the removal of structural domination and practices corrosive of reciprocity; affirmative action may sometimes be required to achieve that, so affirmative action may sometimes be essential to support the flourishing of democracy over time. Political equality illuminates the relationship between affirmative action and constitutional democracy, inviting opponents to consider whether their objection to race-conscious decision-making is so fierce that they are willing to risk the flourishing of democracy. It situates affirmative action within a broader governance regime designed to support the conditions of political equality over time.[54]

EQUALITY DUTIES IN MACHINE LEARNING

Black activists and intellectuals have long recognized that data can be used to support political equality. As Yeshimabeit Milner, the founder of Data for Black Lives, argues, "We can't write an algorithm that's going to solve racism. So we asked ourselves what it would mean to bring together software engineers, data scientists, activists of all races and really think about how we can change . . . these technological innovations." As Cathy O'Neil explains, "Data is not really neutral. In fact, it's the opposite of neutral. It's dynamic and explosive. And it is exposing, it exposes facts that we might not want to look at."[55]

PEDs would require institutions in a defined set of contexts to use race data to advance racial equality. As Salome Vilijoen argues, "Democracy as a normative standard offers criteria for evaluating how data relations are ordered, and should be ordered, by data governance law. It provides one theory of what define[s] unjust data relations and distinguish[es] them from just relations." Consider the p(click) example with which the chapter began. P(click) is trained on data that reflect racial inequalities: Black users tend to click on ads for jobs with lower than the average income and ads for mortgages with poorer terms, and because p(click) is an accurate machine learning model, its predictions reflect those social inequalities. PEDs transform our reasoning about this case. Political equality holds that respecting the equal moral worth of persons requires awareness of and sensitivity to differences that justify differential treatment. If there is a strong basis in evidence that including race or imposing demographic parity on p(click) would narrow persistent racial disparities, respecting the equal worth of Black and white people may require Facebook to do precisely that.[56]

By immunizing Facebook from charges of disparate treatment or violations of equal protection, PEDs would at minimum permit this. PEDs stipulate that where consideration of race is the most effective way to advance racial equality, then institutions are not prohibited from it. By removing the ever-present threat of anticlassification, this alone would transform Facebook's incentive structure.

In contexts as fundamental to the activities of citizenship as finding a home and securing a job, however, PEDs may even impose a positive duty on well-resourced institutions like Facebook to consider how best to use machine learning to advance racial equality. Facebook could be required to demonstrate that it has made reasonable efforts to design its advertising delivery system in the spheres of housing and employment so as to advance racial equality.[57]

This would require Facebook to deploy exactly the kind of comparative analysis of alternatives that Facebook submitted to the court in the imaginary lawsuit we explored in the last chapter. Instead of allowing Facebook to justify p(click) by showing that alternative models would have to use protected characteristics, and so are effectively unavailable, Facebook would be required to explore the full set of alternative ways of designing p(click) to reduce outcome disparities, including by using protected characteristics. The required empirical analysis would explore whether imposing demographic parity on particular models would in practice advance the welfare of disadvantage groups. Incentivizing institutions to explore alternative ways of designing machine learning systems to advance shared goals will be essential for the advancement of racial justice, gender equality, and socioeconomic opportunity as the use of machine learning becomes increasingly common.

Consider another example, the Los Angeles Police Department's PredPol. PEDs would require the LAPD to change how it designs and uses predictive tools in policing. Suppose the LAPD decided to invest resources in developing an approach that would ensure that predictive tools used by law enforcement reduced racial inequalities.

The LAPD developed a training course for police officers and commanders to help them understand the predictions of predictive policing systems. The training illustrates how data capture the outcomes of social processes that are often unjust. Predictive systems use measured arrest data, not actual offenses, and given existing patterns in policing, police forces are more likely to incorrectly arrest blacks and fail to arrest whites. In addition to the training, the LAPD also replaced PredPol with a different system, DemPol. DemPol weights crimes according to their severity, significantly reducing weightings attached to nonviolent crimes. As a result, the LAPD found, fewer police officers were sent to areas with high densities of nonviolent crime, such as possession of drugs or nonviolent robberies; in these areas, additional policing had been more likely to criminalize than to deter future crime. DemPol also included a mechanism for monitoring the effects of sending more police officers to particular neighborhoods, factoring in whether sending police officers was actually reducing crime rates. The system was intentionally designed to weaken the grip of past racial inequalities on future policing.

An interdisciplinary team also experimented with a range of statistical techniques to promote equity. They settled on Cynthia Dwork's "fair affirmative action" combined with a temporary form of demographic parity as the most transparent way to reduce racial inequalities, since both require institutions to be explicit about how they define and implement equal treatment. The team also decided to provide DemPol with data about the racial composition of different neighborhoods to ensure that the system took account of how race itself shapes policing and the measurement of crime in different neighborhoods. The LAPD found that this combination of better training and a redesigned predictive tool transformed the racial disparities produced by predictive policing.[58]

As with Facebook, PEDs would shift the LAPD's incentives. Instead of the blanket prohibitions against the use of protected characteristics that allow the LAPD to insist that its hands are tied, PEDs incentivize the LAPD to invest time and resources in exploring alternative ways of designing and deploying predictive tools to achieve their institutional objective: protecting public safety while reducing persistent racial disparities in policing in Los Angeles.

By altering the incentives that shape how institutions design and deploy machine learning models, PEDs would transform the governance of decision-making. Instead of making it easy for institutions to justify machine learning systems that entrench social inequalities, they would incentivize institutions to explore ways to use machine learning to advance equality. Given the scale and speed at which machine learning can compound and naturalize inequality, we must become more comfortable with policy tools that encourage institutions to work to reduce persistent social inequalities. Political equality offers a compelling justification for such policies by situating them within a regime for governing decision-making whose express purpose is to support the conditions of political equality over time. This refocuses debates over discrimination and affirmative action on what really matters: protecting and strengthening the flourishing of democracy.[59]

An AI Equality Act

In constitutional democracies around the world, there is a pressing need to update and reimagine laws that require institutions to evaluate the impact of their decision procedures on social inequalities.

Imagine a new law called the AI Equality Act (AIEA). The AIEA would set out the duties of public and private institutions as they build and use predictive tools, who has responsibility for monitoring and enforcing those duties, and to whom the duties apply. The act would assert political equality as a guiding principle in the design and deployment of predictive tools and move the governance of decision-making beyond the tort law approach to discrimination, which is centered on individual rights and remedies, and toward ensuring that institutions do not compound structural social inequality and that they sometimes directly address it.[60]

The AIEA would describe the broad content of citizenship and the importance of different sectors in securing the conditions required for citizens to function as political equals.[61] It would establish broad duties for institutions to demonstrate they have made reasonable efforts to ensure that their decision-making systems do not compound social inequalities and that, in some contexts, their systems reduce them. Whereas in the conventional approach laws impose obligations on private companies and public bodies and courts serve as a recourse to rectify failures of compliance, the AIEA would take a different approach. It would restructure the relationship between laws, regulators, and institutions by making regulators, rather than courts, the primary enforcer of these duties.[62]

The AIEA would represent a decisive moment of legislative assertion: Congress or Parliament would offer a picture of what it means to be a citizen of the United States or Britain and describe who has what obligations to remove barriers to establish and secure the political equality of citizens over time. In the United States, this assertion would directly challenge a Supreme Court that has often engaged in the "judicial usurpation of racial policymaking power from the representative branches of government," as the law professor Girardeau Spann argues.[63] It would recognize, as one UK judge put it, that the principle of "treating like cases alike and unlike cases differently is a general axiom of rational behaviour" that each legislature must define for itself:

> Of course persons should be uniformly treated, unless there is some valid reason to treat them differently. But what counts as a valid reason for treating them differently? And, perhaps more important, who is to decide whether the reason is valid or not? Must it always be the courts? The reasons for not treating people uniformly often involve, as they do in this case, questions of social policy on which views may differ. These are questions which the elected representatives of the people have some claim to decide for them-

selves. . . . The fact that equality of treatment is a general principle of rational behaviour does not entail . . . that it should always be the judges who have the last word on whether the principle has been observed. In this, as in other areas of constitutional law, sonorous judicial statements of uncontroversial principle often conceal the real problem, which is to mark out the boundary between the powers of the judiciary, the legislature and the executive in deciding how that principle is to be applied. . . . A self-confident democracy may feel that it can give the last word, even in respect of the most fundamental rights, to the popularly elected organs of its constitution.[64]

The AIEA is exactly the kind of governance regime that predictive tools like machine learning make possible—and necessary. Realizing the ambition that President Barack Obama articulated not long before he left office will require something very like the AIEA: "To avoid exacerbating biases by encoding them into technological systems, we need to develop a principle of 'equal opportunity by design'—designing data systems that promote fairness and safeguard against discrimination from the first step of the engineering process and continuing throughout their lifespan." By creating a governance regime in which private companies and public bodies routinely record, report, and justify disparities in outcomes produced by predictive tools, the AIEA would institutionalize the asking of exactly the moral and political questions that political equality invites and that discrimination encourages us to ignore. For the widespread use of machine learning to support political equality and the flourishing of democracy, we must be ambitious and imaginative about how we govern predictive tools. PEDs and an AI Equality Act offer a vision of how we might begin to do that.[65]

5

Facebook and Google
(The Politics of Machine Learning II)

If newspapers are successful in overthrowing tyrants, it is only to establish a tyranny of their own. The press tyrannizes over public men, letters, the arts, the stage and even over private life.[1]

—JAMES FENIMORE COOPER, *THE AMERICAN DEMOCRAT* (1838)

Modern state-unity depends on technology and far exceeds the limits of face-to-face community.... [T]echnological application ... has revolutionized the conditions under which associated life goes on. This may be known as a fact ... [b]ut it is not known in the sense that men understand it.... They do not understand *how* the change has gone on nor *how* it affects their conduct. Not understanding its "how," they cannot use and control its manifestations.... Whatever obstructs and restricts publicity, limits and distorts public opinion and checks and distorts thinking on social affairs.[2]

—JOHN DEWEY, *THE PUBLIC AND ITS PROBLEMS* (1927)

We are creating a world that all may enter without privilege or prejudice accorded by race, economic power, military force, or station of birth. We are creating a world where anyone, anywhere may express his or her beliefs, no matter how singular without fear of being coerced into silence or conformity.[3]

—JOHN PERRY BARLOW, "A DECLARATION OF INDEPENDENCE OF CYBERSPACE" (1996)

IN MARCH 2016, Kabir Ali posted a video of himself searching for images on Google. When Ali searched for "three black teenagers," Google returned a bunch of mug shots alongside pictures of a few smiling teens. When he searched for "three white teenagers," Google returned only the smiling teens. No mug shots. The video prompted a fierce debate about whether Google's search was racist. "It is society, not Google, that is racist," one article argued.

> The outrage towards Google as a result of those searches makes sense if a person isn't aware of the nature of search engine optimisation (SEO), algorithms, alt tagging and stock photography, but once you have that knowledge, it enables you to direct your outrage more accurately. . . . Google is a search engine; search engines collect data from the internet . . . computers and search engines do not think for themselves. They are . . . a reflection of those who use them—us.[4]

Kabir Ali agreed: "The results were formed through the algorithm they set up. They aren't racist but I feel like they should have more control over something like that."[5]

Facebook and Google do not create content; they build systems that distribute it.[6] Are they therefore responsible for the particular content that appears on their site? Are they a neutral conduit for communication and information with no obligation to monitor what they distribute, like a post office or a newspaper distribution company? On the one hand, Ali seemed to think the answer is yes. Because Google's algorithms reflect what people do, the more people upload and share images that embody racial stereotypes, the more Google's algorithms will return search results that reflect those stereotypes. Google is not responsible for search results; its algorithms simply reflect our social world back to us. And yet, Ali recognized, it is not quite that simple, because Google *sets up* the algorithms. Google builds algorithms that use past search results to predict which images are relevant, so Google controls whether algorithms replicate, ignore, or combat racial stereotypes in the images that people upload and share.[7]

By building systems that shape who sees what, when, and why, Facebook and Google mold the minds of billions of citizens and shape the public spheres of democracies across the world. At stake here is not simply the narrow issue of legal liability—whether Facebook and Google can be held legally responsible for the content they distribute—but a different version of the broader question we have been exploring: What is the nature of Facebook's and Google's power to design machine learning systems that shape what we read and how we talk to one another, even how we feel? And in a democracy, how should that power be governed?

This chapter returns to the politics of machine learning, where we began in chapter 1, but it explores the political character of machine learning in a different context. Instead of looking at how machine learning is used to distribute benefits and burdens in welfare services, the criminal justice system, or digital advertising, the remainder of this book focuses on how Facebook and Google use machine learning to distribute ideas and information. Just as the first half of the book built an argument about fairness, nondiscrimination, and political equality by starting from the political character of machine learning, this half does something similar: it builds an argument about digital infrastructure and the regulation of technology companies by starting with the political character of Facebook's and Google's machine learning systems.

By one measure, over 70 percent of all internet traffic goes through sites owned by Facebook and Google.[8] For those of us born in the 1990s, the internet was never a utopia of unencumbered, self-governing equals, but the space created and controlled by the world's largest companies: Apple, Microsoft, Alphabet (which owns Google), Amazon, and Facebook. The power of these companies is rooted in the technologies they build. How they build and use technology, "how algorithms [are] run, and in whose interest," matters not just for experts and policymakers but for all of us, as citizens, whose democracy they mold and shape.[9]

Drawing on my own experience in the technology industry as well as computer science research, this chapter demystifies this tech infrastructure in explaining how it works and why we all need to understand how it works. What people see when they load Facebook or search on Google is determined by ranking systems that use machine learning to order vast quantities of content and websites, solving what I call the "problem of abundance." This chapter explores how Facebook and Google design these systems. Because the power to design ranking systems is the essence of Facebook's and Google's power, understanding how these systems work and how they are built is critical to exploring how democracies should govern Facebook and Google.[10]

This chapter lays the foundations for a different way of thinking about regulating big technology companies. Instead of asking questions about the implications of technology for democracy, as if we are passive agents subject to the forces of technology and the companies that build it, we should ask what a flourishing of democracy requires from the regulation of technology. Nothing about the technology of prediction determines the effects of Facebook and Google on our society, economy, and democracy. We, the citizens and representatives of democracies across the world, must articulate the responsibilities borne by Facebook and Google to design machine learning systems that support healthy information architectures and thriving civic spaces. We must do what Kabir Ali understood was possible: hold them accountable for the power they exercise.

Facebook

Facebook is really, really big. At the time of writing, three billion people regularly used Facebook or apps owned by Facebook, like WhatsApp, Instagram, and Messenger. Within the populations of developed democracies, Facebook's reach is extraordinary. Seventy percent of adults in the United States use Facebook, three-quarters of whom visit the site every day, and Facebook is the most visited site in Britain. A little over 40 percent of Americans, and 33 percent (or 76 percent on some measures) of Britons get their news from Facebook. Facebook's systems shape the ideas and information encountered every day by billions of citizens across the world.[11]

Newsfeed

Facebook's most important system is newsfeed. It's the first thing you see when you open Facebook, what you spend five minutes scrolling through when you should be doing something else. Here is what I see when I opened mine in April 2020. A *Financial Times* article about the coronavirus lockdown in India. A former colleague in political science at Harvard reflecting on what pandemics mean for democracy. Advice from my local Labor group in Bury, Manchester, to elderly people who were self-isolating. An advert for a pair of gym shorts. A post from someone I met in Israel in 2015, a video of Jesse Lingard's winner in the FA Cup final in 2016, pictures of my in-laws in Alaska, and a doctor describing their experience of treating coronavirus patients. Facebook's newsfeed system determines the order in which these pieces of content appeared on my screen.

Here is how the newsfeed system works. Imagine all the content that Facebook could show each time someone loads the page: every status or photo posted by friends, every news article or video shared by a group they like. On average, 1,500 stories could be shown to each user at any moment, 15,000 to those with larger networks of friends. This is called the inventory, the stock of all content Facebook could display on your newsfeed. Newsfeed is a ranking system that orders this inventory content based on predictions about what content users are most likely to engage with. In a split second, the newsfeed system combines the predictions of hundreds of machine learning models, ranking inventory content from most to least likely to engage a particular user. We rank and order things all the time, from household chores to books on our shelves, but machine learning makes it possible to rank a much, much larger set of objects, more efficiently, in ways that people find useful.

Because ranking systems use multiple machine learning models, they are different from the models we have encountered so far. The COMPAS risk score predicts a specific outcome: the probability that someone up for bail or parole will commit a crime within two years of release. That prediction is used by judges and parole boards to make decisions about bail and parole. By contrast, Facebook's newsfeed system uses hundreds of models, each trained to predict a specific outcome, and the interaction of these models determines the ranking of content. Individual models include the p(click) model we have explored, which predicts the probability that a user will click on a particular piece of content; p(like), which predicts the probability that a user will "like" a particular piece of content; and p(share), p(comment), and so on. The system also uses models that predict more complex outcomes, such as the quality of a piece of content or whether users will find something offensive or objectionable.

Their complexity makes ranking systems harder to reason about than the models we have encountered so far. COMPAS was built to predict a particular outcome because the law requires that decisions about bail and parole be guided by recidivism risk. Every component of the criminal justice system is governed by well-known and well-tested laws. Facebook's newsfeed, which did not exist before 2006, is the product not of a single moment of design, but of a series of tweaks and updates and several more radical transformations, all guided by the pursuit of profit, a relentless desire to disrupt, and a grander ambition to reshape our social and political order. Facebook's newsfeed was built to change existing institutions, not to fit within them.[12]

The best way to understand the newsfeed ranking system is to explore it from the ground up, as we did with more straightforward models, focusing on the outcome, training data, and features. Facebook's patent filing describes the newsfeed system as "machine learning models . . . used for ranking news feed stories presented to users. The news feed ranking model may rank news feeds for a user based on information describing other users connected to the user in the social networking system." That information "includes interactions of the other users with objects associated with news feed stories," such as "commenting on a news feed story, liking a news feed story, or retrieving information, for example, imagines, videos associated with a news feed story."[13]

Let's start with the features of the newsfeed system. In ranking systems, features—the variables used to estimate an outcome—are called "ranking signals." The signals that newsfeed uses to rank content change all the time, but according to Facebook's patent, there are three basic kinds. Signals about content include the type of content (video, status update, photo) and how popular it is (how many likes, comments, or shares it has received). Signals about a user's network are derived from who produced a post (a close friend, a group the user's sister liked, someone they were at school with) and who has engaged with that post (how close those who have engaged with it are to the user). And a user's past behavior—what kind of content they tend to engage with (which news organizations, which kinds of media, which groups)—generates the third kind of signal. In sum, the newsfeed system uses signals about content, a user's network, and their online behavior to rank content in its inventory.

Newsfeed's models are trained on a mind-boggling volume and variety of data. Facebook gathers data about each of these signals to train its newsfeed models: data about content (engagement by the user with different types of content over time), the user's network (the groups their friends tend to engage with), and the user's own past behavior (the content they tend to engage with). Suppose Facebook has 52,000 data points about every user. If the average Facebook user has 338 friends, Facebook has 17,576,000 data points about the average user's network. Suppose Facebook has 1,000 data points about each piece of content. If there are 1,500 pieces of content in the average user's inventory, that's 1.5 million data points about the content that newsfeed could show to each user at any given moment in time. And that's just data for each individual user. If there are 2.8 billion users, that means 4,200,000,000,000,000 data points, a number so large it's almost meaningless. The power of the newsfeed system depends on vast quantities of training data about a self-contained world of human behavior.[14]

Because newsfeed is a ranking system rather than an individual machine learning model, describing the outcome it predicts is more complex. Whereas COMPAS predicts a specific outcome, recidivism risk, newsfeed aims to optimize a top-line metric. Metrics orient the hundreds of machine learning models in a ranking system toward a single, coherent goal. As with individual machine learning models, for which selecting the outcome is often the most significant design choice, defining these metrics is often the most important design choice in ranking. Nobody at Facebook—including Mark

Zuckerberg—knows exactly how all the machine learning models within newsfeed interact: how p(click) affects p(like), how content quality models affect p(share), and so on. But Facebook always knows how each of these models affects the top-line metrics, against which the success of Facebook's engineers and computer scientists is judged. We must therefore evaluate ranking systems in terms of the top-line metrics they aim to optimize, not just the outcomes that individual models are trained to predict.

The way to appreciate the power of these metrics is to observe what happens when they change. In 2013, Facebook users started to notice more attention-grabbing headlines appearing on their newsfeeds: "An Auto Executive Talks up Gas. The Guy Next to Him Who Builds Space Rockets Puts Him in His Place," or "We May Tell Our Kids That Life Isn't Fair, but We Should Actually Listen to Them Talk about Fairness." The change resulted from Facebook's decision to promote more "high-quality" and "relevant" content in newsfeed's top-line metric. Somewhat surprisingly, the company that produced these headlines, Upworthy, began to receive more unique monthly visitors from Facebook than the *New York Times* did. BuzzFeed's Facebook traffic rose by 69 percent. Traffic surged to old articles with eye-catching headlines, such as an old piece in the *Atlantic* titled "Zach Galifianakis Says Everything You Want to Say to Justin Bieber Right to His Face." Within a few weeks of changing newsfeed's top-line metric, Facebook had sealed the fate of news organizations across the world.[15]

These shifts make it easy to see why designing newsfeed is political. As I argued in chapter 1, choices are made in designing machine learning models that prioritize some interests and values over others. These choices matter because machine learning models operate on a significant scale and with unprecedented speed, shaping the world in their image as they naturalize the interests and values they promote. Choices about top-line metrics in Facebook's newsfeed are political in exactly this sense: they rank content in ways that promote some interests and values over others, and yet their politics is obscured behind technical details and superficially neutral objectives.

There was an even more significant shift in newsfeed's top-line metric in 2018. To avoid backlash from news organizations every time it changed the newsfeed system, Facebook decided that newsfeed would optimize for meaningful social interactions (MSIs). Facebook's newsfeed system would maximize active and deliberate forms of engagement, such as comments, shares, and reactions (those smiley or angry or sad faces), above more passive forms of engagement, such as likes, clicks, and views. Machine learning models would be used to predict what content would maximize active engagement from a user and their network, and newsfeed would rank content from most to least likely to provoke active engagement.

The MSI shift clearly benefited some interests over others. While the 2013 update had made Facebook critical for many news organizations—"centraliz[ing] online news consumption in an unprecedented way," as the *New York Times*'s John Herrman put it—the MSI shift increased engagement within Facebook while reducing traffic to external news organizations. Facebook benefited at the expense of traditional media as internal engagement increased by almost 50 percent and referral traffic decreased by almost 40 percent. MSI also benefited some publishers but harmed others. Large publishers like CNN and the BBC often did well, but others lost huge volumes of traffic. Slate's referrals declined from 28.33 million to 3.63 million from January 2017 to May 2018, a drop of 87 percent, and the drop-off in Vox referrals led to the layoff of fifty employees. Although the politics of the MSI shift was not clear-cut—Fox News became the top web publisher by engagement, and LADbible and Breitbart got more engagement than the *Guardian*, but conservative websites complained that the shift was "boosting liberal sites" while "crushing" theirs—it laid bare Facebook's power to shape who wins and who loses in the media industry.[16]

The MSI shift also prioritized some values over others. "We want Facebook to be a place for meaningful interactions with your friends and family—enhancing your relationships offline, not detracting from them," wrote Zuckerberg in a blog post announcing the shift. "After all, that's what Facebook has always been about." The idea was to increase the quality, rather than the quantity, of the time people spend on Facebook by prioritizing "high-value engagement" like comments, reactions, comment replies, or sending something to a friend. "We've gotten feedback from our community that public content . . . is crowding out the personal moments that lead us to connect more with each other," argued Zuckerberg. Facebook's research showed that posts from friends and family are better "for people's well-being" than "passively reading articles or watching videos—even if they're entraining or informative." "Too often, watching video, reading news or getting a page update is just a passive experience." In pursuit of users' happiness and health, Facebook promised to promote content from family or friends and reduce the prevalence of "public content."[17]

Facebook chose to prioritize the social over the public, orienting its newsfeed ranking system toward posts and discussion from family and friends and away from discussions of shared value, such as articles that newspapers judged to be of public concern or reliable, high-quality information about important issues in public debate. One study found that the MSI shift increased "divisiveness" and "outrage" by promoting posts that provoked and animated people, such as stories about the legalization of abortion, celebrity deaths, immigration, and missing children, a good proportion of which were not true.[18]

The choice to change newsfeed's top-line metric makes the political character of Facebook's choices about the design of newsfeed visible, because it reorients what hundreds of machine learning models aim to optimize. The MSI shift prioritized the social over the public and engagement over quality. As Chris Cox wrote when he quit as Facebook's chief product officer (he has since rejoined the company): while "social media's history is not yet written," it is clear that "its effects are not neutral."[19]

Integrity

All kinds of unpleasant things provoke engagement on social media: lies, racism, nudity, pornography, abuse, bullying, spam, and clickbait. Newsfeed gives this stuff reach. More people see it, so more people engage with it, so more people see it, and so on. These things spread on Facebook not because people are liars or racists or lewd, abusive hucksters, but because Facebook has built a ranking system that boosts lies, racism, and lewd, abusive hucksterism. Because Facebook has an enormous inventory of content it can show each user and masses of data to build systems that distribute it, there are countless ways in which Facebook could design newsfeed. Newsfeed has no natural state. If people see too much lying, racism, pornography, and abuse, it is because Facebook built a ranking system that distributes and amplifies them.

While spreading this kind of content provokes emotions that keep people coming back, beyond a certain point people start to feel offended and hurt, drained by the banality and unpleasantness of what they see, and they start blaming—or worse, quit—Facebook. The unofficial aim of the "integrity system" is to stop newsfeed from spreading content that goes beyond this invisible line, counterbalancing its indiscriminate boosting by removing and demoting the kind of content for which people might blame Facebook. What people see on Facebook is determined by a ceaseless struggle between the newsfeed and integrity systems. And Facebook controls which system wins.[20]

The integrity system is also composed of hundreds of machine learning models. Unlike the newsfeed system, each model operates independently,

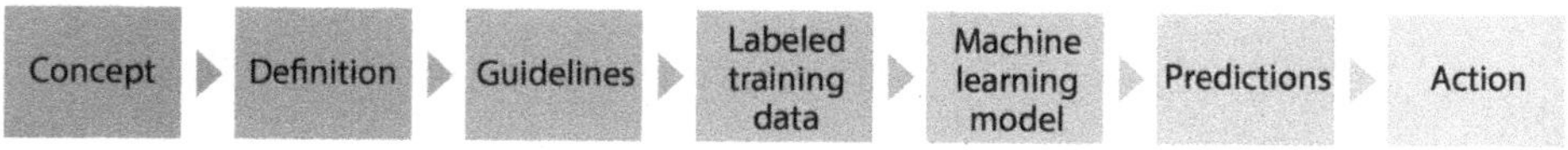

Concept ▶ Definition ▶ Guidelines ▶ Labeled training data ▶ Machine learning model ▶ Predictions ▶ Action

FIGURE 5.1.

rather than being arranged as a ranking system. Each model predicts a particular kind of bad content. The "misinformation" model predicts content that is likely to be false or misleading. The "hate speech" model predicts content that is likely to be hate speech. Different actions result from these predictions. Sometimes models are used to reduce the boosting that newsfeed would otherwise have given it, often called "demotion"; in other cases, models are used to temporarily remove content until a human can decide whether to remove it for good.

An entire book could be written about how these systems are built, but the general process works like this. Facebook first defines a concept that will underpin a machine learning model, such as misinformation or hate speech. To build a machine learning model that approximate this concept, Facebook creates training data sets by hiring human labelers to label hundreds of thousands of pieces of content. These labelers are given labeling guidelines that illustrate what kind of content meets the definition of the concept, such as what constitutes misinformation or hate speech. These data are used to train a model that predicts whether new content resembles the kind of content labeled as misinformation or hate speech in the training data.

Imagine you are a Facebook engineer building a machine learning model to detect "toxic" content. Needing first to define what "toxic" means, you might decide that toxic content is whatever promotes hate or division against a particular social group. To make this vague definition concrete, you will need to write guidelines for labeling content, perhaps using examples that illustrate content that falls just above and just below the threshold. You would then employ labelers to use these guidelines to label hundreds of thousands of pieces of content. Finally, you would train a model on these data to predict whether new pieces of content resemble those labeled as toxic in the training data. Each of these design choices weaves together questions about the meaning of toxicity, how Facebook should exercise its power in predicting it, and how to interpret and express fundamental values in technical systems. Examining these choices in detail unearths the unavoidable political judgments involved in building a simple machine learning model at Facebook and Google.[21]

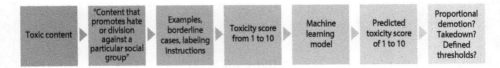

FIGURE 5.2.

Suppose you decide to assign to content a toxicity score from 1 to 10, with 10 being the most toxic. This system assumes that "toxicity" is something scalar that should be judged in terms of units of toxicity, and also that toxicity is linear, such that units of toxicity mean the same across the scale—the difference between content rated 2 and 3 on the toxicity scale is the same as the difference between content rated 7 and 8. Toxicity could be binary, however, such that content is either toxic or not. It could also be nonlinear—for instance, if there is little difference between content that is 2 and 3 on the scale but the difference between content with a score of 7 and 8 is significant.

Assumptions about the concept of toxicity have implications for designing a machine learning model to predict it. Technology companies measure the judgments of human labelers to understand how they interpret the concept of toxicity. Suppose you discover that there is much more agreement among labelers about toxicity scores at the higher end of the range. Moderators are more likely to agree that content deserves a toxicity score of 8, less likely to agree about a score of 7, and then increasingly unlikely to agree on 6 and so on down the scale. Suppose agreement is nonlinear: almost everyone agrees about content with scores above 8, but agreement drops off rapidly below 5, such that there is very little agreement about scores of 4 and below. You must then use this information to decide what action to take on the basis of predicted toxicity scores. If you want to act only when there is reasonable agreement among labelers about the meaning of toxicity, you should act only on content with a score above 8. If the model acts on content with a toxicity score below 5, it would be acting on the basis of an outcome about which there is significant disagreement.

Your design choices also imply assumptions about how to interpret and express fundamental values within technical systems. Suppose you are given a general instruction to build the toxicity model with an unflinching commitment to free speech. There are reasonable disagreements within your team about what this means and how it should be expressed in the design of the model. Some argue that the toxicity model should not be used to remove content but rather to demote content in proportion to the toxicity score it receives. Content with a toxicity score of 1 would not be demoted at all, content with a toxicity score of 5 would receive a moderate demotion, and content with a toxicity score of 10 would be heavily demoted.

Others reject the notion that this is what free speech implies. They argue that since heavily demoted content never in practice appears in anyone's newsfeed, drawing a distinction between heavily demoting content and removing it is disingenuous, like the moderator of a town hall insisting that the rules allow everyone to speak while placing some people too far down the agenda to ever have an opportunity to speak. Instead, they argue, free speech implies that Facebook should act only where there is clear consensus about the meaning of an outcome. Facebook should simply remove content above the threshold for consensus—in this case, a predicted toxicity score of 8—with clear notifications to people that their content has been removed. A final camp rejects the unflinching commitment to free speech altogether, arguing that there is far too much divisive and polarizing content on Facebook. They suggest the removal of content with a predicted toxicity score above 8 *and* the proportional demotion of content with a score below 8.

The gaps of experience, accountability, and language play a significant role in debates like these. I've seen it for myself. Usually those in positions of responsibility cite market research about "what users want," while offering vague general instructions about the importance of a system respecting some value, such as free speech, leaving computer scientists and engineers to interpret and express that value. The experience gap arises when, as often happens, those who design the system are not experienced in ethical reasoning about the values it is supposed to express. The accountability gap becomes a problem when those responsible for the system have little knowledge of the technical choices required to ensure that the system actually expresses the values it is supposed to. The language gap makes it hard to address the experience and accountability gaps, as ethicists experienced in reasoning about values often do not speak the technical language required to reason about how to express those values in the design of machine learning systems. These gaps make it difficult to establish clear structures of internal accountability for the design of machine learning systems. Engineers are often frustrated, not because executives have different value commitments (though sometimes they do), but by how often executives miss the connections between technical choices and particular values. But when engineers spot those connections, they themselves often lack the moral and political language to describe them.

I've also seen disagreements about underlying goals surfacing during the process of building these systems. People explore and clarify their own values by building machine learning systems (as we saw with Allegheny County's AFST), especially in companies like Facebook and Google. Internal discussions get heated because everyone knows that a certain kind of power to shape public debate is being exercised. Building machine learning models to predict toxicity, for instance, may change how engineers think about the concept itself and its relationship to free speech. It has taken me several pages to articulate just a few of the connections between technical choices and values you might encounter as an engineer at Facebook building one imaginary system, the toxicity model. As I argue, to identify and interrogate the political stakes of choices about designing and using these systems we must build structures of accountability that deliberately bridge the gaps of experience, accountability, and language.[22]

Google

Each time you Google something, your search query travels on average 1,500 miles to one of Google's data centers. A thousand computers use machine learning systems to process your search, returning a list of millions of websites ranked from most to least relevant. All in 0.2 seconds.

When Google was founded in September 1998, it processed about 10,000 of these searches a day, most of them in the United States. It now processes 40,000 searches a second, or 3.5 billion a day, from all over the world. Perhaps most remarkably, about 15 percent of searches have never been searched before. Just over half of all external traffic to news websites is driven by Google's search results (another 27 percent comes from Facebook). Half of Americans get news from search engines; one-quarter use search as their main way to access news. Google might be the most powerful company in the world.[23]

Google exists because it solved a problem. To understand the problem, and how Google solved it, imagine you are in a helicopter above an enormous, jostling crowd of a billion people crammed into an area the size of New York City. (You can fit the world's population into surprisingly small spaces—Google it.) The crowd is a mess. A bunch of people are naked or performing some kind of sex act, some are fighting, others are laughing, a few are reading books. Imagine you are on a mission to find something out. After the helicopter drops you at a random point in this crowd, you plan to go from person to person, asking for whoever might have the answer to your query. You would have a tiny chance of finding the right person. This crowd is the internet in the 1990s. Google solved the problem by listening to your query, scanning the enormous crowd, identifying the right people, and arranging them in an orderly line, starting with whoever is probably most relevant. This section describes how Google does this and why it matters.

PageRank

Search is about identifying and organizing sources of information relevant to a query. In the internet, these sources are websites; in our crowd, people are the sources. What made Google unique is PageRank, an algorithm that ranks the relevance of websites to a query.

In the mid-1990s, computer scientists began to use hyperlinks to explore the structure of the web. The content of websites had turned out not to be of much use because, although Harvard.edu is very relevant for queries about Harvard, its content does not often mention "Harvard" or "higher education." Hyperlinks, by contrast, encode a kind of judgment, a gesture about the utility or relevance of a website, usually but not always a positive one. The number of hyperlinks to a page, known as the number of backlinks that page has, reflects its importance.

Mapping hyperlinks could produce a picture of the meta-structure of the web. The "networked structure of a hyperlinked environment," wrote Jon Kleinberg, a computer scientist at Cornell, could be "a rich source of information" about the web. The web was "a hypertext corpus of enormous complexity that expands at a phenomenal rate," and it could "be viewed as an intricate form of populist hypermedia, in which millions of on-line participants, with diverse and often conflicting goals, are continuously creating hyperlinked content." Hyperlinks encoded precisely the "type of judgment" needed because "the creator of page p, by including a link to page q, has in some measure conferred authority on q." In the enormous crowd we are imagining, hyperlinks are like points. Each person points to a finite number of others, so that mapping who points to whom can give us a picture of the meta-structure of the crowd.[24]

Computer scientists found that the web has a giant-in-a-crowd structure. If each point is worth a meter of height, most of the individuals in a billion-strong crowd are a centimeter tall, some are a meter, fewer are two meters, and a very few are giants so tall that they stretch far into the clouds. The small people almost always point to giants; the giants sometimes point to one another, but almost never to the small people. Whereas in the real world height is normally distributed—almost all adults measure between five feet and six feet, five inches, with most people bunched around the middle—backlinks conform to a power law distribution. A very large number of pages have no backlinks at all (the one-centimeter people), a much smaller number have one backlink (the one-meter people), and a tiny number have millions of backlinks (the giants).[25]

Kleinberg described these giants as "authorities." Which giant is the appropriate authority depends on what you want to know. Kleinberg also found that some smaller people were "hubs" who point to all the relevant giants on a particular topic. "A certain type of natural equilibrium exists between hubs and authorities," wrote Kleinberg, in "a mutually reinforcing relationship: a good hub is a page that points to many good authorities; a good authority is a page that is pointed to by many good hubs." The hyperlink structure of the web enables the identification of "a small set of the most 'authoritative' or 'definitive' pages" for a particular topic—the giants who can answer your query. Algorithms could use hyperlinks to estimate the relevance of pages in search.[26]

This was the foundation of PageRank, an algorithm developed by the computer scientists Larry Page and Sergey Brin in 1998. ("PageRank" is a riff on Page's name and webpages.) Page and Brin were working on a citation analysis project at Stanford University, supported by the National Science Foundation. (Google began as http://google.stanford.edu/). Just as citations were used to estimate the impact of scholarly papers, hyperlinks could be used to develop "an approximation of the overall relative importance of web pages," encoding a judgment about relevance and authority.[27]

There are three parts to PageRank. The first is the number of backlinks (the number of hyperlinks to that page). If hyperlinks are affirmations or citations, pages with more backlinks are probably more authoritative than those with few. "The intuition behind PageRank," write Page and Brin, "is that it uses information which is external to the Web pages themselves—their backlinks, which provide a kind of peer review." Important websites (Yahoo.com was their example) "will have tens of thousands of backlinks (or citations) pointing to it," as "many backlinks generally imply that [a page] is quite important."[28]

The second is the quality of backlinks. "Backlinks from 'important' pages," write Page and Brin, "are more significant than backlinks from average pages. This is encompassed in the . . . definition of PageRank." Just as a citation from an important paper with lots of citations might count for more than a citation from a paper that has never been cited, PageRank estimates the quality of

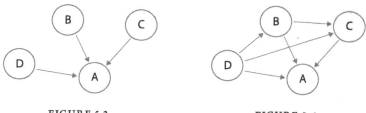

FIGURE 5.3.   FIGURE 5.4.

links "by counting the number and quality of links to a page to determine a rough estimate of how important the website is. The underlying assumption is that more important websites are likely to receive more links from other websites." Hyperlinks from websites that have more backlinks count for more than hyperlinks from websites with few or no backlinks.[29]

The best way to grasp the logic of PageRank is to work through the basic math that underpins it. Imagine there are four websites: *A, B, C,* and *D*. Let's ignore any links from a page to itself, and let's also treat several links from one page to another as a single link. Start by assuming that the PageRank for each page is the same. Assuming a probability distribution from 0 to 1, each page will begin with a PageRank of 1 divided by the total number of pages on the web. In this example, we have four websites, so each page will begin with a PageRank of 0.25.[30]

Imagine a simple model in which the only links are from pages *B, C,* and *D* to *A*. In this case, each webpage would transfer its initial PageRank of 0.25 to *A*, adding a total of 0.75 to *A*'s PageRank. Let's make the case a bit more complex. *A* links to no other page. *B* links to pages *C* and *A*. *C* links to page *A*. And *D* links to *A, B,* and *C*. In this case, *B* transfers half its starting PageRank of 0.25, which is 0.125, to pages *A* and *C*. Page *C* transfers all of its value to *A*, the only page it links to. *D* transfers one-third of its value of 0.25, or 0.083, to *A, B,* and *C*.

Calculating PageRank involves a recursive loop, in which the PageRank of each page is guessed repeatedly, approximating to its true PageRank over time. In our case, we could represent the calculation as follows.

$$PR(A) = \frac{PR(B)}{2} + \frac{PR(C)}{1} + \frac{PR(D)}{3}$$
$$PR(A) = \frac{0.25}{2} + \frac{0.25}{1} + \frac{0.25}{3}$$
$$PR(A) = 0.125 + 0.25 + 0.083$$
$$PR(A) = 0.458$$

This calculation can be represented algebraically. The PageRank of *A* is equivalent to the sum of the PageRank of each page divided by its number of outbound links *L*().

$$PR(A) = \frac{PR(B)}{L(B)} + \frac{PR(C)}{L(C)} + \frac{PR(D)}{L(D)}$$

In more general form, as in Page and Brin's original paper, the PageRank for any page *u* can be expressed as:

$$PR(u) = \sum_{v \in B_u} \frac{PR(v)}{L(v)}$$

Here is what this means in words. The PageRank for a page *u* depends on the PageRank of each page *v* within the set of all pages linking to page *u*, B_u, divided by the number of links $L(v)$ from page *v*. More simply, *u*'s PageRank depends on the number and quality of pages linking to *u*.

Page and Brin described PageRank in terms of someone randomly surfing the web. The surfer starts on a random webpage, then clicks on a link at random. They do the same on the next page, continuing until they have covered the entire web. A website's PageRank is the probability that, starting from a random page, the random surfer will end up on that website after a fixed but reasonably long time. Like being dropped at random into the crowd and then following points at random to find the giants, a person's PageRank is the probability that the user will end up talking to that person after a fixed period of time. PageRank is also a bit like voting. A link to a page counts as a vote of support. PageRank adds up all the votes for each page (the first component: quantity), but votes from pages that themselves got more votes count for more (the second component: quality).

The random surfer brings out a problem with the simple version of PageRank, with its two components of the number and quality of backlinks. A random surfer might get stuck. They could get caught in a loop, clicking on links from page *X* that jump to page *Y*, then clicking on links from page *Y* that jump back to page *X*, then back to *Y*, and so on. Or a random surfer could get stuck on a page that has no outgoing links. Page and Brin call this a rank sink, or link sink—like a couple in the crowd who only talk about and point to one another and refuse to point to anyone else. Instead of continuing in this loop forever, the surfer would probably get bored and jump to another random page. They would give up on talking to the couple and start talking to someone else.[31]

This is why Page and Brin introduced the third factor of PageRank, which models a moment in which the random surfer gets bored after following a defined number of links and jumps to another random page. This is called the dampening factor d, which is a parameter that can be set anywhere from 0 to 1 (usually to 0.85). Confusingly, d is the probability that the surfer will keep surfing, so to model the probability they will get bored and jump to a random page, we subtract d from 1 and divide the result by the total number of webpages. In other words, the probability that the surfer will keep going is assumed to decrease with each additional click. If a major page like the BBC or the *New York Times* links to a page via four "link-hops," the value of that link is dampened in contrast to a page that the BBC links to directly. Adding this dampening factor, the rest of the formula is basically the same:[32]

$$PR(A) = \frac{1-d}{N} + d\left(\frac{PR(B)}{L(B)} + \frac{PR(C)}{L(C)} + \frac{PR(D)}{L(D)} + \cdots \right)$$

In words, the dampening factor is subtracted from 1 and divided by the total number of webpages. The PageRank of A is then calculated by adding that figure to the product of the dampening factor and the sum of the PageRank scores of the pages with links to A. To put this in general form, assume that page A has pages T_1 to T_n linking to it (i.e., page A is referenced by pages T_1 to T_n). The dampening factor is d, which is set from 0 to 1, usually at 0.85. And $L()$ is the number of outbound links. In that case, the PageRank of A will be as follows:

$$PR(A) = \frac{1-d}{N} + d\left(\frac{PR(T_1)}{L(T_1)} + \cdots + \frac{PR(T_n)}{L(T_n)} \right)$$

PageRank models a random surfer who starts on a random webpage, then clicks on hyperlinks at random, never going back but sometimes getting bored and jumping to another page. The probability that the random surfer will visit a particular page is its PageRank. PageRanks constitute a probability distribution over all the pages on the web, the sum of which is 1.[33]

This third component built personalization into PageRank from the start. You can tweak d at a level ranging from one page to a defined group of pages, to all pages on the web. If d is uniform over all webpages, this models a random surfer periodically jumping to a random page, which "is a very democratic choice," since "all web pages are valued simply because they exist." Adjusting d to weight a particular page boosts the PageRanks of that page and the pages surrounding it, effectively adjusting d to model a surfer who is not random but someone about whom you have considerable contextual information, such as their home page and most visited pages. This gives a view of the web "focused and personalized to a particular individual," as Brin and Page wrote in 1998. The farther you get from the home page of the nonrandom surfer, the more similar the PageRanks become, and the more the personalized model converges to the nonpersonalized model in which d is uniform across all webpages. A "personal search engine . . . could save users a great deal of trouble by efficiently guessing a large part of their interests." The idea of a personalized search assistant was built into Google's very first ranking algorithm.[34]

PageRank "represent[s] a collaborative notion of authority or trust," as Page and Brin wrote, "since if a page was mentioned by a trustworthy or authoritative source, it is more likely to be trustworthy or authoritative . . . quality or importance seems to fit within this kind of circular definition."[35] The media scholar Siva Vaidhyanathan compares PageRank to a pragmatist theory of truth. "The truth of an idea is not a stagnant property inherent in it," wrote the philosopher William James. Instead, "truth happens to an idea. It becomes true, it is made true by events. Its verity is in fact an event, a process, the process namely of verifying itself, its verification."[36] Rather than relying on authors to describe their own website, PageRank harnesses the tacit judgment of the community of web authors about the quality of that website. PageRank uses this dynamic, social approach to estimating relevance through a process of experimentation, feedback, and collective discovery, imposing order on the messy network of the web. The essence of this approach is the idea that the number and quality of links to a website are a good guide to its importance, like "the common wisdom that the best roadside diners are the ones with all the big trucks parked outside," as the *New York Times*'s technology journalist, Peter Lewis, put it at the at the time.[37]

Beyond PageRank

Whereas PageRank was an algorithm tweaked and updated by human engineers, like Facebook, Google now uses machine learning to drive almost every component of its ranking system. A few years ago, as PageRank became just one of many factors influencing search results, Google decided to stop allowing people to view each website's approximate PageRank. Google now uses three kinds of signals in its search ranking system: those focused on links, like PageRank; those focused on quality; and those focused on the meaning of search queries.[38]

After links, the second most important component of the ranking system is quality. In the 2010s, many of Google's updates aimed to reduce the ranking of low-quality, spammy websites. Panda, introduced in 2011 and named after its designer, Navneet Panda, reduced low-quality sites like content farms that boost their ranking by using computers to aggregate content from other sites rather than producing their own. Panda also introduced a more expansive approach to evaluating quality, incorporating signals about whether users trusted information on a site, whether that information was original, and whether it was presented clearly. Penguin, introduced in 2012, focused on reducing the rankings of websites that boosted their ranking by using link farms that aggregated large numbers of links from virtually empty websites. Though Panda and Penguin have been effective at combating low-quality sites, some websites always lose from every update.[39]

Google uses machine learning to estimate the quality of websites, much as Facebook uses machine learning in its integrity system. Google defines a concept, writes guidelines for people to label hundreds of thousands of examples, trains machine learning models to estimate whether websites approximate the labeled examples, and then runs experiments and A/B tests to compare results from the old and new ranking systems. Tens of thousands of these experiments are run each year.[40]

As with Facebook, Google's labeling guidelines shape what its models predict. The detailed versions of Google's quality guidelines are closely guarded secrets, but they are sometimes leaked or released in abridged form. Google's "General Guidelines" include 168 pages of guidance for reviewing website quality. "Search engines exist to help people find what they are looking for," the guidelines explain, to "provide a diverse set of helpful, high quality search results, presented in the most helpful order." Different types of search need different kinds of results: medical searches need trustworthy and authoritative results; results for cute animal searches "should be adorable."[41]

Two concepts underpin these guidelines. The first is quality. People are asked to rate the quality of pages "to evaluate how well the page achieves its purpose." Labelers determine a website's purpose, whether sharing information about a topic or providing entertainment, then examine its trustworthiness and expertise, content quality, and ease of navigation to assign a page quality rating ranging from "lowest" to "medium" and "highest." The second concept is utility. People are asked to assign a "needs met" score to pages in response to a particular search query, from "fully meets" to "moderately meets" and "fails to meet." This assessment analyzes the user's intent, distinguishing between "know" queries ("who is the US president?"), "do" queries ("how do I tie a tie?"), website queries ("BBC News"), and visit-in-person queries ("nearest ATM"). Even if pages are high-quality, Google instructs, "useless" results should receive a "fails to meet" score since "useless is useless."[42]

As I have emphasized, machine learning changes the point at which humans exercise control over decision-making. Just as Facebook exercises control not primarily by judging individual pieces of content but by defining a concept, writing labeling guidelines, and building a machine learning model to approximate it, Google exercises control by defining concepts like quality, writing labeling guidelines, and building machine learning models to approximate it. Machine learning does not replace human choices, but rather changes the point at which humans make choices. As choices are made at the level of designing a system rather than about individual websites or pieces of content, machine learning can obscure the interests and values that those choices promote.[43]

The third most important signal in Google's search system is the meaning of queries. My grandparents often type fully formed question into Google: "Could you tell me the best place to get Indian in Manchester?" Most of us type half-formed questions full of ambiguities: "best Indian Manchester." Hummingbird uses machine learning to interpret that you mean "show me good Indian restaurants in Manchester," drawing on semantic search research in computer science to understand meaning by focusing on the whole query rather than just individual words. The long-term goal is conversational search, in which devices like Google Home understand what you are looking for without you having to type anything. RankBrain, introduced in 2015, developed this approach by using "deep learning" for translation, speech, and bioinformatics to match the meaning of users' queries to websites. The future of Google and Facebook will be shaped by the development of machine learning approaches like deep learning.[44]

Google presents updates to its ranking system as part of the inexorable path of progress, but very occasionally the veneer of consumer-driven neutrality crumbles and the political character of these updates becomes easier to see. One such moment explored by the media scholar Tarleton Gillespie came in 2011.[45]

Understanding it requires some context. In 2003, after US senator Rick Santorum compared homosexuality with adultery, polygamy, and incest—comparing homosexual acts to "man on child, man on dog, or whatever" and claiming that such acts undermine the "basic tenets of our society"—the sex columnist Dan Savage announced a contest to redefine the word "Santorum." After receiving thousands of submissions, Savage chose the winner: "Santorum: the frothy mixture of fecal matter and lube that is sometimes the by-product of anal sex." Savage bought the web domain spreadingsantorum.com and used his profile to encourage thousands of his followers to attach hyperlinks from "Santorum" to the site. Spreadingsantorum.com was soon Google's top result in searches for Santorum. Some have even speculated that the site played a role in Santorum's reelection defeat in 2006.[46]

In 2011, Santorum announced he was running for president. Santorum's return to the public spotlight entrenched spreadingsantorum.com's position as the top search result, as journalists linked to the site when discussing whether it was making a difference to Santorum's presidential bid (thereby in a small way ensuring that it would), Stephen Colbert deliberately mentioned it, and users searched for "Santorum" and clicked on spreadingsantorum.com. Santorum was soon asked if he wanted the result removed. After initially refusing to, he then said: "If you're a responsible business, you don't let things like that happen in your business that have an impact on the country," adding, "I suspect if something was up there like that about Joe Biden, they'd get rid of it." There are few charges that Google and Facebook hate more than political bias, for if that charge sticks, politicians might regulate them. Google had to decide what to do.[47]

Publicly, of course, Google refused to do anything: "Google's search results are a reflection of the content and information that is available on the Web. Users who want content removed from the internet should contact the webmaster of the page directly." Google does not "remove content from our search results, except in very limited cases such as illegal content and violations of our webmaster guidelines." In February 2012, however, spreadingsantorum.com disappeared from the first page of results. The Urban Dictionary result, which also defined the sex act, took the top spot.[48]

There are several competing theories about what happened. Instead of deliberately removing the result, Savage's site probably disappeared because Google changed its ranking system. One possibility is that Google updated its SafeSearch system, which ensures that adult results are not returned for non-adult searches. Another may be that Google changed how it boosts the ranking of "official" sites: "Google muddied the water by blaming safe search, but that appears totally untrue. They don't want people to have a potentially strong example of their new 'official page detection' (OPD) algorithm." If spreading-santorum.com had previously been incorrectly identified as an official page, this error would have been corrected in an update to the OPD algorithm. Google's engineers may not actually have known why Savage's site dropped, since how the interactions between hundreds of machine learning models impact individual websites can be almost impossible to discern.[49]

What matters is not which theory is correct but what the episode reveals about the power that Google exercises when it designs its machine learning systems. Before 2012, PageRank had effectively learned that people searching for "Santorum" often were actually looking for spreadingsantorum.com. Page-Rank captures the uncoordinated behavior of web users, aggregating judgments of value and importance to inform search rankings. As Google's head of global communications said at the time: "There definitely are people who are finding this to be the best answer to their question, and they are indicating this by either clicking on this result or linking to this result as the best answer to that question." Just as Kabir Ali said, Google could not be held responsible for its search results, because its ranking system was simply giving users what they wanted.[50]

And yet the site did not disappear because people suddenly decided they weren't interested. If Savage showed that PageRank could be influenced by co-ordinated collective action, then the site's disappearance made clear that de-signing a ranking system necessarily involves judgments about the legitimacy of that collective action. As Tarleton Gillespie writes, Google "must make cat-egorical and *a priori* distinctions about what kinds of results to prioritize, when, and for whom. And it must do so with an eye toward how information provid-ers will then try to emulate these distinctions." Google must decide how to distinguish the normal process of public debate from artificial attempts to boost the ranking of useless websites. Google may not want to make that judgment, but because of its position in our information ecosystem, it has to. Building machine learning systems that rank some sites above others requires judgments about what sites deserve to be ranked above others. Designing machine learn-ing models that rank ideas and information requires judgments about which values should guide the design of the public sphere.[51]

Suppose it was the official page detection model that killed Santorum's site. Think about how Google would design a model that judges the officialness of websites. First Google would have to settle on the principle that official sites deserve to be ranked higher than unofficial ones, a judgment that would be "infused with a particular theory of democracy," as Gillespie argues. "To privilege official sites over unofficial ones is to amplify those official voices in the public square. . . . The algorithm could be designed to do the exact opposite: it could grant 'unofficial' pages (like Savage's) higher standing, precisely because they do not have the benefits of amplification that official information sources usually do. . . . Every design has a theory about quality public discourse embedded within it." Then Google would have to decide what constitutes an official page, using quantifiable criteria that can accurately be predicted, such as the structure of hyperlinks, which would benefit pages that already have large numbers of backlinks. Then Google would have to decide how much of a ranking boost to give official pages: whether to boost pages in proportion to the number of backlinks or to give a fixed boost to all pages judged to be official.[52]

Making these choices is just what Google does. Just as the MSI shift illuminated the politics of designing newsfeed, the disappearance of spreadingsantorum.com illuminated the political character of Google's choices about the design of its search ranking system. Each time Google makes choices about how that system will change, some websites benefit while others lose, and some values are protected while others are violated, and yet the political content of those choices is obscured behind the simple interface of Google's website. Google's ranking systems powered by machine learning—like Facebook's— bake in political choices, naturalizing the web it ceaselessly shapes.

Solving the Problem of Abundance: But How?

Obscuring the Politics

Facebook and Google hide their power behind anodyne techno-babble. What they fear most is a widespread awareness of the political character of their machine learning systems.

"When we talk about integrity," explains Tessa Lyons, who runs Facebook's News Feed integrity team, "we're talking about any attempts to abuse our platform in order to create bad experiences for people." Bad experiences are the kind of content that people blame Facebook for, the invisible line beyond which promoting MSI is no longer in Facebook's interest. The word "integrity" comes from the Latin *integritatem*, meaning wholeness or completeness, purity or blamelessness. Facebook want citizens to believe that its integrity machine learning models are keeping Facebook whole and complete, unsullied by Russian hackers or domestic peddlers of lies and hate. Facebook's power to design these models is thus presented as a kind of generous public service that protects our public sphere. What integrity models actually do is unilaterally impose value-laden definitions on the moderation of public debate. The word "integrity" distracts from the system's real purpose: to reduce the ranking of content causing bad experiences that people might blame Facebook for.[53]

According to Facebook, building machine learning models to moderate public debate is simply a technical challenge of reducing error. Facebook's "Community Standards," Zuckerberg explains, aim "to err on the side of giving people a voice while preventing real world harm and ensuring that people feel safe in our community." "In some cases," according to Monika Bickert, vice president of public policy, "we make mistakes because our policies are not sufficiently clear to our content reviewers. . . . More often than not, however, we make mistakes because our processes involve people, and people are fallible." The best way to reduce error is to reduce the role of people. But people design Facebook's newsfeed and integrity systems too. When people like Bickert blame the obvious form of human control—low-paid contract workers who review individual pieces of content—they distract from the subtler form of human control—high-paid engineers and executives who design machine learning models.[54]

Google also obscures the politics of its machine learning systems. Design choices are presented as being driven by the inexorable pursuit of serving users better: "We can't make a major improvement without affecting rankings for many sites. It has to be that some sites will go up and some will go down. Google depends on the high-quality content created by wonderful websites around the world, and we do have a responsibility to encourage a healthy web ecosystem. Therefore, it is important for high quality sites to be rewarded, and that's exactly what this change does." They articulate vague goals that hide underlying disagreements: "Our goal is to get you the answer you're looking for faster, creating a nearly seamless connection between you and the knowledge you seek" (Facebook's equivalent goal: to "show the right content to the right people at the right time").[55] And they put themselves on the side of users even when they are not. In 2004, after activists alerted Google that a neo-Nazi site was the top result in searches for "Jew," Google posted a notice: "Offensive Search Results. We're disturbed about these results as well." Instead of intervening, Google threw up its hands and proclaimed its horror at the indiscriminate logic of search. But Google isn't in the same position as users. As Kabir Ali recognized, Google controls its ranking system.[56]

Unearthing the Politics

Cutting through this obfuscation requires a resolute focus on points of human choice. As Facebook's and Google's machine learning systems become ever more important to the structure of our public sphere, scholars, policymakers, and citizens must become ever more adept at identifying the points at which human control is exercised over the design of those systems. The next few chapters build an account of how we should understand Facebook's and Google's power to design machine learning systems, so I want to state quite precisely the points of choice involved in designing them.

Facebook's newsfeed and Google's search both solve a problem of abundance. Facebook is useful because its newsfeed system sorts thousands of pieces of content in a user's inventory that could be shown each time they load Facebook, and it ranks them based on which pieces it predicts they will find most engaging. Google is useful because it sorts millions of websites on the internet—Google's search index contains hundreds of billions of webpages and is over one million gigabytes—and ranks them based on which it predicts will be most relevant to a particular search query.[57]

Facebook's and Google's power is rooted in how they use machine learning to solve the problem of abundance. About 31 percent of people click on the first search result that Google displays. People are ten times more likely to click on the first search result than the tenth, and moving from the second to the first search result significantly increases the chance that a website will be clicked on. On average, moving up one spot in Google's search results increases the chance that a website will be clicked on by 31 percent. When Facebook and Google change their ranking systems, they change how a vast quantity of content and websites are filtered, sorted, and ranked, shaping what we see and what we read, what we learn and even how we feel, focusing our attention and determining how and where we spend our time on the internet. As I explore in the next chapter, Facebook's and Google's systems are a kind of super-powered performative prediction: they make their predictions come true, molding our opinions and beliefs, desires and habits, in their own image. Facebook's and Google's power is rooted in how they use machine learning to solve the problem of informational abundance.[58]

There are four crucial points of choice at which Facebook and Google exercise that power. These choices should be the central focus of any approach to governing Facebook and Google.

The first and most fundamental is choosing the underlying values that the ranking system is built to advance. Google's search implies that systems that control access to information should prioritize sources judged by a community to be authoritative and that a community's judgment about authority ought to be respected. Whether right or wrong, this choice takes a particular view about how and by whom information should be distributed in the public sphere. Facebook's newsfeed implies that systems that distribute content should prioritize the social over the public and engagement over quality. Whether right or wrong, that choice also takes a particular view about how content should be distributed in the public sphere. A framework for governing Facebook and Google should focus on the values that guide the design of these ranking systems.

The second point of choice is the top-line metrics that ranking systems seek to optimize. Because ranking systems comprise hundreds of machine learning models, the most salient point of choice is defining the top-line metric that orients those machine learning models. Top-line metrics embed values into ranking systems. By shifting newsfeed's top-line metric to MSI, Facebook changed the objective that hundreds of machine learning models were seeking to optimize, transforming the effects of the system on the people who use newsfeed and the organizations that depend on its traffic. Each time the top-line metric changes, so too does the way the newsfeed ranking system solves the problem of abundance and, as a result, its effects on our public sphere. A framework for governing Facebook and Google should focus on the top-line metrics that these ranking systems seek to optimize.

At the third point of choice is the decision about the concepts that machine learning models are built to approximate. When Facebook builds a machine learning system to detect toxic content, or Google builds a machine learning system to estimate quality, both are making a judgment about what concepts will structure and guide the public sphere and how those concepts should be understood: that content fitting Facebook's definition of toxicity, or information fitting Google's definition of low quality, should be made almost invisible. Whether right or wrong, building machine learning systems to approximate concepts implies a view about what those concepts mean and what role they should play in structuring our public sphere. A framework for governing Facebook and Google should focus on the concepts that Facebook and Google build machine learning models to approximate.

The final, and somewhat more granular, choice concerns the guidelines that Facebook and Google write to shape how people label the examples used to train machine learning models. Concepts like toxicity and quality are abstract, general, and vague; to be useful for ranking or moderating content on a vast scale, they must be turned into data sets that can be used to train machine learning models. Writing and implementing these guidelines involves the exercise of power, often hiding significant judgements about values and interests. These guidelines shape how machine learning systems approximate concepts, implying a view about how those concepts should be interpreted and expressed within machine learning systems, and applied in our public sphere. A framework for governing Facebook and Google should focus on the guidelines used to label the hundreds of thousands of pieces of content and websites that shape the machine learning systems deployed by Facebook and Google.

Because Facebook's and Google's machine learning systems are dynamic, evolving rapidly over time in ways that fundamentally change how they use ranking to solve the problem of informational abundance, what matters is the process that shapes each of these design choices, rather than the individual design choices made at a given moment. Any successful effort to regulate Facebook and Google must focus not on the interests and values that their machine learning systems advance at any given moment, but on the processes and mechanisms of governance used over time to identify and articulate those interests and values, define the concepts, and develop the guidelines.

Governing Facebook and Google is not primarily about *what* systems Facebook and Google build but about *how* Facebook and Google build those systems over time. The processes and mechanisms of governance that shape how Facebook and Google make political choices about the design and deployment of machine learning systems matter more than the particular political choices that Facebook and Google make. The next chapter examines the nature of the power they exercise when they design ranking systems powered by machine learning, setting the foundations for a vision of how to regulate these two tech companies to structure those processes and mechanisms of governance in ways that support the flourishing of democracy.

6

Infrastructural Power

The way to prevent these irregular interpositions of the people is to give them full information of their affairs thro' the channel of the public papers, and to contrive that those papers should penetrate the whole mass of the people. The basis of our governments being the opinion of the people, the very first object should be to keep that right; and were it left to me to decide whether we should have a government without newspapers or newspapers without a government, I should not hesitate a moment to prefer the latter.[1]

—THOMAS JEFFERSON TO EDWARD CARRINGTON
(JANUARY 16, 1787)

Participation in activities and sharing in results . . . demand communication. . . . Wherever there is conjoint activity whose consequences are appreciated as good by all persons who take part in it, and where the realization of the good is such as to effect an energetic desire and effort to sustain it . . . just because it is a good shared by all, there is . . . a community. The clear consciousness of a communal life, in all its implications, constitutes the idea of democracy.[2]

—JOHN DEWEY, *THE PUBLIC AND ITS PROBLEMS* (1927)

The term "public" signifies two closely interrelated but not altogether identical phenomena: It means, first, that everything that appears in public can be seen and heard by everybody and has the widest possible publicity. . . . Second, the term "public" signifies the world itself, insofar as it is common to all of us and distinguished from our privately owned place in it. . . . To live together in the world means essentially that a world of things is between those who have it in common, as a table is located between those who sit around it; the world, like every in-between, relates and separates men at the same time.[3]

—HANNAH ARENDT, *THE HUMAN CONDITION* (1958)

Platforms act as performative intermediaries that participate in shaping the worlds they only purport to represent.[4]

—TAINA BUCHER, *IF . . . THEN: ALGORITHMIC POWER AND POLITICS* (2018)

ON THE MORNING OF February 22, 2018, Tina Adams was nervous. She had planned a march of fellow public teachers on the State Capitol in Charleston, West Virginia, to protest a hike in state health insurance premiums and further delays to a long-promised pay raise. Although thousands had attended the Facebook event, Tina wasn't sure who would show up now. It had been thirty years since teachers in West Virginia last walked out, the state attorney general had declared the strike illegal, and it had been snowing heavily. Soon after she arrived in the parking lot, a huge caravan of school buses rolled in, adorned with colorful decorations and protest signs, honking their horns. Supportive state snowplow drivers had cleared the highway ahead of the caravan, and now hundreds of teachers left the buses and filed into the statehouse. "We just kept yelling: 'We're not gonna take it,'" Tina told me a few months later, beaming. The walkout became known as "Fed-Up Friday," and the whole day was live-streamed on Facebook.[5]

The strike swept across the nation as teachers in Oklahoma, Kentucky, and Arizona walked out too. At first, lawmakers were uncompromising: "I guarantee you," proclaimed the Republican governor of Kentucky, Matt Bevin, that "somewhere in Kentucky today, a child was sexually assaulted that was left at home because there was nobody there to watch them. I'm offended that people so cavalierly, and so flippantly, disregarded what is truly best for children." This rhetoric backfired. After polling suggested that three-quarters of Americans believed that teachers had the right to strike, the GOP-led Kentucky legislature condemned Bevin for his remarks, and both parties rushed to embrace the teachers' agenda, supporting dozens of teachers to run for state legislatures—thirty-four in Kentucky alone. After nine straight days—the longest strike in West Virginia's history—teachers won a 5 percent pay raise and a task force to address problems with state health insurance. Tina sat down and cried. She had won. She had found her voice, organized a political movement, and made change.[6]

Facebook was critical to the movement's success. The West Virginia Public Employees United group, started by teachers to share concerns about planned health insurance cuts, grew in just a few months to twenty-four thousand invitation-only members, or 70 percent of West Virginia's public school teachers. "Facebook contributed to a sense of everyone being in it together," explained Emily Comer, one of the group's founders. "West Virginia can be an isolating place," explained another teacher and group member, Eric Newsome. "Communities can be far from each other. I'm here in southern West Virginia, which is more impoverished than the northern part of the state. But being on Facebook, I'm like, 'Hey, they're ticked off at the same stuff as we are. They're having the same issues too.'" Something similar happened elsewhere across the country. Forty thousand joined the Oklahoma Teachers United group on Facebook, and forty-five thousand joined the Arizona Educators United group.[7]

Facebook made collective action possible, enabling teachers to coordinate across thousands of miles in some of the most rural, impoverished states in America. "West Virginia does have a long history of wildcat strikes," continued Eric Newsome, "but in terms of all fifty-five counties going out, that has never happened, and it would not have happened if it wasn't for social media." Another strike leader concurred: "This strike wouldn't have happened without the grassroots organization through the private Facebook group. The legislative leadership, unions, other organizations, were all helpful. But without question, I don't think this would have reached the critical mass that was needed had they not had the platform of the group to communicate." Facebook was the infrastructure for the political movement that Tina started.[8]

As I spent more time in West Virginia, I was struck by how much and how effectively Tina's community used Facebook. Tina and her husband John, a former coal miner, are from Wyoming County, a mining region whose population has almost halved over the last few decades as persistent unemployment and a shrinking economy have driven many away. For Tina's community, separated by hundreds of miles of poor-quality roads without effective public transport, Facebook is an invaluable tool. Locals use Facebook to buy and sell goods, find work, arrange community events, stay in touch, and ultimately to organize, mobilize, and achieve change. Facebook has become vital infrastructure for many social, economic, and political activities in Tina's community.[9]

Just as these strikes were spreading across the country, Mark Zuckerberg gave his first testimony to Congress. "It is no secret that Facebook makes money off... data through advertising revenue," declared Senator Chuck Grassley from Iowa, "although many seem confused by or altogether unaware of this fact. Facebook... generated $40 billion in revenue in 2017, with about 98 percent coming from advertising across Facebook and Instagram." In pursuit of advertising revenue, explained Senator Christopher Coons from Delaware, Facebook aims above all to "capture [people's] attention."[10]

This chapter uses two analogies to explore the nature of Facebook's and Google's power. By comparing Facebook to a digital public square and Google to a digital public library, I show how and why design choices about their machine learning systems matter. When Facebook and Google design these systems, they exercise a kind of infrastructural power to structure our public sphere and organize our information ecosystem. Because this power is unilateral, subject to neither meaningful economic competition nor effective democratic oversight, citizens lack mechanisms for holding Facebook and Google to account. Political action that depends on Facebook is vulnerable to Facebook's shifting priorities and design decisions. What's more, because Facebook and Google are advertising companies, they design ranking systems to maximize revenue. They solve the problem of informational abundance by designing ranking systems that grab, stimulate, and direct attention in pursuit of profit, producing filter bubbles and social division, limiting the scope for curiosity and random discovery, and ultimately corrupting the public sphere. As Congress interrogated Zuckerberg, thirty thousand teachers gathered at Oklahoma's State Capitol in Oklahoma city after coordinating their protest on Facebook. A newspaper headline captured the irony: "Facebook Is in Crisis Mode. The Teacher Strikes Show It Can Still Serve a Civic Purpose."[11]

This chapter articulates the problem statement for regulating Facebook and Google from the standpoint of democracy. I use my analogies to argue that Facebook's and Google's machine learning systems have become part of the infrastructure of the digital public sphere, shaping what citizens know and believe and how they encounter each other, discuss common aspirations, and forge shared ambitions. That these systems can corrupt the public sphere illuminates the nature of Facebook's and Google's power to design them. Ranking systems like Facebook's newsfeed and Google's search are a case of supercharged performative prediction: they use the power of prediction not just to work out what citizens already want, but to shape what they want, ranking and ordering ideas and information to commandeer attention and mold the public sphere. To support the flourishing of democracy, we must step back and ask how we should govern corporations whose infrastructural power shapes the character of our public sphere and our civic information architecture.

Infrastructural Power

Facebook: The Public Square

The problem with the Cambridge Analytica story was that it made Facebook the solution. Facebook likes the idea that 2016 was about how Russia and Cambridge Analytica stole the US presidential election, because it means that we need Facebook to defend the integrity of our elections: "We at Facebook were far too slow to recognize how bad actors were abusing our platform," explained Samidh Chakrabarti, Facebook's head of civic engagement. "We face determined, well-funded adversaries who will never give up and are constantly changing tactics. It's an arms race and we need to constantly improve.... It's why we're investing heavily in more people and better technology to prevent bad actors misusing Facebook."[12]

Imagine that you live in a town dominated by one public square, perhaps the agora of ancient Rome or the Piazza del Campo in Siena. The square is used for all kinds of activities. Groups of residents from different neighborhoods gather to discuss local issues. Others meet to plan public protests or to swap favorite recipes. Friends and family from opposite sides of the town meet to share memories and talk about what they've been reading. The public square is defined by the presence of stories: "a newspaper, magazine, book, website, blog, song, broadcast station or channel, street corner, theater, conference, government body and more." In the square, people "gather as a mass or associate in smaller groups ... talk and listen ... plan and organize" and "deliberate over matters of public importance." Citizens come to buy and sell goods, meet friends and make plans, discuss the issues of the day, and organize politically. The square is also used for town meetings and public debates. Politicians make speeches, hold campaign rallies, and post adverts, and citizens come together to make collective decisions and select their representatives. Suppose everything about the square is controlled by one corporation. They design the square, shape its architecture and atmosphere, and set the rules about which groups will stand where, who gets to speak, for how long, and about which subjects.[13]

Suppose that after an unexpected election result citizens accused the corporation of failing to remove false pamphlets circulated by foreign agents, which some argued might have tipped the election. What is objectionable here is that the corporation's unilateral control over the architecture and rules of the public square includes the power to tip elections, not simply the use of this power by foreign agents. Similarly, the real story of 2016 was not the malicious forces of Russia and Cambridge Analytica—it was that by shaping what voters saw and heard about different candidates, Facebook's machine learning systems could affect who turned out to vote, and that might have been enough to tip the election. Such an outcome would be especially possible in democracies that use first-past-the-post. "Ultimately," concluded one commentator, "these problems stem not from the platforms' glitches but from their very features." The focus on bad actors distracts from the power that Facebook wields all the time. Facebook is the problem, not the solution.[14]

Let's push the analogy further. Suppose agents of the corporation control what people see when they come into the square by handing out literature like pamphlets, articles, photos, and messages. The corporation does not write this literature, but because of the abundance of pamphlets, articles, photos, and messages that could be shown to each person at any moment)by choosing the content that people see), the corporation shapes what people feel as they enter the square. The corporation also controls what people encounter as they walk around the square, using subtle nudges and clues to guide where they go, the groups they meet, and the conversations they overhear and participate in. The corporation does not control what people say or share with one another, but because of the abundance of voices, stories, and ideas circulating, the corporation shapes what people feel, especially about those they meet, as they walk around.[15]

This is how we should think about Facebook's newsfeed: as infrastructure that ranks information and ideas in the digital public square. How Facebook designs the newsfeed system determines the order in which people see and hear thousands of things that are being said or done at any given moment. Although the corporation cannot determine which pamphlet each individual receives as they enter the square, the corporation doesn't much care about each individual. What it cares about are aggregate effects: how the collective mood responds to different ways of ranking information and ideas. Similarly, Facebook designs newsfeed by considering how best to maximize its top-line metric, not the particular content to show individuals. Rather than rank news from far-flung places or debates about matters of public concern, Facebook chooses to optimize MSI in order to rank pieces of content that provoke reactions and engagement so that more people see and hear them. And because

Facebook's control over this infrastructure is unilateral, it need not account for the square it builds.

This clarifies what makes Facebook different from the *New York Times* and Fox News. The corporation does not determine what is in each pamphlet, which stories the editors of the pamphlet decide to print and which they do not, but it does decide which pamphlets to give people as they enter and walk around the square. Similarly, Facebook's newsfeed does not determine which stories the *New York Times* or Fox News commission, what they decide to print or broadcast, but it determines whether citizens see content from the *New York Times* or Fox News, which stories or videos different people see, and which pieces of content receive the widest circulation. Newspapers and broadcast channels are important components of the public square, but they are not the same kind of underlying infrastructure as Facebook's newsfeed. Facebook does not create content; it determines who sees what content. The power to design Facebook's newsfeed is a more fundamental infrastructural power than the power to decide what to print or broadcast.

Suppose the corporation developed digital signposts that direct people toward groups congregating in the square they might like to join. The corporation found that, when people join like-minded groups, people who live near each other or who read similar books, they tend to visit the square more often. This is like Facebook's group recommendation tool. The corporation also learned that occasionally handing a controversial pamphlet to assembled groups provokes heated discussion that keeps people coming back. This is like Facebook's system for ranking content within groups, which plays an increasingly important role in driving traffic to and within Facebook.[16]

Suppose the corporation also introduced a system for moderating town meetings. On entering the square, everyone would be given headphones with a built-in microphone. By using the extensive information it had gathered about each individual, the corporation could predict whose voices people would most want to hear and then it could stream those voices directly into each person's headphones. For example, the corporation developed a model that predicted each person's tolerance for toxic content and then filtered out toxic content they didn't want to hear. Those who said things that most people would find toxic could be effectively muted without having to physically ban them from the square. Town meetings became a kind of giant, personalized, silent disco.[17]

This is like Facebook's integrity system, and in particular the toxicity model we explored in the last chapter. Just as the corporation might find that its defini-

tion of toxicity punished some groups of citizens more than others by stream-
ing less of the speech produced by those groups into the headphones of others,
in the real world content written in African American English is more likely to
be labeled as toxic, and so machine learning models disproportionately demote
content produced by African Americans. "Abusive language detection systems . . . have a disproportionate negative impact on African-American social
media users," potentially "discriminat[ing] against the groups who are often the
targets of the abuse we are trying to detect," explained one report.[18]

If town meetings become more adversarial, driven by a few angry voices
that provoke outrage and reaction, citizens might begin to feel that town meetings are shaped more by the corporation's interests than the town's. Although
the corporation might insist that citizens are hearing what they want to hear—
that is, town meetings are only angrier and more adversarial because citizens
are—citizens might doubt the corporation's motives, suspecting that the corporation introduced the silent disco system because it boosted the corporation's profit. On the walls surrounding the square, the corporation posts vague
explanations of how its systems decide which speech to stream into people's
headphones, but citizens might still object that its unilateral control over the
infrastructure of their public square hinders their capacity to organize, deliberate, and make collective decisions.

In a bid to address these criticisms, suppose the corporation assembles an
independent panel of experts to oversee town meetings. Citizens can refer
pamphlets or people they find objectionable to the panel, which reviews them
against the corporation's rules and decides whether to burn the pamphlets or
ban the people from the square. After initially welcoming the move, citizens
soon find that the panel of experts makes little difference to the general character of town meetings. Because the panel has jurisdiction only over decisions
about individual pamphlets and people, it does not affect the silent disco system or the distribution mechanism for handing pamphlets to people as they
enter and walk around the square. This scenario describes the problem with
Facebook's Oversight Board. Its jurisdiction over individual content moderation decisions does not touch Facebook's real power: the design of its machine
learning systems.[19]

There are very real ways in which Facebook's power mirrors the corporation's. Like the corporation, Facebook cannot decide what people say and do,
or what editors decide to publish in pamphlets, but because there is an abundance of speech and action, Facebook's systems order and rank ideas and information, shaping who benefits and which values the square embodies. Like

the corporation's silent disco, Facebook can immunize itself from the charge of policing speech because its systems are personalized, different for each user. If a user wants to hear something different, they just have to change the signals they give about what they want to hear.

Facebook's machine learning systems are the infrastructure of the digital public square. The company's newsfeed ranking system shapes what people see as they enter and walk around the square. Facebook's group recommendation and ranking system shapes who people congregate with and what they talk about. Facebook's integrity system delivers personalized town debates to each person, preemptively filtering content before anyone sees it. When Facebook builds or changes these systems, it redesigns the infrastructure of the digital public square, altering its fundamental character, changing who is seen and heard by whom, shaping the course of public debate, and restructuring the tools that citizens have to organize, engage, and make collective decisions.[20]

Part of the point of this analogy is to show what is not the same. A public square is a physical place in which people assemble and from which people can withdraw at will. Facebook enables us to step outside our homes without leaving them, and because its machine learning systems are personalized, it also offers the illusion of publicity, as if what we see and hear is just like what others see and hear, when in fact each citizen participates in their own curated public sphere—a virtual reality public sphere. Whereas in our imaginary public square citizens can see each other wearing headphones and, if they want, can take them off and take back control of their town meetings, the only way to escape Facebook's ranking systems is to leave Facebook.

As more of the activities of citizenship move online, more of what has happened in the physical world will happen in the digital world, and the digital public square will come to matter even more for democracy. "The public square, the place where the ideas of the day are thrashed out," writes the journalist Jamie Bartlett, "is increasingly run on a set of private servers. The owners of those private servers could make decisions—based on shareholder interest, or the political views of the founders—that materially change the nature and balance of public debate: and no one would ever know."[21] Bartlett is right. Except that the important technologies are not "servers" but rather machine learning models. And as such, it is not that owners *could* make decisions that shape the nature of public debate—they already do. Because they have to. That is what it means to use machine learning to design ranking systems that solve the problem of abundance. That is what Facebook does.

Google: The Public Library

How societies organize information shapes their politics: what they do and what they can conceive of doing. Five thousand years ago, the ancient Sumerians of Mesopotamia were the first society we know of to use the technology of writing to organize information. Temple officials created simple pictograms to catalog flows of grain and animals, which had become too large to recall by memory. Because writing was time-consuming and required specialist skills, a powerful elite of scribes infused writing with a kind of mystique, using it to exaggerate their powers of memory and recall. A few thousand years later, Socrates accused the inventors of writing of "declar[ing] the very opposite" of its "true effect." Far from enabling memory, writing "implants forgetfulness" because people cease "to exercise memory," relying instead "on that which is written, calling things to remembrance no longer from within themselves, but by means of external marks." Writing, he argued, is a tool not "for memory, but for reminder."[22]

As a reminder tool, writing turned out to be pretty useful. Using reeds to mark wet clay, scribes developed pictographic sequences into a writing system called cuneiform (the Latin *cuneus* means "wedge"), which used complex phonetic sounds to record stories about war, famine, plague, and love. As these stories proliferated, the utility of writing depended on finding ways to store and organize tablets, scrolls, and books. Humanity's first library, established by the Assyrian ruler Ashurbanipal in what is now Iraq in the seventh century BC, gathered and organized the stories and records of the ancient Sumerians. It contained more than thirty thousand cuneiform tablets organized by subject matter, including archival records, religious and scholarly texts, and notable works of literature, like the *Epic of Gilgamesh*. "According to several religions, there were book collections before the creation of man: the Talmud has it that there was one before the creation of the world, the Vedas say that collections [of books] existed before even the Creator created himself, and the Qur'an maintains that such a collection coexisted from eternity with the uncreated God." Whether scribes or librarians, whoever controls the storage and organization of knowledge shapes who knows what and whose stories are read by whom, exercising the most enigmatic of powers.[23]

Just as libraries are useful because they deploy technologies to index information, Google was useful because PageRank organized websites to help people access what they wanted to know. As we saw in the last chapter, the web in the late 1990s was like an unorganized mass of millions of books—a vast crowd of people talking to one another, with a few giants—in which it was almost impossible to find information. Google became the self-made librarian for the biggest library that mankind had ever seen, as Page and Brin put it, by "bringing order to the web."[24]

Think of the web as something like the Library of Babel, a fictional library from a Jorge Luis Borges story that the legal scholar James Grimmelmann first explored as a helpful analog to the internet more than a decade ago. The Library of Babel is made up of an endless series of hexagonal rooms. In each room, four walls are covered with shelves and the other two lead to a narrow connecting hallway, which runs through a vast air shaft with a winding staircase that stretches up and down as far as the eye can see. On one side of this hallway is a small room where "one may sleep standing up"; a toilet to "satisfy one's fecal necessities" is found in the other. Each of the hexagon's book-covered walls contains five shelves; each shelf contains thirty-five books; each book has four hundred and ten pages, forty lines per page, and eighty words per line.[25]

Think of the books in the Library of Babel as websites. Most are incomprehensible, full of "senseless cacophonies, verbal jumbles and incoherences." One on "circuit 1594" is a "mere labyrinth of letters, but on the next-to-last page says *Oh time thy pyramids.*" Nobody knows what this phrase means. Like the HTML code underlying a webpage, every book is composed of the same elements: the space, the comma, the period, and twenty-two letters of the alphabet. The Library contains every book it is possible to imagine, including all combinations of these 25 orthographic symbols. Although the internet is not infinite, it is unimaginably large: about 4.2 billion pages or about 1.9 billion websites.[26]

The great problem of the Library of Babel is accessing its knowledge. The Library is equipped "with precious volumes" and yet is "useless," for "a library containing all possible books arranged at random might as well have no books. All possible true information cannot be distinguished from all possible false information." "Men reasoned," however, that if the Library contains every possible book, then "on some shelf in some hexagon" there "must exist a book which is the formula and perfect compendium of all the rest," and which "some librarian" must have "gone through." This librarian is the Book-Man.

The Book-Man answers the Library's knowledge organization problem. He promises to bring order to the Library, to make it useful, as PageRank brought order to the web. The Book-Man does not know what is in each book, but he understands how books are organized, the hidden structure of the Library, and so he knows where to find things. Similarly, Google's PageRank system did not know the content of each website, but by leveraging the structure of the links between websites, it organized and made them useful by pointing the user in the right direction. Much as PageRank made surfing the web unnecessary, the Book-Man eliminates the need for librarians to wander around endlessly seeking whatever knowledge preoccupies them. They just ask the Book-Man.

The Book-Man's capacity to direct people confers the power to control access to knowledge. Like Google's mission to "organize the world's information and make it universally accessible and useful," Google's capacity to direct people conferred the power to control access to the web, ranking the information that people were given in response to queries and the principles, structures, and systems according to which information was organized and made useful. Over time, and on an enormous scale, Google shaped the fortunes of websites and the minds of web users, exerting an unrivaled influence over the circulation of information. "Like a god," the Book-Man in effect becomes the Library; so Google in effect became the web.

James Grimmelmann emphasizes two kinds of power that Google and the Book-Man wield: the power of censorship and the power of hidden favorites. In the Library, Purifiers wander around seeking to "eliminate useless works," condemning "whole shelves" that, with "their hygienic, ascetic furor," cause "the senseless perdition of millions of books." But because there are "several hundred thousand imperfect facsimiles" of every book that "differ only in a letter or a comma," censorship is doomed to fail. Hidden favorites are more of a threat. As the Book-Man's "knowledge is based on a source inaccessible to us, surrounded with inherent uncertainties, and subject to his personal discretion," he could give misleading advice to enemies without their knowledge. "Any pattern we think we perceive in his answers could be sandbagging, or it could be an artifact of an imperfect human attempt" to understand his recommendation system. Given these two kinds of power, Grimmelmann concludes, "the more Book-Men, the better," as "competition" will make "it harder . . . to mislead" and "create[s] an incentive . . . to work hard at giving good advice." We need more than one Google.[27]

The Book-Man's power lies in directing people toward books—in who is sent where and why—and Google's power lies in how it designs its ranking system. The exercise of this power always involves having favorites: "Whether consciously or unconsciously, the search engine will be more useful to some users than to others." This is what the Rick Santorum versus Dan Savage case illustrated. Whether or not Google deliberately targeted Savage's site, its choices about the design of its ranking models by definition built in notions of which websites deserved to be ranked highest. If Google's ranking systems are the web's informational infrastructure, how Google builds this infrastructure necessarily benefits some and not others.[28]

Part of what is distinctive about search is that people often do not know what they want to know, and as such, whoever controls and organizes the infrastructure of search wields an awesome kind of power. "The very nature of search is that we ourselves don't entirely know what . . . we're looking for when we ask the question, so that the question could plausibly refer to any of trillions of possible books."[29] As Helen Nissenbaum, a professor of information security, argues, people "tend to treat search-engine results the way they treat the results of library catalogue searches." Because Google's search ranking system addresses a problem of abundance, like "a library containing all the printed books and papers in the world without covers and without a catalogue," Google's search ranking system functions as the web's informational infrastructure, controlling access to "vast amounts of information." In designing that system, Google exercises the power "to highlight and emphasize certain Websites, while making others, essentially, disappear."[30]

When Google designs its search ranking system, it designs part of the vital infrastructure of our civic information ecosystem, structuring how people access information that is fundamental to the activities of citizenship. Decisions about how that infrastructure is built shape the flow of ideas and information in the public sphere. A library authority cannot determine what is written in a library's books, but it can decide how books are indexed; which books are placed where, whether at the front desk or in the basement; and how librarians respond to particular queries and how they present their answers. As one ethnographic study of libraries concludes, "Knowing who the decision-makers, or gatekeepers, are in the decision-making process, whether it is the library boards, library directors, or public officials, is crucial."[31] The same is true of Google. Controlling Google requires controlling how decisions are made about the design of its search ranking system.

The scope and scale of Google's infrastructural power is likely to grow, increasing the stakes of how that power is exercised. Google aspires not just to answer our queries but to guide what we want. As Eric Schmidt said in 2010: "I actually think most people don't want Google to answer their questions. They want Google to tell them what they should be doing next. . . . We know roughly who you are, roughly what you care about, roughly who your friends are." Just as the Book-Man comes to know humanity's hopes and fears by observing what people seek in the Library of Babel, Google created a laboratory for understanding human beings by creating a Book-Man for the web: what people search for and when, their hopes, fears, and dreams. Google is fast becoming a guide to the most basic activities of life: health and well-being, love, childbirth and parenting, where to live and to work, and how to vote. Google aspires not just to find what we want but to decide what we want, to be the librarian of our desires, the infrastructure of our decision-making.[32]

The Corruption Critique

While these analogies help conceptualize Facebook's and Google's infrastructural power, they leave out the most obvious thing about them: they are advertising companies. "Facebook Is Not the Public Square" read the headline of a 2014 *New York Times* editorial.

> Because social media businesses have become such a fixture in modern life many people might think of them as the digital equivalent of the public square. . . . But these companies are more like privately operated malls—the management always reserves the right to throw you out if you don't abide by its rules. . . . As much as free speech advocates would like Facebook and other Internet companies to uphold liberal values, these companies are unlikely to do so if it means sacrificing lucrative business opportunities.[33]

By structuring Facebook's and Google's incentives, the political economy of digital advertising shapes the ends for which they exercise infrastructural power. If the corporation or the Book-Man earned revenue by selling ads, they would be incentivized to get people to spend as much time in the public square and public library as possible. To do this, they might spread untruths and foster an atmosphere of heightened mistrust, circulating ideas and information that provoke addictive emotions like outrage, disgust, and lust. By keeping people in the square and library for as long as possible, the corporation and the Book-Man could observe and track their hopes, fears, and instincts, providing more information to work out how best to provoke addictive emotions and keep people coming back in the future, producing more opportunities to sell ads and generate more revenue.

I call this "the corruption critique." In pursuit of user growth and advertising revenue, Facebook and Google have harvested enormous quantities of data to build powerful ranking systems that addict, manipulate, and control. The argument unfolds in two steps. The first involves a claim about political economy: because Facebook and Google are digital advertising companies, their overriding incentive is to increase the number of people who use their platform, the frequency with which they use it, and the average time they spend on it. The second involves a claim about the corrupting effects of this political economy: by building ranking systems that trade in addiction, Facebook and Google drive polarization, increase social division, spread misinformation, and stifle possibilities for curiosity and random discovery. Focusing on the corrupting effects of Facebook's and Google's systems illuminates the distinctive character of their infrastructural power: using prediction to solve the problem of abundance has created ranking systems that commandeer attention, shaping the preferences and wants of citizens who aspire to govern themselves.[34]

Advertising and Surveillance Capitalism

Franklin Foer, author of one of the best books about the ideas that animate Silicon Valley, makes an argument similar to the *New York Times* editorial's. His piece "The Death of the Public Square" contrasts Facebook and Google with the "real public square," which was never built by anyone, but "just started to organically accrete, as printed volumes began to pile up. . . . Institutions grew, and then over the centuries acquired prestige and authority. Newspapers and journals evolved into what we call media. Book publishing emerged from the printing guilds, and eventually became taste-making, discourse-shaping enterprises." "Nothing was perfect" about this public square, Foer argues; "it could be jealously exclusive, intolerant of new opinion, a guild that protected the privileges of its members and blocked worthy outsiders," but it "provided the foundation for Western democracy. It took centuries . . . to develop—and the technology companies have eviscerated it in a flash."[35]

As technology companies have displaced the traditional institutions of the public sphere, "the values of big tech have become the values of the public sphere." For example, despite "all its power and influence" as "our primary portal to the world, Google can't really be bothered to care about the quality of knowledge it dispenses" and "has no opinion about what it offers, even when that knowledge it offers is aggressively, offensively vapid." By using hyperlinks and clicks to rank websites, Google gives "us what's popular, what's most clicked upon, not what's worthy. You can hurl every insult at the old public sphere, but it never exhibited such frank indifference to the content it disseminated."[36]

In pursuit of advertising revenue, Foer argues, Facebook and Google have corrupted the public sphere. Facebook and Google "want their machines to rouse us in the morning . . . guide us through our days, relaying news and entertainment, answering our most embarrassing questions, enabling our shopping." These systems are not designed to "present us with choices" or "a healthy menu of options," but to "anticipate our wants and needs." "What's so pernicious," he observes, is that "they weaponize us against ourselves. They take our data—everywhere we have traveled on the web, every query we've entered . . . even the posts we begin to write but never publish—and exploit this knowledge to reduce us to marionettes." By developing an "intimate portrait of our brains . . . our anxieties and pleasure points," they use "the cartography of our psyche to array the things we read and the things we watch, to commandeer our attention for as long as possible, to addict us. When our conversation and debate is so intensely and intricately manipulated, can it truly be said to be free?"[37]

Consider what became known as "the contagion study," one of the A/B tests that Facebook uses to measure how design updates affect top-line metrics. In the study, one group of users were shown mostly positive and optimistic content, while another group was shown mostly sad, negative content. Those shown more positive content shared more positive content, and those shown more negative content shared more negative content. "Emotional states can be transferred to others via emotional contagion," the study concluded, "leading people to experience the same emotions without their awareness." Although the study confirmed that newsfeed can shape how people feel on an enormous scale, the more revealing finding, which got little attention at the time, was that users shown content that was neither positive nor negative engaged less with Facebook. They did other things with their time—the worst possible outcome for Facebook. Because social emotions get people to spend more time on Facebook, Facebook boosts content that provokes social emotions.[38]

Shoshana Zuboff describes the profit-driven corruption of the public sphere as surveillance capitalism, "the unilateral claiming of private human experience as free raw material for translation into behavioral data. These data are then computed and packaged as prediction products and sold into behavioral futures markets." As people use Facebook and Google because their systems efficiently sort and rank content and websites in order of relevance, Facebook and Google build these systems to ensure that people visit and spend as much time as possible on their platforms. Facebook and Google are "secretly scraping your private experience as raw material, and [selling] predictions of what you're gonna do. . . . These are bald-faced interventions in the exercise of human autonomy . . . [and] the very material essence of the idea of free will."[39]

The corruption critique centers on the relationship between two kinds of machine learning systems that Facebook and Google build. The first is advertising delivery systems. Advertisers pay to access these systems because they are extremely effective at maximizing the chance that ads will be shown to people who engage with them, resulting in more clicks and shares from an enormous number of users and generating more revenue for advertisers per dollar of ad spend. The second is newsfeed and search ranking systems, which generate the training data that make advertising delivery systems effective. Facebook and Google build ranking systems not as a public service but to generate more data about user behavior on which to train revenue-generating advertising systems by getting people to spend time on and engage with the platforms. This is a self-perpetuating cycle: more users of newsfeed and search generate more data; more data enable the building of more powerful advertising systems; more powerful advertising systems generate more revenue; with more revenue, more highly skilled engineers can be hired to build newsfeed and search systems that better engage users. As Peter Norvig, Google's director of research, is supposed to have said at Google's Zeitgeist in 2011, "We don't have better algorithms than anyone else; we just have more data."[40]

Zuboff persuasively makes the first claim in the corruption critique: that the political economy of advertising structures the incentives that shape the design of Facebook's and Google's machine learning systems. Maximizing advertising revenue requires increasing the number of users, the number of times they visit the platform, and the amount of time they spend there, thus producing more data to improve advertising systems, which become more valuable to advertisers and generate more revenue. Facebook and Google have strong incentives to build finely tuned, attention-grabbing addiction machines.

Prediction, Personalization, and Filter Bubbles

The second step links political economy to the public sphere. Machine learning is the critical, underappreciated component of the corruption critique, because it connects its two steps. The political economy of digital advertising creates incentives for Facebook and Google to build machine learning systems that have undesirable social effects by creating filter bubbles and driving faction, reducing the prospects of curiosity and random discovery, and corrupting the public sphere. The causal mechanism for the effects of digital advertising on the public sphere is machine learning, which increases the scale and speed at which advertising companies mold the character of public debate and structure the information ecosystem.

Everything on Facebook and Google is personalized. When you Google the same query on someone else's phone, you get different results. As we saw, Google's original PageRank algorithm could weight home pages to model a surfer who was not random but was a person with particular preferences and surfing habits. A "personal search engine," Page and Brin promised in 1998, "could save users a great deal of trouble by efficiently guessing a large part of their interests." In terms of our analogy, personalization means that each person has a different Book-Man: where people are sent depends on what they have sought and where they have been before. The Book-Man sends two people asking the same query in entirely different directions. As Marissa Mayer, former executive at Google and CEO of Yahoo!, explained: "We believe the search engine of the future will be personalized and that it will offer users better results."[41]

The same is true of newsfeed. Like the people in the silent disco in the public square listening to different speeches through their headphones, each user has a different newsfeed, and the boundaries between the personal and the public are blurred. As Adam Mosseri, former head of News Feed, explained, "People expect the stories in their feed to be meaningful to them— and we have learned over time that people value stories that they consider informative. Something that one person finds informative or interesting may be different from what another person finds informative or interesting. . . . We're always working to better understand what is interesting and informative to you personally, so those stories appear higher up in your feed. . . . We are not in the business of picking which issues the world should read about. We are in the business of connecting people and ideas—and matching people with the stories they find meaningful." Facebook is "a multitude of Facebooks, appearing to be one public venue but in fact spun out in slightly different versions."[42]

Facebook's and Google's predictions about relevance sort people into groups: people who live in the same area, people who like similar pages, people who click on similar ads, or people who watch similar news channels. As Eli Pariser argued a decade ago, this sorting process can cause "filter bubbles," or "echo chambers," in which similar kinds of people are exposed to similar kinds of content. Think of the informational worlds that newsfeed creates every day. A nation wakes up, opens their phones, looks at Facebook, and learns that somebody resigned from government. My newsfeed shows me: "Government official resigns objecting to illegal use of Presidential power." Someone else sees: "Government official stabs President in the back." We shower, brush our teeth, get in the car, check Facebook again. My newsfeed informs me: "President attacks peaceful protesters." Someone else is told: "Protestors launch violent attack on President." It's not just news that is sorted in this way—it's the culture we are exposed to, the ideas we encounter, the way information is presented and evaluated. Facebook's newsfeed does not make anyone resign or protest, but it affects what the nation knows about the event and how different groups of citizens feel about it.[43]

There is mixed empirical evidence about the existence of filter bubbles and the role of Facebook's and Google's systems in creating and sustaining them. One study showed that even when a political campaign deliberately targeted ads at diverse audiences, Facebook's advertising system tended to deliver similar ads to similar kinds of people. When researchers tried to target campaign ads at those who voted for the opposing party, Facebook's advertising system still tended to deliver ads for Democrat candidates to Democrat audiences and ads for Republican candidates to Republican audiences. This effect was stronger with smaller advertising budgets, because if Democrats are more likely to engage with Democratic ads and Republicans with Republican ads, Facebook's systems will not spend limited resources delivering ads to those less likely to engage with them.[44]

Regardless of what empirical research reveals about particular adverse social effects of Facebooks and Google's systems, the corruption critique's critical insight is that digital advertising incentivizes the two companies to use prediction to rank ideas and information in whatever way most effectively commandeers human attention. Whereas a newspaper is constructed on "the assumption . . . there is a body of important topics that news consumers, as citizens and members of a community, should know," Facebook and Google build the infrastructure they control to engage and enrage each individual as effectively and consistently as possible. The corruption critique clarifies that Facebook and Google have no reason to use the power of prediction to build public infrastructure that supports the flourishing of democracy.[45]

Consider content moderation. Universal forms of content moderation demote content by the same amount for all users; often called "blanket demotion," such forms would demote toxic content the same amount for everyone. This process runs against the advertising imperative, which reasons that, if some people want to see more toxic content than others, showing them more toxic content will boost visits and time spent, generating more data and more revenue. Personalized content moderation demotes objectionable content in proportion to people's appetite for it—that is, Facebook demotes content heavily for people it predicts will not want to see toxic content, but does nothing about, or even promotes, toxic content for people it predicts will find it energizing. Provided they are unaccountable advertising companies, Facebook and Google will structure public debate and build ecosystems of information using personalized predictions about engagement rather than principled, public criteria of what makes for a healthy public sphere and civic information architecture.

The performative character of Facebook's and Google's ranking systems makes the incentives that digital advertising creates especially pernicious. Ranking systems are a case of super-charged performative prediction that effects the outcomes they purport to predict: people engage with content that Facebook predicts they will engage with because Facebook places that content higher on their newsfeed, and people engage with websites that Google predicts they will engage with because Google places those websites higher on their search results. Predictions about engagement shape what each person engages with, which in turn shapes predictions about their engagement, which shape what each person engages with. By placing toxic content higher on the newsfeeds of people Facebook predicts will engage with it, Facebook makes those people more likely to engage with it, increasing the chance they will be shown toxic content in the future.

It's hard to overstate the importance of this point. By homing in on the connections between digital advertising and the design of ranking systems powered by machine learning, the corruption critique helps clarify what is distinctive about the infrastructure that Facebook and Google control: by directing attention they purport to predict, those systems do not simply satisfy citizens' preferences—they shape the preferences that citizens have in the first place.

A Distinct Kind of Infrastructural Power

We are now in a position to articulate the problem statement for regulating Facebook and Google. What makes the challenge of regulating Facebook and Google different is the nature of the power they wield through unilateral control over ranking systems that shape the public sphere in their image. This section focuses on what makes this infrastructural power distinctive.

Prediction and Infrastructural Power

Facebook's and Google's power is rooted in the political character of machine learning. As the communications scholar Mike Ananny argues, any approach to regulating the "sociotechnical infrastructures" of "online speech platforms" must focus on "probabilistic ideas about chance, likelihood, normalcy, deviance, [and] confidence thresholds." The power to design machine learning systems that generate predictions is "at once, a seemingly neutral technique, evidence of power, and a rationalization of risks . . . [that] can reveal attempts to control the world through categories used to define normality and punish deviance." This "is a type of power platform makers have a vested interest in obfuscating, mystifying, and controlling" to "deflect responsibility for the configuration of [their] technical infrastructures."[46]

Facebook and Google often use the language of prediction to "offer a kind of false stability couched in mathematical certainty that is beyond the comprehension of most platform users and regulators (and some makers) but that is routinely offered to provide an illusion of normalcy and predictability." "While computers are consistent . . . people are not always as consistent in their judgments," argues Zuckerberg. "The vast majority of mistakes we make are due to errors enforcing the nuances of our policies rather than disagreements about what those policies should actually be." Instead of asking humans to remove misleading news stories, Tessa Lyons, head of Facebook's newsfeed, explains, Facebook can simply "rank those stories significantly lower" to "cut future views by more than 80 percent." Over the coming years, Zuckerberg has pledged, "we expect to have trained our systems to proactively detect the vast majority of problematic content." While human choices about the design of machine learning models are no less fallible than human content moderation decisions, they are less visible, and less easy to hold to account.[47]

Human content moderation is a distraction from Facebook's power to design machine learning models. Humans remove a tiny fraction of the billions of pieces of content that machine learning models rank and demote every day, yet there is much greater scrutiny of how moderators remove content than of how Facebook's engineers build machine learning models. This is understandable, because content removal is the more tractable form of Facebook's power—but it is also the less important form of power. Consider the decision about whether to ban President Donald Trump from the platform. Whether Trump is banned makes minimal difference to Facebook or to the character of public debate; how newsfeed is designed is central to both. Because Facebook's Oversight Board focuses public debate on individual content moderation decisions and deflects from how the newsfeed and integrity systems are designed, a focus on the Oversight Board suits Facebook. Provided it lacks jurisdiction over the design of machine learning systems, the Oversight Board is a giant exercise in distraction.[48]

Holding Facebook and Google accountable for how they use prediction to structure our public sphere and civic information ecosystem will require us to ask new kinds of questions. For instance, in prediction, mistakes are always political: it matters who the mistakes are about and who gets to decide what counts as a mistake. Consider the toxicity model. If Facebook reports that the model has an accuracy rate of 90 percent, what kinds of content does the model tend to incorrectly classify as toxic? Are particular groups more likely to produce content that Facebook incorrectly classifies as toxic? Who are they? Even asking Facebook to report probability estimates would change how we think about Facebook's power. Imagine posts appearing with labels like, "We're fairly sure this post is toxic," or "We're 80 percent sure this post is toxic," or "We've decided this post is toxic, but there's a 20 percent chance we are wrong." Facebook and Google don't label content this way because doing so would encourage people to ask *how* Facebook and Google generate these predictions. And this would point toward the deliberate human choices involved in machine learning: selecting top-line metrics, choosing concepts to approximate, writing labeling guidelines, and assembling training data. As Mike Ananny argues:

> Probability matters to free speech and free speech platforms precisely because the probabilities governing communication environments shape our collective ability to see and understand unavoidably shared collective outcomes—to discover ourselves as publics and know our chances of self-governance. . . . Probability matters to free speech because it goes to the heart of what it means to realize and govern ourselves. . . . If the chance that our words spread or that we hear others depends on probabilistic systems, then we have a vested interest in seeing probability as a political technology that either helps or hinders our abilities to think, associate, deviate, adapt, resist, or act. And when we limit probability to one type of concept, one particular operationalization or set of values, we limit our ability to imagine new social arrangements.[49]

Opening up our imaginations about how to govern Facebook and Google requires us to wrestle with what is distinctive about their infrastructural power. We must unpack the political character of their machine learning systems more incisively and examine the different kinds of systems they build in a more granular way, distinguishing Facebook's newsfeed from its integrity system, and Google's search from its advertising system. As machine learning becomes an ever more common component of vital infrastructure, citizens, elected representatives, and regulators must ask new types of questions to interrogate the politics of machine learning.

The Challenge for Regulation

There is nothing new about data-driven marketing. In 1974, well before Google or the internet (Eric Schmidt was nineteen), the computer scientist Stafford Beer wrote:

> We shall use the power of computers to undertake an editing process on behalf of the only editor who any longer counts—the client himself. . . . If we can encode an individual's interests and susceptibilities on the basis of feedback which he supplies . . . marketing people will come to use this technique to increase the relatively tiny response to a mailing shot which exists today to a response in the order of 90 percent. . . . The conditioning loop exercised upon the individual will be closed. Then we have provided a perfect physiological system for the marketing of anything we like—not then just genuine knowledge, but perhaps "political truth" or "the ineluctable necessity to act against the elected government."[50]

As Jill Lepore's *If Then* convincingly shows, corporations have long sought to generate advertising revenue by using data to predict behavior. What makes Facebook and Google different is the distinctive infrastructural power involved in designing ranking systems that use machine learning to solve the problem of abundance.[51]

The performativity of ranking is what makes this power distinctive. Compare the performative effects of Facebook's and Google's systems on predictive policing. In predictive policing, more police officers are sent to neighborhoods predicted to be high risk; that leads to more crimes being recorded in those neighborhoods, thus increasing their measured risk and leading to more police officers being sent there in the future. Over time this pattern changes behavior: police officers begin to suspect that residents of high-risk neighborhoods are more prone to crime, and residents begin to feel hostile toward the police. The allocation of police resources serves as the mechanism through which predictions about crime risk themselves influence the future crime risk of different neighborhoods.

Ranking systems also influence the outcomes they purport to predict. If Google predicts that you are likely to engage with left-wing news websites, it ranks those websites higher. That ranking makes you more likely to engage with left-wing news websites and feed in more data that confirm you engage with left-wing news websites; as a result, they will be ranked higher. If Facebook predicts that you are likely to engage with toxic content, it shows you more toxic content, making you more likely to engage with toxic content and feed in data that confirm you engage with toxic content; as a result, you will be shown more toxic content. Slowly but surely, you become the kind of person who engages with left-wing news websites or the kind of person who engages with toxic content. Facebook and Google rank content and websites that are consistent with their predictions above those that are not, shaping behavior in ways that make their predictions come true. Ranking serves as the mechanism through which predictions about engagement themselves influence the ideas and information with which people engage.

Machine learning raises the scale and speed of ranking's performative effects. If ranking systems could sort and order vast quantities of content and websites without machine learning—perhaps by magic—ranking systems would still have this performative character. Its performativity depends on the behavioral consequences of displaying some things above others. But machine learning matters because the scale of Facebook's and Google's ranking systems, the range of citizens they reach and the breadth of the content they structure and order, is part of why they matter for democracy. Imagine that Facebook decides to build a machine learning model to predict which news sources people trust, then ranks news from sources that Facebook predicts people are likely to trust higher than sources it predicts they are not likely to trust. By ranking news from sources that people are predicted to be likely to trust higher, Facebook ensures that people will engage with more news from those sources, and regardless of how trustworthy those news sources actually are, people may come to trust them more. This outcome changes the meaning of trustworthiness itself, because trustworthiness is not the same as popularity: the trustworthiness of a newspaper, for instance, is determined by shared, institutional criteria, not by individual preferences that have made it popular. By using individual predictions to rank news on a vast scale, Facebook's system changes the very meaning of trustworthiness.[52]

Friendship offers another example. As the communications scholar Taina Bucher argues, Facebook's ranking systems "decide which stories should show up on users' newsfeeds, but also, crucially, which friends." Facebook's patent explains that "social networking systems value user connections because better-connected users tend to increase . . . use of the social networking system, thus increasing user-engagement and . . . advertising opportunities." By ranking friends who provoke more engagement above those who do not, Facebook makes it more likely that you will engage with those friends, confirming their place at the top of your newsfeed. As one woman explained, "It does feel as if there is only a select group of friends I interact with on the social network, while I've practically forgotten about the hundreds of others I have on there." Newsfeed purports to predict which friends we want to engage with, but really, it shapes which friends we remember. Ranking friends by engagement shapes how we understand the meaning of friendship.[53]

Facebook's and Google's unilateral control over digital public infrastructure is objectionable in its own right, but a distinctive infrastructural power is at work when that control is exercised through the design of ranking systems powered by machine learning. When people engage with content at the top of Facebook's newsfeed or with websites at the top of Google's search results, they are subject to this infrastructural power. This power influences people's hopes and fears, wants and preferences, shared understandings and common concerns, shaping the capacity of citizens to imagine and choose different futures, debate the ends they wish to pursue, and exercise their collective freedom. To regulate Facebook and Google we must reckon with their power to shape the very agents who must assert their collective agency to regulate Facebook and Google—citizens.

7

Democratic Utilities

Yesterday and ever since history began, men were related to one another as individuals.... To-day, the every-day relationships of men are largely with great impersonal concerns, with organizations, not with other individuals.... The line of demarcation between actions left to private initiative and management and those regulated by the state has to be discovered experimentally.[1]

—JOHN DEWEY, *THE PUBLIC AND ITS PROBLEMS* (1927)

The liberty of a democracy is not safe if the people tolerate the growth of private power to a point where it becomes stronger than the democratic state itself. That in its essence is fascism: ownership of government by an individual, by a group, or any controlling private power.[2]

—FRANKLIN D. ROOSEVELT, "MESSAGE TO CONGRESS ON THE CONCENTRATION OF ECONOMIC POWER" (1938)

The most problematic aspect of Facebook's power is Mark's unilateral control over speech. There is no precedent for his ability to monitor, organize and even censor the conversations of two billion people.[3]

—CHRIS HUGHES, "IT'S TIME TO BREAK UP FACEBOOK" (2019)

Curious why I think FB has too much power? Let's start with their ability to shut down a debate over whether FB has too much power.... I want a social media marketplace that isn't dominated by a single censor.[4]

—SENATOR ELIZABETH WARREN, TWEET (MARCH 12, 2019)

She's right—Big Tech has way too much power to silence Free Speech.[5]

—SENATOR TED CRUZ, TWEET (MARCH 12, 2019)

"IN THESE LAST FOUR YEARS, we have made the exercise of all power more democratic," began President Franklin D. Roosevelt's Second Inaugural Address in 1937, "for we have begun to bring private autocratic powers into their proper subordination to the public's government. The legend that they were invincible above and beyond the processes of a democracy—has been shattered. They have been challenged and beaten. . . . We [have written] a new chapter in our book of self-government."[6]

This chapter reaches into the Progressive and New Deal eras to recover some valuable tools for thinking about how to govern Facebook and Google. In the industrial era, Progressive legal scholars, activists, and reformers argued that democracies must assert public power over corporations that control vital infrastructure. Focusing on the concept of public utilities, I compare recent, overly economistic ideas about public utilities that center on whether companies are natural monopolies with older, more political conceptions that center on the political problems posed by corporate control over vital infrastructure. These political conceptions asserted the authority of democratic states to protect the public interest by subjecting corporate control to dynamic processes of public administration and democratic governance.[7]

Facebook's and Google's unilateral control over ranking systems triggers the central concerns that animated these political conceptions of public utilities. These systems have become part of the infrastructure of the public sphere, an essential tool for citizens to participate as political equals, speak and be heard, access information, organize, and make collective decisions. How Facebook and Google design these systems shapes how citizens encounter and engage with one another and how they develop shared experience and common understandings of public issues and, ultimately, their capacity to exercise collective self-government.

Yet, as scholars have pointed out, Facebook and Google are different from railroads and electricity or telephone providers. Facebook and Google shape "how [content] is organized, how it is monetized, what [is] removed and why," raising "both traditional dilemmas . . . and some substantially new ones, for which there are few precedents or explanations."[8] Unlike railroads and electricity or telephone providers, whose bottleneck power is rooted in their control over public goods, Facebook's and Google's bottleneck power is rooted in the design of ranking systems that use predictions to direct human attention, molding the citizens who aspire to govern themselves. To respond to these new dilemmas, I propose a new category of corporations that should be subject to public oversight and democratic governance: democratic utilities.[9]

Democratic utilities would be corporations whose unilateral control over vital infrastructure shapes the conditions of collective self-government. The democratic utility category recognizes that we need different tools to regulate the distinct kind of power that Facebook and Google exercise. For democracy to assert its authority over new modes of capitalism, we must develop new laws, regulatory institutions, and mechanisms of governance to structure accountability over new forms of infrastructural power. When that power depends on machine learning, the process of designing machine learning systems should be subject to public obligations and mechanisms of governance structured through the democratic utility framework.

Although this chapter engages with US law, my concern is with political strategies and concepts, not legal ones. My argument is not that as a matter of law the public utility concept applies to Facebook and Google, but rather, that by exploring the legal innovation of public utilities that Progressive-era scholars and legal activists developed to confront the challenges of their age, we can illuminate what is distinctive about the challenges of our own. By exploring how public utilities were conceptualized in the past, I hope to illuminate the pressing question of how democracies should govern corporations whose power is rooted in the design of the ranking systems, powered by machine learning, that function as the infrastructure of the digital public sphere.[10]

The Public Utility Concept

A few years into his second term, President Roosevelt gave an address to Congress on "The Concentration of Economic Power." "Among us today a concentration of private power without equal in history is growing," he began, noting that "of all corporations reporting, less than 5 percent of them owned 87 percent of all assets" and "one-tenth of 1 percent of them earned 50 percent of the net income of all of them." "Concentration of economic power in the few," he continued, is an "inescapable problem for modern 'private enterprise' democracy." To address the problem he proposed "a program whose basic purpose is to . . . turn business back to the democratic competitive order."[11]

The under-discussed and under-theorized public utility concept provides rich tools for thinking about how to turn Facebook and Google back to the democratic order. I argue that economistic conceptions of public utilities— corporations with monopoly control over public goods like railroads, electricity, and telephone providers—have come to constrain our imaginations about how and why democracies should regulate different kinds of corporate power. I contrast these conceptions with the broader, more political Progressive-era conception of public utilities, which was motivated by political concerns about the corporate exercise of infrastructural power.

The Origins of Public Utilities

We should start by returning to the fundamentals. Corporations, as the legal scholar William Novak explains, are "artificial entities that governments allow . . . human beings to create in order to accomplish certain ends"; as such, governments have "the authority to determine not only the ends for which corporations might be created but also the means by which they attain . . . those ends." For much of the history of the modern state, states have imposed "standard[s] of public care, public responsibility, and public accountability" that constrain how corporations can pursue those ends.[12]

Public utilities are "one of the more remarkable innovations in the history of democratic attempts to control the . . . corporation." In the Progressive and New Deal eras, the public utility concept was "consciously and constructively" developed to expand the reach of the administrative state in an "extraordinary era of democratic political struggle and corporate regulatory innovation."[13] Public utilities were "in many ways" the "legal foundation" of "the modern American administrative and regulatory state."[14] Those who advocated for public utility regulation recognized the need "to ensure collective, social control over vital industries that provided foundational goods and services on which the rest of society depend . . . [and] whose set of users and constituencies were too vast to be empowered and protected through more conventional methods of market competition, corporate governance, or ordinary economic regulation."[15]

The origins of the public utility concept lie in three distinct bodies of law. The first is English common law, which, since the Middle Ages, has held certain "common callings"—public surgeons, tailors, blacksmiths, innkeepers, common carriers—to distinct legal standards. Because those who practiced these trades were thought to step outside the private household to do business with "the public," it was thought that they should be subject to obligations that protect the public. In his treatise on maritime law—described as "the most famous paragraph in the whole law relating to public services"[16]—the English legal scholar Matthew Hale, known for his judicial impartiality during the Civil War of 1642–1651, wrote:

If the king or subject have a public wharf, unto which all persons that come to that port must come and unlade or lade their goods . . . because they are the wharfs only licensed by the queen . . . or because there is no other wharf in that port . . . there cannot be taken arbitrary and excessive duties for cranage, wharfage, pesage, etc., neither can they be enhanced to an immoderate rate, but the duties must be reasonable and moderate. . . . For now the wharf and crane and other conveniences are affected with a public interest, and they cease to be juris private only as if a man set out a street in new building on his own land, it is now no longer private interest, but is affected with a public interest.[17]

The second origin of the public utility concept was in states' police powers to regulate commerce. The chief justice of Massachusetts, Lemuel Shaw, explained the basis of police powers in *Commonwealth v. Alger* when upholding the legislature's right to restrict the establishment of private property within wharfs:

All property in this commonwealth . . . is served directly or indirectly from the government, and held subject to those general regulations, which are necessary to the common good and general welfare. . . . The power we allude to is rather the police power; the power vested in the legislature by the constitution to make, ordain, and establish all manner of wholesome and reasonable laws, statutes, and ordinances, either with penalties or without, not repugnant to the constitution, as they shall judge to be for the good and welfare of the Commonwealth.[18]

The third and perhaps most important origin of the public utility concept was a shift in how corporations were established. Until the mid-nineteenth century, corporations were established through a special act of legislative charter. This made it obvious that corporations derived their authority and purpose from legislatures and that legislatures could and should impose obligations to guide their purposes and conduct. As Chief Justice John Marshall explained, corporations were "an artificial being, invisible, intangible, and existing only in contemplation of law." Because "the objects for which a corporation is created are universally such as the government wishes to promote," the "right to change them is not founded on their being incorporated, but on their being the instruments of government, created for its purposes. The same institutions, created for the same objects, though not incorporated, would be public institutions, and, of course, be controllable by the legislature."[19]

As general incorporation replaced legislative charter as the primary means of establishing corporations in the mid-nineteenth century, states increasingly governed corporate power through general laws and regulations rather than particularized obligations.[20] As the economic historian Willard Hurst explained: "From the 1780s well into the mid-nineteenth century the most frequent and conspicuous use of the business corporation—especially under special charters—was for one particular type of enterprise, that which we later call *public utility* and put under particular regulation because of its special impact in the community." Public utility regulation was a direct response to this shift in how corporations were established, from state charter to general incorporation.[21]

In bringing together and drawing on these three bodies of law, the Progressive-era public utility concept offered a broad justification for government regulation of corporations to advance the public interest. The public utility concept was part of a broader effort to develop conceptual frameworks and legal tools to "assert democratic control over newly expansive forms of corporate power and concentration," such as the Interstate Commerce Act (1887), the Sherman Act (1890), and the Federal Trade Commission Act (1914). Progressive and New Deal legal scholars, activists, and reformers, arguing that corporate power posed a political as well as an economic problem because unilateral corporate control of vital infrastructure imperils the exercise of collective freedom, developed a dynamic set of tools to hold private powers accountable to the public good. And yet our images of public utilities have since become increasingly narrow, confined by economistic conceptions of what public utilities are that constrain possible justifications for public control over corporate power.[22]

The Economic Conception

When most of us imagine public utilities, we think of railroad companies, which control a single node within a transport network that is essential for downstream social and economic activity, or electricity or telephone companies, which control a cable essential for the activities of businesses and households across the country. These images are generally understood to capture the two central components of what makes a corporation a public utility: first, that the corporation is a "natural monopoly," as occurs when a "single firm can service the entire relevant market at the lowest cost possible thanks to" network effects and economies of scope and scale; and second, that it controls a public good, a non-rival and non-excludable good with high sunk costs in production. On this conception, public utility regulation addresses "the most troubling form of private power" in which monopolistic firms control a non-rival and non-excludable good that is extremely difficult to duplicate.[23]

As one scholar explained in 1940, "Given a monopoly of essential services, governmental activity to perform the regulatory tasks undertaken in other fields by competition would seem almost inevitable. . . . Regulation has been instituted because competition has been conspicuously absent, and the purpose has been, universally, to protect the consumer from exploitation by those in a monopoly position." A company that controls a railroad in a coal field wields power over companies that wish to buy coal and over consumers who depend on fair and equitable access to energy. A company that controls the telephone cable in a small town wields power over businesses and citizens who depend on nondiscriminatory access to telecommunications services.[24]

This narrow conception is the legacy of a deliberate attempt to redefine the meaning of public utilities. Beginning in the mid-twentieth century, law and economics scholars argued that by entrenching a relationship between regulators and corporations, public utility law itself created and sustained monopolies. Once "the policy of state-created, state-protected monopoly" had become "firmly established over a significant portion of the economy," the "public utility status" became "the haven of refuge for all aspiring monopolists who found it too difficult, too costly, or too precarious to secure and maintain monopoly by private action alone." Decades of similar arguments have left us with an image of public utilities as necessary evils: stultifying, ineffective, but essential. Unlike in the Progressive era, when many of the best lawyers practiced and theorized public utility law, until recently public utilities were considered a professional dead end.[25]

Yet the scope and goals of democratic control over corporate power need not depend on whether corporations are natural monopolies that control public goods. There are other ways to reason about what makes corporate power objectionable and about how to govern it. As William Novak argues, "In contrast to the anemic vision of 'public utilities' in contemporary discourse," we should recover an older set of tools for governing corporate power "in which conceptions of public interest, public service, public goods, and public utilities were anything but marginal or aligned, " but instead were "innovative, capacious, and extraordinarily efficacious." In thinking about how to govern Facebook and Google, we should draw on this older, more dynamic set of tools, including the political conception of public utilities, which is concerned above all with how best to prioritize democracy over capitalism.[26]

The Political Conception

In the early twentieth century, as William Novak argues, "the legal concept of public utility was capable of justifying state economic controls ranging from statutory police regulation to administrative rate setting to outright public ownership of the means of production."[27] Legal reformers, institutional economists, and Progressives systematically explored the connections between social, economic, and political power, experimenting with different ways of asserting public power over different kinds of corporate control of social infrastructure. The public utility concept was the crucial prong in a dynamic "movement toward [public] control," as the institutional economist John Maurice Clark argued in 1926; it covered electricity and the telephone, irrigation and flood prevention, radio and aerial navigation, the Federal Reserve system, prison corporations, public health and insurance firms, and even the "democratization of business."[28]

Public utilities "in this broader sense, [are] not a thing or type of entity but an undertaking—a collective project aimed at harnessing the power of private enterprise and directing it toward public ends."[29] As John Cheadle explained in 1920 in his "Government Control of Business," "Monopoly is significant as one among many social and economic situations that may be considered by the legislature in adopting its policy."[30] Or as the legal scholar Nicholas Bagley put it more recently, "A business need not be monopolistic in a strict sense" for it to be treated as a public utility. "An extraordinary range of market features—the costs of shopping around, bargaining inequalities, informational disadvantage, rampant fraud, collusive pricing . . . and more—could all . . . warrant state intervention."[31] Our analysis must consider the political problems associated with the corporate exercise of infrastructural power, not just the economic problems associated with the monopolistic control of public goods.

The roots of what I call the political conception of public utilities lie in the US Supreme Court decision in Munn v. Illinois in 1877, when the Court upheld an Illinois statute that regulated rates charged for storing grain.[32] In a sweeping and foundational defense of the powers of the legislature to regulate corporations through the administrative state, the Court argued that elevators and warehouses that stored grain were "affected with a public interest" and therefore were the legitimate objects of regulatory measures that imposed public control and asserted the common good. The idea that the scope and form of public oversight should depend on how corporate infrastructural power is "affected with a public interest" became a foundational principle for judging when and how corporations should be subject to regulatory oversight.[33]

In the next few decades, the *Munn* doctrine was cited in numerous rulings that upheld diverse forms of regulation. For instance, in an unsuccessful effort to broaden the scope of civil rights regulation in 1883, Justice John Marshall Harlem wrote:

> The doctrines of *Munn v. Illinois* have never been modified by this court, and I am justified, upon the authority of that case, in saying that places of public amusement . . . are clothed with a public interest, because used in a manner to make them of public consequence and to affect the community at large. The law may therefore regulate . . . the mode in which they shall be conducted, and, consequently, the public have rights in respect of such places. . . . It is consequently not a matter of purely private concern.[34]

This idea was best articulated in the seminal text of public utility law, Bruce Wyman's 1,500-page *The Special Law Governing Public Service Corporations*, published in 1911. Wyman synthesized old English common law doctrines of public callings and carriers, public utilities law, and emerging legal developments in public works and public employment. He understood the dynamism and reach of the public utility concept: "What branches of industry will eventually be of such public importance as to be included in the category . . . it would be rash to predict."[35] A few decades later, in 1930, Felix Frankfurter, associate justice on the US Supreme Court from 1939 to 1962, agreed. Justice Frankfurter described the public utility concept as "perhaps the most significant political tendency at the turn of the century." He too understood the concept's radical implications: "Suffice it to say that through its regulation of these tremendous human and financial interests which we call public utilities, the government may in large measure determine the whole socio-economic direction of the future."[36] In a later essay he wrote for the original *Encyclopaedia of the Social Sciences*, Frankfurter explained:

> [The] contemporary separation of industry into businesses that are "public" and hence susceptible to manifold forms of control . . . and all other businesses, which are private, is thus a break with history. But it has built itself into the structure of American thought and law and while the line of division is a shifting one and incapable of withstanding the stress of economic dislocation, its existence in the last half century has made possible, within a selected field, a degree of experimentation in governmental direction of economic activity of vast import and beyond any historical parallel.[37]

On the broader political conception, public utilities are corporations whose exercise of infrastructural power shapes the terms of citizens' common life. This recognizes that when forms of economic regulation are of "limited efficacy in addressing private power concerns when it comes to infrastructural goods," states must draw on other regulatory tools to structure democratic control over corporations that exercise infrastructural power.[38]

The political conception identifies three central characteristics of corporations that should be subject to democratic oversight. First, they provide a good or service that is subject to significant network effects with increasing returns to scale and high sunk costs for competitors, placing limits on the capacity of market competition to discipline and structure accountability. Instead of focusing on the narrow question of natural monopoly, this conception incorporates a wider analysis of how production dynamics shape the nature of a corporation's infrastructural power. Second, such corporations provide a good or service that constitutes a kind of vital infrastructure that is essential for a wide range of economic, social, and political activities. Third, unilateral control over this vital infrastructure gives corporations a bottleneck power that makes downstream users, whether companies, civic organizations, or individual citizens, vulnerable to manipulation, unfair practices, and exploitation.

The political conception captures the concerns about infrastructural power explored in the last chapter. The design of infrastructure shapes who wins and who loses, which values are advanced and which are blocked, implicating racial justice, consumer welfare, labor, productivity, and business. When infrastructure is essential for citizens to govern themselves and function as equals in their social, economic, and political lives, unilateral control over that infrastructure can exacerbate underlying inequalities of participation and power. As the lawyer Sabeel Rahman argues:

> As citizens in a complex and highly unequal economy, we have . . . interests in public values like equal access, non-discrimination, and in stable provision of foundational, infrastructural goods and services—and our concerns extend beyond price to problems of power, control, and accountability. Our challenge is to take these strategies and values to innovate regulatory policies that fulfill these aspirations in the context of modern technological and economic forces.[39]

The political conception of public utilities offers a dynamic and flexible understanding of corporate power, opening up a wide range of regulatory approaches to structure the governance of corporations that control vital social infrastructure. It is concerned not only with concentrated corporate power's ability to crowd out competitors, raise barriers to entry, and stifle innovation, but also with the threat it poses to citizens' liberty and capacity to govern themselves.

Applying the Concept

In 1935, Congress passed the Public Utility Holding Company Act, which aimed to address economic concentration and unfair practices in public utility holding companies. As one senator opened his discussion of the act: "The people of this Nation have been regaled with stories of the railroad manipulation of politics, but in their palmiest days the railroad kings were cheap pikers compared to the clever, ruthless, and financially free-handed political manipulators of the power trust."[40] The act granted the Securities and Exchange Commission (SEC) sweeping powers to analyze and restructure the entire industry. As one SEC secretary explained: "People forget about it, but it really was epochal. . . . Imagine today if Congress gave a government agency the authority to study the entire high-tech industry and the responsibility to reorganize it."[41] The remainder of this book argues that to regulate Facebook and Google, this is precisely what we should do.

This section argues that Facebook's and Google's unilateral control over ranking systems triggers all three components of the political conception of public utilities: they are subject to strong network effects and economies of scope and scale; their ranking systems constitute vital social infrastructure; and unilateral control over those systems has created a corporate bottleneck power that threatens citizens' liberty and exercise of self-government. This is not to argue that, as a matter of law, Facebook and Google should be treated as public utilities, but to demonstrate that we can learn from the regulatory innovations developed by those who devised the public utility concept as we decide how to respond to current concerns about Facebook's and Google's infrastructural power.

The Economics of Machine Learning

Facebook and Google use machine learning to power ranking systems that solve the problem of abundance. Facebook's newsfeed uses predictions about engagement to rank content in a person's inventory, and Google's search ranks use predictions about relevance to rank websites in response to search queries. Facebook's and Google's revenue depends on the ability of these systems to persuade people to visit as often and for as long as possible in order to gather data on which to train advertising systems. Facebook's and Google's production dynamics depend on the economics of machine learning.[42]

The concept of tipping is useful here. Markets prone to tipping tend toward a single, dominant player; known as winner-take-all markets, competition is generally for rather than within these markets. Once a market has tipped, it is extremely difficult for new entrants to depose the dominant firm without policy intervention. In digital markets, "the challenges to effective competition . . . do not come about solely because of platforms' antic-competitive behavior," as Jason Furman, former chair of President Obama's Council of Economic Advisers, explained in a major report. "Their network-based and data-driven platform business models [themselves] tend to tip markets towards a single winner." In markets where the primary product is machine learning systems that organize and structure information, two forces produce a tendency toward tipping.[43]

The first is the network effect of the utility of a service growing as the number of users increases. Facebook and Google are subject to strong network effects. The more people there are on Facebook, the greater the chance you can use Facebook to keep in touch with high school classmates or the people you met while traveling. Similarly, the more websites Google indexes, the greater the chance that Google will find that quote or bit of information you are looking for. The more of our world that Facebook and Google organize and rank, the more useful Facebook and Google become.[44]

Machine learning influences the network effects to which Facebook and Google are subject. The more data Facebook has, the more accurately it can predict which content will engage which users. The more data Google has, the more accurately it can predict which websites will be relevant to which search queries. As newsfeed and search systems improve, more data for training is acquired by advertising delivery systems, and better advertising delivery systems generate more revenue. There is a compounding dynamic to the economics of machine learning: more data leads to better machine learning systems, which create more revenue, enabling Facebook and Google to capture an ever higher share of global digital advertising, a market likely to be worth over $580 billion by the end of 2025.[45]

The second force that produces a tendency toward tipping arises from economies of scope and scale. Because there are minimal physical distribution costs, the costs of building a machine learning model are similar whether there are 10 million or 100 million users, and each additional user represents a declining marginal cost. Facebook and Google have an incentive to grow and scale incredibly fast (it took five years, from 2004 to 2009, for Facebook to go from 1 million to 350 million users) by investing in the fixed costs of establishing a large user base to reduce the average cost per user and increase the utility of the product.[46] The size of this user base makes it extremely hard for new firms to compete. They cannot develop comparably effective machine learning systems without the data that come from scale, and they cannot develop comparable scale without developing comparably effective machine learning systems.[47]

Here again, the production dynamics depend on machine learning. The more data Facebook and Google have, the better their ranking systems will be at predicting engagement and relevance. Having more data also makes it easier to build new machine learning models, which enable Facebook and Google to enter new markets with much better products than those of existing competitors. (Imagine the machine learning models you could build by combining data from Google's maps, mail, and search systems.) As people come to "rely more and more on a platform to organize their lives through their online social, cultural, or economic activity, their data become more informative about their future choices and firms are willing to pay to influence those choices . . . a few 'gatekeeper' firms [will be left] in a position to control the tracking and linking of . . . behaviors across platforms, online services, and sites."[48]

There are obvious potential harms to consumers. Market power in digital advertising may result in markups paid for by advertisers, reducing consumers' access to ads. By using behavioral techniques like framing, nudges, and defaults, Facebook and Google can influence the outcomes they predict, enabling them to display the most profitable ads rather than those that provide the most long-term value to consumers. Facebook and Google "understand that in some settings they can obtain higher margins if they either make all of the necessary complements themselves, or position themselves as a mandatory bottleneck between partners and customers," reducing the possibility of successful challenge by competitors and stifling future innovation.[49]

Yet the political conception of public utilities we are applying to Facebook and Google is concerned above all with political problems, not economic ones. We must fold this analysis of production dynamics into a broader evaluation of Facebook's and Google's infrastructural power.

Machine Learning as Infrastructure

The second component of the political conception is that the good or service a company provides has become a kind of vital infrastructure. Facebook's and Google's machine learning systems have come to dominate "both our economic landscape and the structure of the public sphere itself."[50]

"Like a road system" or "a telecommunications network," whose benefits "are generated at the ends," Facebook's and Google's social value depends on "the wide variety" of activities they facilitate. The two companies support a dizzying range of "commercial, educational, social, [and] political" activities of "individuals, corporations, government actors, or other entities."[51]

The public interest conception pays particular attention to social and political activities. The value of Facebook's and Google's ranking systems as "public and social infrastructure ... dwarfs [their] value as commercial infrastructure" because of "the range of capabilities [they provide] for individuals, firms, households and other organizations to interact with each other and to participate in various activities and social systems." Although these activities often evade "observation or consideration within conventional economic" measures, they have "significant effects on fundamental social processes and resource systems that generate value" because they enable "end-users [to] interact with each other to build, develop, produce, and distribute public and social goods. Public participation in such activities not only benefits the participants directly ... [but] also results in external benefits that accrue to society as a whole, both online and offline."[52]

Several scholars have observed that Facebook's and Google's ranking systems have become part of the infrastructure of the public sphere. As early as 2010, Microsoft researcher Danah Boyd wrote that Facebook had become a service that people "feel is an essential part of their lives, one that they need more than want.... Facebook never wanted to be a social network site; it wanted to be a social utility.... Nor will most people give up Facebook, regardless of how much they grow to hate [it]." Boyd argues:

> If Facebook is a utility—and I strongly believe it is—the handful of people who are building cabins in the woods to get away from the evil utility companies are irrelevant in light of all the people who will suck up and deal with the utility to live in the city.... When people feel as though they are wedded to something because of its utilitarian value, the company providing it can change but the infrastructure is there for good. Rather than arguing about the details of what counts as a utility, let's move past that to think about what it means that regulation is coming.[53]

Zuckerberg has said as much himself. In a letter written in 2017, he mentions "infrastructure" twenty-six times and "social infrastructure" fifteen times:

> History is the story of how we've learned to come together in ever greater numbers—from tribes to cities to nations. At each step, we built social infrastructure like communities, media and governments to empower us to achieve things we couldn't on our own. . . . In times like these, the most important thing we at Facebook can do is develop the social infrastructure . . . for community—for supporting us, for keeping us safe, for informing us, for civic engagement, and for inclusion of all. . . . I am reminded of President Lincoln's remarks during the American Civil War: "We can succeed only by concert. It is not 'can any of us imagine better?' but, 'can we all do better?' . . . As our case is new, so we must think anew, act anew." . . . There are many of us who stand for bringing people together and connecting the world. I hope we have the focus to . . . build the new social infrastructure to create the world we want for generations to come.[54]

Some scholars resist the description of Facebook's and Google's systems as vital infrastructure. Although some "increasingly speak of larger social media platforms like Facebook as a sort of 'social utility' or a 'social commons' and claim that they are essential to one's social existence . . . the reality is that such sites are not essential to survival, economic success, or online life . . . unlike water and electricity, life can go on without Facebook or other social networking services."[55] But infrastructure need not be necessary for survival for us to consider it and regulate it as vital infrastructure, since railroads, electricity, and telephones are not essential for survival either.

Consider the concept of "pervasiveness." Courts have upheld the regulation of corporations that distribute information in the public sphere when those corporations control a pervasive kind of infrastructure, such as radio frequencies or broadcasting channels.[56] The Supreme Court has rejected the idea that the internet constitutes a pervasive kind of infrastructure because "the receipt of information on the Internet requires a series of affirmative steps more deliberate and directed than merely turning a dial. . . . The special factors recognized . . . as justifying regulation of the broadcast media . . . —the scarcity of available frequencies at its inception; and its "invasive" nature—are not present in cyberspace."[57] Yet if we distinguish Facebook's and Google's ranking systems from the internet as a whole, "when we consider that a user can suddenly, unexpectedly, and involuntarily encounter something as disturbing as a live-streamed murder or suicide in one's news feed in very much the same way that one can unexpectedly be exposed to foul language on the radio, it does seem that a compelling case for pervasiveness could be made."[58]

There are two reasons why Facebook's and Google's ranking systems may be pervasive. First, by ordering abundant quantities of content or websites, ranking systems direct citizens' attention. People are more likely to engage with the content that Facebook predicts they are more likely to engage with because that content is displayed at the top of their newsfeed. People are more likely to read the websites that Google predicts they are more likely to read because those websites are displayed at the top of their search results. As we have seen, far from involving deliberate and directed steps, ranking systems make their predictions come true, shaping the circulation of ideas and information in the public sphere in their own image. Second, by solving the problem of abundance, ranking systems impose a kind of scarcity on the distribution of content. Although there are thousands of pieces of content in a user's Facebook inventory and billions of websites indexed on Google, by ordering and sorting this material, ranking systems make this abundance practically inaccessible. The scarcity is artificial, the product of ranking rather than the physical characteristics of public goods, but its effects on citizens are no less profound. Facebook's and Google's ranking systems may be just as pervasive as television and radio.

Facebook's and Google's systems also support a wide range of activities that are fundamental to citizenship, as the Supreme Court recently seems to have recognized. "While in the past there may have been difficulty in identifying the most important places . . . for the exchange of views," the Court continued, "today the answer is clear. It is cyberspace."

> Seven in ten American adults use at least one Internet social networking service. . . . On Facebook, for example, users can debate religion and politics with their friends and neighbors or share vacation photos. . . . While we now may be coming to the realization that the Cyber Age is a revolution of historic proportions, we cannot appreciate yet its full dimensions and vast potential to alter how we think, express ourselves, and define who we want to be. . . . Social media allows users to gain access to information and communicate with one another about it on any subject that might come to mind. . . . [Social media] are [for many people] the principal sources for knowing current events, checking ads for employment, speaking and listening in the modern public square, and otherwise exploring the vast realms of human thought and knowledge. These websites can provide perhaps the

most powerful mechanisms available to a private citizen to make his or her voice heard. They allow a person . . . to "become a town crier with a voice that resonates farther than it could from any soapbox."[59]

Facebook's and Google's machine learning systems are a pervasive kind of infrastructure that support activities that are vital to citizenship. These activities are political not just in the obvious sense of enabling citizens to fight elections, organize civic campaigns, or distribute political material, but in the deeper sense of enabling citizens to encounter and engage with one another, develop shared experience and a common understanding of public issues, and access shared resources of information and record. Exerting public control over the design of the infrastructure that supports those activities is fundamental to protect the liberty and self-government of citizens.[60]

Bottleneck Power

The final component of the political conception is that companies exercise a kind of bottleneck power. Because Facebook's and Google's ranking systems impose artificial scarcity on abundant quantities of content and websites, unilateral corporate control over those systems leads to an especially objectionable kind of bottleneck power.

Bottleneck power is "a situation where consumers . . . rely upon a single service provider, which makes obtaining access to those consumers . . . by other service providers prohibitively costly."[61] As the Furman report explains: "One, or in some cases two firms in certain digital markets have a high degree of control and influence over the relationship between buyers and sellers. . . . As these markets are frequently important routes to market, or gateways for other firms, such bottlenecks are then able to act as a gatekeeper between businesses and their prospective customers."[62]

There are sound economic reasons to regulate companies with bottleneck power: "The bottleneck firm has the incentive and ability to harm competition. . . . These firms require extra monitoring to be sure they are not violating antitrust, or other laws, because of the uncertainties in technology and demand, the speed at which platforms tip, the irreversibility of tipping, and the need for expert evaluation of the design of algorithms." This is what supports nondiscrimination rules: "For almost a century, public utility companies and common carriers had one common characteristic: all were required to offer their customers service under rates and practices that were just, reasonable, and non-discriminatory." In the case of Facebook and Google, "non-discrimination rules [could] foster entry and diversity, create potential sources of disruptive innovation and protect start-ups and other entrants," preventing "a digital business with bottleneck power from exercising it" to preempt competitors and "expropriate[e] rents."[63]

When corporations distribute information in the public sphere, there are more political reasons for regulating bottleneck power. Before the American Revolution, the British Crown concentrated control over communications platforms, enabling the Crown's postmaster to refuse to deliver newspapers sympathetic to revolutionaries. Congress responded after the Revolution, in 1792, by passing the Postal Service Act, which guaranteed equal access rights and prohibited the Postal Service from discriminating.[64] Similarly, after Western Union consolidated control over telegraph lines across the country during the Civil War, Congress moved in 1866 to prevent it from favoring its own clients in its service provision by passing the Telegraph Act, which prohibited any corporation from acquiring monopoly control over this vital infrastructure of communication.[65]

Imposing nondiscrimination requirements on Facebook and Google would "help ensure the inclusiveness of the platform public sphere by making it harder for the big tech companies to use their economic power to squelch disfavored voices and viewpoints . . . a duty of fair, reasonable, and non-discriminatory dealing would also provide regulators a legal hook they could use to regulate the operation of these companies in all sorts of other ways. . . . It is generative, open-ended, and dynamic."[66] When Senator Warren argued that Google's search should be required to meet such a standard of fair, reasonable, and nondiscriminatory dealing, she was "signaling she believes concentrated power of tech giants needs to be combated not only by the antimonopoly tool of antitrust but also by the antimonopoly tool of public utility regulation."[67]

The public interest conception is centrally concerned with the ways in which bottleneck power threatens political liberty and the exercise of collective self-government. "Public utility laws," as Genevieve Lakier argues, "are designed to protect the public's right of access to important goods and services—to goods and services that one must have access to if one wishes to participate fully in society. It should be obvious that the goods and services that platform companies provide are goods of this kind." As the infrastructure of our digital public square, Facebook's machine learning systems are a kind of bottleneck in citizens' common life as they use the platform, which is a critical tool for communication and organization, political expression, and collective-decision-making. As the infrastructure of our digital public library, Google's machine learning systems are a bottleneck in citizens' information ecosystem: they shape what citizens learn and know, as well as how public knowledge is structured, organized, and distributed.[68]

Here again, it is critical to recognize the pivotal importance of the dynamics of machine learning. Facebook's newsfeed and Google's search solve the problem of abundance by using the predictions of hundreds of finely tuned machine learning models to rank the vast quantity of content and websites that could be displayed. Facebook's and Google's bottleneck power is rooted in the design of these ranking systems: "Those who control what might be described as the access apparatus—the ability to meaningfully sort through huge databases and to organise them in meaningful and useful ways—act as gatekeepers to the information trove. . . . While those with access to the internet can access a range of content, they cannot . . . create their own organisational utilities."[69] Benjamin Barber drew the obvious conclusion in *The Nation* in 2011: "For new media to be potential equalizers, they must be treated as public utilities, recognizing that spectrum abundance (the excuse for privatization) does not prevent monopoly ownership of . . . software platforms and hence cannot guarantee equal civic, education, and cultural access to citizens."[70]

The bottleneck power that Facebook and Google exercise by designing ranking systems is also critical as a matter of law, because bottleneck power is central to the interaction between public utility regulation and the First Amendment. The Supreme Court has repeatedly ruled that private companies that exercise editorial control over speech cannot be required to restrict the flow of speech, except "when there is good reason to believe that doing so is necessary to prevent the property owner from exercising bottleneck control over an important medium of communication."[71] The Supreme Court upheld forced access laws in broadcasting because the local television industry was dependent on cable companies to carry their programming, such that cable operators exercised "control over most (if not all) of the television programming that is channeled into the subscriber's home [and could] thus silence the voice of competing speakers with a mere flick of the switch."[72] Several scholars have argued that while Facebook and Google are "dominant platforms," they "do not enjoy anywhere close to this level of dominance. There is no switch they can flick that can prevent disfavored speakers from disseminating their message on other, less dominant platforms."[73]

Yet this is precisely what Facebook and Google have. With a redesign of their machine learning systems—not so far from the flick of a switch—Facebook and Google can silence whoever they want on whatever basis they want. In our imaginary public square, people whose voices are not streamed into others' headphones could still in principle be heard if someone wandered around for hours trying to find them, but in practice they are silenced by the corporation's power to determine which speech gets streamed into whose headphones. In the Library of Babel, books that the Book-Man refuses to point toward could still in principle be accessed by chance or by sheer force of will, but in practice those books are rendered inaccessible by the Book-Man's power to decide which books to point people toward. Facebook's and Google's ranking systems are bottlenecks in the digital public sphere. Designing those systems involves the exercise of an especially pernicious bottleneck power because ranking makes its predictions come true, shaping what most of us see and hear for a huge proportion of the time we spend on the internet.

Perhaps the clearest example is *Marsh v. Alabama,* a case in which the Supreme Court held that the First Amendment prohibited a corporation from punishing a resident of a company-owned town for distributing religious literature. In applying a "public function" test—in which the First Amendment applies if a private corporation exercises powers traditionally reserved to the state—the Court focused on the functions of the infrastructure that the corporation controlled (the streets, sidewalks, public buildings) rather than the fact of its private ownership: "Whether a corporation or a municipality owns or possesses the town[,] the public in either case has an identical interest in the functioning of the community in such manner that the channels of communication remain free." The corporation should not be permitted "to govern a community of citizens" in a way that "restricts their fundamental liberties."[74]

Let me end by considering an objection. "Social media services are not physical resources with high fixed costs, and they do not possess 'bottlenecks' in any conventional sense," argues one paper:

> Even if network externalities exist that reward larger social media platforms, and even if an existing social media platform denies a competitor use of its "facility," competitors can duplicate such platforms. . . . The challenge comes down to the challenge of building a user base, not building infrastructure. The infrastructure needed to compete is essentially code, computers and services. This digital infrastructure represents a huge distinction from the physical infrastructure required in other industries, where creating

competing facilities requires a massive capital investment. Rolling out a new version of code simply doesn't entail anywhere near the same fixed costs as rolling out new physical towers, wires, and distribution hardware that are used in traditional communications networks.[75]

This objection illustrates the importance of understanding that Facebook's and Google's infrastructural power is exercised through the design of machine learning systems. The two companies' greatest asset is not code; it is machine learning systems and the data on which they depend. Facebook and Google use ranking systems powered by machine learning to organize news, information, content, and websites. The power of these systems depends on the volume of data on which they are trained, and that depends on the number of users Facebook has or the number of websites Google has indexed. Acquiring the data needed to develop a newsfeed system like Facebook's or a search system like Google's would be practically impossible for another company. Those systems are what constitute vital infrastructure, and control over those systems is where an objectionable kind of corporate bottleneck power resides.[76]

The political conception provides a framework for reasoning about when and how public control should be asserted over corporate control of vital infrastructure that supports the basic activities of citizenship. Applying this political conception to Facebook and Google would, as Rahman argues, make public utility regulation once again "vital for regulating those private actors operating in goods and services whose provision" appears "to require some degree of market concentration and consolidation—and whose set of users and constituencies were too vast to be empowered and protected through more conventional methods of market competition, corporate governance, or ordinary economic regulation."[77]

My purpose here is not to argue that because Facebook and Google crowd out competitors, raise barriers to entry, and stifle innovation they should as a matter of law be regulated as public utilities. It is to argue that Facebook's and Google's power triggers many of the concerns that animated the legal scholars and reformers who articulated the political conception of public utilities in the early twentieth century. The power to build ranking systems that function as the infrastructure of our digital public sphere poses not just economic problems but also political problems, because it threatens the capacity of citizens to exercise political liberty and collectively govern themselves. As Rahman argues, "The problem of private power [is] best understood as not just economic, but a political problem of . . . the accumulation of arbitrary authority unchecked by the ordinary mechanisms of political accountability."[78]

By ranking content based on predictions about relevance, Facebook and Google exercise a pervasive and pernicious infrastructural power that shapes the conditions for the exercise of collective self-government. How we regulate Facebook and Google should depend on how best to ensure that the exercise of this infrastructural power supports the flourishing of democracy.

Democratic Utilities

Although Facebook's and Google's ranking systems trigger many of the concerns that animated the political conception of public utilities, we should not regulate the two companies as we have regulated traditional public utilities. To see why, consider a proposal put forward in an op-ed in the *Financial Times* by Tristan Harris, a technologist and former Google ethicist. Harris proposed that Facebook and Google should be regulated as "attention utilities"—that is, platform businesses "that have created vital public digital infrastructure."[79]

The regulations that Harris argues we should impose resemble the kinds of regulations imposed on traditional public utilities. Attention utilities should be "required to operate in the public interest, according to rules and licences that guide their business models." They should "be required to convert to a monthly licence free model a bit like the BBC or a subscription model like Netflix," and they should submit "to the terms of an operating licence framed by a duty of care," as suggested by the EU's antitrust commissioner, Margrethe Vestager.[80] Attention utilities would be subject to a social impact assessment that evaluates "new products . . . for their potential impact on mental health, social isolation, fake news, polarisation and democracy. This pre-clearance would be akin to an environmental impact assessment or safety protocols used for medical devices."[81]

Harris's proposal illustrates a common but misguided way of using the public utility framework to think about how to regulate Facebook and Google. This begins by comparing Facebook and Google to industrial-era public utilities, then proposes different ways to subject Facebook and Google to obligations that resemble those developed in the industrial era. Critics rightly respond that industrial-era public utility regulations may prove ineffective and counterproductive when applied to Facebook's and Google's processes for designing dynamic machine learning systems.

Beyond Traditional Public Utilities

Consider one of Harris's proposals: requiring utilities to pre-clear products with a dedicated regulator. The intuition behind such a proposal comes from how physical infrastructure is regulated: a railroad company is required to pre-clear plans for a new pricing structure, and a telephone company is required to pre-clear plans for a new 5G network. In these cases, pre-clearance checks the corporate control over public goods, allowing regulators to impose public values like equity and safety. As Tom Wheeler, former chairman of the Federal Communications Commission (FCC), has argued, pre-clearance was characteristic of industrial-era "rigid utility-style regulation," because regulatory "micromanagement" was the most effective way to protect the public interest.[82]

Proposals like this have been subject to forceful criticisms. Consider one from the Harvard lawyer Susan Crawford. Despite their size and evident market power, argues Crawford, it's a misclassification to treat Facebook and Google as public utilities, because they do not own or operate a "physical network" franchised by the government, and unlike electricity, gas, communications, or water, they are not regulated by public utility commissions. People can "#deletefacebook and still live respectably," which is much "harder" to do when seeking "transport, power, communications, water, and sewer services. Because Facebook is not a physical, tangible network and is not on the same level of necessity as a 'real' utility," Crawford concludes, "it isn't one." Designating Facebook and Google as utilities risks letting "real" utilities off the hook and stifling future innovation.[83]

Peter Swire, a former member of President Obama's Review Group on Intelligence and Communications Technologies, makes a similar argument. Swire argues that as we evaluate the costs of a lack of regulation, our regulatory proposals must also consider "government imperfections in regulation," which can be "especially steep in industries that otherwise would continue to innovate." He uses the "old public utility approach" of pre-clearance as an example, arguing that it had "numerous flaws" because it "does not adapt readily to high-innovation markets where competition is typically based on factors other than price."[84]

It is easy to see the force of this critique. Imposing industrial-era proposals like pre-clearance on Facebook and Google may well prove ineffective or counterproductive. For one thing, Facebook's and Google's ranking systems are already well established, so requiring pre-clearance for future updates to those systems may not make much difference. For another, requiring a regulator to pre-clear machine learning models may slow future innovation. More importantly, the regulator tasked with making decisions about whether Facebook's newsfeed or Google's search violates a duty of care would have immense discretionary power. Pre-clearance may do little to orient Facebook's and Google's infrastructural power toward the public interest.

This is the wrong conversation to be having. Traditional public utility regulation is not suitable for governing Facebook and Google because Facebook and Google are not traditional public utilities. The purpose of exploring the concerns that animated Progressive legal reforms is to open our imaginations about when and how democracies should assert their authority over corporate control of vital infrastructure. Examining why Progressive legal reformers responded to the problems of their age by developing the public utility concept can illuminate the kinds of regulatory concepts we need to address the problems of our own age. Applying the concerns that animated these reformers to the specific nature of Facebook's and Google's power suggests that we may need our own regulatory innovations to regulate Facebook and Google.

We need to move beyond industrial-era images of public utilities and reach for underlying principles. For instance, as Tom Wheeler argues, the "responsibility to proactively identify and mitigate potential harms" characteristic of public utility regulation "is as valid today as it ever was." However, "its implementation" through "prior approval mechanisms is inappropriate for the application of fast-moving digital technology. In its place, a new agile regulatory model should be adopted."[85] Transplanting proposals devised in a different era of production makes it too easy for Facebook and Google to argue that regulation would stifle innovation and fail to protect the public interest. Instead, we should "return" to "the basic principles" of the Progressive-era public interest conception of public utilities and consider how "a new regulatory process" could best give effect to those principles. As corporate power is increasingly exercised through the design of predictive tools, we need to innovate the frameworks we draw on to govern this new kind of corporate power.[86]

Because Facebook and Google are different from traditional public utilities, critics are right that many of the obligations placed on traditional utilities may not work if imposed on Facebook and Google. Instead of rejecting the relevance of the traditional public utility framework—and with it, the possibilities for regulating Facebook and Google to address the political problems they pose—the political conception invites conceptual and regulatory innovation to assert democratic oversight of new kinds of corporate infrastructural power.

Different forms of corporate power pose different kinds of political problems that require different kinds of regulation. As FDR argued, democracy is not a static political system, but a process of innovation in which each generation must reimagine the institutional structures that embody the ideals of democracy to meet the concrete challenges of their age. That is what we must do with Facebook and Google.

The Possibilities of Self-Governance

The need for regulatory innovation should not surprise us. The political problems posed by Facebook and Google are different from the political problems posed by railroads or by electricity or telephone providers. Instead of confining the relevance of the public utility concept to the companies we currently think of and regulate as public utilities, we should reach for the broader, richer, and deeper set of ideals that underpin the Progressive-era political conception of public utilities. The most compelling argument for regulating Facebook and Google is not that we need a technocratic solution to protect competition or consumers, but that we need regulatory experimentalism to structure the exercise of self-rule in conditions of data-driven capitalism.

I propose a new category of corporations that should be subject to processes of public control and democratic governance: democratic utilities. Democratic utilities are corporations whose infrastructural power shapes the possibilities of collective self-government itself. The motivating purpose of regulating democratic utilities is to protect the flourishing of democracy.

Facebook and Google are both a distinctive kind of democratic utility that structures our public sphere and organizes our information ecosystem. Their infrastructural power is rooted not in the control of public goods like railroads or electricity or telephone cables, but in the design of ranking systems that impose an artificial form of scarcity, direct citizens' attention, and shape the exercise of self-governance. By using ranking to determine what appears where on which people's newsfeeds and search results, Facebook and Google shape the ideas and information that citizens engage with on a vast scale. The two companies' unilateral control over these ranking systems concentrates social and political as well as economic power, shaping how we understand and interpret the world around us, discuss fundamental matters of common concern, organize social and political groups, and make collective choices.

The democratic utility concept focuses our attention on the dynamic and pervasive power of a company that designs infrastructural ranking systems. It targets regulatory responses toward the functions of those ranking systems in a flourishing democracy, exploring the activities they support, who they affect and make vulnerable, and how best to empower citizens to design them to support a healthy public sphere and civic information architecture. The next chapter explores the obligations and mechanisms of governance that should be imposed on Facebook and Google to ensure that they build infrastructural ranking systems to support the flourishing of democracy.[87]

8

Regulating for Democracy

The many, who are not as individuals excellent men, nevertheless can, when they have come together, be better than the few best people, not individually but collectively.... For each individual among the many has a share of excellent and practical wisdom, and when they meet together, just as they become in manner one man, who has many feet, and hands, and senses, so too with regard to their character and thought.... Hence the many are better judges than a single man ... for some understand one part, and some another, and among them they understand the whole.[1]

—ARISTOTLE (350 BCE)

Ancient peoples are no longer a model for modern ones.... You are neither Romans, nor Spartans; you are not even Athenians. Leave aside these great names that do not suit you. You are Merchants, Artisans, Bourgeois, always occupied with their private interests, with their work, with their trafficking, with their gain; people for whom even liberty is only a means for acquiring without obstacle and for possessing in safety.... This situation demands maxims particular to you. Not being idle as ancient Peoples were, you cannot ceaselessly occupy yourselves with the Government as they did: but by that very fact that you can less constantly keep watch over it, it should be instituted in such a way that it might be easier for you to see its intrigues and provide for abuses. Every public effort that your interest demands ought to be made all the easier for you to fulfill since it is an effort that costs you and that you do not make willingly. For to wish to unburden yourselves of them completely is to wish to cease being free. "It is necessary to choose," says the beneficent Philosopher, "and those who cannot bear work have only to seek rest in servitude."[2]

—JEAN-JACQUES ROUSSEAU (1764)

The task of democracy is forever that of creation of a freer and more humane experience in which all share and to which all contribute.[3]

—JOHN DEWEY, "CREATIVE DEMOCRACY" (1939)

ON OCTOBER 5, 2021, Frances Haugen, a former Facebook product manager, testified before the US Senate. She argued that to regulate Facebook and Google, "there needs to be a dedicated oversight body, because right now the only people in the world who are trained . . . to understand what's happening inside of Facebook are people who grew up inside of Facebook." This oversight body would be a new "regulatory home" with the knowledge and authority to create structures of oversight of technology companies like Facebook and Google. To design and establish this body, we must "break out of previous regulatory frames . . . privacy protections or changes to Section 230 alone will not be sufficient . . . [because] they will not get to the core of the issue, which is that no one truly understands . . . [the] choices made by Facebook."[4]

This book has focused on one kind of choice made by organizations like Facebook: choices about the design and integration of machine learning systems. When organizations like child welfare agencies or police departments make choices about the design and use of these systems, they exercise a distinctive kind of power: the power to predict. Haugen was among the first whistleblowers to recognize the importance of the political character of this power for regulating Facebook and Google. Time and again, she argued, the most important choices that Facebook and Google make are value-laden choices about the design of machine learning systems that function as part of the infrastructure of the public sphere, such as Facebook's newsfeed or Google's search. Governing these choices will require moving beyond existing regulatory frameworks. Building on the analysis of the political character of Facebook and Google's systems in chapter 5, of the infrastructural power they wield in designing them in chapter 6, and of the democratic utility framework in chapter 7, this chapter develops a constructive alternative approach to regulation that is rooted in a concern for the flourishing of democracy.

As you read this chapter, imagine you are a US senator charged with developing proposals for regulating Facebook and Google. Because you are concerned above all with the flourishing of democracy, as all US senators ought to be, you begin by articulating a set of principles to guide the design of Facebook's and Google's systems to ensure that they support a healthy public sphere and civic information ecosystem. I describe three, which would serve as yardsticks against which to evaluate the design of Facebook's and Google's systems: anti-corruption, diversity, and shared experience. Exploring what these principles mean in practice sharpens some of the most important and interesting questions about regulating Facebook and Google: How should Facebook design a newsfeed system to enable diverse citizens to encounter one another in conditions of respect and equality and to actually come to know one other? How should Google design a search system to support the formation of shared knowledge and a resilient civic information architecture? How should democracies ensure that Facebook and Google build systems that support the social and informational conditions of collective self-government? These questions remind us that the connection between political values and choices in machine learning is at the heart of regulating Facebook and Google.

As I have argued in this book, disagreements about political values and how to embed them in machine learning systems are both unavoidable and desirable. There will always be contests over what principles should guide the design of our public sphere and how those principles are to be expressed in the design of machine learning systems. What matters is that we regulate Facebook and Google to institutionalize the process of asking and answering the right questions—those being questions that force us to articulate what a healthy public sphere and information ecosystem look like and to justify how we design machine learning systems in light of that vision. I have been lucky enough to work with talented legislators, regulators, and technologists striving to do just that, and what I have learned above all is that a great deal of humility is required. What we need is a governance regime that invites intentional experimentation and reflection and keeps alive the possibility of change and revision in the design of machine learning systems that function as digital infrastructure to support the social and informational conditions of collective self-government.[5]

I argue that this approach requires two crucial shifts in how we think about regulating Facebook and Google. The first is a shift from a focus on technical explanations to a focus on institutional justifications. We need structures of accountability that require Facebook and Google to justify how the systems they build advance shared goals, such as the principles of anticorruption, diversity, and shared experience. Those justifications do not require technical explanations of the inner logic of machine learning models, as many privacy-focused regulatory proposals suggest, but principled justifications that surface the political values built into technical choices. The second is a shift from technocratic to participatory decision-making. We need to involve civil society actors and public bodies with relevant knowledge and expertise in ongoing judgments about how to advance shared goals in the design of Facebook's and Google's machine learning systems. I argue that we should do so by creating a new platform regulator, the AI Platforms Agency (APA), to develop mechanisms of empowered participatory governance.

The regulation of Facebook and Google is an opportunity for regulatory innovation. By combining structural reforms to corporate governance and the administrative state with scrutiny through participatory decision-making, the approach I describe would not only regulate Facebook and Google but also introduce a much-needed shift in how we approach regulation itself, abandoning the search for stable, technocratic solutions and embracing institutional experimentalism as part of the urgent project of democratic reform.

Goals

At the center of the Pynx, the hill in Athens opposite the Acropolis, is a raised platform called the *bema*. The *bema* was designed to elevate and project the speech of leaders like Pericles and Demosthenes to the several thousand citizens of ancient Athens assembled to make decisions about matters of war, taxation, and punishment.[6] In ancient Rome, the Forum was designed to be the center of political activity: it housed government buildings and was the site of elections and public speeches as well as Rome's commercial center.[7] In seventeenth-century London, coffeehouses were designed as places where citizens could read newspapers, discuss affairs of state, and trade in goods and gossip.[8]

All healthy political societies design public spaces to advance shared goals because the design of these spaces affects the texture of daily life. We should think of the machine learning systems that are part of the infrastructure of the digital public sphere in a similar way. If designing these systems involves the exercise of infrastructural power, as I have argued, we should ensure that they are designed to support the social and informational conditions of collective self-government.

Three Principles

As a US senator, you have decided to articulate a few principles that capture those conditions. These principles will guide the choices that Facebook and Google make about the design of their ranking systems powered by machine learning: the values those systems express, the top-line metrics they optimize, the concepts they approximate, and the guidelines that shape the labeling of the data on which they are trained. I explore three: anticorruption, which holds that Facebook and Google should design systems that prioritize the public interest above advertising revenue; diversity, which holds that those systems should promote a diversity of voices and values in the public sphere by encouraging serendipitous encounters among citizens; and shared experience, which holds that those systems should forge shared experience through a civic information architecture.

These principles flesh out what it means to be a good democratic utility—one that intentionally designs machine learning systems to advance the principles of anticorruption, diversity, and shared experience. Exploring what these principles look like in practice illustrates the kind of ongoing discussion we must have about how Facebook's and Google's machine learning systems should support the flourishing of democracy.[9]

I must emphasize at the outset that while our public sphere would be much healthier if Facebook and Google deliberately designed systems to advance these principles, there is no technical solution to the hard, face-to-face work of sustaining democracy and co-creating our common life. Whenever I feel uneasy about the technocratic character of technical solutions to democratic problems, I recall a speech given by John Dewey in 1939, on the eve of the Second World War:

> Democracy . . . is the sole way of living which believes wholeheartedly in the process of experience as end and as means; as that which is capable of generating the . . . emotions, needs, and desires so as to call into being the things that have not existed in the past. For every way of life that fails in its democracy limits the contacts, the exchanges, the communications, the interactions by which experience is steadied while it is enlarged and enriched. The task of this release and enrichment is one that has to be carried on day by day. Since it is one that can have no end till experience itself comes to an end, the task of democracy is forever that of creation of a freer and more humane experience in which all share and to which all contribute.
>
> Democracy as a way of life is controlled by personal faith in personal day-by-day working together with others. Democracy is the belief that even when needs and ends or consequences are different for each individual, the habit of amicable cooperation—which may include, as in sport, rivalry and competition—is itself a priceless addition to life . . . to treat those who disagree—even profoundly—with us as those from whom we may learn, and in so far, as friends.[10]

ANTICORRUPTION

There is nothing new about private control over the infrastructure of the public sphere. The Roman Forum was a center of commercial as well as political activity; London's coffeehouses were owned by private proprietors but served a function that was in part public. The democratic utility concept invites us to examine the kinds of social and political interactions and activities that machine learning systems support, and then to derive goals that orient the design of those systems toward creating a healthy public sphere and resilient civic information ecosystem.[11]

The anticorruption principle holds that those who build vital infrastructure should consider and seek to advance the public interest rather than simply focusing on private gain. The anticorruption principle treats the public interest as a pragmatic ideal, forged through the process of deliberation, participation, and collective decision-making, and insists that the outcome of that process should have implications for the appropriate exercise of power in the performance of public functions, such as the design of ranking systems that solve the problem of abundance. Public goals need not be wholly insulated from commercial imperatives, but a continuous effort should be made to orient the building of vital infrastructure toward public goals rather than merely the accrual of private wealth. The pursuit of private gain is not itself corrupt, but we must ensure that it involves sincere and ongoing consideration of the public interest. The anticorruption principle responds to the corruption critique, which argues that the political economy of digital advertising encourages Facebook and Google to build systems that capture and retain attention, corrupting the public sphere in pursuit of profit.[12]

To see what the anticorruption principle might mean in practice, consider different ways of paying for the public sphere. There are taxes, in which the entire public pays for public assets like pavements, parks, schools, and, previously, post offices; fines, paid by a subset of the public who violate a set of rules; and fees, paid by a subset of the public who use a particular service, such as buses and now post offices. Facebook and Google use advertising to pay for the public sphere they build. This is not itself new. In 1833, the *New York Sun* caused a sensation by charging one cent for each newspaper, promising "to lay before the public ... the news of the day" and "to offer an advantageous medium for advertisements." What makes Facebook and Google different is the way the "business model has infected and driven the pathologies of ... digital and private informational infrastructure." The anticorruption principle would require Facebook and Google to better separate the incentives of digital advertising from the design of informational infrastructure.[13]

One way to do this would be to ban targeted advertising altogether, encouraging companies like Facebook and Google to shift toward a subscription business model. With an annual revenue of $85 billion and 2.8 billion users, Facebook earns about $30 per user per year. Facebook could charge a fee that varies according to where a user lives or what they earn. A ban on targeted ads falls squarely within the tradition of fair and just pricing rules. "As with non-discrimination and common carriage, the ban would place limits on the kinds of practices legally available to information platforms . . . alter[ing] the revenue-generating strategy of the firms themselves." Margarethe Vestager, the EU's antitrust commissioner, has proposed something similar, arguing that Facebook and Google should be required to charge users for services.[14]

A better option might be to impose a structural firewall between advertising systems and ranking systems that distribute ideas and information, insulating the process of designing systems that function as public infrastructure from the process of designing digital advertising systems. Such a firewall would be like separating the risky securitization arms of financial institutions from core banking functions, or banning a railroad company from controlling related services, such as the production of coal. The newspaper industry pioneered a similar firewall in insulating editorial judgments from commercial imperatives. Where broadcasters fail to faithfully serve the public interest, the Supreme Court has even suggested that private ownership can be rescinded.[15]

In the democratic utilities approach, structural firewalls would isolate the component of Facebook and Google that functions as social infrastructure and subject that component—and only that component—to obligations and mechanisms of governance designed to support a healthy public sphere and information ecosystem. It would separate ranking systems that solve a problem of informational abundance, like Facebook's newsfeed and Google's search, from advertising delivery systems that determine who sees which ads. The democratic utilities approach would separate choices about the design of machine learning systems that serve as infrastructure from choices about the design of systems that serve simply commercial, revenue-raising functions.[16]

This approach mirrors Tim Wu's proposals for imposing a separations principle on what he calls "information monopolies": companies that "traffic in forms of individual expression" and are "fundamental to democracy." Wu describes his separations principle not as

> a regulatory approach but rather [as] a constitutional approach to the information economy . . . a regime whose goal is to constrain and divide all power that derives from the control of information. . . . A separations Principle would mean the creation of a salutary distance between each of the major functions or layers in the information economy. It would mean

that those who develop information, those who control the network infrastructure on which it travels, and those who control the tools or venue of access must be kept apart from one another.[17]

By transforming the political economy of Facebook and Google, structural firewalls would better align the two companies' incentives with the public interest. Facebook's newsfeed would be structurally separated from Facebook's advertising system, and Google's search would be structurally separated from GoogleAds. Advertising delivery systems would not be subject to the obligations and mechanisms of governance entailed by regulation as a democratic utility and would instead be subject to requirements designed to protect economic competition. Establishing these firewalls would ensure that Facebook and Google adequately consider the public interest as they design and operate machine learning systems that are part of the infrastructure of the digital public sphere.[18]

In practice, this structural separation could take various forms. One would be a firewall within each company between the governance structures that control the ranking and advertising systems, separating the engineers, data scientists, policy teams, and vice presidents who build Facebook's newsfeed and Google's search from those who build the companies' advertising delivery systems. The companies could create entirely separate corporate decision-making structures for each system by establishing different boards for each, with different composition and representation requirements. Another option would go further, requiring firewalls between the data that Facebook uses to build its newsfeed, and Google its search system, and the data they use to train advertising delivery systems. With a firewall between these data repositories, each system could be subject to different portability, interoperability, and transparency requirements.

A firewall between data systems may also require a different way to pay for ranking systems that serve as infrastructure. One option would be a tech tax targeted at profits. Revenues could be spent not only on running Facebook's newsfeed or Google's search but also on building and operating the physical spaces that Dewey argued were critical to democratic life.[19]

DIVERSITY

In flourishing democracies, citizens with different experiences and identities encounter one another not merely as objects in books or films or plays, but as people with different perspectives they try to understand and appreciate as they get to know one another. As the Harvard lawyer Cass Sunstein argues, citizens need "exposure to materials, topics, and positions [they] would not have chosen in advance" and "a range of positions" on "substantive questions of policy and principle." Such exposure was among James Madison's central concerns. Madison feared that social groups that become siloed, insulated from each other's opinions and ways of thinking, could solidify into what he called "factions"—groups that place the welfare of other group members above the welfare of the nation.[20]

Madison's solution to faction was the geographic structure of representation. By dispersing diverse social groups across a large nation, representatives in each district or region would be required to make judgments about how best to filter and sift different views to forge the national interest. As the divides in modern democracies become ever more strongly correlated with geography, Madison's solution to the problem of faction has become increasingly strained. We need new ways to sustain robust institutions of social learning that avert the problem of faction.[21]

The principle of diversity requires that institutions operating as information bottlenecks work to ensure that citizens are exposed to opinions and ways of thinking that differ from their own. The principle of diversity is intimately bound up with serendipity, the fortuitous encounter with people or ideas we did not expect to find in a forum we trust. It encourages us to think about the creation of spaces in which citizens come together without quite knowing what to expect. This is the very opposite of Facebook's newsfeed and Google's search, which, because they are ranking systems, make people more likely to engage with the content or websites that they are predicted to engage with. Instead of influencing the behavior they claim to predict, ranking systems would be required by the diversity principle to proactively promote diverse sources of ideas and information.

To apply this principle Facebook and Google would have to redesign the digital public sphere. Facebook could introduce a serendipity button: "Imagine if you could flip a switch on Facebook and turn all the conservative viewpoints that you see into liberal viewpoints, or vice versa. You'd realize that your news might look nothing like your neighbor's."[22] Or better, Facebook and Google could change ranking systems themselves. Imagine if they built ranking systems that predict not the content people want to see, but the content they do not want to see—what they don't tend to click on, like, or share. Facebook and Google could use those systems to occasionally show users content that they're not predicted to engage with. They could present this content in appealing ways and notify users that, while they might not agree with it, they might still find it interesting, suggesting "Try this" or "Here is a different view" or "Have you thought about this?" or "Here is what others think." A serendipity button would build diversity and chance into the infrastructure of the digital public sphere, pushing against the performative power of prediction by mimicking the unexpected interactions in the streets, in bars, or reading the newspaper.

We could borrow from James Madison and use geography to advance the diversity principle. If place is critical to bridging across diverse citizens, we could embed place in the regulation of Facebook and Google. Ranking systems could be designed to promote engagement and information flows across different geographies by distributing content with thresholds for geographic diversity, deliberately exposing people to content and websites produced by fellow citizens who live in places they might otherwise not encounter. This approach would mirror other policy proposals for weakening the force of parochial ties and building alternative structures for controversial political views, such as introducing a new version of the draft or establishing geographic lotteries for admission to elite colleges. If one of the informational conditions of democracy is that individuals are unexpectedly exposed to the opinions and attitudes of others, machine learning systems that shape our informational ecosystem should be built to support and secure this condition.[23]

We could also draw inspiration from the fairness doctrine, a regulatory obligation previously applied to broadcasting. The fairness doctrine required broadcasters to "(1) devote a reasonable portion of broadcast time to the discussion and consideration of controversial issues of public importance," and it further stipulated "(2) that in doing so, [they be] fair—that is . . . affirmatively endeavor to make . . . facilities available for the expression of contrasting viewpoints held by responsible elements with respect to the controversial issues presented." The doctrine was not simply an equal airtime regulation but also a statement of a positive duty to consider "what the appropriate opposing viewpoints were on these controversial issues, and who was best suited to present them." The fairness doctrine could be reimagined as a design principle for infrastructural ranking systems like newsfeed or search.[24]

The constitutionality of the fairness doctrine has been a subject of intense debate. The constitutionality of the FCC's imposition of public interest criteria hinged on the inevitable scarcity of radio frequencies. "Because of the scarcity of radio frequencies, the Government is permitted to put restraints on licensees in favor of others whose views should be expressed on this unique medium. But the people as a whole retain their interest in free speech by radio and their collective right to have the medium function consistently with the ends and purpose of the First Amendment. It is the right of the viewers and listeners, not the right of the broadcasters, which is paramount."[25] As the media scholar Philip Napoli argues, the fairness doctrine "rested on the notion that the proportion of audience attention controlled by these networks was so large that the public interest in diversity and competition was served by requiring the networks to allow other content creators to have access to this massive accumulation of audience attention."[26]

Although no First Amendment analogy quite captures Facebook's and Google's distinctive infrastructural power, they are certainly more like radio stations than newspapers. By solving the problem of abundance, Facebook's and Google's machine learning systems impose an artificial scarcity on citizens' informational ecosystem. As I have argued, their ranking systems shape access to newspapers and determine who reads what news, but they are not like newspapers themselves. Facebook and Google use this point to argue against all regulation—we should not be regulated because we are not information producers—but it is really an argument against regulation that treats Facebook and Google as information producers. Like broadcasters, if Facebook and Google exercise bottleneck power over the flow of information and ideas, they may have a corresponding duty to ensure a diversity of information sources and viewpoints. We could reimagine the fairness doctrine as a design principle of infrastructural ranking systems like Facebook's newsfeed and Google's search.[27]

SHARED EXPERIENCE

A self-governing people must be conscious of themselves as a people, a collective that shares experiences, feelings, attitudes, habits, and hopes. As some die, others are born, and the composition and character of a citizenry change, the existence and consciousness of the ultimate agent in a democracy, the people, depends on collective memory. Some of the most interesting bits of seminal texts in the history of political thought are discussions about the common experiences and commitments that political societies need to endure over time.[28]

There are four benefits to shared experiences and information. First, whether a presidential TV debate, a new movie, or a sports event, people enjoy shared experiences. The very fact that something is enjoyed by many people at once is a source of its value. Second, shared experiences support social interactions, providing common topics, memories, and concerns that enable people from diverse backgrounds to communicate and engage. The offerings of public broadcasting channels like the British Broadcasting Corporation (BBC) and televised sporting events provide a focal point for people to discuss and interpret experiences, a kind of social glue that helps forge a civic culture and information ecosystem. Third, shared experiences underpin social trust. Not only is social trust a feeling of solidarity, a view of others as fellow citizens engaged in the shared enterprise of self-government, but it undergirds collective action, whether adhering to Covid-19 restrictions, fighting a war, or supporting those who have suffered misfortunes. Fourth, information also has a valuable social property: when one person knows something, others have the opportunity to learn it too, enabling each person to function as an information conduit in a connected social web. Shared experiences forge a nation: public holidays symbolize moments of shared significance (one reason we should make elections into public holidays), as does the coronation of a monarch.[29]

The shared experience principle requires that the institutions occupying bottleneck positions in our information ecosystem support shared experiences and widely disseminate public information to promote common purpose across diverse citizens.

The principle of shared experience could focus on time. Democracies rely on shared memories of certain moments: the assassination of JFK in 1963, the passage of the Civil Rights Act of 1964, 9/11, the invasion of Iraq, the night of the 2016 presidential election, the Black Lives Matter protests in the summer of 2020, and the storming of the Capitol on January 6, 2021. Or in the United Kingdom: the 1966 World Cup Final, the race riots of 1981, the funeral of Princess Diana in 1997, the 7/7 London bombings or the Manchester Arena attack in 2017, the opening ceremony of the London Olympics, and the night in June 2016 when the British learned that they had voted to leave the European Union. Whether the passing of legislation or significant sporting events, at particular moments a society comes together to share an experience. Because they read different opinion columns or watch different news stations, citizens interpret that experience through different lenses, of course, but the experience itself is required to have the bridging conversations with others who interpret it differently. Like the diversity principle, the shared experience captures a basic informational condition of collective self-government. The two principles work in tandem. The shared experience principle ensures that citizens receive information about events or topics of public importance, while the diversity principle ensures adequate diversity in the sources of that information.

If shared experiences at particular moments help forge common purpose, Facebook's and Google's ranking systems could be built to ensure the widespread distribution of information about significant events and moments in time. Facebook and Google could create a content category for information about events, topics, culture, and issues of widespread public importance, then build ranking systems that display that content higher in people's newsfeeds or search results. The two companies could design community debate pages or subsidize advertising to enable government officials or local representatives to disseminate information and engage in public argument, especially at moments of great public import. They could create pages that provide public education about important topics—not just about elections, but about other topics of historical, political, or cultural significance—and monitor and update them over time.

There are two objections to the idea of imposing shared goals—such as the three principles we have explored—on the design of Facebook's and Google's machine learning systems. First, doing so risks a kind of censorship. There is an "insoluble tension between an obligation to regulate [media] in the public interest while simultaneously avoiding censorship," and as such, "public interest [obligations] can be used to advance partisan or private interest."[30] Because the concept of a singular public interest is a fiction, whoever makes judgments about the public interest imposes a kind of censorship. "If the government is empowered to advance the public interest online, it will necessarily affect the moderation decisions of private companies.... Given the history of partisan abuse of the public interest ... the burden of proof should rest with those advocating for public interest standard[s] for the internet to show that their rules would not impose new restrictions on free speech." Second, imposing shared goals risks creating a powerful infrastructure for propaganda that would concentrate too much power in the hands of whoever interprets these principles in the design of Facebook's and Google's machine learning systems.[31]

These objections do not appreciate what Facebook and Google already do. As we have seen, by solving the problem of information abundance, ranking systems impose an artificial kind of scarcity on vast quantities of content and websites, and the design of those systems inevitably imposes restrictions on who is seen and heard by whom. Building a ranking system is by definition a kind of censorship. Similarly, the top-line metrics, values, and concepts built into the design of ranking systems inevitably impose a certain way of structuring the flow of information and ideas in the public sphere. Facebook's and Google's systems are already infrastructure for propaganda. The question is simply whether we wish to stand back and permit the unavoidable power of censorship and propaganda involved in building Facebook's and Google's systems to be exercised in pursuit of advertising revenue, or to step up and work to ensure that these systems support the flourishing of democracy.[32]

Beyond Competition

I want to consider a more persuasive objection, one that has lurked in the background of the last few chapters. Readers versed in antitrust or competition policy might think that the problem with the approach I have described is that it would forestall economic competition. Jason Furman's report on competition policy in the digital era begins: "Some people argue that digital platforms are natural monopolies where only a small number of firms can succeed, making competition impossible. The logical conclusion of that view is utility-like regulation of the type used for electricity distributors. . . . We disagree . . . seeing greater competition among digital platforms as not only necessary but also possible—provided the right policies are in place."[33]

I have already argued that it is a mistake to apply industrial-era conceptions of public utilities to Facebook and Google. The political conception of public utilities developed in the Progressive era focuses not simply on whether corporations are natural monopolies, but on the political problems posed by the corporate exercise of infrastructural power. The fact that Facebook and Google are different from traditional utilities should prompt us to focus on the underlying concerns that motivate the political conception, not to reject the concept of public utilities outright. Just as competition policy must be developed in an age of data-driven capitalism, so too must other areas of regulation, including public utility law. Although this point goes some way to addressing Furman's objections, it is a little too quick. We should dwell a while longer on the relationship between competition policy and the democratic utility framework I have proposed.[34]

I have some sympathy with the view that the economics of machine learning is likely to make Facebook and Google natural monopolies. Google, for instance, accounts for nearly 90 percent of all search queries in the United States, and almost 95 percent on mobile devices. But when and how a democracy regulates corporations should not hinge on whether they are natural monopolies, but on the nature of the power they wield; in particular, regulation should be aimed at ensuring that the exercise of that power supports the flourishing of democracy. If Facebook and Google cease to wield the infrastructural power I have explored—perhaps because they are eclipsed by some other social network or search provider, or because they are broken up by successful antitrust suits—they no longer need to be regulated as democratic utilities. The democratic utility approach does not depend on—and is agnostic toward—debates about whether Facebook and Google are natural monopolies.[35]

A deeper challenge of Furman's argument is that public utility regulation would give up on, and even prevent, economic competition. On this view, asking the corporation that controls our imaginary public square to ensure that there is no hate speech or to fact-check every pamphlet would entrench its dominance by creating a kind of dependency. Similarly, requiring Facebook and Google to advance the principles of anticorruption or diversity or shared experience would establish a symbiotic relationship that leaves the state dependent on the two companies to advance the goals it lays down. The result, at best, would be a disincentive for the state to enforce competition policy, and at worst, a corrupt institutional dependency that makes Facebook forever the dominant social network and Google the dominant search provider. This outcome would fail to achieve the purpose of public utility regulation: to protect political liberty and the exercise of self-government.[36]

We should appreciate the force of this point. There may indeed prove to be tensions between competition policy and the imposition of shared goals on the design of infrastructural machine learning systems. The more goals governments impose on Facebook and Google, the more governments may come to depend on Facebook and Google to advance those goals, especially given the technical expertise required to build machine learning systems. This is one reason why incentives like tax breaks and government subsidies may be a better way to begin regulating Facebook and Google than the imposition of specific legal duties focused on different kinds of permissible and impermissible content. But these tensions should not be overstated. Imposing shared goals that orient the exercise of infrastructural power need not entrench the dominance of Facebook and Google. One good piece of evidence for this is found in Furman's own proposals.

Furman proposes that a special legal category should be created for corporations like Facebook and Google: firms with strategic market status (SMS). SMS firms would be subject to a code of anticompetitive conduct, enforced by a new regulator "that sets out how [an] SMS [firm is] expected to behave in relation to activity motivating its SMS designation." By "defin[ing] the boundaries of anti-competitive conduct in digital markets," the code of conduct seeks to protect competition among SMS firms. Determinations about which firms fall into the SMS category should "be an evidence-based economic assessment as to whether a firm has substantial, entrenched market power in at least one digital activity, providing the firm with a strategic position (meaning the effects of its market power are likely to be particularly widespread and/or significant)"; this assessment would focus "on assessing the very factors which may give rise to harm, and which motivate the need for regulatory intervention."[37]

There are striking similarities between the SMS concept and the concept of democratic utilities, and judgments about whether to treat a corporation as an SMS firm are similar to judgments about whether to treat a corporation as a democratic utility. Whether or not Facebook and Google are natural monopolies, the economics of machine learning makes it extremely difficult for competitors to challenge their power. That is why SMS determinations consider whether a corporation's power has "widespread and/or significant effects," including, presumably, effects on the distribution of ideas and information. Furman's own argument suggests that we need *some* special category that responds to the distinctive power of Facebook and Google; the only question is what criteria warrant inclusion in that category and what kinds of obligations follow.

My argument is concerned with how we approach regulation that supports the flourishing of democracy, rather than what legal category we assign to public utilities. Given the pervasive effects of Facebook's and Google's systems on the digital public sphere, democracies should seek to ensure that those systems are designed to support the flourishing of democracy. Nothing hangs on the term "public utilities"; I just happen to think that the concerns that prompted Progressive-era legal reformers to develop the public utility concept illuminate how democracies should regulate Facebook and Google. You could describe my approach as "sector-specific regulation" that applies to firms with "strategic democratic status" (SDS) and the motivating argument would still obtain, because it focuses on the nature of the infrastructural power that democratic utilities exercise. Like mine, Furman's proposals recognize that there are some corporations whose position in digital markets is not likely to change anytime soon and that the power of those corporations should be subject to a distinct set of regulatory obligations.[38]

The difference is that Furman's rules aim to protect competition, whereas mine aim to support the flourishing of democracy. This is the point pressed by the democratic utility approach. While the idea that economic competition itself protects political liberty has historically been among the most potent arguments for antitrust reform and enforcement, the democratic utility approach insists that the obligations and structures of governance imposed on Facebook and Google should aim to do more than simply protect economic competition.[39]

Insofar and for as long as Facebook and Google exercise an infrastructural power that shapes conditions of collective self-government, Facebook and Google should design machine learning systems to protect the public interest, promote exposure to a diversity of sources of information ideas, and forge shared experience and civic information architectures. In the age of data-driven capitalism, we should regulate Facebook and Google as democratic utilities *and* we should require Facebook and Google to respect pro-competition rules. The democratic utility approach is not opposed to competition policy; it simply holds that competition policy is not sufficient. If proponents of competition policy insist on an insoluble tension between these two approaches, we should remember that democracy comes before capitalism, not the other way around.

Practice

Anticorruption, diversity, and shared experience are not meant to be definitive statements of the principles that characterize a healthy public sphere. I have chosen these principles in order to illustrate the vital importance of focusing on the connections between political values and choices in machine learning if we are to regulate Facebook and Google to support the flourishing of democracy. As a US senator, you understand that contests over political values and how best to express them in technical systems are part of what it means to live in a flourishing democracy. What you therefore seek is an approach to regulating Facebook and Google that institutionalizes the asking and answering of the right questions—those being questions that force different actors to articulate what they believe a healthy public sphere looks like and how they will design machine learning systems to support it. You want regulatory structures that embed processes of experimentation and collective learning about different duties and obligations and different ways of designing technical systems to advance them.

This section explores how we might do this in practice. I argue for two shifts in how we think about regulating Facebook and Google. The first is a shift from technical explanations to institutional justifications. Facebook and Google should be required to justify the concrete choices they make in designing their machine learning systems, not to provide technical explanations of the inner logic of those systems, as required by many regulatory approaches focused on privacy. The second is a shift from technocratic to participatory decision-making. To ensure that Facebook and Google build infrastructural machine learning systems to advance shared goals, the right actors must be in the room, including civil society groups and public bodies with relevant experience and expertise. I argue that we should create a new regulator, the AI Platforms Agency (APA), to support this shift to participatory decision-making by developing mechanisms of empowered participatory governance.

Accountability

We need to start with institutional structures that enable elected representatives, citizens, and regulators to evaluate whether Facebook's and Google's machine learning systems advance shared goals, such as the principles of anticorruption, diversity, and shared experience. Exploring how to achieve this returns us to one of this book's central themes: the gaps in experience, accountability, and language.

Recall when I asked you in chapter 5 to imagine that you were a Facebook engineer who wanted to change the newsfeed ranking system by introducing the toxicity model. After you ran experiments to determine the content that different people tended to find toxic, and then hired people to label thousands of pieces of content, you used A/B tests to evaluate how the model would affect newsfeed's top-line metrics; finally, you presented your findings to product managers, policy teams, and vice presidents. These higher-ups held a thirty-minute meeting to review your evidence, evaluate alternative ways of designing the model, and decide whether to give the green light or send your team back to the drawing board.

To whom does Facebook owe a justification about how it has designed this machine learning model? And how should Facebook offer that justification? What information should Facebook provide to citizens, representatives, and regulators? Imagine a journalist asking your boss, the vice president responsible for the toxicity model, how it was built. There is a good chance that your boss will know little about the model, because they lack your engineering experience or the time to understand it. A journalist might listen to the vice president's generalities—"it gives people more of what they want to see"—and be none the wiser about whether the model advances the principles of diversity and shared experience. This is the experience gap: the journalists skilled in making judgments about how information should be distributed in the public interest are not the ones who make choices about the design of machine learning models that distribute information in the public sphere. And it is also the accountability gap: the vice president responsible for the effects of a model does not understand how the engineer designed it.

This raises a problem about how to structure accountability. How can we ensure that the vice president's uninformed answers actually reflect technical choices made in machine learning? If the vice president does understand those technical choices, how can we ensure that the vice president explains them in ways that actually inform journalists, citizens, and regulators, many of whom do not speak the language of computer science? How should Facebook and Google be held accountable for ensuring that they design their systems to sustain a healthy public sphere and information ecosystem?

JUSTIFICATION > EXPLANATION

Many scholars of privacy law have argued that accountability requires Facebook and Google to provide technical explanations of the inner logic of their machine learning models. Because machine learning models are often nonlinear, nonmonotonic, and discontinuous and use large numbers of inputs, it can be extremely hard to understand why a model produces a particular prediction.[40] They argue that inscrutability blocks accountability, because citizens' lives are shaped by the predictions of models whose logic they cannot understand, and so Facebook and Google should be required to explain the inner logic of their machine learning systems.[41]

The thought underpinning this idea is simple. Accountability requires that citizens justify to one another how the technologies they build affect their common life. Accountability is part of how citizens authorize the complex decision-making procedures to which they are subject. Because the systems built by Facebook and Google have become part of the infrastructure of the digital public sphere, these companies should be required to justify to citizens and representatives how they design these systems to advance shared goals. On this view, whoever designs a machine learning model must explain how the model works in order to justify the model to those whose lives it shapes. Accountability requires justification, and justification requires explanation.[42]

To probe this reasoning, consider an example. Suppose a woman is involved in a car crash that leaves her paralyzed from the waist down. After she wakes up in the hospital, she asks: "Why did I crash?" Ford, the company that made her car and serviced it a few weeks earlier, sends a crash investigator, who leaves a report by her bed. It explains: "The velocity of your car produced a centrifugal force on the wheel hub, which gradually produced a rotating motion on the wheel stud, which, in turn, loosened the front left wheel from the chassis. The resulting force made your vehicle swerve to the left. The particles of the central barrier then came into contact with the polymers on the left side of the vehicle, breaking the molecular structure of the polymer on the driver's side, and rapidly reducing the speed of your vehicle to a halt. The rapid reduction and speed caused the bones in your upper spine to crack, resulting in the injuries you have today."

This explanation is clearly unsatisfactory. Although it might be accurate, answering the victim's question with an account of microphysics is beside the point. It is an explanation at the wrong level. What the victim wants to know is why her wheel came off. She wants Ford to justify why her wheel came off even though its mechanics serviced the vehicle the previous month. Ford's account of the microphysics of the car crash not only misunderstands what the victim wants to know but evades institutional responsibility by failing to justify what happened.

To those subject to the predictions of Facebook's and Google's machine learning models, offering explanations of their inner logic is a little like offering an account of the microphysics of a car crash to the victim of that crash. The right form of explanation can be crucial to the giving and receiving of justifications, but the wrong form can undermine it. The demand for technical explanations of Facebook's and Google's systems conceives of explanation at the wrong level—and more precisely, at a level not relevant to justification and therefore to accountability. We should not adopt technical solutions to explanation without thinking through what is required to structure accountability over time.

Two shifts in focus from technical explanations are implied here. First, to clarify *what* is being justified, the focus should be on how Facebook and Google design and use machine learning systems, not on the technical details of those systems. What matters is not how their systems work but why they work as they do. Second, *to whom* the justification is offered should be shifted: Facebook and Google should justify their choices about those systems not to individual citizens but to empowered regulators. Less emphasis should be placed on the rights of isolated individuals who are expected to understand complicated technical models and more on how to structure institutional accountability.

WHAT SHOULD BE JUSTIFIED?

As I have argued throughout this book, machine learning is a process that involves concrete choices made by humans. The focus on whether and how to provide technical explanations of a machine learning model obscures the prior question: How did the machine learning model come to be designed this way? That is a question about the justification of institutional choices that is both prior to and more significant than the question of how the model works. In these choices lie trade-offs about discrimination and fairness, who wins and who loses, the values built into a model, and the concepts it approximates, along with a host of other normative and epistemological assumptions, some of which we have explored with the toxicity example.

Shared goals like the principles of anticorruption, diversity, and shared experience should serve as yardsticks against which to evaluate the specific design choices I identified in chapter 5. First, Facebook and Google should be required to justify the top-line metrics that their ranking systems are built to optimize or the target variable that individual machine learning models are trained to predict. The choice of top-line metrics or target variables embeds important moral and political choices that profoundly shape the interests and values advanced by machine learning systems. Second, Facebook and Google should justify the concepts that machine learning systems approximate and the guidelines that shape how those concepts are interpreted and applied, such as toxicity, hate speech, and trustworthiness. Third, Facebook and Google should provide summary statistics about the training data sets they have assembled to train machine learning systems.[43]

These choices shape the systems that Facebook and Google build. For citizens, civil society groups, and regulators to evaluate whether these systems are advancing a healthy public sphere and civic information architecture, the companies' concrete choices must be identified, surfaced, explained, and evaluated against shared goals. Explanations conducive to accountability would illuminate Facebook's and Google's choices about top-line metrics and target variables, concepts and guidelines, and training data, because these are the choices through which Facebook and Google exercise infrastructural power.

TO WHOM SHOULD JUSTIFICATIONS BE OFFERED?

If our goal is to regulate Facebook and Google to support the conditions of collective self-government, their justifications must be offered not to isolated individuals but to empowered regulators. Like most concerns about machine learning, justifications can be evaluated only with an aggregate analysis of the impact of machine learning systems. To structure the kind of accountability that supports experimentation and reflection, Facebook and Google should justify their choices about the design of their machine learning systems to an empowered, well-resourced regulator that can execute this aggregate analysis.

We should separate two distinct sets of justificatory requirements. Those in the first set are designed to empower citizens by ensuring that democratic utilities explain the processes and principles they use to make choices in the design of important machine learning systems. Facebook and Google could relatively easily outline the basic principles that underpin the design of their newsfeed and search systems—such as their top-line metrics, concepts and guidelines, and summary statistics about training data—as well as provide aggregate information summarizing what kinds of content or websites are being shown to whom, which could be examined by technologists, academics, journalists, policy experts, and the broader public. The complexity of machine learning is not an excuse for failing to provide basic information that illuminates what machine learning systems are designed to do.

The second set of justificatory requirements would be aimed at a well-resourced regulator, such as the AI Platforms Agency, which would be empowered to obtain the information needed to make judgments about whether Facebook's and Google's design choices are in practice advancing shared goals. They could request technical information, including the data sets used to train machine learning models, top-line metrics and target variables, and the inputs they use, and require that Facebook and Google provide information to academic and civil society researchers. As the legal scholar Margot Kaminski argues, rather than "arguing over" the "instrumental value of individual notice, or publicly releasing source code," we should structure "accountability across a firm's decision-making, over time."[44]

BEYOND PRIVACY

To structure the accountability of democratic utilities we must focus on principled justifications of design choices in machine learning, not technical explanations of the inner logic of machine learning models. An institutional approach to establishing and structuring accountability must move beyond the framework of personal privacy.

Consider an example. Facebook's "Why Am I Seeing This?" tool, known as WAIST, promises to explain to individuals why newsfeed displays a particular piece of content. When someone clicks on the tool, they see explanations like: "You are friends with the person who produced this post" or "You are in your 30s" or "You have liked posts similar to this one in the past." To the question "Why am I seeing this?" the tool answers, "Because you are friends with the person who produced this post, you are in your 30s, and you have liked similar posts."

That explanation may be true, but it is beside the point. Citizens want to know why Facebook built newsfeed the way it did, not what categories are relevant to why they saw an individual post. Why is newsfeed's top-line metric meaningful social interactions, and how is MSI defined? What kind of content would a user see if Facebook chose a different top-line metric? What are the concepts that newsfeed's machine learning models invoke in the moderation of public debate? How are those concepts defined? On what information are those models trained? According to what guidelines? The kind of explanation required to justify newsfeed's ranking system focuses on choices and principles, not on technical explanations of the inner logic of its machine learning models.[45]

Tools like WAIST allow Facebook to claim that it has justified the design of newsfeed. The focus on technical explanations suits Facebook, because it distracts from prior, more fundamental choices about the values and interests advanced by its design of its newsfeed system, which draw attention to Facebook's pervasive infrastructural power. The danger is that many citizens will react to WAIST's explanations by no longer feeling any need to press for answers to the harder, more fundamental question of why newsfeed was built the way it was. Technical explanations can distract from institutional justifications. Knowing how a machine learning model works is not itself a check on the power of those who decide how it works. Algorithmic explanation does not constitute institutional justification.

The widespread focus on technical explanations has been driven by an uncritical bent toward transparency, which is thought to matter because to see is to know, and knowledge is power, as if the provision of information inexorably fosters effective oversight. On this view, technical explanations of machine learning models provide information that individuals can use to challenge the power of those who designed those models. This assumption is a mistake. Transparency is a means, not an end in itself, an instrumental good that has value if and when it furthers accountability. As the conditions in which transparency furthers accountability are more limited than is often supposed, the drive toward transparency often produces regulatory regimes that fail to achieve accountability over time. If technical explanations deflect from the need for institutional justification, the uncritical bent toward transparency suits Facebook and Google.[46]

Transparency is valuable insofar as it furthers the aim of accountability, but it must be put in its place. Transparency may be necessary for some forms of accountability, but it neither constitutes nor is sufficient for accountability. The same goes for individual explanations of the logic of machine learning systems. They are valuable if and when they enable institutions to justify those systems to individuals and regulators. Accountability requires justification, and justification requires explanation. The form of each should determine the form of the other.[47]

The focus on transparency stems from the origins of many proposals for regulating Facebook and Google in privacy law. The idea is that if knowledge is power, and to see is to know, transparency ensures that individuals can see institutions, and privacy ensures that institutions cannot see individuals. Transparency checks the power of institutions, and privacy protects the power of individuals. Scholars who cut their teeth as privacy lawyers have transplanted their tendency to reach for transparency to address a wide range of ills in debates about how to regulate Facebook and Google.[48]

We cannot let the limits of the privacy debate influence how we structure accountability in the regulation of Facebook and Google. The privacy debate has been hemmed in by its focus on individual consent, a concept that has proved to be a mirage, both in theory and in practice. As a result, that debate has overlooked more fundamental challenges about how to structure accountability over the exercise of institutional power. The danger is that individual "understanding" of a machine learning model takes the role that individual "consent" is supposed to play in securing institutional accountability. Individual understanding may be just as much of an illusion as individual consent. If individual-understanding-of-machine-learning-models becomes the new individual-consent-to-the-use-of-personal-data, we should expect a wholesale failure to hold Facebook and Google to account.[49]

Institutional justification, not algorithmic explanation, is essential to the accountability constitutive of collective self-government. The technical explanation of machine learning models is never sufficient for, is often unnecessary to, and sometimes actively distracts from the structuring of accountability to citizens, administrative officials, and elected representatives. Holding the goal of supporting the flourishing of democracy at the front of our minds requires a laserlike focus on points of choice in the face of apparent technical inevitability. Facebook and Google must be required to justify the choices they made in building infrastructural machine learning systems, and we must not be distracted by whizzy technical explanations of how those systems work.

Democratic Experimentalism

The approach I have described would transform the governance of Facebook and Google. Both companies would be required to justify to a well-resourced regulator the concrete choices made in the design of infrastructural ranking systems against the yardstick of shared goals, such as the principles of anticorruption, diversity, and shared experience. But to structure processes of deliberate experimentation and reflection about how best to design these systems to advance shared goals, we need to answer a further question: Who should make judgments about whether Facebook's and Google's systems are being satisfactorily designed to advance shared goals? We must shift away from technocratic forms of decision-making toward mechanisms of empowered participatory governance.

By starting with the creation of a regulator with the technical skills to understand and evaluate how Facebook and Google build machine learning systems—what I have proposed calling the AI Platforms Agency—we can establish an institutional home for the skill of bridging the language and experience gaps to surface the political values involved in machine learning. Rather than dwell on the details of this regulator, I want to explore one of the vital things that a regulator like an APA could do: structure innovative mechanisms of empowered participation that involve civil society groups and public bodies with relevant knowledge and expertise, alongside citizens, in the design and evaluation of Facebook's and Google's systems. I explore how citizen assemblies involving legislators and regulators could be used to devise the obligations to which Facebook and Google are subject; how mini-publics involving public bodies like the National Archives or the FCC and civil society groups could be used to scrutinize choices about the design of particular machine learning systems; and how citizen juries could be used to decide whether those systems are in practice advancing shared obligations.[50]

Here my proposals differ sharply from conventional approaches to regulating Facebook and Google. If our goal is to support the conditions of collective self-government, the structures of governance we establish should empower citizens, regulators, elected representatives, and civil society to co-design the infrastructure of the public sphere and co-create the obligations against which that infrastructure is evaluated. As a recent report explained, "Although how people use social media and other digital platforms has negatively affected the practice of democratic citizenship, we can redesign these platforms and their uses to support, rather than erode, our constitutional democracy and sense of common purpose." By intentionally experimenting with innovative mechanisms of deliberative democracy to design the infrastructure of the digital public sphere, we can reorient and restructure Facebook and Google to support the flourishing of democracy.[51]

This approach would constitute a radical experiment in democratic and administrative reform as it builds mechanisms of empowered participation into the governance of corporations that exercise the distinctive kind of infrastructural power I have explored. It would ensure that the administrative structures created to regulate Facebook and Google do not "create veils of legitimacy that . . . dampen the critical and participatory energies of the public . . . thwarting citizen control rather than enhancing it." The regulation of Facebook and Google should enhance, not diminish, collective action and democratic power.[52]

Two decades of research and experiments in deliberative democracy have developed myriad innovative structures for enhancing participation and deliberation. This research has found that people are social problem-solvers who reason in groups. When people know that deliberation will result in decisions with real stakes, they are remarkably willing to deliberate, especially those "turned off by standard partisan and interest group politics." Providing reasons and listening respectfully have been shown to reinforce each other. Deliberation may slow things down, but it may also generate sustainable solutions to common problems by injecting sites of listening into political and regulatory processes. Introducing mechanisms of empowered participation would make the structures through which Facebook and Google are governed more participatory and more responsive, part of a wider strategy of democratic reform "that puts the citizen at the center."[53]

These mechanisms are very different from self-imposed corporate governance tools like Facebook's Oversight Board. First, they would be structured by an accountable public regulator, the APA, rather than being at the whim of shareholders and CEOs like Mark Zuckerberg. Second, and crucially, they would have jurisdiction over the design and evaluation of machine learning systems, including Facebook's newsfeed and integrity systems and Google's search, not just individual content moderation decisions. As I have argued, unless governance tools like Facebook's Oversight Board have jurisdiction over the design of machine learning systems, rather than just individual content moderation decisions, they are little more than a distraction.[54]

Three mechanisms of empowered participation could be used in the governance of Facebook and Google to broaden the kinds of actors involved in the different decisions involved in the design and evaluation of different machine learning systems.

First, because citizen assemblies are most effective when they address complex matters of considerable public importance, citizen assemblies would be well suited to devising and developing the broad obligations imposed on Facebook and Google. These assemblies could include elected representatives deliberating alongside experts from regulatory bodies and then submitting recommendations. For instance, to develop the obligations guiding the design of Google's search ranking system, the APA could invite public bodies like the National Archives and the American Library Association to periodically examine how effectively particular obligations are ensuring that the search ranking system is advancing the principles of anticorruption, diversity, and shared experience, and these bodies could update those obligations if necessary. As diverse actors with different perspectives co-create the goals that infrastructural search ranking systems are required to advance, they would be building legitimacy and widening participation.[55]

Second, mini-publics could be used to scrutinize the actual design of Facebook's and Google's machine learning systems; by providing a forum for gathering information and synthesizing evidence, they could serve as an effective tool to connect corporate decisionmakers with the concerns of civil society actors, experts, and citizens. As a forum for contestation and the scrutiny of experts, a mini-public brings diverse perspectives to the otherwise technical domains of building and evaluating infrastructural machine learning systems, and these different perspectives can inform and widen public deliberation.[56] The APA could convene monthly mini-publics that bring together the FTC, the FCC, and civil society bodies like Upturn and the American Civil Liberties Union to examine major updates to Facebook's newsfeed system. When Facebook announces significant updates to its integrity system—for instance, if they were to introduce the toxicity model we have explored—the APA could convene a mini-public to examine the design principles that underpin the model and evaluate evidence about its likely impact. The mini-public's deliberations would broaden the information base that Facebook uses to design its core machine learning systems, producing better decisions as well as greater legitimacy.[57]

Third, citizen juries could be used to make controversial decisions about individual cases, whether they involve particular machine learning systems or individual content moderation decisions. Citizen juries build legitimacy for their judgments and educate citizens by empowering them to participate in decisions about important issues of public concern. This function is critical because citizens' "capacities to deliberate and make public decisions atrophy when left unused, and participation in these experiments exercises those capacities more intensely than conventional democratic channels," enabling citizens "to develop and deploy their pragmatic political capabilities." The APA could use citizen juries to make high-stakes individual decisions, like whether to ban President Trump from Facebook, whether to demote Dan Savage's spreadingsantorum.com site, or how to respond to egregious search results or hate groups operating on Facebook and Google. Citizen juries could also be used for visible binary decisions, such as whether Facebook should be allowed to deploy a model that moderates public debate using personalized predictions about toxicity.[58]

What motivates these reforms is the urgent need for democratic reform and experimentation. As modern states have become larger and more diverse and the problems they face more complex, the institutions of nineteenth-century representative democracy have become increasingly distanced from the ideals that animate democracy: the active involvement of the citizenry, collective action and decision-making, and public debate on issues of common concern. To combat the "erosion of democratic vitality" and the "withering of democracy," we may need to embrace radical experiments in the design of political and administrative institutions.[59]

By exploring different ways of organizing decision-making in corporations and the administrative state, my approach aims to encourage the kind of institutional experimentation that can reinvigorate democracy. Being more granular about the machine learning systems built by Facebook and Google opens up possibilities for using mechanisms of empowered participation to involve civil society groups and public bodies in making different kinds of decisions about the design and evaluation of these systems. We should not sap the energy from these experiments by overengineering them, handing too much control to experts, using complicated polls, or restricting the decisions that participants can make. Doing so would undermine their purpose—they are experiments, after all. The point is to do them, to see what works and what doesn't, and to learn.

Regulating Facebook and Google is an opportunity to recover the lost art of institutional design and experimentation. As the classicist Josiah Ober argues, "An enhanced capacity for institutional innovation in the face of . . . change is a central feature of" resilient democracies; "the capacity for institutional innovation is promoted by growing sophistication and sustained diversity of participants, whilst sophistication and diversity are, in turn, promoted by well-designed institutions." We will sometimes be uneasy as we embrace experimentalism, or even frightened. But we must embrace the uncertainty of democratic reform, which, after all, is what democracy is all about. We must forge our future by taking a leap in the dark, together—the very opposite of prediction.[60]

Conclusion

Above all come together. You are ruined without resource if you remain divided. And why would you be divided when such great common interests unite you? . . . In a word, it is less a question of deliberation here than of concord; the choice of which course you will take is not the greatest question: were it bad in itself, take it all together; by that alone it will become the best, and you will always do what needs to be done provided that you do so in concert.[1]

—JEAN-JACQUES ROUSSEAU,
LETTERS WRITTEN FROM THE MOUNTAIN (1764)

At the bottom of all the tributes paid to democracy is the little man, walking into the little booth, with a little pencil, making a little cross on a little bit of paper—no amount of rhetoric or voluminous discussion can possibly diminish the overwhelming importance of that point.[2]

—WINSTON CHURCHILL (1944)

HACKATHONS—MARATHONS OF hacking—bring together a group of technologists to solve a problem or develop an idea. Facebook's Like button and its messaging tool were created at hackathons, as was GroupMe, a messaging app acquired by Skype for $50 million. Another spawned TrumpScript, a now-discontinued programming script that emulated Trump's language and forbade the use of fractions or decimals because "America never does anything halfway."[3]

In 2017, The Fourth Group hosted a hackathon with an unusual aim: automating politicians. The team that won, Civic Triage, created a chat bot that

212

would replace weekly surgeries, when British MPs meet their constituents, by offering an automated, continuous messaging service to listen to constituents' concerns and direct them toward relevant services.[4]

Technologists have also begun to apply machine learning to politics. The US company Kimera aims to build "artificial general intelligence": all-knowing, general-purpose systems that, instead of learning to predict a well-defined target variable, aspire to perform every cognitive task as well as humans. In practice, artificial general intelligence remains elusive, even delusional, a subject more for journalists and corporate PR than computer scientists. But our fascination with these systems, and their possible applications to politics, is revealing. Mounir Shita, Kimera's CEO, is working on a system called Nigel that will "assist you in political discussions and elections [by] figuring out your goals and what reality looks like to you . . . assimilating paths to the future to reach your goals . . . constantly trying to push you in the right direction."[5]

By learning to predict your political views, Nigel aims to tell you how to vote. Nigel "might push you to change your views, if things don't add up in the algorithm, [but] the whole purpose of Nigel is to figure out who you are. . . . If you are a racist, Nigel will become a racist. If you are a left-leaning liberal, Nigel will become a left-leaning liberal. There is no political conspiracy behind this." Another technologist, Thomas Frey, is building AI systems that learn which voters tend to pick candidates who "are good looking and make us feel better" and which tend to vote for "elected officials who make the best decisions," so that we can "add more value to the votes of those who are better informed, better educated or more involved."[6]

Many hope that AI might correct democracy's worst vices. If democracy's problem is disinformation and demagoguery, AI promises rationalism and consistency; after all, it's "hard to brainwash an AI." For others, like César Hidalgo, director of the Collective Learning group at MIT's Media Lab, democracy's problem is its "user interface." Politicians are meant to "aggregate the views and needs of constituents," but in practice, politics is "filled with compromises." Ideally, we would vote on everything ourselves, but in practice, citizens have a "cognitive bandwidth problem." To get around this, Hidalgo suggests, we should automate voting. Each voter would have a digital delegate, their very own political avatar, that would gather information about their needs, views, and opinions. To start with, these avatars could vote on laws proposed by real politicians and get feedback from citizens on how they voted. If this worked, "an algorithm could be developed" to "write laws that would get a certain percentage of approval," creating "a world in which direct democracy and software agents are a viable form of participation." An automated Congress or Parliament would have as many legislators as citizens.[7]

These proposals might seem far-fetched, but there is nothing inevitable about how we do democracy today. There are numerous ways of institutionalizing the ideals of political equality and collective self-government. Across the history of democracy, how we select those who rule us has changed considerably. Ancient Athenians selected officeholders by lottery, and when America was founded, elections were considered an aristocratic constraint on an unpredictable demos, not the essence of democracy. How we vote has changed too. A century ago, few democracies had secret ballots; now, as postal and online voting become more common, we are moving ever closer to holding elections in the privacy of our homes. Democracy changes more often, and more radically, than we might imagine.

The representative element of modern democracy was deliberately designed to curtail the demos because, for most of democracy's history, political elites have not really trusted the majoritarian judgments of citizens. For James Madison, the purpose of legislatures was to refine and enlarge citizens' views "by passing them through the medium of a chosen body of citizens," not to give people a voice but to speak in their stead. Similarly, much of twentieth-century social science focused on the apparent stupidity and irrationality of voters. Joseph Schumpeter, the Austrian-born American economist, argued that, "if results that prove in the long run satisfactory to the people at large are made the test of government for the people, then government by the people . . . would often fail to meet it." For the political scientist William Meyer, "the wants and desires of the common man are inextricably out of line with what he really needs and ought to have." More recently, Christopher Achen and Larry Bartels have argued that voters do not have coherent preferences, pay little attention to politics, and generally vote for strange and often contradictory reasons. "Election outcomes," they write, "turn out to be largely random events from the viewpoint of contemporary democratic theory." Democracy is a world in which "unexpected events . . . insufficient information, hurried and audacious choices, confusions about motives and interests, plasticity and even identification of political identities, as well as the talents of specific individuals . . . are frequently decisive in determining the outcomes."[8]

Given that democracy is so rubbish, it should be no surprise that so many seem to want to automate it. If machine learning can eliminate prejudice and arbitrariness from the decisions of judges, why not the decisions of voters too? Surely democracy free from disinformation and demagoguery would be better democracy? Why is rule by prediction such a terrible idea?

There are some obvious answers. For one thing, predictive tools make mistakes. Voting is hard to predict because narratives and stories matter in politics. For another, individualized predictions overlook the collective character of voting: it's not just about predicting how one person votes in isolation, but about how citizens vote as a collective. The most troubling aspect of these proposals, however, is their attitude to freedom: what it means to make free choices as a community of self-governing political equals.

Hidalgo's proposal makes democracy itself an exercise in performative prediction. To have a legislature of political avatars that vote on bills written using predictions about what bills will pass would be to have citizens' votes determined by patterns of behavior and the writing of laws determined by predictions about how citizens will vote. Predictions about citizens' votes themselves would shape what citizens vote on. Predictions about how citizens will vote would come true, not because they capture what citizens want their future to look like, or because they capture any judgment about what their future should look like, but because those predictions themselves have shaped the bills that citizens get to vote on. Using prediction to automate democracy misunderstands the nature of both prediction and democracy. By taking the relationship between them to an extreme, these proposals can teach us something about both.

Democracy in the Age of AI

Let's start with prediction. At first glance, prediction seems oriented toward the future. The word itself comes from the Latin *praedicere*, which means "to foretell" or "to give notice," to declare something before it happens. Prediction is the power of foreknowledge, the capacity to use knowledge of the future to make decisions that shape it.

Yet, as I have argued in this book, prediction is more about the past than the future. By predicting the risk of a child suffering abuse and neglect, AFST revealed persistent patterns of racial and socioeconomic inequality in the provision of welfare services in Allegheny County, Pennsylvania. By predicting the probability that Facebook users will click on ads for different jobs, p(click) reproduced enduring inequalities of race and gender in the US labor market. By using hyperlinks to predict the relevance of websites in search, Google's search reinforced the dominance of websites that were already dominant. We imbue machine learning models with an almost mythical power to predict the future, but we all too easily forget that they learn from the past.

Performativity is often the mechanism through which predictions shape the future. Because police officers record a higher proportion of crimes in the neighborhoods they are sent to, predictive policing tools effect the outcomes they predict. Because people are more likely to click on content or websites at the top of their newsfeed or search results, Facebook's and Google's ranking systems make predictions about engagement come true. Performativity can change people's behavior. Police officers who begin to feel suspicious toward residents of high-risk neighborhoods, or toward residents who act out when unfairly surveilled, are subject to prediction's performative power. So are people who read left-wing news websites that Google predicts they want to read, or people who engage with toxic content that Facebook predicts they want to engage with. Instead of offering knowledge of the future, prediction often traps us in the past.

And that's the thing: prediction can *only* be based on the past. As recounted in chapter 1, I grab my coat when there are dark and ominous clouds because when there have been dark and ominous clouds in the past, it has tended to rain. The reason I stocked up on gas when the United States declared war on Iraq is that when the United States has gone to war with oil-producing states in the past, the price of oil has tended to go up. AFST is useful only if the characteristics of parents who have abused or neglected their children in the past are similar to the characteristics of parents who will abuse or neglect their children in the future. Facebook's toxicity model is useful only if similar kinds of people tend to find similar kinds of content toxic over time. Data that support valid statistical inference must not only be a representative sample of the population but capture a past world that is roughly like the future. For the predictions of machine learning models to be useful, the future cannot be too different; otherwise, training data provide no information about the future. To the extent that the future is radically different from the past, prediction is a poor guide to the future.

In the realm of decision-making, the assumption that the future will look like the past is not neutral, for it bakes in a set of moral and political judgments. Performative prediction illustrates that making decisions on the assumption that the future will look like the past makes it more likely that the future will in fact come to look like the past. Whether in child welfare services, predictive policing, or Facebook's and Google's ranking systems, I have shown that when the past is not neutral—because some social groups have wielded power over others, some values have been prioritized, some voices have been unfairly silenced, or some sources of information have been mistakenly overlooked—

the choice to base decisions on unconstrained predictions cannot be neutral either. It is a choice to structure our decisions in ways that project the past into the future, and the more decisions we base on prediction, the more of our world will come to be shaped by that choice.

That's the first thing that these proposals get wrong. Aspiring to use prediction to automate democracy forgets that prediction doesn't just estimate the future—it assumes that the future will look like the past. If we delegate too many decisions to prediction, we will *make* the future look like the past.

Freedom is the opposite of prediction. At an individual level, when we make choices using our knowledge of the past, we assume that our choices are not determined by the past. Human freedom depends on the possibility of breaking with the past, sometimes radically. Immanuel Kant was struck by this in 1784. After studying data about the marriage patterns of Prussians, Kant observed that in "registers of these events in great countries," choices about who to marry seemed to display "as much conformity to the laws of nature as the oscillations of the weather," as if human choices are "as much under the control of universal laws of nature as any other physical phenomena." Kant's political philosophy sought to understand what it means to describe humans as free given these apparently inexorable patterns. He argued that freedom is not something we can observe but something we must assert, that it is a moral standpoint we take when we act as humans. The assertion of human freedom is what makes us human.[9]

Freedom is also the opposite of prediction in a collective sense. Democracy is the exercise of our collective freedom to choose the rules we live by, and the exercise of collective freedom also depends on the possibility of breaking with the past, sometimes radically. This is what happens in revolutions when people adopt a new constitution and system of government. Whereas the metric of prediction is accuracy, the metric of democracy is collectively made choices. The collectiveness of the choice is what makes the choice legitimate. The authority of a constitution or government flows from it being chosen by the people, whether or not it was the best option on the table, or it produces the most economic growth, or it expresses the best moral principle.

And this understanding of the origin of authority points to the second thing that these proposals get wrong. They treat democracy as a mechanism for preference aggregation, a decision rule for accurately approximating the policy preferences of a citizenry, whereas in fact democracy is a form of collective agency. My point is not to argue against these specific proposals, but to reflect on what these proposals tell us about the meaning of democracy in an age of ubiquitous prediction.

Reforming Democracy?

For democracy to flourish in an age of ubiquitous data-driven decision-making, we must ensure that the institutions we develop to regulate machine learning empower us to wrestle with its political character, rather than burying it beneath superficially neutral technocratic objectives.

In the first half of the book, I explored the political character of the machine learning systems used to distribute benefits and burdens in child welfare agencies, banks, and law enforcement. Using predictions to allocate benefits and burdens can compound the social inequalities encoded in data, entrenching the obstacles to living and participating as political equals encountered by some citizens. The danger is that we will embrace superficially neutral solutions, like mathematical definitions of fairness or nondiscriminatory duties, that prohibit institutions from using categories of disadvantage to address disadvantage. In our imaginary lawsuit, when p(click) excluded race and gender but compounded inequalities of race and gender, it was found not to be a discriminatory practice, but when Facebook sought to use race to deliberately address racial inequality, the law prevented it from doing so. Instead, I argued, the ideal of political equality should guide the governance of decision-making, supporting positive duties to advance equality enforced by regulators rather than courts. I described a new AI Equality Act that would institutionalize ongoing consideration of ways to interpret and apply the ideal of political equality across decision-making systems in different institutions that affect different social groups.

In the second half, I explored the political character of the Facebook and Google machine learning models used to make decisions about the distribution of information and ideas. Using predictions to rank ideas and information doesn't simply enable people to access what they want—it shapes what they want, corroding the capacity of citizens to exercise their collective freedom to debate the ends they wish to pursue. Although competition and privacy law may protect consumers from obvious harms, they may also hinder our capacity to debate and experiment with designing infrastructural ranking systems that support a healthy public sphere and civic information ecosystem. Instead, I argued for a new AI Platforms Agency that would embed mechanisms of empowered participatory governance every step of the way in the design and evaluation of Facebook's and Google's machine learning systems, supporting collective experimentation and learning about designing those systems that will best support the flourishing of democracy.

By exploring these two cases alongside each other, my purpose has been to show that debates about fairness and nondiscrimination and the regulation of Facebook and Google are wrestling with problems that are fundamentally to do with democracy. In both cases, regulatory responses that seek to exercise state power with purported neutrality would actually ensure that prediction entrenches the status quo. Instead of reaching for stable technocratic solutions, we should articulate the guiding ideals that capture the characteristics of a flourishing democracy and establish institutional structures that will enable us to continually ask questions about how to achieve these ideals and that will leave open the possibility of changing our answers. By holding the flourishing of democracy as my goal, I have imagined different ways of responding to these problems that aim to ensure that the governance of institutions that build and use predictive tools advances political equality and supports the exercise of collective self-government. That is what it means for democracy to push against the grip of prediction.

Let me end by drawing out two wider lessons, one straightforward and one more challenging. The straightforward lesson is that there is no neutral way to make collective choices. To co-create a future that is different from the past we must consciously invoke political ideals and ceaselessly debate how to interpret and apply them in practice. The exercise of collective power involved in establishing regulatory structures unavoidably benefits some more than others and protects some values while violating others. Just as choices in machine learning have this political character, so too do choices about how we govern machine learning. To ensure that predictive tools are used to create a different future—a more equal future where all have the opportunity to flourish and diversity supports common purpose—we must intentionally embed the asking of political questions in the governance of predictive tools. If data captured a different world, then perhaps we could govern predictive tools and the institutions that use them by requiring fair and nondiscriminatory decision-making and by protecting competition and privacy. But that is not our world.

This conclusion suggests the second lesson: embedding the asking of political questions in regulatory structures will require reforming the administrative state and changing how we think about policymaking itself. Instead of seeking to identify optimal policy solutions, regulation should structure processes of experimentation and collective learning in order to support the intentional iteration of policy responses to shared challenges. The aim of regulation is not settled solutions but co-ownership over the process of describing a problem and co-creation of imaginative solutions to addressing it. Instead of efficiency and optimization, the goal is to secure the foundations of legitimacy and to empower a population to work toward solutions in the knowledge that they can develop them. If democracy is to flourish in the age of AI, we must reform the structure of the administrative state.[10]

The first step is a renewed appreciation for the political goals of regulation. Consider antitrust law. The stated motivation behind recent efforts to reform antitrust law is to respond to new challenges: "There is an urgent need to develop a new pro-competition regulatory regime for online platforms . . . given the fast-moving, complex nature of the markets we have reviewed, and the wide-ranging, self-reinforcing problems we have identified," read one report. Such an antitrust regime would be "better suited to the challenges of the Digital Age," concluded another.[11] Although antitrust law is indeed outdated, it has become a blunt tool for regulating Facebook and Google because it has been caught in a technocratic mindset in public policy. As the historian Richard Hofstadter observed: "Once the United States had an antitrust movement without antitrust prosecutions; in our time there have been antitrust prosecutions without an antitrust movement." We have lost an appreciation that antitrust aims "to keep concentrated private power from destroying democratic government."[12] As argued by Senator John Sherman—after whom the Sherman Act is named—regulation "constitute[s] an important means of achieving freedom from corruption and maintaining freedom of independent thinking, political life, a treasured cornerstone of democratic government."[13]

The goal of the two regulatory approaches I have described is not to identify optimal policy solutions, but to advance political equality and support the conditions of collective self-government. Achieving these ends will require us to approach regulation not as a static set of rules but as a tool for continuously structuring and restructuring the organization of power in social, economic, and political institutions in ways that support the flourishing of democracy.[14] As the philosopher Alain de Benoist writes:

It is one thing to surround oneself with technicians and experts, and quite another to charge these people with identifying the objectives to be pursued. To wish to put the government into the hands of "experts" is to forget the act that the judgment of experts must itself be reassessed and reevaluated, as political decision-making implies both conflicts of interest and a number of possible choices. Now, our age, which has previously bowed to the *myth* of decision-making via "technical knowledge," is increasingly forgetful of all this. An acceptance of the *operative* role of experts may thus quickly lead to the legitimatising of *technocracy*. Under the pretext that the increasing complexity of public affairs makes politics necessarily dependent upon "those who know," the people are being stripped of their sovereignty, while the very notion of politics goes up in smoke.[15]

Or as Ian Shapiro articulates the challenge: "We all have an interest in our decisions being informed by the best available knowledge. But we should not succumb to the illusion that technical expertise can displace politics or render it redundant. This is not so much because experts usually know less than they claim or believe, though this is often true. It is because technical knowledge is never neutral in its applications."[16]

My exploration of the politics of machine learning makes this clear. Precisely because technical choices involve the exercise of power, if we are to govern predictive tools to ensure that they support, rather than corrode, democratic ideals, we must acknowledge and intentionally structure regulation to keep its political goals alive. What matters is not which particular values or interests predictive tools prioritize at any given moment, but the processes and mechanisms of governance used to surface and interrogate those values and interests over time. Institutionalizing continuous processes of experimentation, reflection, and revision will force us to ask how best to advance political equality and support the conditions of collective self-government over time. As the use of prediction in decision-making becomes ever more common, we must embed the active consideration of how best to realize democratic ideals in the governance of predictive tools.

That is why democracy cannot be automated. Not even for the most complex function it is possible to imagine is democracy about optimization. It is about deciding to make history together. If democracies can summon the political energy, the widespread use of prediction offers the opportunity for greater intentionality and openness about the goals of decision-making and greater legislative direction to ensure that institutions support the conditions of political equality and collective self-government. We must seize this opportunity and embed active consideration of democratic ideals in the heart of the regulatory state.

ACKNOWLEDGMENTS

I want to thank the individuals and institutions that helped me write this book and think politically about how we govern technology.

The book began at Harvard University, where I was lucky enough to form relationships with brilliant and supportive scholars in political theory, computer science, and law. The enthusiasm of Michael Sandel and Danielle Allen for political theory that is informed by other disciplines and schools, combined with their talent for teaching the skills of listening and learning required to produce it, was the propeller that drove this book. I learned so much from their commitment to rigorous scholarship that engages a wider public through writing, speaking, and emotional intelligence. Cynthia Dwork taught me how to read and speak the language of computer science, but her humanity and analytic brilliance also pushed me to think critically about how I do political theory and engage with policy debates. Jonathan Zittrain's appetite for playful conceptual innovation and legal argument, alongside his encyclopedic knowledge of US jurisprudence and constitutional law, was vital in developing the book's argument and probing the policy ideas that emerged from it.

Many other colleagues and friends gave their time and patience to help me write this book. The Edmond J. Safra Center for Ethics has been my home for the best part of three years, and I owe a great deal to its proudly interdisciplinary community: Meira Levinson, Mathias Risse, Ben Eidelson, and Archon Fung, and others who attended a manuscript workshop in December 2021; Maggie Gates, Emily Bromley, and Jess Miner, who organized the workshop; and many other scholars and staff there who have expanded my professional and personal horizons. Cynthia Dwork and her reading group of computer scientists, especially Yo Shavit and Christina Ilvento, gave invaluable feedback on draft chapters and taught me how to navigate computer science; several from this group have become close collaborators and friends. Martha Minow, Talia Gillis, Tina Eliassi-Rad, Solon Barocas, and Finale Doshi-Velez have been generous with their time and knowledge, allowing me to join classes and comment on their manuscripts. And finally, I received endless energy and support from so many in Harvard's Department of Government, including Avishay Ben Sasson-Gordis, Justin Pottle, Jacob Hoerger, Briitta van Staalduinen, Alex Mierke-Zatwarnicki, Eric Beerbohm, Katrina Forrester, Jennifer Hochschild, and Peter Hall.

Much of how I think about the politics of technology I learned outside my graduate career. Sylvana Tomaselli, Helen Thompson, David Runciman, and Judith Gardom taught me how to think and write about politics as an undergraduate at Cambridge University, and we have since shared much laughter and thought as friends. I have also learned much from many members of Facebook's Responsible AI team, including Elliot Schrage, Isabel Kloumann, Joaquin Quiñonero Candela, Sam Corbett Davies, Jonathan Tannen, Becky White, and Chloé Bakalar. Their talent and appetite for confronting enormous obstacles have often been energizing and educational.

I owe a great debt to Matt Rohal, whose support and insight gave this project shape and form at a very early stage, along with the entire editorial and production team at Princeton University Press, particularly Jill Harris and Cindy Buck, and to Peter Strauss, who continues to push my thinking and writing to make it exciting and interesting to the widest possible audience.

The person who made this book is my wife, Leah Downey. While I researched and wrote it, we met, got married, had our first child, completed our PhDs, and moved across the Atlantic. Before that, we swapped dissertation topics, she from writing about the politics of prediction to the politics of monetary policy, and me from monetary policy to prediction, and we've since shared all our most important ideas and problems. Leah is a sharp and creative scholar, the only person I know who can see moral and political philosophy in theoretical mathematics, but more importantly, she has a dazzling soul full of courage and joy. I will forever associate this book with her.

NOTES

Introduction

1. Virginia Eubanks, *Automating Inequality: How High-Tech Tools Profile, Police, and Punish the Poor* (New York: St. Martin's Press, 2018), 158.

2. In 2018, 1,770 children are estimated to have died from abuse and neglect in the United States. Children's Bureau, *Child Maltreatment 2018* (Washington, DC: US Department of Health and Human Services, Children's Bureau, 2018), https://www.acf.hhs.gov/cb/report/child-maltreatment-2018; Eubanks, *Automating Inequality*, 132.

3. Eubanks, *Automating Inequality*, 160; Dan Hurley, "Can an Algorithm Tell When Kids Are in Danger?," *New York Times*, January 2, 2018, https://www.nytimes.com/2018/01/02/magazine/can-an-algorithm-tell-when-kids-are-in-danger.html.

4. Initially, cases assigned a risk score of 18 or higher (the riskiest 15 percent of calls) were flagged as "mandatory screen-ins," which were automatically sent for investigation. That threshold has since been lowered to a risk score of 16 (the riskiest 25 percent of calls). Hurley, "Can an Algorithm Tell When Kids Are in Danger?"; Alexandra Chouldechova, Emily Putnam-Hornstein, Diana Benavides-Prado, Oleksandr Fialko, and Rhema Vaithianathan, "A Case Study of Algorithm-Assisted Decision Making in Child Maltreatment Hotline Screening Decisions," *Proceedings of Machine Learning Research* 81 (2018): 134–48; Rhema Vaithianathan, Emily Putnam-Hornstein, Nan Jiang, Parma Nand, and Tim Maloney, *Developing Predictive Risk Models to Support Child Maltreatment Hotline Screening Decisions: Allegheny County Methodology and Implementation* (Pittsburgh, PA: Allegheny County Analytics, March 2019, updated April 2019), https://www.alleghenycountyanalytics.us/wp-content/uploads/2019/05/16-ACDHS-26_PredictiveRisk_Package_050119_FINAL-2.pdf.

5. Eubanks, *Automating Inequality*, 167.

6. Davide Panagia, "On the Possibilities of a Political Theory of Algorithms," *Political Theory* 49, no. 1 (2021): 109–33; Taina Bucher, *If . . . Then: Algorithmic Power and Politics* (New York: Oxford University Press, 2018); Cathy O'Neil, *Weapons of Math Destruction: How Big Data Increases Inequality and Threatens Democracy* (New York: Crown, 2016).

7. Chouldechova et al., "A Case Study of Algorithm-Assisted Decision Making."

8. Hurley, "Can an Algorithm Tell When Kids Are in Danger?"

9. Salomé Viljoen, "Democratic Data: A Relational Theory for Data Governance," *Yale Law Journal* 131, no. 2 (November 2021): 573; Aristotle, *The Politics, and the Constitution of Athens* (Cambridge: Cambridge University Press, 1996); Josiah Ober, *Demopolis: Democracy before*

Liberalism in Theory and Practice, John Robert Seeley Lectures (Cambridge: Cambridge University Press, 2017).

10. GOV.UK, "Investigatory Powers Act," March 1, 2016, updated December 18, 2017, https://www.gov.uk/government/collections/investigatory-powers-bill.

11. Shoshana Zuboff, "The Coup We Are Not Talking About," *New York Times*, January 29, 2021, https://www.nytimes.com/2021/01/29/opinion/sunday/facebook-surveillance-society-technology.html; Karen Hao, "How Facebook Got Addicted to Spreading Misinformation," *MIT Technology Review*, March 11, 2021, https://www.technologyreview.com/2021/03/11/1020600/facebook-responsible-ai-misinformation/.

12. Most of the law I explore is from the United States and the United Kingdom, simply because those are the cases I know best, but the underlying arguments apply more broadly. Because my focus is democracy, I assume that the democratic nation-state is the appropriate unit of analysis.

Chapter 1. The Politics of Machine Learning I

1. Langdon Winner, "Do Artifacts Have Politics?," *Daedalus* 109, no. 1 (1980): 121–36.

2. These data include "adult probation, the bureau of drug and alcohol services, the housing authority, the county jail, the juvenile probation office, the Allegheny County police department, the state office of income maintenance, the office of mental health and substance abuse services, the office of unemployment compensation, and almost 20 local school districts." The annual cost of managing the warehouse, through a contract with Deloitte, totals about $15 million, or about 2 percent of DHS's annual budget. Virginia Eubanks, *Automating Inequality: How High-Tech Tools Profile, Police, and Punish the Poor* (New York: St. Martin's Press, 2018), 134–35.

3. Ibid., 140; David Zucchino, *Myth of the Welfare Queen: A Pulitzer Prize–Winning Journalist's Portrait of Women on the Line* (New York: Scribner, 1997); Khalil Gibran Muhammad, *The Condemnation of Blackness—Race, Crime, and the Making of Modern Urban America* (Cambridge, MA: Harvard University Press, 2010).

4. These disparities are present in other states and counties too. In 2011 in Alaska, 51 percent of children in foster care were Native American, but Native Americans made up 17 percent of the youth population. In Illinois, 53 percent of children in foster care were African American, but they made up 16 percent of the youth population. Eubanks, *Automating Inequality*, 153.

5. Winner, "Do Artifacts Have Politics?"

6. Edna Ullmann-Margalit, "Big Decisions: Opting, Converting, Drifting," in Edna Ullmann-Margalit, *Normal Rationality: Decisions and Social Order*, edited by Avishai Margalit and Cass R. Sunstein (Oxford: Oxford University Press, 2017).

7. James Manyika and Jacques Bughin, "AI Problems and Promises," McKinsey Global Institute, October 15, 2018, https://www.mckinsey.com/featured-insights/artificial-intelligence/the-promise-and-challenge-of-the-age-of-artificial-intelligence.

8. The Royal Society, *Machine Learning: The Power and Promise of Computers That Learn by Example*, April 2017, 86, https://royalsociety.org/~/media/policy/projects/machine-learning/publications/machine-learning-report.pdf.

9. David Autor, David Dorn, Lawrence F. Katz, Christina Patterson, and John Van Reenen, "The Fall of the Labor Share and the Rise of Superstar Firms," *Quarterly Journal of Economics*

135, no. 2 (2020): 645–709; Tyler Cowen, "Superstar Firms and Market Concentration," *Marginal Revolution*, December 4, 2019, https://marginalrevolution.com/marginalrevolution/2019/12/superstar-firms-and-market-concentration.html; Manyika and Bughin, "AI Problems and Promises."

10. "Faneuil Hall Boston: The Ethics of Apps and Smart Machines," 2016, https://www.youtube.com/watch?v=6UScJ080uAA&t=17s. Judges are perhaps the best-known example of inconsistent decision-makers. A study of judicial rulings in Israel found that the longer it had been since judges' last meal, the less lenient they became, and that soon after eating breakfast or lunch, judges gave considerably more lenient sentences. Shai Danziger, Jonathan Levav, and Liora Avnaim-Pesso, "Extraneous Factors in Judicial Decisions," *Proceedings of the National Academy of Sciences* 108, no. 17 (2011): 6889–92.

11. Royal Society, "Machine Learning," 86.

12. Kim Strong, "Can a Computer Program Save More Children from Abuse and Neglect?," *York Daily Record*, June 24, 2021, https://www.ydr.com/story/news/2021/06/24/allegheny-countys-child-welfare-algorithm-hoped-save-children/5318550001/.

13. Solon Barocas and Andrew D. Selbst, "Big Data's Disparate Impact," *California Law Review* 104, no. 3 (June 1, 2016): 677. Arthur Samuel, an IBM engineer, coined the term "machine learning" in 1959. Machine learning is different from algorithms that computer scientists developed before the 1990s. Algorithms code a series of explicit steps, often in the form of "if-then" statements. Think of autonomous driving: if you sense a green light, go; if it's red, stop. These steps quickly become immensely complicated: if you see a child in the road, swerve right; if there's a wall to the right, swerve left; if there's an elderly couple crossing on the left . . . spontaneously combust? A better approach might be to ask: What would a human do? Machine learning answers that question by using billions of data points acquired from human drivers. Tom M. Mitchell, *Machine Learning* (New York: McGraw-Hill, 1997); Trevor Hastie, Robert Tibshirani, and Jerome Friedman, *The Elements of Statistical Learning: Data Mining, Inference, and Prediction* (New York: Springer New York, 2009); Stuart J. Russell and Peter Norvig, *Artificial Intelligence: A Modern Approach* (Upper Saddle River, NJ: Prentice-Hall, 2010); David Kelnar and Asen Kostadinov, *The State of AI 2019: Divergence*, MMC Ventures, 2019, https://iec2021.aaru-confs.org/The-State-of-AI-2019-Divergence.pdf.

14. Judith Donath, "Commentary: The Ethical Use of Powerful Words and Persuasive Machines," *Journal of Marketing* 85, no. 1 (2021): 160–62.

15. Cynthia Dwork and Deirdre Mulligan, "It's Not Privacy, and It's Not Fair," *Stanford Law Review* 66 (September 2013): 35. Humans can supervise the learning of algorithms, but they don't have to. In supervised learning, a computer is given a large set of data to learn from and the "correct" answer about an outcome of interest is labeled. This is its training data. A human selects an algorithm that determines how the computer approaches the data and sometimes specifies the parameters relevant to identifying the outcome of interest. In unsupervised or semi-supervised learning, a human does not specify an outcome or relevant parameters before the data are examined. Analysts often use unsupervised learning to get an initial sense of the structures within data, before turning to more precise forms of supervised learning to perform a specific task. This book is mostly about supervised learning because that is the form of machine learning used in most of the examples we explore. Maithra Raghu and Eric Schmidt, "A Survey of Deep Learning for Scientific Discovery," arXiv:2003.11755v1 [cs.LG], March 26, 2020,

https://doi.org/10.48550/arXiv.2003.11755; Vahe Tshitoyan, John Dagdelen, Leigh Weston, Alexander Dunn, Ziqin Rong, Olga Kononova, Kristin A. Persson, Gerbrand Cederand, and Anubhav Jain, "Unsupervised Word Embeddings Capture Latent Knowledge from Materials Science Literature," *Nature* 571, no. 7763 (2019): 95–98.

16. Janine continued: "I trust the caseworker more. . . . You can talk and be like, 'You don't see the bigger problems?'" Eubanks, *Automating Inequality*, 168.

17. I mostly use the term "target variable." Sometimes I refer to the "outcome" that a model is trained to predict, by which I mean the target variable—the proxy for the outcome of interest—rather than the outcome of interest itself. There are different types of target variables in supervised learning: classification tasks, which involve a discrete outcome; estimation tasks, which involve a continuous variable; and prediction tasks, which involve either a discrete outcome or a continuous variable, but for values in the future. A multitude of difficult issues about what "probability" means continue to plague theoretical computer science. Philip Dawid, "On Individual Risk," *Synthese* 194, no. 9 (2017): 3445–74; A. Philip Dawid, Monica Musio, and Rossella Murtas, "The Probability of Causation," *Law, Probability, and Risk* 16, no. 4 (2017): 163–79; Ian Hacking, *The Taming of Chance* (Cambridge: Cambridge University Press, 1990); Judea Pearl, *Causal Inference in Statistics: A Primer* (Chichester, UK: John Wiley & Sons, 2016); Brian Skyrms, *Choice and Chance: An Introduction to Inductive Logic* (Stamford, CT: Wadsworth, 2000); Jan von Plato, *Creating Modern Probability: Its Mathematics, Physics, and Philosophy in Historical Perspective* (Cambridge: Cambridge University Press, 1994).

18. The term "spam" comes from *Monty Python's Flying Circus*: in a skit, characters reading a restaurant menu descend into endlessly repeating the word "spam." The term was picked up by online gamers and discussion groups. Many of the spam filtering techniques that Google deploys combine supervised learning, like support-vector machines (SVMs), and unsupervised learning, including neural networks that teach themselves new criteria for accurately detecting spam without having to be retrained. Emmanuel Gbenga Dada, Joseph Stephen Bassi, Haruna Chiroma, Shafi'i Muhammad Abdulhamid, Adebayo Olusola Adetunmbi, and Opeyemi Emmanuel Ajibuwa, "Machine Learning for Email Spam Filtering: Review, Approaches, and Open Research Problems," *Heliyon* 5, no. 6 (2019): e01802; Michael Crawford, Taghi M. Khoshgoftaar, Joseph D. Prusa, Aaron N. Richter, and Hamzah Al Najada, "Survey of Review Spam Detection Using Machine Learning Techniques," *Journal of Big Data* 2, no. 1 (2015): 1–24.

19. In 2012, for instance, the share of long-term workers with tenure of ten or more years was about two points higher for men than women. Francine Blau and Lawrence Kahn, "The Gender Wage Gap: Extent, Trends, and Explanations," Working Paper 21913, National Bureau of Economic Research, January 2016, 37; Erling Barth, Sari Pekkala Kerr, and Claudia Olivetti, "The Dynamics of Gender Earnings Differentials: Evidence from Establishment Data" Working Paper 23381, National Bureau of Economic Research, May 2017.

20. Murad Ahmed, "Is Myers-Briggs Up to the Job?," *Financial Times*, February 11, 2016, https://www.ft.com/content/8790ef0a-d040-11e5-831d-09f7778e7377.

21. The act defines abuse and neglect as "the physical or mental injury, sexual abuse, negligent treatment, or maltreatment of a child . . . by a person who is responsible for the child's welfare under circumstances which indicate that the child's health or welfare is harmed or threatened." Vaithianathan et al., *Developing Predictive Risk Models*; Anne C. Petersen, Joshua Joseph, and Monica Feit, "Describing the Problem," in *New Directions in Child Abuse and Neglect*

Research, edited by Anne C. Petersen, Joshua Joseph, and Monica Feit (Washington, DC: National Academies Press, 2014).

22. Vaithianathan et al., *Developing Predictive Risk Models*.

23. Four percent of call referrals are also likely to be intentionally false. As Virginia Eubanks explains: "The activity that introduces the most racial bias into the system is the very way the model defines maltreatment." Eubanks, *Automating Inequality*, 144, 155.

24. Chouldechova et al., "A Case Study of Algorithm-Assisted Decision Making."

25. Andrew Pickering, *Science as Practice and Culture* (Chicago: University of Chicago Press, 1992); Chris Anderson, "The End of Theory: The Data Deluge Makes the Scientific Method Obsolete," *Wired*, June 23, 2008, https://www.wired.com/2008/06/pb-theory/; Jim Bogen, "Theory and Observation in Science," *Stanford Encyclopedia of Philosophy*, January 6, 2009, revised January 11, 2013, https://plato.stanford.edu/archives/spr2013/entries/science-theory-observation/; Sabina Leonelli, "What Distinguishes Data from Models?," *European Journal for Philosophy of Science* 9, no. 2 (2019): 1–27.

26. Hacking, *The Taming of Chance*, 1–3.

27. Michele Banko and Eric Brill, "Scaling to Very Very Large Corpora for Natural Language Disambiguation," Proceedings of the Thirty-Ninth Annual Meeting of the Association for Computational Linguistics, Toulouse, France, July 6–11, 2001; Scott Cleland, "Google's 'Infringenovation' Secrets," *Forbes*, October 3, 2011, https://www.forbes.com/sites/scottcleland/2011/10/03/googles-infringenovation-secrets/; James E. Short and Steve Todd, "What's Your Data Worth?," *MIT Sloan Management Review* 58, no. 3 (2017): 17; Ajay Agrawal, *Prediction Machines: The Simple Economics of Artificial Intelligence* (Boston: Harvard Business Review Press, 2018); Agrawal, *Prediction Machines*, 27.

28. Neil M. Ferguson et al., on behalf of the Imperial College COVID-19 Response Team, "Impact of Non-Pharmaceutical Interventions (NPIs) to Reduce COVID-19 Mortality and Healthcare Demand," March 16, 2020, 19, https://www.imperial.ac.uk/media/imperial-college/medicine/sph/ide/gida-fellowships/Imperial-College-COVID19-NPI-modelling-16-03-2020.pdf.

29. There were several other ambiguities in counting Covid-19 deaths. For instance, the death rate depends significantly on the capacity of local hospital systems, but that proved hard to predict too. Ventilators, for instance, turned out to be much less important than was initially thought. Silvia Aloisi, Deena Beasley, Gabriella Borter, Thomas Escritt, and Kate Kelland, "Special Report: As Virus Advances, Doctors Rethink Rush to Ventilate," *Reuters*, April 23, 2020, https://www.reuters.com/article/us-health-coronavirus-ventilators-specia-idUSKCN2251PE. Notable political contests centered on how governments calculated their Covid-19 infection and death counts. Sharon Begley, "Trump Said Covid-19 Testing 'Creates More Cases.' We Did the Math," *STAT*, July 20, 2020, https://www.statnews.com/2020/07/20/trump-said-more-covid19-testing-creates-more-cases-we-did-the-math/; Julian E. Barnes, "CIA Hunts for Authentic Virus Totals in China, Dismissing Government Tallies," *New York Times*, April 2, 2020, https://www.nytimes.com/2020/04/02/us/politics/cia-coronavirus-china.html; Sarah Kliff and Julie Bosman, "Official Counts Understate the US Coronavirus Death Toll," *New York Times*, April 5, 2020, https://www.nytimes.com/2020/04/05/us/coronavirus-deaths-undercount.html.

30. Jonas Lerman, "Big Data and Its Exclusions," *Stanford Law Review* 66 (September 2013), https://www.stanfordlawreview.org/online/privacy-and-big-data-big-data-and-its-exclusions/.

31. Kate Crawford, "Think Again: Big Data—Foreign Policy," *Foreign Policy*, May 10, 2013, http://foreignpolicy.com/2013/05/10/think-again-big-data/; David J. Hand, "Classifier Technology and the Illusion of Progress," *Statistical Science* 21, no. 1 (February 2006): 7.

32. The prospects of acquiring private health insurance data are slim, however, as middle-class families would not stand for it. Eubanks, *Automating Inequality*, 157–58.

33. Stella Lowry and Gordon Macpherson, "A Blot on the Profession," *British Medical Journal* 296, no. 6623 (1988): 657.

34. Barocas and Selbst, "Big Data's Disparate Impact," 682.

35. Latanya Sweeney, "Discrimination in Online Ad Delivery," *ACM Queue* 11, no. 3 (2013); Barocas and Selbst, "Big Data's Disparate Impact," 683; Sweeney, "Discrimination in Online Ad Delivery"; Safiya Umoja Noble, *Algorithms of Oppression: How Search Engines Reinforce Racism* (New York: New York University Press, 2018); Barocas and Selbst, "Big Data's Disparate Impact," 683.

36. "Features" and "attributes" are often used to mean the same thing, but there is a subtle difference. An attribute is a particular type of data. Each data point (such as a call referral record in AFST) contains several attributes (name, address, criminal record, gender, race, and so on). A feature can simply refer to an attribute, but it can also refer to the internal representation of the data generated by a machine learning model. Neural networks, for instance, create features that are useful in predicting outcomes that are often combinations of particular attributes, often at an extremely high level of abstraction. This so-called feature extraction is used in detecting audio signals, engineering, and understanding text. Edward T. Nykaza, Arnold P. Boedihardjo, Zhiguang Wang, Tim Oates, Anton Netchaev, Steven Bunkley, and Matthew G. Blevins, "Deep Learning for Unsupervised Feature Extraction in Audio Signals: Monaural Source Separation," *Journal of the Acoustical Society of America* 140, no. 4 (2016): 3424; Yi-Zhou Lin, Zhen-Hua Nie, and Hong-Wei Ma, "Structural Damage Detection with Automatic Feature-Extraction through Deep Learning," *Computer-Aided Civil and Infrastructure Engineering* 32, no. 12 (2017): 1025–46; Hong Liang, Xiao Sun, Yunlei Sun, and Yuan Gao, "Text Feature Extraction Based on Deep Learning: A Review," *EURASIP Journal on Wireless Communications and Networking* 2017, no. 1 (2017): 1–12.

37. Toon Calders and Indrė Žliobaitė, "Why Unbiased Computational Processes Can Lead to Discriminative Decision Procedures," in *Discrimination and Privacy in the Information Society*, edited by Bart Custers, Toon Calders, Bart Schermer, and Tal Zarsky (Berlin: Springer, 2013), 47.

38. Barocas and Selbst, "Big Data's Disparate Impact," 688; Julia Angwin, Jeff Larson, Lauren Kirchner, and Surya Mattu, "Car Insurance Companies Charge Higher Rates in Some Minority Neighborhoods," *Consumer Reports*, April 21, 2017, https://www.consumerreports.org/consumer-protection/car-insurance-companies-charge-higher-rates-in-some-minority-neighborhoods/.

39. Barocas and Selbst, "Big Data's Disparate Impact," 689; Lior Strahilevitz, "Privacy versus Antidiscrimination," Public Law and Legal Theory Working Paper 174, University of Chicago Law School, 2007, 364, https://chicagounbound.uchicago.edu/public_law_and_legal_theory/235.

40. For instance, the AFST team found that race did not significantly improve accuracy, and so it was excluded from the models. The original AFST model was trained on 76,964 referrals received from April 2010 to July 2014, involving 47,305 distinct children. These data included variables about each person involved in a call referral, ranging from information about their demographics, past interactions with welfare authorities and county prisons, receipt of public

benefits, juvenile probation, and behavioral health. The team tested eight hundred variables, eventually including seventy-one weighted variables in the model that predicts the probability that a child will be placed conditional on being screened in and fifty-nine weighted variables in the model that predicts the probability that a child will be re-referred conditional on being screened out. Chouldechova et al., "A Case Study of Algorithm-Assisted Decision Making."

41. Cynthia Dwork, Moritz Hardt, Toniann Pitassi, Omer Reingold, and Rich Zemel, "Fairness through Awareness," arXiv:1104.3913v2 [cs.CC], April 20, 2011, revised November 29, 2011, 226, https://doi.org/10.48550/arXiv.1104.3913.

42. Barocas and Selbst, "Big Data's Disparate Impact," 691.

43. Andrea Romeri and Salvatore Ruggieri, "A Multidisciplinary Survey on Discrimination Analysis," *Knowledge Engineering Review* 29, no. 5 (2014): 223–24.

44. Kevin P. Murphy, *Machine Learning: A Probabilistic Perspective* (Cambridge, MA: MIT Press, 2012), 22.

45. Chouldechova et al., "A Case Study of Algorithm-Assisted Decision Making"; Hastie, Tibshirani, and Friedman, *The Elements of Statistical Learning*, 222; Vaithianathan et al., *Developing Predictive Risk Models*, sec. 7; Alex Beutel, Jilin Chen, Tulsee Doshi, Hai Qian, Allison Woodruff, Christine Luu, Pierre Kreitmann, Jonathan Bischof, and Ed H. Chi, "Putting Fairness Principles into Practice: Challenges, Metrics, and Improvements," arXiv:1901.04562v1 [cs.LG], January 14, 2019, https://doi.org/10.48550/arXiv.1901.04562; Jon Kleinberg and Sendhil Mullainathan, "Simplicity Creates Inequity: Implications for Fairness, Stereotypes, and Interpretability," Working Paper 25854, National Bureau of Economic Research, May 2019.

46. Jon Kleinberg, Himabindu Lakkaraju, Jure Leskovec, Jens Ludwig, and Sendhil Mullainathan, "Human Decisions and Machine Predictions," *Quarterly Journal of Economics* 133, no. 1 (2017): 237–93.

47. Chouldechova et al., "A Case Study of Algorithm-Assisted Decision Making."

48. Thirteen percent of those cases that were investigated led to a child being placed in foster care within two years. When a call screener receives an allegation of abuse or neglect, they do not have time to examine the case history of each person named on a call, of their siblings or parents, and of others living at the same address. Institutions have a strong incentive to create centralized databases that can be used to develop predictive systems for use in decision-making. Chouldechova et al., "A Case Study of Algorithm-Assisted Decision Making"; Barbara D. Underwood, "Law and the Crystal Ball: Predicting Behavior with Statistical Inference and Individualized Judgment," *Yale Law Journal* 88, no. 7 (1979): 1408–48; Paul E. Meehl, *Clinical versus Statistical Prediction: A Theoretical Analysis and a Review of the Evidence* (Minneapolis: University of Minnesota Press, 1954); Kleinberg et al., "Human Decisions and Machine Predictions." Predictive tools offer the seductive promise of replacing the folk theories of causality, social processes, and race that often characterize the decisions of resource- and time-scarce street-level bureaucrats—for instance, the tropes about black motherhood often invoked in decisions about welfare. Dorothy E. Roberts, *Shattered Bonds: The Color of Child Welfare* (New York: Basic Books, 2002); Bernardo Zacka, *When the State Meets the Street: Public Service and Moral Agency* (Cambridge, MA: Harvard University Press, 2017).

49. Sometimes machine learning creates decisions that never actually existed before. Many of the machine learning models that Facebook and Google use to rank and order vast quantities of information do this. Chouldechova et al., "A Case Study of Algorithm-Assisted Decision Making."

50. Ibid.

51. Further analysis discovered that after an initial period of leaning heavily on the tool's predictions, caseworkers reverted to exercising their own judgment and rates of manager override remained high. This suggests the interesting conclusion that people may at first defer to the predictions of statistical tools but then revert to exercising their own judgment. Eubanks, *Automating Inequality*, 142; Chouldechova et al., "A Case Study of Algorithm-Assisted Decision Making."

52. Chouldechova et al., "A Case Study of Algorithm-Assisted Decision Making"; Vaithianathan et al., *Developing Predictive Risk Models*.

53. O'Neil, *Weapons of Math Destruction*, 21; Noble, *Algorithms of Oppression*, chap. 1.

54. The racial disparities in the data also record the prejudice of human call screeners. Research has demonstrated that Black children are more likely than white children to be screened in, even when the risk to Black children is lower than the risk to white children. Caseworkers may be implicitly applying different risk thresholds, or they may overestimate the risk for Black children relative to white children. Alan J. Dettlaff, Stephanie L. Rivaux, Donald J. Baumann, John D. Fluke, Joan R. Rycraft, and Joyce James, "Disentangling Substantiation: The Influence of Race, Income, and Risk on the Substantiation Decision in Child Welfare," *Children and Youth Services Review* 33, no. 9 (2011): 1630–37, https://doi.org/10.1016/j.childyouth.2011.04.005.

55. These decisions can often surface tensions among an institution's purposes. DHS both delivers important welfare programs to families and keeps children safe. The tension between these purposes drives the trade-offs that underpin choices involved in designing the machine learning models used in the provision of child protection services. Emily Putnam-Hornstein and Barbara Needell, "Predictors of Child Protective Service Contact between Birth and Age Five: An Examination of California's 2002 Birth Cohort," *Children and Youth Services Review* 33, no. 8 (2011): 1337–44; Eubanks, *Automating Inequality*; Vaithianathan et al., *Developing Predictive Risk Models*. Those who designed the first version of AFST were interested in predicting child maltreatment from the moment a child is born. In a 2011 paper, Barbara Needell and Emily Putnam-Hornstein wrote: "A risk assessment tool that could be used on the day of birth to identify those children at greatest risk of maltreatment hold great value. . . . Prenatal risk assessments could be used to identify children at risk . . . while still in the womb." That approach was rejected by Allegheny County. Putnam-Hornstein and Needell, "Predictors of Child Protective Service Contact," 1343; Eubanks, *Automating Inequality*, 137; Vaithianathan et al., *Developing Predictive Risk Models*.

56. Eubanks, *Automating Inequality*, 151–52.

57. Virginia Eubanks calls this the new "digital poorhouse." Ibid., chap. 5.

58. O'Neil, *Weapons of Math Destruction*, 91.

59. Bucher, *If . . . Then*, 3–4.

60. Viljoen, "Democratic Data," 9.

61. Winner, "Do Artifacts Have Politics?"

62. Juan Perdomo, Tijana Zrnic, Celestine Mendler-Dünner, and Moritz Hardt, "Performative Prediction," arXiv:2002.06673v1 [cs.LG], February 16, 2020, https://doi.org/10.48550/arXiv.2002.06673.

63. Ibid.

64. As Hardt puts it, measurement error "narrows the regime in which fairness criteria cause decline." When a bank's unconstrained pursuit of profit "is misaligned with individual out-

comes, fairness criteria are better for minority than majority group, because they pull the utility curve into a shape consistent with the outcome curve." The interests of both groups may differ from the bank's interests: "What would be desirable from the perspective of the decision maker is a certain equilibrium where the model is optimal for the distribution it induces. . . . Performativity therefore suggests a different perspective on retraining, exposing it as a natural equilibrating dynamic rather than a nuisance." Ibid.

65. O'Neil, *Weapons of Math Destruction*, 204.

66. Richard T. Wright and Scott H. Decker, *Armed Robbers in Action: Stickups and Street Culture* (Boston: Northeastern University Press, 1997), 84–85; Brendan O'Flaherty, *Shadows of Doubt: Stereotypes, Crime, and the Pursuit of Justice* (Cambridge, MA: Harvard University Press, 2019), 59–60. "From the 1890s through the first four decades of the twentieth century Black criminality would become one of the most commonly cited and longest-lasting justifications for black inequality and mortality in the modern urban world." Muhammad, *The Condemnation of Blackness*; O'Flaherty, *Shadows of Doubt*, 31.

67. Brent A. Staples, *Parallel Time: Growing Up in Black and White* (New York: Pantheon Books, 1994), 202. This episode inspired the title of Claude Steele's excellent book on the role of stereotypes in perpetuating racial injustice, *Whistling Vivaldi: How Stereotypes Affect Us and What We Can Do* (New York: W. W. Norton & Co., 2011).

68. Staples, *Parallel Time*, 204.

69. One reason arrest rates for robbery are higher than for other crimes of theft, like burglary or larceny, is that robbery is a street crime carried out in public. Paul Guerino, Paige Harrison, and William J. Sabol, "Prisoners in 2010," NCJ 236096, US Department of Justice, Bureau of Justice Statistics, December 2011, revised February 9, 2012, https://bjs.ojp.gov/content/pub/pdf/p10.pdf; Rajiv Sethi, "Crime and Punishment in a Divided Society," in *Difference without Domination*, edited by Danielle Allen and Rohini Somanthan (Chicago: University of Chicago Press, 2020), 93–114.

70. Dorothy Roberts, "Digitizing the Carceral State," *Harvard Law Review* (2019): 1714; Andrew Guthrie Ferguson, "Illuminating Black Data Policing," *Ohio State Journal of Criminal Law* 15, no. 2 (2018): 513–14; Elizabeth E. Joh, "Feeding the Machine: Policing, Crime Data, and Algorithms," *William and Mary Bill of Rights Journal* 26, no. 2 (2017): 287–302. For a long time racial disparities in crime data were interpreted as evidence of natural racial differences in propensity toward violence, and in the early twentieth century these disparities were often explained by genetic propensities. William J. Bennett, *Body Count: Moral Poverty—and How to Win America's War against Crime and Drugs* (New York: Simon & Schuster, 1996); Ta-Nehisi Coates, "The First White President," *Atlantic*, October 2017, https://www.theatlantic.com/magazine/archive/2017/10/the-first-white-president-ta-nehisi-coates/537909/; W.E.B. Du Bois, "The Spawn of Slavery: The Convict-Lease System in the South," in *Race, Crime, and Justice: A Reader*, edited by Shaun L. Gabbidon and Helen Taylor Greene (New York: Taylor and Francis/Routledge, 2005), 5.

Chapter 2. Fairness

1. "If we were not provided with the knack of being wrong, we could never get anything useful done. We think our way along by choosing between right and wrong alternatives, and the wrong choices have to be made as frequently as the right ones. We get along in life this way. We

are built to make mistakes, coded for error." Lewis Thomas, "To Err Is Human," in Lewis Thomas, *The Medusa and the Snail: More Notes of a Biology Watcher* (New York: Viking Press, 1979), 30–32.

2. Julia Angwin, Jeff Larson, Surya Mattu, and Lauren Kirchner, "Machine Bias," *ProPublica*, May 23, 2016, https://www.propublica.org/article/machine-bias-risk-assessments-in-criminal -sentencing.

3. Aristotle, *The Politics, and the Constitution of Athens*, chaps. III.9, III.12; Danielle S. Allen, *The World of Prometheus: The Politics of Punishing in Democratic Athens* (Princeton, NJ: Princeton University Press, 2000), chap. 11.

4. To my knowledge, few computer scientists who develop these mathematical definitions see themselves as attempting to "automate" fairness. That is something of a straw man. The fair machine learning debate is better understood and engaged with by scholars from other disci-plines as an effort to develop tools for the inspection, interrogation, and communication of the patterns that predictive tools unearth and replicate. Sandra Wachter, Brent Mittelstadt, and Chris Russell, "Why Fairness Cannot Be Automated: Bridging the Gap between EU Non-Discrimination Law and AI," *Computer Law and Security Review 41 (July 2021)*: 105567, https://www.sciencedirect.com/science/article/abs/pii/S0267364921000406.

5. Jeff Larson, Surya Mattu, Lauren Kirchner, and Julia Angwin, "How We Analyzed the COMPAS Recidivism Algorithm," *ProPublica*, May 23, 2016, https://www.propublica.org /article/how-we-analyzed-the-compas-recidivism-algorithm.

6. ProPublica's analysis focused specifically on scores produced at the pretrial stage for use in decisions about whether to release a defendant on bail, since that is how the tool is mostly used in Broward County, Florida, where the data ProPublica used in their analysis were from. Ibid.

7. Jeff Larson and Julia Angwin, "Bias in Criminal Risk Scores Is Mathematically Inevitable, Researchers Say," *ProPublica*, December 30, 2016, https://www.propublica.org/article/bias-in -criminal-risk-scores-is-mathematically-inevitable-researchers-say; Angwin et al., "Machine Bias."

8. Many of these fairness definitions were first articulated by psychologists and criminolo-gists exploring the use of predictive tools in the middle of the twentieth century. Meehl, *Clinical versus Statistical Prediction*; T. Anne (Theresa Anne) Cleary, "Test Bias: Validity of the Scholastic Aptitude Test for Negro and White Students in Integrated Colleges," Educational Testing Service, June 1966; Richard B. Darlington, "Another Look at 'Cultural Fairness,'" *Journal of Edu-cational Measurement 8*, no. 2 (1971): 71–82; Underwood, "Law and the Crystal Ball"; Robyn M. Dawes, David Faust, and Paul E. Meehl, "Clinical versus Actuarial Judgment," *Science 243*, no. 4899 (1989): 1668–74.

9. Using data to make predictions often forces the imposition of categories that ignore salient differences between people. Many of the artificial binaries that modern states have constructed—Black and white, men and women—are rooted in attempts to predict and control. I describe these categories as binaries not because they are binaries, but to illustrate how prediction forces the ascription of labels that are unrepresentative and often unjust. I explore this issue in more detail in chapter 4.

10. Models that predict a continuous target variable can be turned into classifiers by impos-ing discrete thresholds. Consider AFST, which estimates the probability distribution, from 0 to 1, that a child will be placed in foster care within two years of an allegation of abuse and neglect.

AFST could be turned into a binary classifier by applying thresholds. The model could answer the question "Will this child be placed in foster care within two years of receiving this call?" by returning the answer "Yes" if a prediction falls above a certain threshold in the estimated probability distribution. A host of important and foundational questions ask what it actually means to predict individual risk. Dawid, "On Individual Risk"; Dawid, Musio, and Murtas, "The Probability of Causation."

11. There is no guarantee that this requirement will actually help narrow a gap between two social groups. Suppose that two groups each have one hundred applicants, fifty-eight of whom are well qualified in one group but only two of whom are in the other. If a company plans to hire thirty applicants and satisfy the equality of TPR condition, twenty-nine would be hired from the first group and only one from the other. Given all the resources in income and education that would be accrued by the twenty-nine applicants from the first group, this might do little over time to advance equality between the two groups. Moritz Hardt, Eric Price, and Nathan Srebro, "Equality of Opportunity in Supervised Learning," October 7, 2016, https://home.ttic .edu/~nati/Publications/HardtPriceSrebro2016.pdf; Muhammad Bilal Zafar, Isabel Valera, Manuel Gomez Rodriguez, and Krishna P. Gummadi, "Fairness beyond Disparate Treatment and Disparate Impact: Learning Classification without Disparate Mistreatment," arXiv:1610.08452v2 [stat.ML], October 26, 2016, revised March 8, 2017, https://doi.org/10.1145 /3038912.3052660.

12. The FPR is calculated by dividing the number of negative events incorrectly predicted to be positive (incorrect predictions of default) by the total number of events predicted to be positive (predictions of default), correctly or incorrectly. $FPR = FP/(FP + TP)$. Hardt, Price, and Srebro, "Equality of Opportunity in Supervised Learning."

13. Ibid.; Zafar et al., "Fairness beyond Disparate Treatment and Disparate Impact."

14. Jeffrey Reiman and Ernest Van Den Haag, "On the Common Saying That It Is Better That Ten Guilty Persons Escape than That One Innocent Suffer: Pro and Con," *Social Philosophy and Policy* 7, no. 2 (1990): 226–48. In civil law, where the cost of false positives is more finely balanced, the evidentiary standard is less strict, requiring a verdict based "on balance of probabilities." Deborah Hellman, "Measuring Algorithmic Fairness," Public Law and Legal Theory Research Paper 2019–39 (Charlottesville: University of Virginia School of Law, 2019), 26–27.

15. ProPublica calculated the positive predictive value (PPV) for the general recidivism model rather than the true positive rate (TPR). The two measures are similar. PPV tends to be used for the evaluation of medical tests. Because TRP is intrinsic to these tests, PPV depends also on prevalence. ProPublica also analyzed accuracy. The general recidivism model was correct in its predictions 61 percent of the time overall, while the violent recidivism model was correct in its predictions 20 percent of the time. The general recidivism model was correct about as often across Blacks and whites: 63 percent for Blacks and 59 percent for whites. Results for the violent recidivism model were similar. The FPR was 38 percent for Blacks and 18 percent for white. The FNR was 63 percent for whites and 38 percent for Blacks. Black defendants were twice as likely as white defendants to be misclassified as high risk of violent recidivism. Larson et al., "How We Analyzed the COMPAS Recidivism Algorithm."

16. William Dietrich, Christina Mendoza, and Tim Brennan, "COMPAS Risk Scales: Demonstrating Accuracy Equity and Predictive Parity," Northpointe Inc., July 8, 2016, https://go .volarisgroup.com/rs/430-MBX-989/images/ProPublica_Commentary_Final_070616.pdf.

17. Notice that the predictor $\hat{Y}$ and the target variable Y have swapped places from definitions focused on errors. The FPR conditions the predictor $\hat{Y}$ on the value of the target variable Y. A false positive is a positive prediction $\hat{Y}$ (will default on loan) when the true value of the target variable Y is in fact negative (does not default on loan). Calibration reverses this, focusing on the rate at which the target variable Y is in fact positive (the rate of actual loan defaults) when the predictor issues a prediction $\hat{Y}$ within a given bucket (say, a 10 percent change in loan default). When subgroup calibration is satisfied, it provides confidence that the predictions of a machine learning model mean the same thing across protected groups. In the loan default case, when the model predicts a 10 percent chance of loan default, subgroup calibration ensures that this means the same thing across Blacks and whites. AFST would be well calibrated with respect to race if for each risk score (1 to 20) the proportion of cases that result in placement is the same across Blacks and whites. There is more to be said about the distinction between positive and negative predictive values, which apply to score functions or binary classifiers, and calibration, which applies to predicted probabilities. In this case, positive and negative predictive values would apply to a classifier that predicts "default" or "no default," for instance, by imposing a threshold on the estimated probability distribution of default. Solon Barocas, Moritz Hardt, and Arvind Narayanan, *Fairness and Machine Learning: Limitations and Opportunities* (fairmlbook.org, 2019), chap. 2, http://www.fairmlbook.org; Sam Corbett-Davies and Sharad Goel, "The Measure and Mismeasure of Fairness: A Critical Review of Fair Machine Learning," September 11, 2018, https://www.5harad.com/papers/fair-ml.pdf.

18. At the time of writing, researchers are trying to understand AFST's miscalibration at the top end of the estimated probability distribution. AFST actually overestimates the risk for white children compared to Black children. In the top two scores, a white child who receives a score of 20 has a risk of placement comparable to that of a Black child who scores around 18. Chouldechova et al., "A Case Study of Algorithm-Assisted Decision Making"; Corbett-Davies and Goel, "The Measure and Mismeasure of Fairness." The only cases in which it may not be a good thing to satisfy subgroup calibration are those in which calibration is satisfied using deliberately crude information to intentionally harm protected groups. In redlining, for instance, a bank could deliberately use coarse variables like zip code while ignoring more granular individual attributes like income and credit history. Assuming that Black and white households defaulted at similar rates within particular neighbourhoods, the predictor would have been well calibrated and yet would also have predicted an unnecessarily high risk of default for creditworthy minorities who lived in high-risk neighborhoods. Corbett-Davies and Goel, "The Measure and Mismeasure of Fairness"; Jon Kleinberg, Jens Ludwig, Sendhil Mullainathan, and Ashesh Rambachan, "Algorithmic Fairness," *AEA Papers and Proceedings* 108 (2018): 22–27; Jennifer Skeem, John Monahan, and Christopher Lowenkamp, "Gender, Risk Assessment, and Sanctioning: The Cost of Treating Women Like Men," *Law and Human Behavior* 40, no. 5 (2016): 580–93.

19. Nina Grgić-Hlača, Muhammad Bilal Zafar, Krishna P. Gummadi, and Adrian Weller, "The Case for Process Fairness in Learning: Feature Selection for Fair Decision Making," in Symposium on Machine Learning and the Law, Twenty-Ninth Conference on Neural Information Processing Systems (NIPS), Barcelona, 2016; Francesco Bonchi, Sara Hajian, Bud Mishra, and Daniele Ramazzotti, "Exposing the Probabilistic Causal Structure of Discrimination," *International Journal of Data Science and Analytics* 3, no. 1 (2017): 1–21.

20. Put differently, correlations between the membership of protected groups and other variables are the norm, not the exception. Dwork et al., "Fairness through Awareness," 214–26.

21. Sam Corbett-Davies and Sharad Goel show that for one recidivism prediction model, women with a score of 7 recidivate less than 50 percent of the time, whereas men with the same score recidivate over 60 percent of the time. Women with a recidivism risk score of 7 reoffend about as frequently as men with a score of 5. This gap is consistent across a range of risk scores. Corbett-Davies and Goel, "The Measure and Mismeasure of Fairness." Interestingly, several states now use separate risk assessment tools to predict recidivism for men and women. The Wisconsin Supreme Court supported the use of gender-specific prediction models in sentencing because they promote "accuracy that ultimately inures to the benefit of the justice system including defendants." Loomis v. Wisconsin, 882 N.W.2d 749 (Wis. 2016); Skeem, Monahan, and Lowenkamp, "Gender, Risk Assessment, and Sanctioning"; Matthew Demichele, Peter Baumgartner, Michael Wenger, Kelle Barrick, Megan Comfort, and Shilpi Misra, "The Public Safety Assessment: A Re-Validation and Assessment of Predictive Utility and Differential Prediction by Race and Gender in Kentucky," April 25, 2018, http://dx.doi.org/10.2139/ssrn .3168452; Betsy Anne Williams, Catherine F. Brooks, and Yotam Shmargad, "How Algorithms Discriminate Based on Data They Lack: Challenges, Solutions, and Policy Implications," *Journal of Information Policy* 8 (2018): 78–115.

22. Requiring the positive acceptance rate to be equal across groups is equivalent to requiring the predictive distribution to be independent of protected attributes. James E. Johndrow and Kristian Lum, "An Algorithm for Removing Sensitive Information: Application to Race-Independent Recidivism Prediction," arXiv:1703.04957v1 [stat.AP], March 15, 2017, 3, https:// arxiv.org/pdf/1703.04957.pdf; Michael Feldman, Sorelle A. Friedler, John Moeller, Carlos Scheidegger, and Suresh Venkatasubramanian, "Certifying and Removing Disparate Impact," arXiv:1412.3756v3 [stat.ML], July 16, 2015, 259–68, https://arxiv.org/pdf/1412.3756v3.pdf; Benjamin Fish, Jeremy Kun, and Ádám D. Lelkes, "A Confidence-Based Approach for Balancing Fairness and Accuracy," arXiv:1601.05764v1 [cs.LG], January 21, 2016, https://doi.org/10.48550 /arXiv.1601.05764; Rich Zemel, Yu (Ledell) Wu, Kevin Swersky, Toniann Pitassi, and Cynthia Dwork, "Learning Fair Representations," Thirtieth International Conference on Machine Learning, Atlanta, June 17–19, 2013, *Journal of Machine Learning Research* (W&CP) 28 (2013): 325–33, https://www.cs.toronto.edu/~toni/Papers/icml-final.pdf.

23. Barocas, Hardt, and Narayanan, *Fairness and Machine Learning*, chap. 2; Reuben Binns, "Fairness in Machine Learning: Lessons from Political Philosophy," *Proceedings of Machine Learning Research* 81 (October 2017): 149–59.

24. Applied to hiring, the four-fifths rule stipulates that if women are hired at less than 80 percent of the rate at which men are hired, there is a presumptive claim of disparate impact. Suppose that 40 percent of men who apply to a company are hired, and 20 percent of women who apply are hired. The hiring ratio here would be 40:20. The rate of hiring for female applicants would be 50 percent of the rate of hiring for male applicants, supporting a presumptive claim of disparate impact. These requirements focus on averages, constraining the permissible disparity between the probability that the average woman and the average man are hired. Feldman et al., "Certifying and Removing Disparate Impact"; Calders and Žliobaitė, "Why Unbiased Computational Processes Can Lead to Discriminative Decision Procedures."

25. Solon Barocas, Moritz Hardt, and Arvind Narayanan rightly point to an ambiguity in how we should think about this result. If gender were truly irrelevant to the classification task, training data for one group would be of equal predictive value for both. And yet, the very fact that we designate gender as a protected attribute suggests that it is in fact relevant to all kinds of classification tasks. Barocas, Hardt, and Narayanan, *Fairness and Machine Learning*, chap. 2; Dwork et al., "Fairness through Awareness."

26. Dwork et al., "Fairness through Awareness," 2.

27. There are actually two assumptions that underpin the result: (1) that base rates are unequal across social groups, and (2) that the predictor is imperfect. Alexandra Chouldechova, "Fair Prediction with Disparate Impact: A Study of Bias in Recidivism Prediction Instruments," *Big Data* 5, no. 2 (2017): 153–63, doi:10.1089/big.2016.0047; Jon Kleinberg, Sendhil Mullainathan, and Manish Raghavan, "Inherent Trade-offs in the Fair Determination of Risk Scores," arXiv:1609.05807v2 [cs.LG], September 19, 2016, revised November 17, 2016, https://doi.org/10.48550/arXiv.1609.05807; Geoff Pleiss, Manish Raghavan, Felix Wu, Jon Kleinberg, and Kilian Q. Weinberger, "On Fairness and Calibration," arXiv:1709.02012v2 [cs.LG], September 6, 2017, revised November 3, 2017, https://doi.org/10.48550/arXiv.1709.02012.

28. Hardt, Price, and Srebro, "Equality of Opportunity in Supervised Learning."

29. Larson and Angwin, "Bias in Criminal Risk Scores Is Mathematically Inevitable."

30. Barocas, Hardt, and Narayanan, *Fairness and Machine Learning*, chap. 2; Kleinberg, Mullainathan, and Raghavan, "Inherent Trade-offs in the Fair Determination of Risk Scores"; Chouldechova, "Fair Prediction with Disparate Impact." Corbett-Davies and Goel show that if two groups have different base rates, their risk distributions with respect to the target variable will necessarily differ, regardless of the form of model or the features used to predict risk. "Because the risk distributions of protected groups will in general differ, threshold-based decisions will typically yield error metrics that also differ by group." In other words, optimal thresholds for the welfare of both groups will differ from the optimal thresholds that satisfy demographic parity or equal error rates. Imposing group fairness constraints can "hurt majority and minority groups alike." Corbett-Davies and Goel, "The Measure and Mismeasure of Fairness," 11–12.

31. O'Flaherty, *Shadows of Doubt*; Danielle S. Allen, *Cuz: The Life and Times of Michael A.* (New York: Liveright, 2017); Michelle Alexander, *The New Jim Crow: Mass Incarceration in the Age of Colorblindness*, rev. ed. (New York: New Press, 2012); Muhammad, *The Condemnation of Blackness.*

32. Noble, *Algorithms of Oppression.*

33. Aristotle, *Nicomachean Ethics*, translated by Roger Crisp (Cambridge: Cambridge University Press, 2000), book V; Allen, *The World of Prometheus*, chap. 11; Frederick Schauer, "On Treating Unlike Cases Alike," paper presented at symposium on *Settled versus Right: A Theory of Precedent* by Randy Kozel, University of Richmond School of Law, April 20–21, 2018.

34. As Corbett-Davies and Goel explain: "The numerator of the false positive rate (the number of defendants who do not reoffend) remains unchanged while the denominator (the number of detained defendants who do not reoffend) increases." Corbett-Davies and Goel, "The Measure and Mismeasure of Fairness," 15.

35. Kleinberg, Mullainathan, and Rambachan continue: "Absent legal constraints, one should include variables such as gender and race for fairness reasons. As we show in an empirical

example below, the inclusion of such variables can increase both equity and efficiency." The next chapter considers why the law may require an action—the removal of protected traits—that may harm the welfare of protected groups, and what we should do about it. Kleinberg et al., "Algorithmic Fairness," 22–23. This requirement also indicates that the fairness of machine learning models cannot be evaluated separately from the broader decision-making process of which they are a component. Dwork and others have shown that individual models that satisfy certain fairness definitions may nonetheless form part of a decision "pipeline" that violates the same definitions. We should reason about fairness at the level not of individual machine learning models but of decision-making systems that deploy machine learning models, whether in criminal justice, child protection, loan default, or hiring. Moreover, how the principle of equal treatment should be applied in machine learning should depend in part on how machine learning models are being used to make decisions. Cynthia Dwork, Christina Ilvento, and Meena Jagadeesan, "Individual Fairness in Pipelines," arXiv:2004.05167v1 [cs.CY], April 12, 2020, https://doi.org/10.48550/arXiv.2004.05167; Cynthia Dwork and Christina Ilvento, "Fairness under Composition," arXiv:1806.06122v2 [cs.LG], November 20, 2018, https://arxiv.org/pdf/1806.06122.pdf.

36. Broward County judge John Hurley, who oversees most bail hearings, said that scores were helpful when he was a new judge, but that now, with more experience, he relies on his own judgment. "I haven't relied on COMPAS in a couple years." Again, this is just as we saw with AFST: screeners initially leaned quite heavily on the risk scores, but then fell back on their own judgment. It may be that after a while humans rely less on the predictions of statistical systems than we might expect. How humans use predictions over time to make high-stakes decisions requires further research. Angwin et al., "Machine Bias"; Danielle Keats Citron, "Technological Due Process," *Washington University Law Review* 85, no. 6 (2008): 1249–1313.

37. Aristotle, *The Politics, and the Constitution of Athens,* chaps. III.9, III.12Allen, *The World of Prometheus,* chap. 11; Michael J. Sandel, *The Tyranny of Merit: What's Become of the Common Good?* (New York: Farrar, Straus and Giroux, 2020).

38. On Dwork's individual fairness approach, which I explore later, the bank could achieve something similar by training a distance metric that saw credit scores of 60 for Black applicants as "similar" to credit scores of 80 for white applicants. In an unjust world, Dwork argues, such deliberate adjustments may be "society's current best approximation to the truth," and as such it may be "desirable to 'adjust' or otherwise 'make up' a metric." Dwork uses the example of "adding a certain number of points to SAT scores of students in disadvantaged groups" for distance metrics imposed on the classifiers used in college admissions. Dwork et al., "Fairness through Awareness," 3; Lily Hu and Yiling Chen, "A Short-Term Intervention for Long-Term Fairness in the Labor Market," arXiv:1712.00064v2 [cs.GT], November 30, 2017, revised February 21, 2018, https://doi.org/10.48550/arXiv.1712.00064.

39. Sorelle Friedler and her coauthors make a similar point: imposing fairness constraints requires the analyst to take a view about what is driving observed disparities. The reason we treat individuals from different groups differently is precisely because we think that the membership of a protected group is relevant to the disparities we observe between protected groups. Sorelle Friedler, Carlos Scheidegger, and Suresh Venkatasubramanian, "On the (Im)Possibility of Fairness," arXiv:1609.07236v1 [cs.CY], September 23, 2016, https://doi.org/10.48550/arXiv.1609.07236.

40. Dwork et al., "Fairness through Awareness."

41. Aristotle, *The Politics, and the Constitution of Athens*, chaps. III.9, III.12; Allen, *The World of Prometheus*, chap. 11.

42. Many papers cite individual fairness in the first few pages, then set it aside because of the difficulty of defining a distance metric. For instance: "One line of work called individual fairness rests on the view that similar examples should receive similar predictions; but this leaves open the question of similarity." Beutel et al., "Putting Fairness Principles into Practice."

43. Christina Ilvento, "Metric Learning for Individual Fairness," arXiv:1906.00250v2 [cs.LG], June 1, 2019, revised April 2, 2020, https://doi.org/10.48550/arXiv.1906.00250; Christopher Jung, Michael Kearns, Seth Neel, Aaron Roth, Logan Stapleton, and Zhiwei Steven Wu, "Eliciting and Enforcing Subjective Individual Fairness," arXiv:1905.10660v2 [cs.LG], October 15, 2019, https://arxiv.org/pdf/1905.10660.pdf. Developing consistent and efficient ways to define distance metrics is an important challenge for future research in fair machine learning. Other approaches postulate a fairness oracle with direct knowledge of fairness "truth" from which a distance metric can be approximated. Cynthia Dwork, Christina Ilvento, Guy N. Rothblum, and Pragya Sur, "Abstracting Fairness: Oracles, Metrics, and Interpretability," arXiv:2004.01840v1 [cs.LG], April 4, 2020, https://doi.org/10.48550/arXiv.2004.01840. Other approaches aim to learn distance metrics directly from relationships in the data rather than from consulting the judgments of domain experts. Zemel et al., "Learning Fair Representations"; Preethi Lahoti, Krishna Gummadi, and Gerhard Weikum, "IFair: Learning Individually Fair Data Representations for Algorithmic Decision Making," arXiv:1806.01059v2 [cs.LG], June 4, 2019, https://doi.org/10.48550/arXiv.1806.01059; Anian Ruoss, Mislav Balunović, Marc Fischer, and Martin Vechev, "Learning Certified Individually Fair Representations," arXiv:2002.10312v2 [cs.LG], February 24, 2020, revised November 20, 2020, https://doi.org/10.48550/arXiv.2002.10312.

Chapter 3. Discrimination

1. Justice John Marshall Harlan dissent, Plessy v. Ferguson, 163 U.S. 537 (1896).

2. Martin Luther King Jr., speech, June 15, 1963, Washington, DC.

3. Justice Harry Blackmun concurrence, Regents of the University of California v. Bakke, 438 U.S. 265 (1978).

4. Justice Antonin Scalia concurrence, Ricci v. DeStefano, 557 U.S. 557 (2009).

5. Stop LAPD Spying, "Before the Bullet Hits the Body: Dismantling Predictive Policing in Los Angeles," May 8, 2018, 38, https://stoplapdspying.org/wp-content/uploads/2018/05/Before-the-Bullet-Hits-the-Body-May-8-2018.pdf.

6. Ibid., 38–39.

7. These models vary in the length of time over which predictions are meant to be valid, from a day to almost a month; whether they focus on the crime risk of neighborhoods or individuals; and what kind of data they use as inputs. Hannah Couchman, "Policing by Machine: Predictive Policing and the Threat to Our Rights," Liberty, January 2019, https://www.libertyhumanrights.org.uk/wp-content/uploads/2020/02/LIB-11-Predictive-Policing-Report-WEB.pdf; Walt L. Perry, *Predictive Policing: The Role of Crime Forecasting in Law Enforcement Operations* (Santa Monica, CA: RAND, 2013).

8. O'Neil, *Weapons of Math Destruction*, 87; Ruha Benjamin, *Race after Technology: Abolitionist Tools for the New Jim Code* (Medford, MA: Polity, 2019), 82; Caroline Haskins, "The Los

Angeles Police Department Says It Is Dumping a Controversial Predictive Policing Tool," *BuzzFeed News*, April 21, 2020, https://www.buzzfeednews.com/article/carolinehaskins1/los -angeles-police-department-dumping-predpol-predictive. Those who build these systems argue that a greater police presence reduces crime, thereby in the long run reducing disparities in crime rates between high-risk and other neighborhoods. If police record only a small fraction of total crime, however, predictive policing systems simply affect where crime gets recorded, not whether overall crime is reduced. Perdomo et al., "Performative Prediction"; Danielle Ensign, Sorelle A. Friedler, Scott Neville, Carlos Scheidegger, and Suresh Venkatasubramanian, "Runaway Feedback Loops in Predictive Policing," arXiv:1706.09847v3 [cs.CY], June 29, 2017, https://doi.org/10.48550/arXiv.1706.09847.

9. I primarily use "discrimination law" so that I can distinguish sharply between "nondiscrimination" and "antidiscrimination law" at the end of the chapter. Hannah Arendt, "Reflections on Little Rock," *Dissent* 6, no. 1 (1959): 45; Benjamin Eidelson, *Discrimination and Disrespect* (Oxford: Oxford University Press, 2015), chap. 6; Kasper Lippert-Rasmussen, *Born Free and Equal? A Philosophical Inquiry into the Nature of Discrimination* (Oxford: Oxford University Press, 2014), chap. 11; Eidelson, *Discrimination and Disrespect*; Lippert-Rasmussen, *Born Free and Equal?*; Tarunabh Khaitan, *A Theory of Discrimination Law* (Oxford: Oxford University Press, 2015); Sophia Moreau and Deborah Hellman, eds., *Philosophical Foundations of Discrimination Law* (Oxford: Oxford University Press, 2013).

10. While UK discrimination law appears to be more far-reaching, unburdened by the narrow anti-classification principle, I argue that similar problems quickly become apparent when applying UK discrimination law to machine learning.

11. Deborah Hellman, "Indirect Discrimination and the Duty to Avoid Compounding Injustice," in *Foundations of Indirect Discrimination Law*, edited by Hugh Collins and Tarunabh Khaitan (Oxford: Hart Publishing, 2018), 105–22; Sandra G. Mayson, "Bias In, Bias Out," *Yale Law Journal* 128, no. 8 (2019): 2218.

12. It is important to distinguish two components of Facebook's advertising system. The first is the targeting system, in which advertisers explicitly select the audiences they want to reach, based on demographic and behavioral characteristics. The second is the delivery system, which is powered by machine learning. The advertising system involves a complex bidding process that optimizes for "impressions," which involve different kinds of engagement, including clicks, likes, shares, applications, and purchases. The bidding process factors in the "quality" of particular bids from advertisers, which is estimated using machine learning models trained on data from user satisfaction surveys. Dawid, "On Individual Risk"; Dawid, Musio, and Murtas, "The Probability of Causation"; Pearl, *Causal Inference in Statistics*; Skyrms, *Choice and Chance*.

13. Muhammad Ali, Piotr Sapiezynski, Miranda Bogan, Aleksandra Korolova, Alan Mislove, and Aaron Rieke, "Discrimination through Optimization: How Facebook's Ad Delivery Can Lead to Biased Outcomes," *Proceedings of the Association for Computer Machinery on Human-Computer Interaction* 3, no. CSCW (2019): 1–30; Amit Datta, Michael Carl Tschantz, and Anupam Datta, "Automated Experiments on Ad Privacy Settings," *Proceedings on Privacy Enhancing Technologies* 1, no. 1 (2015): 92–112.

14. Perdomo et al., "Performative Prediction"; Lydia T. Liu, Sarah Dean, Esther Rolf, Max Simchowitz, and Moritz Hardt, "Delayed Impact of Fair Machine Learning," *Proceedings of the Thirty-Fifth International Conference on Machine Learning, Stockholm, PMLR*, no. 80 (March 12, 2018): 3150–58; Dwork, Ilvento, and Jagadeesan, "Individual Fairness in Pipelines."

Much has been written about the partially analogous case of racial profiling. Eidelson, *Discrimination and Disrespect*, chap. 6; Lippert-Rasmussen, *Born Free and Equal?*, chap. 11; Mathias Risse and Richard Zeckhauser, "Racial Profiling," *Philosophy and Public Affairs* 32, no. 2 (2004): 131–70; Frederick F. Schauer, *Profiles, Probabilities, and Stereotypes* (Cambridge, MA: Belknap Press of Harvard University Press, 2003).

15. This ambition has always had limits. For instance, the "Mrs. Murphy Exception" to the Fair Housing Act (FHA) provides that if a dwelling has four or fewer rental units and the owner lives in one of those units, the home is exempt from the FHA. Democracies have always recognized that the burdens of the pursuit of justice should fall unevenly across institutions, depending on their resources and what they do. Danielle S. Allen and Jennifer S. Light, *From Voice to Influence: Understanding Citizenship in a Digital Age* (Chicago: University of Chicago Press, 2015), chap. 11; Khaitan, *A Theory of Discrimination Law*.

16. In 2010, the United Kingdom's various equality and antidiscrimination laws were brought under a single framework, the Equality Act (EA). The analysis in the notes to this chapter draws several points of comparison between EA jurisprudence and constitutional debates in the US centered on Title VII and the Fourteenth Amendment. *Equality Act 2010: Chapter 15* (2010), http://www.legislation.gov.uk/ukpga/2010/15/pdfs/ukpga_20100015_en.pdf.

17. Rick Perlstein, "Exclusive: Lee Atwater's Infamous 1981 Interview on the Southern Strategy," *The Nation*, November 13, 2012, https://www.thenation.com/article/archive/exclusive-lee-atwaters-infamous-1981-interview-southern-strategy/.

18. In the United Kingdom, direct discrimination is defined as: "A person (A) discriminates against another (B) if, because of a protected characteristic, A treats B less favourably than A treats or would treat others." The act also defines a set of exceptions. "If the protected characteristic is age, A does not discriminate against B if A can show A's treatment of B to be a proportionate means of achieving a legitimate aim; If the protected characteristic is disability, and B is not a disabled person, A does not discriminate against B only because A treats or would treat disabled persons more favourably than A treats B." And "if the protected characteristic is sex . . . (b) in a case where B is a man, no account is to be taken of special treatment afforded to a woman in connection with pregnancy or childbirth." Equality Act 2010, sec. 13.

19. This is a notable difference between US and UK law; in the latter, motive is irrelevant to direct discrimination. Lord Goff defined a straightforward test: "Would the complainant have received the same treatment . . . but for his or her sex?" James v. Eastleigh Borough Council (1990) 2 AC 751, 774. The decision in R (on the application of E) v. Governing Body of JFS (UKSC, 2009), 15, confirmed that courts will impose this objective test instead of requiring proof of discriminatory intent. In the United States, recent attempts to adjust evidential rules to assume discriminatory intent if certain objective criteria are satisfied have largely been reversed by courts. St. Mary's Honor Center v. Hicks, 509 U.S. 502 (1993), 519; McDonnell Douglas Corp v. Green, 411 U.S. 792 (1973) 802–3; Sheila Foster, "Causation in Antidiscrimination Law: Beyond Intent versus Impact," *Houston Law Review* 41, no. 5 (2005): 1469–1548; David Strauss, "Discriminatory Intent and the Taming of Brown," *University of Chicago Law Review* 56, no. 3 (1989): 935. There are important debates in the United States about the scope of disparate treatment, including whether disparate treatment prohibits the use of obvious proxies for protected classes and whether it includes taste-based or statistical discrimination—for instance, if

a man is hired over a woman for a position because the CEO prefers male colleagues, or because customers prefer to be served by men rather than women. David Strauss, "The Law and Economics of Racial Discrimination in Employment: The Case for Numerical Standards," *Georgetown Law Journal* 79, no. 6 (1991): 1619–57; Cass R. Sunstein, "Why Markets Won't Stop Discrimination," *Social Philosophy and Policy* 8, no. 2 (1991): 22–37.

20. US Department of Housing and Urban Development v. Facebook, Inc., "Charge of Discrimination," March 28, 2019, https://www.hud.gov/sites/dfiles/Main/documents/HUD _v_Facebook.pdf; Rebecca Slaughter, "The First 100 Days: Tech in the Biden Administration," *protocol*, 2021, https://www.protocol.com/the-first-100-days-tech-in-the-biden-administration; Kleinberg et al., "Discrimination in the Age of Algorithms," 27; Cass R. Sunstein, "Algorithms, Correcting Biases," *Social Research: An International Quarterly* 86, no. 2 (2019): 7; Charles A. Sullivan, "Employing AI," *Villanova Law Review* 63, no. 3 (2018): 405.

21. HUD's proposed rule stated that a defendant could rebut a discrimination claim by showing that "none of the factors used in the algorithm rely in any material part on factors which are substitutes or close proxies for protected classes under the Fair Housing Act." Sec. (c)(2)(i) in HUD, "HUD's Implementation of the Fair Housing Act's Disparate Impact Standard: Supplementary Information: This Proposed Rule," Pub. L. No. 84 FR 42854, Docket No. FR-6111-P-02 24 CFR 100 (2019), https://www.federalregister.gov/documents/2019/08/19/2019-17542 /huds-implementation-of-the-fair-housing-acts-disparate-impact-standard#h-9; Andrew D. Selbst, "A New HUD Rule Would Basically Permit Discrimination by Algorithm," *Slate*, August 19, 2019, https://slate.com/technology/2019/08/hud-disparate-impact-discrimination -algorithm.html; Kleinberg and Mullainathan, "Simplicity Creates Inequity"; Dwork et al., "Fairness through Awareness."

22. Calders and Žliobaitė, "Why Unbiased Computational Processes Can Lead to Discriminative Decision Procedures," 54; Dwork et al., "Fairness through Awareness."

23. Some argue that the "but for" test provides a straightforward answer: if the decision-maker would have decided differently had they perceived the person to be of a different race or gender, they made the decision because of race or gender. I find this an unconvincing account of both what it means to make decisions "because of" someone's race or gender and what makes it morally wrong to discriminate. Kleinberg et al., "Discrimination in the Age of Algorithms," 16; Samuel R. Bagenstos, "Implicit Bias' Failure," *Berkeley Journal of Employment and Labor Law* 39, no. 1 (2018): 51.

24. Indirect discrimination is defined as: "(1) A person (A) discriminates against another (B) if A applies to B a provision, criterion or practice which is discriminatory in relation to a relevant protected characteristic of B's. (2) For the purposes of subsection (1), a provision, criterion or practice is discriminatory in relation to a relevant protected characteristic of B's if—(a) A applies, or would apply, it to persons with whom B does not share the characteristic; (b) it puts, or would put, persons with whom B shares the characteristic at a *particular disadvantage* when compared with persons with whom B does not share it; and (c) it puts, or would put, B at that disadvantage, and A cannot show it to be a *proportionate means* of achieving a *legitimate aim*." Equality Act 2010, sec. 19. An indirect discrimination case effectively involves two stages: Can the claimant establish a prima facie case of indirect discrimination? If so, can the defendant objectively justify the provisions, criteria, or practices (PCPs) by showing that it is a proportionate means of achieving a legitimate aim?

25. There is a distinction between statistical disparities and adverse impact; statistical disparities may be evidence of adverse impact, but they are not sufficient to demonstrate it. As Lady Hale explains: "It is commonplace for the disparate impact, or particular disadvantage, to be established on the basis of statistical evidence." Lady Hale, Essop v. Home Office (UKSC 2017). This is true in both the United States and the United Kingdom, despite a lot of misguided criticism in the United Kingdom of the four-fifths test. The differences between the underlying legal requirements in the United Kingdom and the United States are not as great as many suppose: the four-fifths test is a rule of thumb rather than a legal requirement, and under US law businesses that preemptively adjust statistical systems to fit the four-fifths test will not be immune from disparate impact suits. As one US recent paper explains: "Whilst outcome disparities are important . . . discrimination and the 4/5 rule should not be conflated." Manish Raghavan, Solon Barocas, Jon Kleinberg, and Karen Levy, "Mitigating Bias in Algorithmic Hiring: Evaluating Claims and Practices," arXiv:1906.09208v3 [cs.CY], December 6, 2019, 15, https://arxiv.org/pdf/1906.09208.pdf. And as Lady Hale said in the United Kingdom: "It cannot have been contemplated that 'particular disadvantage' might not be capable of being proved by statistical evidence." Keely v. Westinghouse Electric Corp., 32 Pa. D. and C. 4th 67 (1996); Catherine Barnard and Bob Hepple, "Indirect Discrimination: Interpreting Seymour-Smith," Cambridge Law Journal 58, no. 2 (1999): 408.

26. See 42 US Code, sec. 2000e-2(k)(1); Louis Kaplow, "On the Design of Legal Rules: Balancing versus Structured Decision Procedures," Harvard Law Review 132, no. 3 (2019): sec. III.

27. "Congress has now provided that tests or criteria for employment or promotion may not provide equality of opportunity merely in the sense of the fabled offer of milk to the stork and the fox. On the contrary, Congress has now required that the posture and condition of the job seeker be taken into account. It has—to resort again to the fable—provided that the vessel in which the milk is proffered be one all seekers can use. The Act proscribes not only overt discrimination, but also practices that are fair in form, but discriminatory in operation. The touchstone is business necessity. If an employment practice which operates to exclude Negroes cannot be shown to be related to job performance, the practice is prohibited." Chief Justice Warren Burger opinion, Griggs v. Duke Power Co., 401 U.S. 424 (1971); Jake Elijah Struebing, "Reconsidering Disparate Impact under Title VII: Business Necessity as Risk Management," Yale Law and Policy Review 34, no. 2 (2016): 499–531; Christine Jolls, "Antidiscrimination and Accommodation," Harvard Law Review 115, no. 2 (2001): 642–99; Richard A. Primus, "Equal Protection and Disparate Impact: Round Three," Harvard Law Review 117, no. 2 (2003): 493; Owen M. Fiss, "Groups and the Equal Protection Clause," Philosophy and Public Affairs 5, no. 2 (1976): 107–77.

28. A court might dispute cases in which a target variable is a crude proxy for the underlying outcome of interest. For instance, suppose COMPAS uses the probability that a person will be arrested or detained within two years of release as a proxy for the real outcome of interest, whether or not they actually commit a crime within two years of release. This proxy is unevenly racially distributed. Because African Americans are stopped and searched at disproportionate rates, white Americans are much less likely to be caught for crimes they commit after release. But even here courts will face obvious constraints. What could COMPAS have been trained to predict instead? We almost never have direct measures of the things we care about, whether true crime rates, what makes for a good employee, or, in Facebook's case, the true value of an individual seeing an ad. Even though the variables that a model is trained to predict are enor-

mously important for the outcomes it produces, it would take an enormously confident and technical court to dispute a business's account of whether an outcome was a reasonable proxy for a legitimate trait. Michael Selmi, "Was the Disparate Impact Theory a Mistake?," *UCLA Law Review* 53 (2006): 701–1549.

29. Don Peck, "They're Watching You at Work," *Atlantic*, December 2013, https://www .theatlantic.com/magazine/archive/2013/12/theyre-watching-you-at-work/354681/. Models trained on data that are biased (in the statistical sense), mislabeled, or unrepresentative might produce a model so error-strewn that it doesn't predict what it is supposed to predict. For instance, COMPAS might use features that are better predictors of the true outcome for one race over another, such as credit history or particular questionnaire responses. Or it might use training data that have been mislabeled for one group, such as often happens when rearrests are not recorded for whites, resulting in the uneven distribution of systematic errors across protected groups. But again, assuming the absence of discriminatory intent, businesses have no incentive to design and adopt error-strewn models. They want models that accurately predict what they are supposed to predict. Barocas and Selbst, "Big Data's Disparate Impact," 709; Selmi, "Was the Disparate Impact Theory a Mistake?"

30. Kleinberg et al., "Discrimination in the Age of Algorithms"; Kevin Tobia, "Disparate Statistics," *Yale Law Journal* 126, no. 8 (2017): 2382–2420; Barocas and Selbst, "Big Data's Disparate Impact"; Cass R. Sunstein, "The Anticaste Principle," *Michigan Law Review* 92 (August 1, 1994): 2410–2649; Strauss, "Discriminatory Intent and the Taming of *Brown*"; Fiss, "Groups and the Equal Protection Clause." In UK law, cases involving machine learning may more frequently reach the objective justification stage of indirect discrimination, and in particular the question of whether a PCP is a necessary means of achieving a legitimate aim. Lady Hale notes that at present there is often "considerable reluctance to reach" this final stage, "yet there should not be. There is no finding of unlawful discrimination unless all . . . elements of the definition [of indirect discrimination] are met. The requirement to justify a PCP should not be seen as placing an unreasonable burden upon respondents. Nor should it be seen as casting some sort of shadow or stigma upon them. There is no shame in it. There may well be very good reasons for the PCP in question . . . a wise employer will monitor how his policies and practices impact upon various groups and, if he finds that they do have a disparate impact, will try and see what can be modified to remove that impact while achieving the desired result." Hale, Essop v. Home Office, 12.

31. In establishing this final part of the process, the Supreme Court ruled in *Albermarle Paper Co. v. Moody* in 1975 that a defendant could "show that other tests or selection devices, without a similarly undesirable racial effect, would also serve the employer's legitimate interest." Albemarle Paper Co. v. Moody, 422 U.S. 405 (1975). The Civil Rights Act of 1991 codified this requirement as the "alternative employment practice" requirement. Recent judgments have argued that a plaintiff can win a disparate impact case by demonstrating there exists "an available alternative employment practice that has less disparate impact and serves the employer's legitimate needs." Justice Scalia, Ricci v. DeStefano, 557 at 578. The United Kingdom's EA combines the final two stages of the disparate impact process, asking: Is there an "objective justification" of PCPs that subjects protected groups to a relative disadvantage? Employers are required to demonstrate legitimate reasons for the PCP (the job-related requirement in US law), usually on the grounds that it is "proportionate" and "reasonably necessary" to achieve a "legitimate aim" that could not be achieved through less discriminatory means (the less discriminatory alternative in US law).

32. Knowledge of disparate impact in the design of a policy or procedure is not always sufficient to demonstrate discriminatory intent in US law. To demonstrate a violation of the Equal Protection Clause, for instance, a plaintiff must show that the state adopted a policy or practice with the *deliberate purpose* of discriminating against the protected class. By contrast, in Title VII the absence of a business justification for such a practice is assumed to be sufficient grounds for inferring discriminatory intent. Washington v. Davis, 426 U.S. 229 (1976); Chief Justice Burger, Griggs v. Duke Power Co., 401. In UK law, the appropriateness requirement of objectively justifying a PCP as a proportionate means of achieving a legitimate aim may also effectively serve as a tool for enforcing best practice in machine learning.

33. In the United Kingdom, Lord Nicholls has argued that the evaluation of the legitimacy of a PCP should happen at the objective justification stage: "[a] responsible employer takes into account such disparate impact, if there be any, when considering which scheme to adopt, and so at the justification stage, the employer must discharge the burden of proof." Barry v. Midland Bank (1999) I.R.L.R. 581, H.L. at 581. The question will often be how courts should reason about whether the use of machine learning to achieve a legitimate objective is "proportionate" in a particular case. That question addresses considerations similar to those explored in this third "reasonable alternative" stage of disparate impact cases. "Finding an aim that is considered legitimate for the purposes of objective justification is much less difficult than showing that the means chosen to achieve this aim are appropriate and necessary." Cases involving machine learning will increasingly hinge on what counts as an "objective justification" of a PCP that is prima facie, indirectly or directly. Christa Tobler, for the European Network of Legal Experts in the Nondiscrimination Field, "Limits and Potential of the Concept of Indirect Discrimination" (Brussels and Utrecht: European Commission, September 2008), 43; Dee Masters and Robin Allen, *Regulating for an Equal AI: A New Role for Equality Bodies* (Brussels: Equinet, 2020), 43, 46, https://ai-lawhub.com/wp-content/uploads/2020/06/Equinet-published-report.pdf; Wachter, Mittelstadt, and Russell, "Why Fairness Cannot Be Automated."

34. In the United Kingdom, our judge might apply the "but for" test. In this case, the joint causes of the disparity between the average incomes offered in job ads shown to men and women are: (a) Facebook's choice to show users whichever ad p(click) predicts they are most likely to click on, (b) the patterns of job ads that men and women tend to click on, and (c) the disparities in the incomes attached to the job ads that men and women tend to click on. The reasons for (c) are complex and multifaceted, but they are irrelevant for establishing prima facie indirect discrimination. It is enough that were it not for (a) or (b), the particular disadvantage would not occur.

35. There is a difference between saying that a feature is recoverable and saying that it is actually used to make predictions. A feature might in principle be recoverable by a model given the training data but not actually used by the model to make predictions. An argument like HUD's would require successfully making both claims. Doing so is extremely difficult without access to the training data and may also require access to the model itself.

36. In the United Kingdom, some might argue that a case like p(click) constitutes a "proxy case" of direct discrimination on the grounds that p(click) subjects women to the particular disadvantage of the "greater risk" of being shown a job ad with a lower average income than those shown to men. Consider Lady Hale's judgment in *Coll*: "The question of comparing like with like must always be treated with great care—men and women are different from one another in

many ways, but that does not mean that the relevant circumstances cannot be the same for the purpose of deciding whether one has been treated less favourably than the other. Usually, those circumstances will be something other than the personal characteristics of the men and women concerned, something extrinsic rather than intrinsic to them. In this case, the material circumstances are that they are offenders being released on licence on condition that they live in an AP. Those circumstances are the same for men and women. But the risk of being placed far from home is much greater for the women than for the men." Lady Hale, R (on the application of Coll) v. Secretary of State for Justice (UKSC, May 24, 2017). There are two problems with the application of *Coll* to cases like p(click). First, in *Coll* the location of the Approved Premises (AP) in which prisoners released on parole are housed is within the control of the defendant; by contrast, the factors that cause the disadvantage in Facebook's case are not, whether the gendered click behavior of social media users or the average income attached to the job ads men and women tend to click on. The second and more fundamental problem arises from the "exact correspondence" test. Not *all* women suffer the relative disadvantage of being shown lower-paid job ads— in fact, those who click on ads for jobs with higher average incomes than those men tend to click on may be shown job ads with a higher average income than those shown to men. Because the machine learning system is personalized, the disadvantage is centered on averages: women *on average* are shown job ads with lower average incomes than the average incomes in ads shown to men. Machine learning systems will rarely meet the "exact correspondence" test. Hale, R (on the application of Coll) v. Secretary of State for Justice, 40; Dee Masters, "Identifying Direct Discrimination in 'Proxy Cases' after R (on the Application of Coll) v. Secretary of State for Justice," *Cloisters News*, May 31, 2017, https://www.cloisters.com/identifying-direct-discrimination-in-proxy-cases-after-r-on-the-application-of-coll-v-secretary-of-state-for-justice/.

37. This bill supports proposals that would require institutions designing and using predictive tools to complete and report an assessment of reasonable alternatives. Assembly Member Chau, "Personal Rights: Automated Decision Systems," Assembly Bill No. 2269, introduced February 14, 2020, California Legislature—2019–2020 Regular Session, https://leginfo.legislature.ca.gov/faces/billTextClient.xhtml?bill_id=201920200AB2269; Logan Graham, Abigail Gilbert, Josh Simons, and Anna Thomas, with Helen Mountfield, "Artificial Intelligence in Hiring: Assessing Impacts on Equality," Institute for the Future of Work, April 2020, https://static1.squarespace.com/static/5aa269bbd274cb0df1e696c8/t/5ea831fa76be55719d693076/1588081156980/IFOW+-+Assessing+impacts+on+equality.pdf.

38. In the United Kingdom, greater emphasis on proportionality may also require more direct confrontation with the distinct moral and political purposes that underpin equality law: on the one hand, the traditional liberal aspiration for neutrality and blindness in the allocation of social benefits and burdens; and on the other, the more substantive aspiration for democratic citizens to relate to one another as equals, with all the concomitant implications for moderating social and economic inequality. If indirect discrimination provides few internal resources to guide that reasoning, greater emphasis on proportionality may unearth the "surprising" fragility of "the concept of indirect discrimination." Sandra Fredman, "Addressing Disparate Impact: Indirect Discrimination and the Public Sector Equality Duty," *Industrial Law Journal* (London) 43, no. 3 (2014): 349.

39. Victoria F. Nourse and Jane S. Schacter, "The Politics of Legislative Drafting: A Congressional Case Study," *New York University Law Review* 77, no. 3 (2002): 575; Richard L. Hasen,

"Vote Buying," *California Law Review* 88, no. 5 (2000): 1323–71; David A. Strauss, *The Living Constitution* (Oxford: Oxford University Press, 2010).

40. Jack M. Balkin and Reva B. Siegel, "The American Civil Rights Tradition: Anticlassification or Antisubordination," *Issues in Legal Scholarship* 2, no. 1 (2003); Strauss, "Discriminatory Intent and the Taming of *Brown*"; Pamela L. Perry, "Two Faces of Disparate Impact Discrimination," *Fordham Law Review* 59, no. 4 (March 1, 1991): 523–95; Barocas and Selbst, "Big Data's Disparate Impact." The UK Supreme Court has described the distinct purposes of prohibitions against direct and indirect discrimination: "The rule against direct discrimination aims to achieve *formal equality of treatment*: there must be no less favourable treatment between otherwise similarly situated people on grounds of colour, race, nationality or ethnic or national origins. Indirect discrimination looks *beyond formal equality* towards a more *substantive equality of results*: criteria which appear neutral on their face may have a disproportionately adverse impact upon people of a particular colour, race, nationality or ethnic or national origins. Direct and indirect discrimination are mutually exclusive." R v JFS, at 57 (emphasis in original). Other reasons have been proffered for what motivates the set of prohibited grounds, such as the social meaning and perceived divisiveness of classifications based on race. Benjamin Eidelson, "Respect, Individualism, and Colorblindness," *Yale Law Journal* 129, no. 6 (2020); Reva B. Siegel, "From Colorblindness to Antibalkanization: An Emerging Ground of Decision in Race Equality Cases," *Yale Law Journal* 120, no. 6 (2011): 1278–1366; Sophia Moreau, "What Is Discrimination?," *Philosophy and Public Affairs* 38, no. 2 (2010): 143–79.

41. The structure of these three kinds of cases is drawn from Owen Fiss, whose argument I consider in more depth later. Fiss, "Groups and the Equal Protection Clause," 171.

42. Kleinberg et al., "Algorithmic Fairness," 108; Pauline T. Kim, "Data-Driven Discrimination at Work," *William and Mary Law Review* 58, no. 3 (2017): 904; Barocas and Selbst, "Big Data's Disparate Impact."

43. Eidelson, *Discrimination and Disrespect*, chap. 2; Moreau and Hellman, *Philosophical Foundations of Discrimination Law*; Fiss, "Groups and the Equal Protection Clause"; Dwork et al., "Fairness through Awareness"; Kleinberg and Mullainathan, "Simplicity Creates Inequity"; Dwork et al., "Fairness through Awareness."

44. This narrowing has been less pronounced in the United Kingdom. Lady Hale writes: "It is instructive to go through the various iterations of the indirect discrimination concept because it is inconceivable that the later versions were seeking to cut down or to restrict it in ways which the earlier ones did not. The whole trend of equality legislation since it began in the 1970s has been to reinforce the protection given to the principle of equal treatment." "The prohibition of direct discrimination aims to achieve equality of treatment. Indirect discrimination assumes equality of treatment—the PCP is applied indiscriminately to all—but aims to achieve a level playing field, where people sharing a particular protected characteristic are not subjected to requirements which many of them cannot meet but which cannot be shown to be justified. The prohibition of indirect discrimination thus aims to achieve equality of results in the absence of such justification. It is dealing with hidden barriers which are not easy to anticipate or to spot." Hale, Essop v. Home Office at 10.

45. Several scholars made this point in the late 1980s and early 1990s. Stephen Guest and Alan Milne, eds., *Equality and Discrimination: Essays in Freedom and Justice* (London: University College London, 1985); Iris Marion Young, *Justice and the Politics of Difference* (Princeton, NJ:

Princeton University Press, 1990), 194–98; Christopher Mccrudden, "Institutional Discrimination," *Oxford Journal of Legal Studies* 2, no. 3 (1982): 303–67.

46. Lily Hu, "What Is 'Race' in Algorithmic Discrimination on the Basis of Race?," *Journal of Moral Philosophy*, forthcoming.

47. Moreau and Hellman, *Philosophical Foundations of Discrimination Law*; George Rutherglen, "Concrete or Abstract Conceptions of Discrimination?," in *Philosophical Foundations of Discrimination Law*, edited by Deborah Hellman and Sophia Moreau (Oxford: Oxford University Press, 2013); Eidelson, *Discrimination and Disrespect*; Hugh Collins and Tarunabh Khaitan, *Foundations of Indirect Discrimination Law* (Oxford: Hart Publishing, 2018); Eidelson, "Respect, Individualism, and Colorblindness."

48. Robin West, *Civil Rights: Rethinking Their Natural Foundation* (Cambridge: Cambridge University Press, 2019); Reva B. Siegel, "The Constitutionalization of Disparate Impact—Court-Centered and Popular Pathways," *California Law Review* 106, no. 6 (2018): 2001–22; Susan D. Carle, "A Social Movement History of Title VII Disparate Impact Analysis," *Florida Law Review* 63, no. 1 (2011): 251–300.

49. Nadya Labi, "Misfortune Teller," *Atlantic*, January/February 2012, https://www.theatlantic.com/magazine/archive/2012/01/misfortune-teller/308846/.

50. As Morris Abram, a former member of the US Commission on Civil Rights under President Ronald Reagan, wrote in 1986 in the *Harvard Law Review*: "Because groups—black, white, Hispanic, male and female—do not necessarily have the same distribution of, among other characteristics, skills, interest, motivation, and age, a fair shake system may not produce proportional representation across occupations and professions, and certainly not at any given time. This uneven distribution, however, is not necessarily the result of discrimination." Morris Abram, "Affirmative Action: Fair Shakers and Social Engineers," *Harvard Law Review* 99, no. 6 (1986): 1315; Balkin and Siegel, "The American Civil Rights Tradition"; Siegel, "The Constitutionalization of Disparate Impact"; Reva B. Siegel, "Blind Justice: Why the Court Refused to Accept Statistical Evidence of Discriminatory Purpose in *McCleskey v. Kemp*—and Some Pathways for Change," *Northwestern University Law Review* 112, no. 6 (2018): 1269–91; Balkin and Siegel, "The American Civil Rights Tradition"; Fiss, "Groups and the Equal Protection Clause."

51. Balkin and Siegel, "The American Civil Rights Tradition," 10.

52. Ibid., 32–33.

53. Ibid., 27.

54. Jeremy Waldron, "Indirect Discrimination," quoted in Mccrudden, "Institutional Discrimination," 304–5.

55. Guest and Milne, *Equality and Discrimination*, 61.

56. Hu, "What Is 'Race' in Algorithmic Discrimination on the Basis of Race?"; Eidelson, *Discrimination and Disrespect*, 55; Young, *Justice and the Politics of Difference*, 194–98.

57. Balkin and Siegel, "The American Civil Rights Tradition," 10.

58. Ibid., 14. As the legal scholar Nancy Down argues: "Discrimination analysis is designed to ensure that no one is denied an equal opportunity within the existing structure; it is not designed to change the structure to the least discriminatory, most opportunity-maximizing pattern." Ronnie J. Steinberg, *Applications of Feminist Legal Theory to Women's Lives: Sex, Violence, Work, and Reproduction* (Philadelphia: Temple University Press, 2012), 560.

59. A similar—but less examined—tension underpins UK discrimination law. Khaitan, *A Theory of Discrimination Law*, chap. 6; Bob Hepple, "The European Legacy of *Brown v. Board of Education*," *University of Illinois Law Review* 2006, no. 3 (2006): 605–23; Danielle S. Allen, *Talking to Strangers: Anxieties of Citizenship since* Brown v. Board of Education (Chicago: University of Chicago Press, 2004); Strauss, "Discriminatory Intent and the Taming of Brown."

60. The government could encourage this ex ante comparison of reasonable alternatives by including a requirement that alternatives be explored as part of procurement contracts. This might encourage companies like Northpointe to explore how best to minimize the disparate impact of risk prediction tools like COMPAS before they are purchased by police departments or courts. In our p(click) case, shifting the burden of proof would require Facebook to invest resources in examining a range of alternative models to predict click probability, including the trade-offs with accuracy produced by different ways of imposing fairness constraints to reduce outcome disparities. Facebook is one of the world's most valuable technology companies—it would not be all that difficult for it to minimize the extent to which its machine learning models exacerbate social inequalities across protected groups.

61. This idea is drawn from Louis Kaplow's distinction between balanced and structured decision-making processes. The disparate impact process is a structured decision-making process, which separates decisions into a series of stages, each isolating a particular component part of the decision. A balanced decision-making process simply weighs the pros and cons of a particular decision, taking all the factors into account in a single moment of decision. Kaplow persuasively argues that structured decision-making is almost always inferior to balanced decision-making. It leads to the assignment of liability when benefits outweigh harms and the failure to assign liability when harms outweigh benefits, and it prohibits the consideration of evidence that is expressly comparative by assigning it to separate stages in the decision-making process. Kaplow, "On the Design of Legal Rules"; Louis Kaplow, "Balancing versus Structured Decision Procedures: Antitrust, Title VII Disparate Impact, and Constitutional Law Strict Scrutiny," *University of Pennsylvania Law Review* 167 (2019). We often use structured decision-making because it turns difficult and uncomfortable questions of judgment into a series of thresholds tests. That is, we often use structured decision-making to make questions of *political* judgment into a questions of *legal* standards about specified thresholds. To some extent, this is inevitable. Laws like antitrust, strict scrutiny in constitutional law, and discrimination law always involve difficult judgments about how particular cases bear on the pursuit of a political goal, but we have become overly fond of obscuring the political judgments required to achieve collective political goals. As Kaplow writes of the second stage of disparate impact, "It seems possible that part of the ambiguity [about] the meaning of the enigmatic requirement of job relatedness and business necessity reflects a reluctance to address contentious issues openly." Kaplow, "Balancing versus Structured Decision Procedures," sec. III; Justice Scalia, Ricci v. DeStefano, 557; Tobia, "Disparate Statistics," 2408; Seigel, "The Constitutionalization of Disparate Impact"; Balkin and Siegel, "The American Civil Rights Tradition."

62. In Hoffman's excellent overview, she cites three such tendencies: "(1) an emphasis on discrete 'bad actors,' (2) single-axis thinking and the centering of disadvantage, and (3) inordinate focus on a limited set of goods," which she then shows crop up in "parallel limits in attempts to address problems of unfairness and bias and data-based discrimination." Anna Lauren Hoff-

mann, "Where Fairness Fails: Data, Algorithms, and the Limits of Antidiscrimination Discourse," *Information, Communication, and Society* 22, no. 7 (2019): 903.

63. Khaitan, *A Theory of Discrimination Law*; Moreau and Hellman, *Philosophical Foundations of Discrimination Law*. This is one of many reasons why Indian ideas of antidiscrimination and equality deserve greater study. B. R. Ambedkar, *Annihilation of Caste: The Annotated Critical Edition*, edited by S. Anand (New Delhi: Navayana, 2014); Sunil Khilnani, *The Idea of India* (New Delhi: Penguin, 2004); Kalpana Kannabirān, *Tools of Justice: Non-Discrimination and the Indian Constitution* (New York: Routledge, 2012).

64. Selmi, "Was the Disparate Impact Theory a Mistake?"; Moreau and Hellman, *Philosophical Foundations of Discrimination Law*, 259. Stokely Carmichael labeled systems that reproduce racial domination as institutional racism, which he described as "less overt, far more subtle, less identifiable in terms of specific individuals committing the acts.... [Institutional racism] originates in the operation of established and respected forces in the society, and thus receives far less public condemnation.... When a black family moves into a home in a white neighborhood and is stoned, burned or routed out, they are victims of an overt act of individual racism which many people will condemn—at least in words. But it is institutional racism that keeps black people locked in dilapidated slum tenements, subject to the daily prey of exploitative slumlords, merchants, loan sharks and discriminatory real estate agents. The society either pretends it does not know of this latter situation or is in fact incapable of doing anything meaningful about it." Stokely Carmichael, *Black Power: The Politics of Liberation in America* (New York: Vintage Books, 1967), 4.

Chapter 4. Political Equality

1. Thomas Jefferson, "Notes on the State of Virginia," in *The Life and Selected Writings of Thomas Jefferson*, edited by Adrienne Koch and William Peden (New York: Modern Library, 1944), 243.

2. Samuel Cornish and John Brown Russwurm, "To Our Patrons," *Freedom's Journal*, March 16, 1827, 1; Melvin L. Rogers, "Race, Domination, and Republicanism," in *Difference without Domination*, edited by Danielle Allen and Rohini Somanthan (Chicago: University of Chicago Press, 2020), 17.

3. W. E. B. Du Bois, *The Souls of Black Folk* (Boston: University of Massachusetts Press, 2018), 11.

4. Nayyirah Waheed, *Salt* (San Bernardino, CA: Nayyirah Waheed, 2013), 140.

5. Meta, "Where We Stand: Actions We're Taking to Advance Racial Justice in Our Company and on Our Platform," Facebook Business, June 21, 2020, https://www.facebook.com /business/news/where-facebook-stands-racial-equality-justice.

6. Kleinberg and Mullainathan, "Simplicity Creates Inequity"; Raghavan et al., "Mitigating Bias in Algorithmic Hiring"; Perdomo et al., "Performative Prediction"; Liu et al., "Delayed Impact of Fair Machine Learning"; Corbett-Davies and Goel, "The Measure and Mismeasure of Fairness"; Chouldechova, "Fair Prediction with Disparate Impact"; Dwork et al., "Fairness through Awareness."

7. Meira Levinson, *No Citizen Left Behind* (Cambridge, MA: Harvard University Press, 2012); Danielle Allen, "A New Theory of Justice: Difference without Domination," in *Difference*

without Domination: Pursuing Justice in Diverse Democracies, edited by Danielle Allen and R. Somanathan (Chicago: University of Chicago Press, 2020); Young, *Justice and the Politics of Difference*; Elizabeth Anderson, *The Imperative of Integration* (Princeton, NJ: Princeton University Press, 2010).

8. Ober, *Demopolis*; Ian Shapiro, *Politics against Domination* (Cambridge, MA: Belknap Press of Harvard University Press, 2016).

9. Allen, *Talking to Strangers*.

10. This notion of co-creation as the grounding of political equality is distinct from the other grounding of political equality, the moral equality of persons. These groundings are not mutually exclusive, but the idea of co-creation adds to the moral equality grounding an explanation of why citizens are political equals in *this* community rather than *that* one. Citizens are moral equals who co-create a common, collectively forged destiny. David Runciman, *How Democracy Ends* (London: Profile Books, 2018), 178; Allen, "A New Theory of Justice"; Pierre Rosanvallon, *The Society of Equals* (Cambridge, MA: Harvard University Press, 2013); Thomas Christiano, *The Constitution of Equality: Democratic Authority and Its Limits* (Oxford: Oxford University Press, 2008).

11. Runciman, *How Democracy Ends*; M. S. Lane, *The Birth of Politics: Eight Greek and Roman Political Ideas and Why They Matter* (Princeton, NJ: Princeton University Press, 2014).

12. Allen, "A New Theory of Justice," 36.

13. Ibid., 38. Not all kinds of domination are equally serious, as Philip Pettit's account of domination often fails to recognize but Ian Shapiro rightly identifies. Pettit defines domination in terms of the capacity for arbitrary interference in the choices of others, without offering tools to distinguish between the content of those choices or how important they are to those who make them. He briefly remarks: "Domination in some areas is likely to be considered more damaging than it is in others; better be dominated in less central activities, for example, rather than in more central ones." He never says, however, what he means. Philip Pettit, *Republicanism: A Theory of Freedom and Government* (Oxford: Oxford University Press, 1997), 58; Pettit, *Republicanism*; Philip Pettit, *Just Freedom: A Moral Compass for a Complex World* (New York: W. W. Norton & Co., 2014); Ian Shapiro, "On Non-Domination," *University of Toronto Law Journal* 62, no. 3 (2012): 293–336, https://doi.org/10.3138/utlj.62.3.293.

14. Levinson, *No Citizen Left Behind*, 48.

15. Consider the different relationships of domination and discrimination to freedom. Nondiscrimination constrains freedom; nondomination is itself a kind of freedom. Nondiscrimination is a negative concept that says nothing about the goals of decision-making beyond avoiding prohibited conduct. By contrast, nondomination is a positive in that it requires a particular kind of freedom to be established and secured. Freedom from domination is freedom from a particular kind of threat to political equality, so nondomination requires the removal of obstacles to political freedom. Allen, "A New Theory of Justice"; Niko Kolodny, "Being under the Power of Others," in *Republicanism and the Future of Democracy*, edited by Genevieve Rousseliere and Yiftah Elazar (Cambridge: Cambridge University Press, 2019); Niko Kolodny, "Rule over None II: Social Equality and the Justification of Democracy," *Philosophy and Public Affairs* 42, no. 4 (2014): 287–336; Shapiro, *Politics against Domination*; Patchen Markell, "The Insufficiency of Non-Domination," *Political Theory* 36, no. 1 (2008): 9–36; Pettit, *Just Freedom*; Philip Pettit, *On the People's Terms: A Republican Theory and Model of Democracy* (Cambridge: Cambridge University Press, 2012).

16. Allen, "A New Theory of Justice," 41.

17. Here it is also helpful to draw the contrast with discrimination. Nondiscrimination duties prohibit the same kind of conduct universally, regardless of the scope of power of a particular institution or the role it plays in reproducing relationships of social and economic equality. The logic of nondiscrimination pits citizens against one another. In a discrimination suit, a court embodying the neutral state must judge whether one party has wronged another; if it has, the court must decide how that party should repay the wronged party. This logic keeps citizens locked in a perpetual state of mutual watchfulness. Political equality derives responsibilities from exploring the role an institution plays in shaping citizens' common life, regardless of whether that institution has committed particular wrongs. It is collective, concrete, and particular. Mike Noon and Edmund Heery, "Institutional Discrimination," in *A Dictionary of Human Resource Management*, edited by Mike Noon and Edmund Heery (Oxford: Oxford University Press, 2008); Ronald L. Craig, *Systemic Discrimination in Employment and the Promotion of Ethnic Equality*, vol. 91 of International Studies in Human Rights (Boston: Martinus Nijhoff, 2007); Khaitan, *A Theory of Discrimination Law*; Moreau and Hellman, *Philosophical Foundations of Discrimination Law*.

18. Justice John Roberts, plurality opinion, Parents Involved in Community Schools v. Seattle School District, 551 U.S. 701 (2007). As one US judge argued, if an institution "provides benefits to some members of our society and denies benefits to others based on race or ethnicity . . . except in the narrowest of circumstances, the Constitution bars such classifications as a denial to particular individuals, of any race or ethnicity, of 'the equal protection of the laws.' The dangers of such classifications are clear. They endorse race-based reasoning and the conception of a nation divided into racial blocs, thus contributing to an escalation of racial hostility and conflict. . . . Such policies may embody stereotypes that treat individuals as the produce of their race, evaluating their thoughts and efforts—their very worth as citizens—according to a criterion barred to the Government by history and the Constitution." Miller v. Johnson, 515 U.S. 900 (1995); Shaw v. Reno, 509 U.S. 630 (1993).

19. William Shakespeare, *The Merchant of Venice*, edited by John Drakakis (London: Arden Shakespeare, 2011), act III, scene I, 49–61.

20. Ibram X. Kendi, *How to Be an Antiracist* (New York: One World, 2019), 9.

21. Beverly Daniel Tatum, *Why Are All the Black Kids Sitting Together in the Cafeteria? And Other Conversations about Race* (New York: Basic Books, 1997), 12.

22. Justice Sonia Sotomayor dissent, Schuette v. Coalition to Defend Affirmative Action, 572 U.S. 291 (2014).

23. Fiss, "Groups and the Equal Protection Clause," 129, 135. As Elizabeth Anderson writes, the color-blind principle "has no direct application in our nonideal world. The best way to achieve it may even be to adopt race-conscious integrative policies." Anderson, *The Imperative of Integration*, 156. Anderson quotes one assertion by Supreme Court justice Potter Stewart in 1980: "The color of a person's skin and the country of his origin are immutable facts," he begins, "that bear no relation to ability, disadvantage, moral culpability, or any other characteristics of constitutionally permissible interest to government." The first assertion is true but not obviously important. The second is patently false. As the disparities produced by machine learning models often illustrate, the color of a person's skin is closely related to ability, disadvantage, and other relevant characteristics like the risk of default, crime rates, or click probability, because for much

of American history race has been a category on the basis of which Black people have been treated differently and made subject to structures of domination and oppression. Fullilove v. Klutznick, 448 U.S. 448 (1980).

24. Sandra Fredman, "Equality: A New Generation?," *Industrial Law Journal* (London) 30, no. 2 (2001): 223–25.

25. Evadné Grant, "Dignity and Equality," *Human Rights Law Review* 7, no. 2 (2007): 320.

26. Justice Blackmun, Regents of the University of California v. Bakke, 438.

27. Anderson, *The Imperative of Integration*, 158; Hu, "What Is 'Race' in Algorithmic Discrimination on the Basis of Race?" Ronald Dworkin describes this as the difference between equality before the law and equality through law. Ronald Dworkin, "What Is Equality? Part 3: The Place of Liberty," *Iowa Law Review* 73 (1987): 1.

28. Justice Scalia, Ricci v. DeStefano, 557; Reva B. Siegel, "The Constitutionalization of Disparate Impact—Court-Centered and Popular Pathways," *California Law Review* 106, no. 6 (2018): 2001–22; Siegel, "Blind Justice."

29. Aristotle, *Nicomachean Ethics*, bk. V; Allen, *The World of Prometheus*, chap. 11; Schauer, "On Treating Unlike Cases Alike"; Sandra Fredman, "Substantive Equality Revisited," *International Journal of Constitutional Law* 14, no. 3 (2016): 712–38; Catharine A. MacKinnon, "Substantive Equality Revisited: A Reply to Sandra Fredman," *International Journal of Constitutional Law* 14, no. 3 (2016): 739–46; Sandra Fredman, "Substantive Equality Revisited: A Rejoinder to Catharine MacKinnon," *International Journal of Constitutional Law* 14, no. 3 (2016): 747–51; Catharine A. MacKinnon, "Substantive Equality Revisited: A Rejoinder to Sandra Fredman," *International Journal of Constitutional Law* 15, no. 4 (2017): 1174–77.

30. Renée Lewis, "Black British History Is Just as Important as African American History," *Orbital*, October 23, 2020, https://theorbital.co.uk/black-british-history-is-just-as-important-as -african-american-history/; Dave Gunning and Abigail Ward, "Tracing Black America in Black British Culture," *Atlantic Studies* 6, no. 2 (2009): 149–58. Another example is the term "BAME" (Black, Asian, and minority ethnic), which is commonplace in well-meaning British society. To put Indians and Pakistanis in the same category would be laughable in India and Pakistan. Richard Ford, "Ethnicity Labels Are Divisive, Says Phillips," *The Times*, May 21, 2015, https:// www.thetimes.co.uk/article/ethnicity-labels-are-divisive-says-phillips-qptswxk3l93; Lawrence A. Blum, *"I'm Not a Racist, but . . .": The Moral Quandary of Race* (Ithaca, NY: Cornell University Press, 2002); George M. Fredrickson, *Racism: A Short History* (Princeton, NJ: Princeton University Press, 2015); Carol Chapnick Mukhopadhyay, *How Real Is Race? A Sourcebook on Race, Culture, and Biology* (Lanham, MD: Rowman & Littlefield, 2014); Levinson, *No Citizen Left Behind*, chap. 2. Whites are much less likely to see themselves as being defined by their race and to acknowledge the ways in which their own experiences are shaped by race. Thomas M. Shapiro, *The Hidden Cost of Being African American: How Wealth Perpetuates Inequality* (New York: Oxford University Press, 2004); Reni Eddo-Lodge, *Why I'm No Longer Talking to White People about Race* (London: Bloomsbury, 2018); Hayward Clarissa Rile, *How Americans Make Race: Stories, Institutions, Spaces* (New York: Cambridge University Press, 2013); Kjartan Páll Sveinsson, "A Tale of Two Englands: 'Race' and Violent Crime in the Press," Runnymede Trust, 2008.

31. Du Bois, *The Souls of Black Folk*, 4.

32. Levinson, *No Citizen Left Behind*, 85.

33. Justice Scalia, Ricci v. DeStefano, 557.

34. Michael C. Lens, "Measuring the Geography of Opportunity," *Progress in Human Geography* 41, no. 1 (2017): 3–25; Philip McCann, *The UK Regional-National Economic Problem: Geography, Globalisation, and Governance* (London: Routledge, 2016); Peter Edward and Andy Sumner, "The Geography of Inequality: Where and by How Much Has Income Distribution Changed since 1990?," Working Paper 341 (Washington, DC: Center for Global Development, September 2013), https://www.cgdev.org/sites/default/files/edward-sumner-geography-of-inequality_1_2.pdf; Abhijit V. Banerjee and Esther Duflo, *Good Economics for Hard Times* (New York: Public Affairs, 2019); Benjamin Austin, Edward Glaeser, and Lawrence Summers, "Jobs for the Heartland: Place-Based Policies in 21st-Century America," *Brookings Papers on Economic Activity* (Spring 2018): 151–255. Susan Sturm offers a compelling account of how to reframe affirmative action in education by "(1) nesting it within an effort to transform institutions to ensure full participation, (2) shifting from rewarding privilege to cultivating potential and increasing mobility, and (3) building partnerships and enabling systemic approaches to increasing educational access and success. . . . These structural approaches are less likely to trigger strict scrutiny from the courts, and will foster the inquiry needed to document the need for affirmative action in admissions and expand the justifications for race-conscious approaches." Susan P. Sturm, "Reframing Affirmative Action: From Diversity to Mobility and Full Participation," *University of Chicago Law Review* (October 30, 2020), https://lawreviewblog.uchicago.edu/2020/10/30/aa-sturm/.

35. Danielle Allen, "Talent Is Everywhere: Using ZIP Codes and Merit to Enhance Diversity," in *The Future of Affirmative Action: New Paths to Higher Education Diversity after Fisher v. University of Texas*, edited by Richard D. Kahlenberg (New York: Century Foundation Press, 2014), 151; Michael J. Sandel, *The Tyranny of Merit: What's Become of the Common Good?* (New York: Farrar, Straus and Giroux, 2020).

36. Paul A. Jargowsky and Natasha O. Tursi, "Concentrated Disadvantage," in *International Encyclopedia of the Social and Behavioral Sciences*, 2nd ed., edited by James D. Wright (Amsterdam: Elsevier, 2015).

37. Roberts, "Digitizing the Carceral State," 1704–7; Dorothy E. Roberts, *Shattered Bonds: The Color of Child Welfare* (New York: Basic Books, 2002); Armando Lara-Millán, "Public Emergency Room Overcrowding in the Era of Mass Imprisonment," *American Sociological Review* 79, no. 5 (2014): 866–87.

38. Ian Shapiro, "On Non-Domination," *University of Toronto Law Journal* 62, no. 3 (2012): 294; Shapiro, *Politics against Domination*; Ian Shapiro, *Democratic Justice* (New Haven, CT: Yale University Press, 1999).

39. Ian Shapiro, *The Real World of Democratic Theory* (Princeton, NJ: Princeton University Press, 2011), 255–56.

40. See the excellent book by Chiara Cordelli, *The Privatized State* (Princeton, NJ: Princeton University Press, 2020). Virginia Eubanks, "A Child Abuse Prediction Model Fails Poor Families," *Wired*, January 15, 2018, https://www.wired.com/story/excerpt-from-automating-inequality/.

41. These judgments are fraught, not least because "Blacks can use public services" has been an all too common response to allegations of discrimination and redlining, often accompanied by the systematic defunding of those very public services. Another salient consideration is the

cost of getting it wrong, which is clearly much less severe in the Uber case. Another consideration might be how easily power conferred by a good or service can be translated from one sphere to another. Another might be whether there are commercial incentives for a service that addresses racial disparities, such as an app that caters to Black passengers by hiring drivers who do not hold racial stereotypes. Michael Walzer, *Spheres of Justice: A Defense of Pluralism and Equality* (New York: Basic Books, 1983), chaps. 1, 12.

42. Aileen McColgan, *Discrimination, Equality, and the Law* (London: Hart Publishing/ Bloomsbury Publishing, 2014), 97. McColgan continues: "If equality demands unequal treatment in proportion to inequality, the fact of pre-existing disadvantage, under-representation and/ or particular need can be regarded as justifying, even demanding, positive action." Michael Feldman, Sorelle Friedler, John Moeller, Carlos Scheidegger, and Suresh Venkatasubramanian, "Certifying and Removing Disparate Impact," arXiv:1412.3756v3 [stat.ML], December 11, 2014, revised February 29, 2015, and July 16, 2015, 259–68, https://doi.org/10.48550/arXiv.1412.3756; Zachary C. Lipton, Alexandra Chouldechova, and Julian McAuley, "Does Mitigating ML's Impact Disparity Require Treatment Disparity?," arXiv:1711.07076v3 [stat.ML], November 19, 2017, revised February 28, 2018, and January 11, 2019, https://doi.org/10.48550/arXiv.1711.07076.

43. Jeff Jacoby, "California's Colorblind Proposition," *Boston Globe*, August 27, 1996, http://www.jeffjacoby.com/8987/california-colorblind-proposition; Mike Comeaux, "Initiative Revives Debate on Affirmative Action," *Los Angeles Daily News*, January 30, 1995; Matthew D. Reade, "Talking about Affirmative Action," introduction to "Affirmative Action at a Crossroads" series, *University of Chicago Law Review*, October 30, 2020, https://lawreviewblog.uchicago.edu/2020/10/30/aa-series/; Assemblyman Bernie Richter and Mayor Willie Brown, "California Civil Rights Initiative Debate," *C-SPAN*, October 27, 1996, https://www.c-span.org/video/?76283-1/california-civil-rights-initiative-debate; Reade, "Talking about Affirmative Action."

44. Tobler, "Limits and Potential of the Concept of Indirect Discrimination," 51; Justice Ackermann, majority opinion, National Coalition for Gay and Lesbian Equality v. Minister of Justice and Others (Constitutional Court of South Africa, 1998); McColgan, *Discrimination, Equality, and the Law*, 78, quoting Minister of Finance and Other v. Van Heerden, CCT 63/03 (2004); Fredman, "Addressing Disparate Impact"; McColgan, *Discrimination, Equality, and the Law*, chap. 3, and 8–9. PEDs could be modeled on the UK Equality Act's provisions for deliberately advancing equality, although it would significantly extend them. Until the Equality Act of 2010, UK law approached positive action, positive duties, and other measures explicitly designed to promote substantive equality as exceptions to the "general principle of non-discrimination." "UK law [did] not permit 'reverse discrimination'" other than for narrowly defined purposes, such as "positive measures to afford access to training and to encourage under-represented groups to take up employment." The EA then established the public sector equality duty (PSED), which applied to public bodies and nonpublic bodies performing public functions in relation to those functions. The PSED requires such bodies to give "due regard" to a number of statutory needs, including the need to eliminate unlawful discrimination, advance equality of opportunity, and foster good relations between persons defined by reference to protected characteristics. No matter which functions the relevant bodies are performing, adequate consideration must be given to equality defined in terms of these statutory needs. Catherine Barnard and Bob Hepple, "Substantive Equality," *Cambridge Law Journal* 59, no. 3 (2000): 576.

45. George Stephanopoulos, Christopher F. Edley, and US Executive Office of the President, *Affirmative Action Review: Report to the President* (Washington, DC: Executive Office of the President, 1995); John Valery White, "What Is Affirmative Action?," *Tulane Law Review* 78 (2004): 2117–2329.

46. Eubanks, *Automating Inequality*, 190.

47. Tobler, "Limits and Potential of the Concept of Indirect Discrimination," 52.

48. As Girardeu Spann convincingly argues, there is a long history of Supreme Court decisions blocking permissible actions to advance racial justice, by both public and private actors. "In the 1842 case of *Prigg v. Pennsylvania*, the Court invoked the fugitive slave provisions of the Constitution and a federal statute to invalidate a Pennsylvania law that prohibited the forceable removal from the state of any person claimed to be an escaped slave without a prior hearing to establish ownership. The decision enabled continuation of the practice depicted in the 2013 historical movie *12 Years a Slave*, whereby White slave dealers would kidnap free Blacks in the North and sell them into slavery in the South. In the infamous 1857 *Dred Scott v. Sandford* decision, the Court . . . held that Blacks could not be citizens within the meaning of the United States Constitution. The decision was one of the factors that lead to the Civil War, and its citizenship holding was overruled by the Fourteenth Amendment's grant of natural-born citizenship—a grant that President Trump has said he would like to end." Girardeu A. Spann, "Good Trouble," *University of Chicago Law Review*, October 30, 2020, https://lawreviewblog.uchicago.edu/2020/10/30/aa-spann/.

49. There are three kinds of affirmative action: facilitative, preferential, and indirect. Facilitative affirmative action affects who is at the starting line, picking out members of disadvantaged groups to broaden the pool of applicants to a job or college program. This was the original meaning of affirmative action in the United States. Preferential affirmative action affects who wins the race, by favoring individuals who are members of protected groups at the moment of decision-making. This can be achieved through quotas; through tiebreaker rules, in which a candidate from a protected group is favored over another candidate when both are equally well qualified; by offering numerical advantages to members of a protected group by boosting their scores; or by considering group membership as one factor among others in an individualized process. Finally, indirect affirmative action policies are facially neutral but targeted at disadvantaged groups, either by preferential policies, such as using geography as a proxy for race, or by creating conditions of inclusion that benefit disadvantaged groups, like building ramps in public spaces or offering gender-neutral parental leave. Algorithmic affirmative action is the preferential kind. Urs Linder, "A Society of Equals: Affirmative Action beyond the Distributive Paradigm," in *Difference without Domination*, edited by Danielle Allen and Rohini Somanthan (Chicago: University of Chicago Press, 2020).

50. I do not intend to suggest the normative irrelevance of history, but simply to locate the content of the substantive obligation in a set of relations to obtain between citizens going forward. The injustices of the past may well be relevant to filling out the content of that obligation in particular times and particular places. It is not that the past should not matter in justifying affirmative action, but that the way it should matter should be defined by reference to the future.

51. Linder, "A Society of Equals."

52. Allen, "Talent Is Everywhere."

53. Sturm, "Reframing Affirmative Action."

54. "There is no sound reason in justice or constitutional law why any agency in a position to dismantle unjust systems of racial stratification may not do so using race conscious means, whether these systems are their own creation or that of other agents, and even if these systems are not illegal. The state has interests in justice and democracy in counteracting legal 'discrimination in contact' by actively promoting the racial integration of schools and workplaces." Anderson, *The Imperative of Integration*, 167.

55. Alan Smith and Federica Cocco, "Race and America: Why Data Matters," *Financial Times*, July 23, 2020, https://www.ft.com/content/156f770a-1d77-4f6b-8616-192fb58e3735; Whitney Battle-Baptiste and Britt Rusert, eds., *W.E.B. Du Bois's Data Portraits: Visualizing Black America* (Princeton, NJ: Princeton Architectural Press, 2018).

56. Viljoen, "Democratic Data."

57. PEDs point to an underlying tension between privacy and the advancement of equality. At present, privacy laws that prohibit institutions from gathering and processing protected data constrain the practical application of statistical techniques that promote equity in machine learning. There is good evidence that requiring the collection of sensitive data reduces inequalities over time, because it forces organizations to acknowledge and confront those inequalities. For instance, following amendments to the Home Mortgage Disclosure Act (HMDA) that required the collection of sensitive data, mortgage lending to low-income and minority communities increased, as did public scrutiny and oversight of lending practices. This is intuitive: what is not seen cannot be addressed. More permissive privacy laws will not guarantee that organizations implement these techniques, but without access to sensitive data for clearly defined purposes, they cannot. Miranda Bogen and Aaron Rieke, "Awareness in Practice: Tensions in Access to Sensitive Attribute Data for Antidiscrimination," conference on Fairness, Accountability, and Transparency, Barcelona, January 2020, 9, https://doi.org/10.1145/3351095.3372877.

58. Dwork et al., "Fairness through Awareness," 2, 11–12.

59. Because PEDs would enable organizations to apply context-sensitive judgments about equal treatment, they would need to be accompanied by more robust structures for securing accountability, auditability, and transparency. These could draw on existing frameworks from government action uses of affirmative action that focus on evidence-based assessment and on whether the use of protected characteristics to reduce outcome disparities has a strong basis in evidence. Institutions could be required to explain to citizens and regulators in concrete terms how they are interpreting and implementing equal treatment in their decision-making—for instance, by using sandboxing structures that permit industry to innovate and experiment with methods of building machine learning models that advance racial justice and gender equality, while enabling regulators to set defined parameters, observe the process of experimentation, and interrogate the results. Daniel E. Ho and Alice Xiang, "Affirmative Algorithms: The Legal Grounds for Fairness as Awareness," *University of Chicago Law Review*, October 30, 2020, https://lawreviewblog.uchicago.edu/2020/10/30/aa-ho-xiang/.

60. The AIEA could establish duties similar to notices issued by the Consumer Financial Protection Bureau (CFPB), except that the AIEA would aim to protect people as citizens rather than simply as consumers. CFPB, "Consumer Financial Protection Bureau Issues No Action Letter to Facilitate the Use of Artificial Intelligence for Pricing and Underwriting Loans," November 30, 2020, https://www.consumerfinance.gov/about-us/newsroom/consumer-financial-protection-bureau-issues-no-action-letter-facilitate-use-artificial-intelligence-pricing-and

-underwriting-loans/; Yvette D. Clarke, Cory Booker, and Ron Wyden, "Algorithmic Accountability Act of 2019," Pub. L. No. H.R. 2231 (2019), https://www.wyden.senate.gov/imo/media/doc/Algorithmic%20Accountability%20Act%20of%202019%20Bill%20Text.pdf; Josh Simons, Anna Thomas, and Abigail Gilbert, "Mind the Gap: The Final Report of the Equality Task Force," Institute for the Future of Work, October 26, 2020, https://www.ifow.org/publications/mind-the-gap-the-final-report-of-the-equality-task-force.

61. Civil rights define the content of the goods and services necessary for citizens to participate as equals in their political community. West, *Civil Rights*, 85. Civil rights are best understood as "rights of inclusion in civil society, or rights to enter, which are necessary for individual flourishing and dependent on positive law for their enjoyment." West, *Civil Rights*, 81; Anderson, *The Imperative of Integration*; Elizabeth Anderson, *Private Government: How Employers Rule Our Lives (and Why We Don't Talk about It)* (Princeton, NJ: Princeton University Press, 2017).

62. The AIEA could involve more widespread use of equality impact assessments (EIAs). There is mixed evidence about the practical efficacy of EIAs, but they illustrate the salient characteristics of an evaluation of the equality and civil rights implications of a machine learning system. EIAs would include an explicit statement of the aim of a decision-making system; how the outcome that a model predicts relates to that aim; summaries of the model's accuracy, performance, and calibration; and basic summary statistics about outcomes across different social groups. Danielle Citron and Frank Pasquale, "The Scored Society: Due Process for Automated Predictions," *Washington Law Review* 89, no. 1 (2014): 1–33; Gerard Ritsema van Eck, "Algorithmic Mapmaking in Smart Cities: Data Protection Impact Assessments as a Means of Protection for Groups," in *Good Data*, edited by Angela Daly, S. Kate Devitt, and Monique Mann (Amsterdam: Institute of Network Cultures, 2019), https://www.rug.nl/research/portal/en/publications/algorithmic-mapmaking-in-smart-cities(c48e4f1c-b668-469a-abc8-71069b7af6ec).html; Dillon Reisman, Jason Schultz, Kate Crawford, and Meredith Whittaker, "Algorithmic Impact Assessments: A Practical Framework for Public Agency Accountability," AI Now, April 2018, https://ainowinstitute.org/aiareport2018.pdf; Simon Reader, "Data Protection Impact Assessments and AI," Information Commissioner's Office (ICO), October 23, 2019, https://ico.org.uk/about-the-ico/news-and-events/ai-blog-data-protection-impact-assessments-and-ai/; Swee Leng Harris, "Data Protection Impact Assessments as Rule of Law Governance Mechanisms," *Data and Policy* 2 (2020); Reuben Binns, "Data Protection Impact Assessments: A Meta-Regulatory Approach," *International Data Privacy Law* 7, no. 1 (2017): 22–35.

63. If the "passion for racial equality" is to evolve "into meaningful social change," the legislature must "retrieve its social policymaking power," recognizing that it too has "a moral obligation, a mission and a mandate, to speak up, speak out and get in good trouble." Spann, "Good Trouble"; Ibram X. Kendi, "Pass an Anti-Racist Constitutional Amendment," *Politico*, 2019, https://politico.com/interactives/2019/how-to-fix-politics-in-america/inequality/pass-an-anti-racist-constitutional-amendment/; West, *Civil Rights*.

64. "The United Kingdom has traditionally done so; perhaps not always to universal satisfaction, but certainly without forfeiting its title to be a democracy." Lord Hoffman, Matadeen v. Pointu (AC 1999).

65. Executive Office of the President, "Big Data: A Report on Algorithmic Systems, Opportunity, and Civil Rights," May 2016, https://obamawhitehouse.archives.gov/sites/default/files/microsites/ostp/2016_0504_data_discrimination.pdf.

Chapter 5. Facebook and Google (The Politics of Machine Learning II)

1. James Fenimore Cooper, *The American Democrat*, quoted in Michael Schudson, *Discovering the News: A Social History of American Newspapers* (New York: Basic Books, 1978), 13.

2. John Dewey, *The Public and Its Problems: An Essay in Political Inquiry* (Athens, OH: Swallow Press, 2016), 132.

3. John Perry Barlow, "A Declaration of Independence of Cyberspace," Electronic Frontier Foundation, February 8, 1996, https://www.eff.org/cyberspace-independence.

4. Antoine Allen, "The 'Three Black Teenagers' Search Shows It Is Society, Not Google, That Is Racist," *Guardian*, June 10, 2016, https://www.theguardian.com/commentisfree/2016/jun/10/three-black-teenagers-google-racist-tweet.

5. Elle Hunt, "'Three Black Teenagers': Anger as Google Image Search Shows Police Mugshots," *Guardian*, June 9, 2016, https://www.theguardian.com/technology/2016/jun/09/three-black-teenagers-anger-as-google-image-search-shows-police-mugshots.

6. This book was written before Facebook changed its name to Meta, and its argument refers to the Facebook platform, on mobile and desktop, not to other Meta products.

7. Noble, *Algorithms of Oppression*.

8. Senator Elizabeth Warren caused some controversy by citing this statistic during her presidential campaign. It comes from analysis of Parse.ly's network by a blogger in 2017. There are several ways to measure how Facebook and Google exert power over other websites and publishers, all of which have different strengths and weaknesses. Elizabeth Warren, "Here's How We Can Break up Big Tech," *Medium*, March 8, 2019, https://medium.com/@teamwarren/heres-how-we-can-break-up-big-tech-9ad9e0da324c; André Staltz, "The Web Began Dying in 2014, Here's How," October 30, 2017, https://staltz.com/the-web-began-dying-in-2014-heres-how.html; Alec Stapp, "Any Way You Measure It, Warren Is Wrong to Claim 'Facebook and Google Account for 70% of All Internet Traffic,'" Truth on the Market, October 2, 2019, https://truthonthemarket.com/2019/10/01/any-way-you-measure-it-warren-is-wrong-to-claim-facebook-and-google-account-for-70-of-all-internet-traffic/.

9. A lot of writing about Facebook and Google mentions their technologies in passing. Jamie Bartlett, for instance, mentions this "mysterious . . . tech infrastructure" in a footnote in the middle of *The People vs. Tech*, He recognizes the importance of the logic of "one of the most powerful and least-understood aspects of online life," but overlooks the vital importance of debating how we should exercise control over this tech infrastructure in regulating companies like Facebook and Google. Jamie Bartlett, *The People vs. Tech: How the Internet Is Killing Democracy (and How We Save It)* (London: Penguin, 2018), 153–54.

10. This chapter stands on the shoulders of several excellent books that explore Facebook's and Google's machine learning models and ranking systems. Frank Pasquale, *New Laws of Robotics: Defending Human Expertise in the Age of AI* (Cambridge, MA: Belknap Press of Harvard University Press, 2020); Tarleton Gillespie, *Custodians of the Internet: Platforms, Content Moderation, and the Hidden Decisions That Shape Social Media* (New Haven, CT: Yale University Press, 2018); Siva Vaidhyanathan, *Antisocial Media: How Facebook Disconnects Us and Undermines Democracy* (New York: Oxford University Press, 2018); Siva Vaidhyanathan, *The Googlization of Everything (and Why We Should Worry)* (Berkeley: University of California Press, 2011); Noble, *Algorithms of Oppression*; Alexander M. Campbell Halavais, *Search Engine Society* (Cam-

bridge: Polity Press, 2017); Helen Fay Nissenbaum, *Privacy in Context: Technology, Policy, and the Integrity of Social Life* (Stanford, CA: Stanford Law Books, 2010).

11. Elisa Shearer and Katerina Eva Matsa, "News Use across Social Media Platforms 2018," Pew Research Center, September 10, 2018, https://www.journalism.org/2018/09/10/news-use -across-social-media-platforms-2018/; Jigsaw Research, *News Consumption in the UK: 2018*, Ofcom, 2018, https://www.ofcom.org.uk/__data/assets/pdf_file/0024/116529/news -consumption-2018.pdf.

12. Franklin Foer, *World without Mind: The Existential Threat of Big Tech* (New York: Penguin Press, 2017).

13. Max Gubin, Wayne Kao, David Vickrey, and Alexey Maykov, "News Feed Ranking Model Based on Social Information of Viewer," US Patent 9582786B2, issued February 28, 2017, https:// patents.google.com/patent/US9582786B2/en.

14. Adam Green, "Facebook's 52,000 Data Points on Each Person Reveal Something Shocking about Its Future," KimKomando, September 17, 2018, https://www.komando.com/social -media/facebooks-52000-data-points-on-each-person-reveal-something-shocking-about-its -future/489188/.

15. From August to November 2013. Robinson Meyer, "Why Are Upworthy Headlines Suddenly Everywhere?," *Atlantic*, December 8, 2013, https://www.theatlantic.com/technology /archive/2013/12/why-are-upworthy-headlines-suddenly-everywhere/282048/; Charlie Warzel, "Facebook Drives Massive New Surge of Traffic to Publishers," *BuzzFeed News*, November 20, 2013, https://www.buzzfeednews.com/article/charliewarzel/out-of-the-blue-facebook -is-now-driving-enormous-traffic-to; Varun Kacholia and Minwen Ji, "Helping You Find More News to Talk About," Meta, December 3, 2013, https://about.fb.com/news/2013/12/news-feed -fyi-helping-you-find-more-news-to-talk-about/.

16. John Herrman, "Inside Facebook's (Totally Insane, Unintentionally Gigantic, Hyperpartisan) Political-Media Machine," *New York Times Magazine*, August 24, 2016, https://www .nytimes.com/2016/08/28/magazine/inside-facebooks-totally-insane-unintentionally -gigantic-hyperpartisan-political-media-machine.html; Nicholas Diakopoulos, *Automating the News: How Algorithms Are Rewriting the Media* (Cambridge, MA: Harvard University Press, 2019), fig. 5.2; Will Oremus, "The Great Facebook Crash," *Slate*, June 27, 2018, https://slate.com /technology/2018/06/facebooks-retreat-from-the-news-has-painful-for-publishers-including -slate.html; George Upper and G. S. Hair, "Confirmed: Facebook's Recent Algorithm Change Is Crushing Conservative Sites, Boosting Liberals," *Western Journal*, March 13, 2018, https://www .westernjournal.com/confirmed-facebooks-recent-algorithm-change-is-crushing-conservative -voices-boosting-liberals/.

17. Mark Zuckerberg, "Meaningful Social Interactions," Facebook post, January 11, 2018, https://www.facebook.com/zuck/posts/10104413015393571.

18. Lara Hazard Owen, "One Year in, Facebook's Big Algorithm Change Has Spurred an Angry, Fox News–Dominated—and Very Engaged!—News Feed," Nieman Lab, March 15, 2019, https://www.niemanlab.org/2019/03/one-year-in-facebooks-big-algorithm-change-has -spurred-an-angry-fox-news-dominated-and-very-engaged-news-feed/.

19. Social media, Cox continued, "is tied up in the richness and complexity of social life. As its builders we must endeavor to understand its impact—all the good, and all the bad—and take up the daily work of bending it towards the positive, and towards the good. This is our

greatest responsibility." Chris Cox, "Farewell Note," Facebook post, March 14, 2019, https://www.facebook.com/photo.php?fbid=10104525464389883&set=a.692319249513&type=3&theater.

20. Vaidhyanathan, *Antisocial Media*, chaps. 1, 7; Gillespie, *Custodians of the Internet*, 7; Michael A. Devito, "From Editors to Algorithms: A Values-Based Approach to Understanding Story Selection in the Facebook News Feed," *Digital Journalism* 5, no. 6 (2017): 753–73; Taina Bucher, "Want to Be on the Top? Algorithmic Power and the Threat of Invisibility on Facebook," *New Media and Society* 14, no. 7 (2012): 1164–80.

21. This hypothetical example comes from a system used by Google. Ivan Mehta, "Google's AI to Detect Toxic Comments Can Be Easily Fooled with 'Love,'" The Next Web, September 11, 2018, https://thenextweb.com/artificial-intelligence/2018/09/11/googles-hate-speech-ai-easily-fooled/; Joni Salminen, Sercan Sengün, Juan Corporan, Soon-gyo Jung, and Bernard J. Jansen, "Topic-Driven Toxicity: Exploring the Relationship between Online Toxicity and News Topics," *PLOS ONE* 15, no. 2 (February 21, 2020): e0228723. Research suggests that examples are particularly important in guiding the judgments of human content moderators. Minna Ruckenstein and Linda Lisa Maria Turunen, "Re-humanizing the Platform: Content Moderators and the Logic of Care," *New Media and Society*, September 19, 2019, https://doi.org/10.1177/1461444819875990.

22. John Rawls, "The Sense of Justice," *Philosophical Review* 72, no. 3 (1963): 281–305.

23. Jeffrey Dean (Google Senior Fellow), "Building Software Systems at Google and Lessons Learned," talk at Stanford University, November 10, 2010, https://www.youtube.com/watch?v=modXC5IWTJI; John Battelle, *The Search: How Google and Its Rivals Rewrote the Rules of Business and Transformed Our Culture* (New York: Portfolio, 2005), chap. 1; Jon Mitchell, "How Google Search Really Works," readwrite, February 29, 2012, https://readwrite.com/2012/02/29/interview_changing_engines_mid-flight_qa_with_goog/; Parse.Ly, "Parse.Ly's Network Referrer Dashboard," https://www.parse.ly/resources/data-studies/referrer-dashboard (accessed March 29, 2020); Diakopoulos, *Automating the News*, 179; Media Insight Project, "How Americans Get Their News," American Press Institute, March 17, 2014, https://www.americanpressinstitute.org/publications/reports/survey-research/how-americans-get-news/; Nic Newman, with Richard Fletcher, Antonis Kalogeropoulos, David A. L. Levy, and Rasmus Kleis Nielsen, *Reuters Institute: Digital News Report 2017*, University of Oxford, Reuters Institute for the Study of Journalism, 2017), https://reutersinstitute.politics.ox.ac.uk/sites/default/files/Digital%20News%20Report%202017%20web_0.pdf.

24. Jon Kleinberg, "Authoritative Sources in a Hyperlinked Environment," *Journal of the ACM* 46, no. 5 (1999): 604, 606.

25. This image is adapted and expanded from Halavais, *Search Engine Society*, 103. The basic structure of the power law distribution is that frequency is inversely proportional to rank, as in earthquakes or city populations. In the context of web results, the top page appears twice as often as the second result, which appears twice as often as the third result, which appears twice as often as the fourth result, and so on. B. A. Huberman, *The Laws of the Web: Patterns in the Ecology of Information* (Cambridge, MA: MIT Press, 2001); Halavais, *Search Engine Society*, 101–3.

26. Kleinberg, "Authoritative Sources in a Hyperlinked Environment," 607, 611.

27. The longer history to PageRank begins in the 1940s with efforts to model the relative importance of different sectors in the US economy, which Kleinberg cited in his "hubs" and

"authorities" paper (ibid.). Page and Brin then drew on Kleinberg. Massimo Franceschet, "PageRank: Standing on the Shoulders of Giants," *Communications of the ACM* 54, no. 6 (2011): 92–101.

28. Lawrence Page, Sergey Brin, Rajeev Motwani, and Terry Winograd, "The PageRank Citation Ranking: Bringing Order to the Web," Technical Report (Stanford, CA: Stanford InfoLab, 1999), 15, 2, http://ilpubs.stanford.edu:8090/422/.

29. Ibid., 15. Google, "Facts about Google and Competition: About Search," November 4, 2011, https://web.archive.org/web/20111104131332/https://www.google.com/competition/howgooglesearchworks.html.

30. In its original form, each page had an initial PageRank of 1, because the sum of PageRank over all the pages was equal to the total number of pages on the web. This soon developed into a probability distribution that summed to 1.

31. Page et al., "The PageRank Citation Ranking," 4.

32. Ibid., 5–6.

33. Sergey Brin and Lawrence Page, "The Anatomy of a Large-Scale Hypertextual Web Search Engine," *Computer Networks and ISDN Systems* 30, no. 1 (1998): 107–17.

34. Page et al., "The PageRank Citation Ranking," 11–12.

35. Ibid., 11.

36. William James, *The Meaning of Truth* (London: Longmans, Green and Co., 1909), preface.

37. Peter H. Lewis, "State of the Art; Searching for Less, Not More," *New York Times*, September 30, 1999, https://www.nytimes.com/1999/09/30/technology/state-of-the-art-searching-for-less-not-more.html.

38. Google has put PageRank through myriad evolutions—for instance, allowing links higher up in a page to count for more. The search engine optimization (SEO) industry examines Google's patents and makes inferences about how Google's search ranking system works. Francesca Arrigo, Desmond Higham, and Vanni Noferini, "Non-Backtracking PageRank," *Journal of Scientific Computing* 80, no. 3 (2019): 1419–37; Bill Slawski, "Google's Reasonable Surfer: How Link Value May Differ Based on Link and Document Features and User Data," *SEO by the Sea*, May 11, 2010, http://www.seobythesea.com/2010/05/googles-reasonable-surfer-how-the-value-of-a-link-may-differ-based-upon-link-and-document-features-and-user-data/; Jennifer Slegg, "Google Removing PageRank from Google Toolbar," The SEM Post, March 8, 2016, http://www.thesempost.com/google-removing-pagerank-from-toolbar/; John Mueller, *English Google Webmaster Central Office-Hours Hangout*, Google, 2014, https://www.youtube.com/watch?v=-GlxLlpm3Ew&feature=emb_title.

39. Google Search Central, "More Guidance on Building High-Quality Sites," May 6, 2011, https://webmasters.googleblog.com/2011/05/more-guidance-on-building-high-quality.html; Pete Walter, "Google Penguin Nearly Killed My Business," *Telegraph*, December 1, 2014, https://www.telegraph.co.uk/finance/businessclub/sales/11265882/Google-Penguin-nearly-killed-my-business.html.

40. Paško Bilić notes that in 2012 Google ran 118,812 content quality evaluations, 665 of which were eventually approved for launch and included within the ranking algorithm—almost two a day. Paško Bilić, "Search Algorithms, Hidden Labour, and Information Control," *Big Data and Society* 3, no. 1 (2016): 6.

41. Google, *General Guidelines*, December 5, 2019, 6, https://static.googleusercontent.com /media/guidelines.raterhub.com/en//searchqualityevaluatorguidelines.pdf.

42. Ibid., 8.

43. Bilić, "Search Algorithms, Hidden Labour, and Information Control"; Gillespie, *Custodians of the Internet*, chaps. 5, 7; Devito, "From Editors to Algorithms."

44. Several types of deep learning approaches are used at Google, including convolutional neural networks (CNNs). Instead of developing machine learning models trained to interpret each component of an image—the edges, colors, shapes, and so on—CNNs themselves learn the best approach to identifying the features of an image that matter most. CNNs are useful for understanding or classifying data that have a very large number of dimensions. Before RankBrain was introduced, Google's search was mostly powered by signals chosen and refined by engineers. After an experiment in which Google's machine learning team used clicks to evaluate how well a website matches a query, they found machine learning to be a powerful tool; machine learning has now eclipsed information retrieval as the core focus of Google's computer scientists. Google and Facebook now fiercely compete for graduates in computer science who specialize in machine learning and are experienced in math and statistics rather than in writing lines of code. Steven Levy, "How Google Is Remaking Itself as a 'Machine Learning First' Company," *Wired*, June 22, 2016, https://www.wired.com/2016/06/how -google-is-remaking-itself-as-a-machine-learning-first-company/. Google also harnesses our collective ability to spell by grouping near-misses, sometimes correcting British to American English. Roberto De Virgilio, Francesco Guerra, and Yannis Velegrakis, *Semantic Search over the Web* (Berlin: Springer, 2012).

45. Tarleton Gillespie, "Algorithmically Recognizable: Santorum's Google Problem, and Google's Santorum Problem," *Information, Communication, and Society: The Social Power of Algorithms* 20, no. 1 (2017): 63–80.

46. Santorum was defending laws against private sexual acts. Associated Press, "Excerpt from Santorum Interview," April 23, 2003, https://usatoday30.usatoday.com/news/washington /2003-04-23-santorum-excerpt_x.htm. After Savage denounced the comments in the *New York Times*, a reader suggested that Savage respond by naming a sex act after Santorum. Savage received three thousand suggestions from his readers and followers. Dan Savage, "GOP Hypocrisy," *New York Times*, April 25, 2003, https://www.nytimes.com/2003/04/25/opinion/gop -hypocrisy.html; Dan Savage, "Savage Love," The Stranger, June 12, 2003, https://www .thestranger.com/seattle/SavageLove?oid=14566.

47. John Sutter, "Santorum Asks Google to Clean up Search Results for His Name," CNN, September 21, 2011, https://www.cnn.com/2011/09/21/tech/web/santorum-google-ranking /index.html; Alexander Burns, "Santorum: Google Spreads 'Filth'," *Politico*, September 20, 2011, https://www.politico.com/story/2011/09/santorum-google-spreads-filth-063952.

48. Sutter, "Santorum Asks Google to Clean up Search Results for His Name."

49. Google contacted one SEO expert to blame the SafeSearch tweak. Gillespie, "Algorithmically Recognizable," 72; Miranda Miller, "Spreading Santorum Loses Its Frothy Spot Atop Google," Search Engine Watch, March 1, 2012, https://www.searchenginewatch.com/2012/03 /01/spreading-santorum-loses-its-frothy-spot-atop-google/.

50. Laura Sydell, "How Rick Santorum's 'Google Problem' Has Endured," *NPR*, January 6, 2012, https://www.npr.org/2012/01/06/144801671/why-santorums-google-problem-remains.

On this view, Google, by showing spreadingsantorum.com, was working exactly as it should, either because most users were looking for that site or, more ambitiously, because the word "Santorum" had actually come to mean "a frothy mixture. . . ." Gillespie, "Algorithmically Recognizable," 70–71.

51. Gillespie, "Algorithmically Recognizable," 73.

52. Ibid., 74.

53. Sam Harnett, "How Facebook Wants to Improve Your News Feed in Time for the Midterm Elections," *KQED*, June 5, 2018, https://www.kqed.org/news/11672059/how-facebook-wants-to-improve-your-news-feed-in-time-for-the-midterm-elections; Katie Harbath and Samidh Chakrabarti, "Expanding Our Efforts to Protect Elections in 2019," Meta Newsroom, January 28, 2019, https://newsroom.fb.com/news/2019/01/elections-2019/; Karl Henrik Smith, "Facebook, the EU, and Election Integrity," *Medium*, July 20, 2019, https://medium.com/swlh/facebook-the-eu-and-election-integrity-46918679bdc4.

54. Meta Transparency Center, "Facebook Community Standards," https://www.facebook.com/communitystandards/ (accessed March 8, 2019); Mark Zuckerberg, "A Blueprint for Content Governance and Enforcement," Facebook post, November 15, 2018, https://www.facebook.com/notes/mark-zuckerberg/a-blueprint-for-content-governance-and-enforcement/10156443129621634/?hc_location=ufi; Monika Bickert, "Publishing Our Internal Enforcement Guidelines and Expanding Our Appeals Process," Meta, April 24, 2018, https://about.fb.com/news/2018/04/comprehensive-community-standards/.

55. Google Official Blog, "Finding More High-Quality Sites in Search," February 24, 2011, https://googleblog.blogspot.com/2011/02/finding-more-high-quality-sites-in.html; Varun Kacholia and Minwen Ji, "Helping You Find More News to Talk About," Meta Newsroom, December 3, 2013, https://about.fb.com/news/2013/12/news-feed-fyi-helping-you-find-more-news-to-talk-about/.

56. Google was responding to a struggle between Jewish activists, who encouraged people to link the word "jew" to a Wikipedia article, and neo-Nazi groups, who tried to link the word back to jewwatch.com, which describes itself as "An Oasis of News for Americans Who Presently Endure the Hateful Censorship of Zionist Occupation." Ultimately the Wikipedia page prevailed. "Jew Watch," Wikipedia, February 3, 2020, https://en.wikipedia.org/w/index.php?title=Jew_Watch&oldid=938960765; John Brandon, "Dropping the Bomb on Google," *Wired*, May 11, 2004, https://www.wired.com/culture/lifestyle/news/2004/05/63380/; James Grimmelmann, "The Google Dilemma," *New York Law School Law Review* 53, no. 4 (2009): 943.

57. US Department of Justice, "Complaint," United States of America v. Google LLC, filed October 20, 2020, 9, https://www.justice.gov/opa/press-release/file/1328941/download.

58. Facebook users are also much more likely to engage with content that appears higher up in their newsfeed, although data are harder to come by. Brian Dean, "We Analyzed 5 Million Google Search Results. Here's What We Learned about Organic Click Through Rate," Backlinko, August 27, 2019, https://backlinko.com/google-ctr-stats; Matt Southern, "Over 25% of People Click the First Google Search Result," *Search Engine Journal*, July 14, 2020, https://www.searchenginejournal.com/google-first-page-clicks/374516/; Nathaniel Persily and Joshua A. Tucker, *Social Media and Democracy: The State of the Field, Prospects for Reform* (Cambridge: Cambridge University Press, 2020), chap. 10.

Chapter 6. Infrastructural Power

1. Thomas Jefferson, *The Papers of Thomas Jefferson—January 1787 to August 1787*, vol. 11, edited by Julian P. Boyd (Princeton, NJ: Princeton University Press, 2018), 49.

2. John Dewey, *The Public and Its Problems* (New York: Henry Holt and Company, 1927), 152.

3. Hannah Arendt, *The Human Condition* (Chicago: University of Chicago Press, 1998), 50–53.

4. Bucher, *If . . . Then*, 1.

5. Patrick Morrisey, "AG Patrick Morrisey Statement on Unlawful Work Stoppage," Facebook post, February 21, 2018, https://m.facebook.com/story.php?story_fbid=1683059798419467&id=291667837558677.

6. Interview with the author, April 2018; Joel Warner, "'We're Not Gonna Take It!': Can Trump Country Withstand the Grassroots Teachers Movement Sweeping the Nation?," *Newsweek*, July 12, 2018, https://www.newsweek.com/2018/07/20/teachers-trump-grassroots-trump-country-uprising-fed-friday-education-west-1019677.html.

7. Caroline O'Donovan, "Facebook Played a Pivotal Role in the West Virginia Teacher Strike," *BuzzFeed News*, March 7, 2018, https://www.buzzfeednews.com/article/carolineodonovan/facebook-group-west-virginia-teachers-strike.

8. Ibid.

9. Wyoming County has a median household income of about $38,000. The US average is almost $62,000.

10. "Transcript of Mark Zuckerberg's Senate Hearing," *Washington Post*, April 11, 2018, https://www.washingtonpost.com/news/the-switch/wp/2018/04/10/transcript-of-mark-zuckerbergs-senate-hearing/.

11. Alexia Fernández Campbell, "Facebook Is in Crisis Mode. The Teacher Strikes Show It Can Still Serve a Civic Purpose," *Vox*, April 12, 2018, https://www.vox.com/policy-and-politics/2018/4/12/17198404/facebook-zuckerberg-testimony-teacher-strikes; Shoshana Zuboff, *The Age of Surveillance Capitalism: The Fight for a Human Future at the New Frontier of Power* (New York: Public Affairs, 2019); Engin Bozdag and Jeroen van den Hoven, "Breaking the Filter Bubble: Democracy and Design," *Ethics and Information Technology* 17, no. 4 (2015): 249–65.

12. "Hard Questions: What Effect Does Social Media Have on Democracy?," Meta Newsroom, January 22, 2018, https://about.fb.com/news/2018/01/effect-social-media-democracy/; "Removing Bad Actors on Facebook," Meta Newsroom, July 31, 2018, https://about.fb.com/news/2018/07/removing-bad-actors-on-facebook/; Vaidhyanathan, *Antisocial Media*, 161–69. The argument that Cambridge Analytica swung the 2016 election is not persuasive. Cambridge Analytica's claim that it used a data set of 5,000 data points on 230 million Americans to develop psychographic profiles and tailor campaign ads has never been substantiated. Nor is there persuasive evidence that psychographic profiling works better than other data-intensive methods regularly used in election campaigns. Jamie Bartlett argues that Cambridge Analytica "probably was decisive" because "Trump won Pennsylvania by 44,000 votes . . . Wisconsin by 22,000 and Michigan by 11,000 . . . less than one per cent of the votes. . . . If those states had gone to Clinton, as projected, she would have been elected president." The fact of narrow margins does not demonstrate that any of the myriad factors that could have changed the vote by those narrow margins was in fact determinative, and it tends to obscure the underlying structures that make

elections close in the first place. Bartlett, *The People vs. Tech*, 100, 73, 88; Frederike Kaltheuner, "Cambridge Analytica Explained: Data and Elections," Privacy International, April 13, 2017, https://medium.com/privacy-international/cambridge-analytica-explained-data-and-elections -6d4e06549491; "The Persuasion Machine," *Secrets of Silicon Valley*, BBC, August 13, 2017, https://www.bbc.co.uk/programmes/b091zhtk; Carole Cadwalladr, "The Great British Brexit Robbery: How Our Democracy Was Hijacked," *Guardian*, May 7, 2017, https://www.theguardian .com/technology/2017/may/07/the-great-british-brexit-robbery-hijacked-democracy.

13. "What Is Story? What Is the Public Square?," Pell Center for International Relations and Public Policy, https://www.pellcenter.org/what-is-story-what-is-the-public-square/; Lucas D. Introna and Helen Nissenbaum, "Shaping the Web: Why the Politics of Search Engines Matters," *The Information Society* 16, no. 3 (2000): 179.

14. Joshua A. Geltzer, "Russia Didn't Abuse Facebook—It Simply Used It as Intended," *Wired*, March 11, 2018, https://www.wired.com/story/bad-actors-are-using-social-media -exactly-as-designed/; Nicholas Diakopoulos, Daniel Trielli, and Jennifer Stark, "I Vote For— How Search Informs Our Choice of Candidate," in *Digital Dominance: Implications and Risks*, edited by Martin Moore and Damian Tambini (Oxford: Oxford University Press, 2018); Jonathan Zittrain, "Facebook Could Decide an Election without Anyone Ever Finding Out," *New Republic*, June 1, 2014, https://newrepublic.com/article/117878/information-fiduciary-solution -facebook-digital-gerrymandering.

15. "The system is exquisitely tuned to detect any existing demand and bring content into existence to satisfy it. To be clear, this is not "demand" in the neoclassical economic sense of the rational preferences of an autonomous actor. Instead, call it "viral demand": anything that anyone can be seduced or tricked into paying attention to. The internet is now a giant machine for creating whatever shiny things are necessary to catch people's eyes." James Grimmelmann, "The Platform Is the Message," *Georgetown Law Technology Review* 2, no. 2 (2018): 229.

16. Ryan Mac and Craig Silverman, "Facebook Quietly Suspended Political Group Recommendations Ahead of the US Presidential Election," *BuzzFeed News*, October 30, 2020, https:// www.buzzfeednews.com/article/ryanmac/facebook-suspended-group-recommendations -election.

17. Zuckerberg, "A Blueprint for Content Governance and Enforcement."

18. Sean MacAvaney, Hao-Ren Yao, Eugene Yang, Katina Russell, Nazli Goharian, and Ophir Frieder, "Hate Speech Detection: Challenges and Solutions," *PLOS ONE* 14, no. 8 (2019): e0221152; Thomas Davidson, Debasmita Bhattacharya, and Ingmar Weber, "Racial Bias in Hate Speech and Abusive Language Detection Datasets," arXiv:1905.12516v1 [cs.CL], May 29, 2019, https://doi.org/10.48550/arXiv.1905.12516; Maarten Sap, Dallas Card, Saadia Gabriel, Yejin Choi, and Noah A. Smith, "The Risk of Racial Bias in Hate Speech Detection," Proceedings of the Fifty-Seventh Annual Meeting of the Association for Computational Linguistics, Florence, August 2, 2019, 1668–78.

19. Nick Clegg, "Charting a Course for an Oversight Board for Content Decisions," Meta Newsroom, January 28, 2019, https://newsroom.fb.com/news/2019/01/oversight-board/; Nick Clegg, "Referring Former President Trump's Suspension from Facebook to the Oversight Board," Meta Newsroom, January 21, 2021, https://about.fb.com/news/2021/01/referring -trump-suspension-to-oversight-board/; Evelyn Douek, "Facebook's 'Oversight Board': Move Fast with Stable Infrastructure and Humility," *North Carolina Journal of Law and Technology*

21, no. 1 (2019), https://ncjolt.org/wp-content/uploads/sites/4/2019/10/DouekIssue1_Final_.pdf.

20. Facebook sets the rules that others must follow: like the committee chair in Robert Dahl's study of New Haven, Connecticut, it sets the agenda for discussion and decision-making and exerts control over the prevailing culture and ideology of the platform—thus exercising all three faces of power. Robert A. Dahl, *Who Governs? Democracy and Power in an American City* (New Haven, CT: Yale University Press, 1961); Steven Lukes, *Power: A Radical View* (Houndmills, Basingstoke, UK: Macmillan, 1974); John Gaventa, *Power and Powerlessness: Quiescence and Rebellion in an Appalachian Valley* (Urbana: University of Illinois Press, 1980); Peter Bachrach and Morton S. Baratz, "Two Faces of Power," *American Political Science Review* 56, no. 4 (1962): 947–52; Steven Lukes, *Power: A Radical View* (Basingstoke, UK: Macmillan, 1974).

21. Bartlett, *The People vs. Tech*, 147.

22. Plato, *Phaedrus* (London: Penguin Books, 2005), sec. 274e.

23. Ernest Cushing Richardson, *The Beginnings of Libraries* (Princeton, NJ: Princeton University Press, 1914), 11. The translation of stories from this library in the nineteenth century transformed Western understandings of human history. The Bible was no longer the oldest written text, or even particularly original. The Fall of Man and the Great Flood were not literal events dictated by God, but Mesopotamian myths embellished by Hebrew scribes: the Garden of Eden was the *Enuma Elish*, the Book of Job was the *Ludlul-Bēl-Nimēqi*, and *The Love Song of Shu-Sin* was the oldest love poem, not the Song of Solomon. Will Durant, *Our Oriental Heritage: Being a History of Civilization in Egypt and the Near East to the Death of Alexander, and in India, China, and Japan from the Beginning to Our Own Day* (New York: Simon & Schuster, 1954); Peter T. Daniels, "The First Civilizations," in *The World's Writing Systems*, edited by Peter T. Daniels and William Bright (New York: Oxford University Press, 1996).

24. Page and Brin's work grew out of the existing field of information retrieval, which drew on studies of academic citation and library indexing systems. Page et al., "The PageRank Citation Ranking"; Halavais, *Search Engine Society*, 17.

25. James Grimmelmann, "Information Policy for the Library of Babel," *Journal of Business and Technology* 3, no. 29 (2008). Several websites have tried to re-create the experience of the Library of Babel. Jonathan Basile et al., "Library of Babel," https://libraryofbabel.info/ (accessed April 8, 2020). Computer scientists have also built machine learning systems that model the Library of Babel. Stephen Mayhew, "The Machine Learning Model Library of Babel," February 9, 2020, https://mayhewsw.github.io/2020/02/09/model-library-of-babel/.

26. Borges developed the themes of the Library of Babel in his 1939 essay "The Total Library," in which he drew on similar ideas developed by Kurd Lasswitz in his 1901 "The Universal Library." Borges described "the universal orthographic symbols, not the words of a language" that Lasswitz arrived at, "whose recombinations and repetitions encompass everything possible to express in all languages. The totality of such variations would form a Total Library of astronomical size. Lasswitz urges mankind to construct that inhuman library, which chance would organize and which would eliminate intelligence." Jorge Luis Borges, *The Total Library: Non-Fiction 1922–1986* (London: Penguin, 2000), 214–16.

27. Grimmelmann, "Information Policy for the Library of Babel," 37.

28. Grimmelmann, "The Platform Is the Message," 39; Halavais, *Search Engine Society*, 118.

29. Grimmelmann, "Information Policy for the Library of Babel," 36.

30. The web is "a public space and a political good" because of "its capacity as a medium for intensive communication among and between individuals and groups in just about all the permutations that one can imagine." Introna and Nissenbaum, "Shaping the Web," 177–80; Laura A. Granka, "The Politics of Search: A Decade Retrospective," *The Information Society* 26, no. 5 (2010): 371.

31. Jennifer Elaine Steele, "Censorship of Library Collections: An Analysis Using Gatekeeping Theory," *Collection Management* 43, no. 4 (2018): 229–48. Grimmelmann persuasively argues that the public interest is generally equivalent to the interest of readers because all possible books already exist, so "no further incentive is required to bring them into being." Grimmelmann, "Information Policy for the Library of Babel," 30.

32. Ryan Chittum, "Google as Big Brother," *Columbia Journalism Review*, August 16, 2010, https://www.cjr.org/the_audit/google_as_big_brother_schmidt_wsj.php.

33. *New York Times*, "Facebook Is Not the Public Square" (editorial), *New York Times*, December 25, 2014, https://www.nytimes.com/2014/12/26/opinion/facebook-is-not-the-public -square.html.

34. Sarah Haan, "Profits v. Principles," in *The Perilous Public Square: Structural Threats to Free Expression Today*, edited by David Pozen (New York: Columbia University Press, 2020); Zuboff, *The Age of Surveillance Capitalism*; James Williams, *Stand Out of Our Light: Freedom and Resistance in the Attention Economy* (Cambridge: Cambridge University Press, 2018); Judson Brewer, "How Your Smartphone Was Engineered to Outsmart You" (review of Adam Alter, *Irresistible: The Rise of Addictive Technology and the Business of Keeping Us Hooked*), *American Journal of Psychology* 131, no. 4 (2018): 506–10; Foer, *World without Mind*; Tim Wu, *The Attention Merchants: The Epic Scramble to Get inside Our Heads* (New York: Knopf, 2016); Joseph Turow, *The Daily You: How the New Advertising Industry Is Defining Your Identity and Your Worth* (New Haven, CT: Yale University Press, 2011); *The Social Dilemma* (documentary), Netflix, 2020, https://www .thesocialdilemma.com/.

35. Franklin Foer, "The Death of the Public Square," *Atlantic*, July 6, 2018, https://www .theatlantic.com/ideas/archive/2018/07/the-death-of-the-public-square/564506/.

36. Ibid.

37. Ibid.

38. Meta Business Help Center, "About A/B Testing," https://en-gb.facebook.com/business /help/1738164643098669 (accessed March 23, 2020); Adam D. I. Kramer, Jamie E. Guillory, and Jeffrey T. Hancock, "Experimental Evidence of Massive-Scale Emotional Contagion through Social Networks," *Proceedings of the National Academy of Sciences* 111, no. 24 (2014): 8788–90. Much of the reaction to the experiment focused on the ethics of running experiments on people's emotions without their knowledge. This may have seemed strange to Facebook's engineers, who already understood that its systems shape users' emotions all the time. That is what newsfeed does. James Grimmelmann, "The Law and Ethics of Experiments on Social Media Users," *Colorado Technology Law Journal* 13, no. 2 (2015): 271; Vaidhyanathan, *Antisocial Media*, chap. 1; Zuboff, *The Age of Surveillance Capitalism*; Williams, *Stand Out of Our Light*; Wu, *The Attention Merchants*.

39. John Laidler, "High Tech Is Watching You," *Harvard Gazette*, March 4, 2019, https://news .harvard.edu/gazette/story/2019/03/harvard-professor-says-surveillance-capitalism-is -undermining-democracy/; Sam Biddle, "'A Fundamentally Illegitimate Choice': Shoshana

Zuboff on the Age of Surveillance Capitalism," *Intercept*, February 2, 2019, https://theintercept
.com/2019/02/02/shoshana-zuboff-age-of-surveillance-capitalism/.

40. I cannot find verification that Norvig actually said this. Alon Halevy, Peter Norvig, and
Fernando Pereira, "The Unreasonable Effectiveness of Data," *IEEE Intelligent Systems* 24, no. 2
(2009): 8–12; Michele Banko and Eric Brill, "Scaling to Very Very Large Corpora for Natural Language Disambiguation," Proceedings of the Thirty-Ninth Annual Meeting of the Association for
Computational Linguistics, Toulouse, France, July 6–11, 2001; Xavier Amatriain, "In Machine Learning, What Is Better: More Data or Better Algorithms," KDnuggets, June 2015, https://www
.kdnuggets.com/in-machine-learning-what-is-better-more-data-or-better-algorithms.html/.

41. Page et al., "The PageRank Citation Ranking," 11–12.

42. Gillespie, *Custodians of the Internet*, 195; Adam Mosseri, "Facebook Improves News Feed
Integrity," Meta Journalism Project, May 19, 2017, https://www.facebook.com/journalismproject
/facebook-improves-news-feed-integrity; Vaidhyanathan, *The Googlization of Everything*, 183;
Halavais, *Search Engine Society*, 77–78; Tobias D. Krafft, Michael Gamer, and Katharina A.
Zweig, "What Did You See? A Study to Measure Personalization in Google's Search Engine," *EPJ
Data Science* 8, no. 1 (2019): 1–23; Anikó Hannák, Piotr Sapieżyński, Arash Molavi Khaki, David
Lazer, Alan Mislove, and Christo Wilson, "Measuring Personalization of Web Search,"
arXiv:1706.05011v1 [cs.CY], June 15, 2017, https://doi.org/10.48550/arXiv.1706.05011; Eli
Pariser, *The Filter Bubble: What the Internet Is Hiding from You* (New York: Penguin Press, 2011);
Adam Mosseri, "Building a Better News Feed for You," Meta Newsroom, June 29, 2016, https://
about.fb.com/news/2016/06/building-a-better-news-feed-for-you/; Tauel Harper, "The Big
Data Public and Its Problems: Big Data and the Structural Transformation of the Public Sphere,"
New Media and Society 19, no. 9 (2017): 1424–39; David Conroy, "Re-examining the Public
Sphere: Democracy and the Role of the Media," PhD thesis, McGill University, Department of
Political Science, 2002, https://escholarship.mcgill.ca/concern/theses/mg74qm55s.

43. Pariser, *The Filter Bubble*.

44. Facebook's systems may stifle the ability of political campaigns to deliberately target ads,
as some have proposed, making it harder for campaigns to exert control over the audience they
reach and ceding even more control to Facebook's machine learning systems. Muhammad Ali,
Piotr Sapiezynski, Aleksandra Korolova, Alan Mislove, and Aaron Rieke, "Ad Delivery Algorithms: The Hidden Arbiters of Political Messaging," arXiv:1912.04255v3 [cs.CY], December 9,
2019, revised December 10 and 17, 2019, https://doi.org/10.48550/arXiv.1912.04255. The em-
pirics are challenging because it's hard to compare offline and online worlds—for instance, it's
difficult to distinguish the relative importance of well-documented psychological traits like
confirmation bias. For how little we still know, see especially Persily and Tucker, *Social Media
and Democracy*, chaps. 2, 3; Axel Bruns, "Filter Bubble," *Internet Policy Review* 8, no. 4 (2019);
Daniel Geschke, Jan Lorenz, and Peter Holtz, "The Triple-Filter Bubble: Using Agent-Based
Modelling to Test a Meta-Theoretical Framework for the Emergence of Filter Bubbles and Echo
Chambers," *British Journal of Social Psychology* 58, no. 1 (2019): 129–49; Pariser, *The Filter Bubble*.

45. Matt Carlson, "Facebook in the News," *Digital Journalism* 6, no. 1 (2017): 2017.

46. Mike Ananny, "Probably Speech, Maybe Free: Toward a Probabilistic Understanding of
Online Expression and Platform Governance," Columbia University, Knight First Amendment
Institute, August 21, 2019, https://knightcolumbia.org/content/probably-speech-maybe-free
-toward-a-probabilistic-understanding-of-online-expression-and-platform-governance. Face-

book and Google use the language of prediction to deflect attention from their power: "A company that reviews a hundred thousand pieces of content per day and maintains a 99 percent accuracy rate may still have up to a thousand errors." Monika Bickert, "Defining the Boundaries of Free Speech on Social Media," in *The Free Speech Century*, edited by Geoffrey R. Stone and Lee C. Bollinger (New York: Oxford University Press, 2019), 269. Twitter's Del Harvey admits that, "given the context of the scale we're dealing with, if you're talking about a billion tweets, and everything goes perfectly right 99.99% of the time, then you're still talking about 10,000 tweets where everything might not have gone right." Tarleton Gillespie, "Platforms Are Not Intermediaries," *Georgetown Law Technology Review*, no. 1 (July 2018): 198, https://georgetownlawtechreview.org/platforms-are-not-intermediaries/GLTR-07-2018/.

47. Tessa Lyons, "Hard Questions: What's Facebook's Strategy for Stopping False News?," Meta Newsroom, May 23, 2018, https://about.fb.com/news/2018/05/hard-questions-false-news/; Josh Constine, "Facebook Will Change Algorithm to Demote 'Borderline Content' That Almost Violates Policies," TechCrunch, November 15, 2018, http://social.techcrunch.com/2018/11/15/facebook-borderline-content/; Zuckerberg, "A Blueprint for Content Governance and Enforcement." As one commentator summed up the "Trending Topics" controversy in 2016: "The bottom line is that humans, unlike algorithms, have hearts. And the company can't know for sure what was in the hearts of the workers who were selecting certain stories while rejecting others," explained one CNN reporter. Brian Stelter, Hope King, and Laurie Segall, "Did Facebook Suppress Conservative News?," CNNMoney, May 9, 2016, https://money.cnn.com/2016/05/09/media/facebook-trending-conservative-news/index.html; Carlson, "Facebook in the News"; Rebecca Stewart, "Facebook to Tweak Trending Topics Following Allegations of Bias," The Drum, May 24, 2016, https://www.thedrum.com/news/2016/05/24/facebook-tweak-trending-topics-following-allegations-bias; Colin Stretch, "Response to Chairman John Thune's Letter on Trending Topics," Meta Newsroom, May 23, 2016, https://about.fb.com/news/2016/05/response-to-chairman-john-thunes-letter-on-trending-topics/. Facebook's response conveniently helps it portray itself as a technology company. As Sheryl Sandberg, Facebook's chief operating officer, told CNN: "We're clear about the industry we're in—we're a tech company. We're not a media company, so we're not trying to hire journalists, and we're not trying to write news." Carlson, "Facebook in the News," 13.

48. Clegg, "Referring Former President Trump's Suspension from Facebook."

49. Ananny, "Probably Speech, Maybe Free"; Gillespie, "Algorithmically Recognizable," 75; Jane I. Guyer, "Percentages and Perchance: Archaic Forms in the Twenty-First Century Platforms," in *Legacies, Logics, Logistics: Essays in the Anthropology of the Platform Economy* (Chicago: University of Chicago Press, 2016), 140, 148; Philip M. Napoli, "Automated Media: An Institutional Theory Perspective on Algorithmic Media Production and Consumption," *Communication Theory* 24, no. 3 (2014): 344.

50. Evgeny Morozov, "Capitalism's New Clothes," *The Baffler*, February 4, 2019, https://thebaffler.com/latest/capitalisms-new-clothes-morozov.

51. Jill Lepore, *If Then: How the Simulmatics Corporation Invented the Future* (New York: W. W. Norton & Co., 2020). Although Zuboff recognizes the importance of machine learning for understanding the implications of Facebook's and Google's systems for democracy, her argument does not explore in much detail how machine learning matters. Zuboff refers to these systems as

"prediction products." She writes: "Surveillance capitalists' interests have shifted from using automated machine processes to know about your behavior to using machine processes to shape your behavior according to their interests . . . [taking] us from automating information flows about you to automating you." Thinking about machine learning systems as products is firmly rooted in the logic of capitalism that her book seeks to critique. Our only option is to reject these systems in a new social movement that helps us, as consumers, better resist their invasions. All we can do is forge a better capitalism. We must build on Zuboff's critique to develop a compelling account of how we, as citizens, should collectively govern Facebook and Google. Zuboff, *The Age of Surveillance Capitalism*, 215. "By seeking to explicate, and denounce, the novel dynamics of surveillance capitalism," argues one cogent review of Zuboff's book, "Zuboff normalizes too much in capitalism itself." Morozov, "Capitalism's New Clothes." As the technologist Cory Doctorow argues, "The surveillance capitalism hypothesis—that Big Tech's products really work as well as they say they do and that's why everything is so screwed up—is way too easy on surveillance and even easier on capitalism." "Why," he asks, are things "so screwed up? Capitalism. Specifically, the monopolism that creates inequality and the inequality that creates monopolism . . . because our governments are in thrall to . . . the ideology that says monopolies are actually just fine. . . . Surveillance doesn't make capitalism rogue. Capitalism's unchecked rule begets surveillance. Surveillance isn't bad because it lets people manipulate us. It's bad because it crushes our ability to be our authentic selves—and because it lets the rich and powerful figure out who might be thinking of building guillotines and what dirt they can use to discredit those embryonic guillotine-builders before they can even get to the lumberyard." Cory Doctorow, "How to Destroy 'Surveillance Capitalism,'" *OneZero*, August 26, 2020, https://onezero.medium.com/how-to-destroy-surveillance-capitalism-8135e6744d59.

52. "We decided that having the community determine which sources are broadly trusted would be most objective." Mark Zuckerberg, "Trustworthy News," Facebook post, January 19, 2018, https://www.facebook.com/zuck/posts/10104445245963251?pnref=story.

53. Bucher, *If . . . Then*, 7–9.

Chapter 7. Democratic Utilities

1. Dewey, *The Public and Its Problems*.

2. Franklin D. Roosevelt, "Message to Congress on the Concentration of Economic Power," speech before the U.S. Congress, April 29, 1938, https://publicpolicy.pepperdine.edu/academics/research/faculty-research/new-deal/roosevelt-speeches/fr042938.htm.

3. Chris Hughes, "It's Time to Break Up Facebook," *New York Times*, May 9, 2019, https://www.nytimes.com/2019/05/09/opinion/sunday/chris-hughes-facebook-zuckerberg.html.

4. Elizabeth Warren, "Curious why I think FB has too much power? . . . ," Twitter, March 11, 2019, https://twitter.com/ewarren/status/1105256905058979841.

5. Ted Cruz, "First time I've ever retweeted . . . ," Twitter, March 12, 2019, https://twitter.com/tedcruz/status/1105523954087849984.

6. Franklin D. Roosevelt, "Inaugural Address," January 20, 1937, American Presidency Project, https://www.presidency.ucsb.edu/documents/inaugural-address-7.

7. William J. Novak, "The Public Utility Idea and the Origins of Modern Business Regulation," in *Corporations and American Democracy*, edited by Naomi R. Lamoreaux and William J.

Novak (Cambridge, MA: Belknap Press of Harvard University Press, 2017), 139–76; Viljoen, "Democratic Data"; Eric A. Posner, *Radical Markets: Uprooting Capitalism and Democracy for a Just Society* (Princeton, NJ: Princeton University Press, 2018), chap. 5.

8. "We do not have a sufficiently precise language for attending to these kinds of interventions and their consequences." Gillespie, *Custodians of the Internet*, 360.

9. Philip M. Napoli, *Social Media and the Public Interest: Media Regulation in the Disinformation Age* (New York: Columbia University Press, 2019), 358; William J. Novak, "Law and the Social Control of American Capitalism," *Emory Law Journal* 60 (2010): 377–1437; Naomi R. Lamoreaux and William J. Novak, *Corporations and American Democracy* (Cambridge, MA: Belknap Press of Harvard University Press, 2017).

10. John Samples and Paul Matzko, "Social Media Regulation in the Public Interest: Some Lessons from History," Columbia University, King First Amendment Institute, May 4, 2020, https://knightcolumbia.org/content/social-media-regulation-in-the-public-interest-some-lessons-from-history; K. Sabeel Rahman and Zephyr Teachout, "From Private Bads to Public Goods: Adapting Public Utility Regulation for Informational Infrastructure," Columbia University, King First Amendment Institute, February 4, 2020, https://knightcolumbia.org/content/from-private-bads-to-public-goods-adapting-public-utility-regulation-for-informational-infrastructure.

11. "Is the vociferation that our liberties are in danger justified by the facts? . . . If there is that danger, it comes from that concentrated private economic power which is struggling so hard to master our democratic government. It will not come, as some (by no means all) of the possessors of that private power would make the people believe—from our democratic government itself." Roosevelt, "Message to Congress on the Concentration of Economic Power."

12. Lamoreaux and Novak, *Corporations and American Democracy*, 5–9.

13. Ibid., 19, 139.

14. William Boyd, "Public Utility and the Low-Carbon Future," *UCLA Law Review* 61, no. 6 (2014): 1635.

15. K. Sabeel Rahman, "The New Utilities: Private Power, Social Infrastructure, and the Revival of the Public Utility Concept," *Cardozo Law Review* 39, no. 5 (2018): 1639.

16. Bruce Wyman, *The Special Law Governing Public Service Corporations: And All Others Engaged in Public Employment*, vol. 1 (New York: Baker/Voorhis, 1911), "Historical Introduction."

17. There are two related justifications for regulating corporate power here: the idea that wharfs are licensed by the queen and the idea that there is no other wharf in the port. Matthew Hale, "De Portibus Maris," in *A Collection of Tracts Relative to the Law of England, from Manuscripts. Now First Edited*, edited by Francis Hargrave (Dublin: E. Lynch et al., 1787), 77–78; Breck P. McAllister, "Lord Hale and Business Affected with a Public Interest," *Harvard Law Review* 43, no. 5 (1930): 759–91.

18. Commonwealth of Pennsylvania v. Alger, 61 Mass 53 (1851). This argument was also rooted in a wider shift in English political theory from social contract theory to a thicker notion of the legitimacy and purposes of state power, beginning with David Hume's critique of social contract theory, through Jeremy Bentham's *Fragment on Government*, and entering American jurisprudence through John Dewey's *Liberalism and Social Action*. Late nineteenth-century US reformers transplanted the concepts of *salus populi* and *res publica* from common law into

274 NOTES TO CHAPTER 7

modern public utility regulation by treating corporations whose activities affected the public interest as utilities that ought to be subject to obligations designed to advance the public interest. David Hume, *A Treatise on Human Nature* (London: Longmans, Green and Co., 1874); Jeremy Bentham, *Bentham: A Fragment on Government* (Cambridge: Cambridge University Press, 1988); A. V. Dicey and Richard A. Cosgrove, *The Period of Benthamism or Individualism* (London: Routledge, 1981); Graham Wallas, "Jeremy Bentham," *Political Science Quarterly* 38, no. 1 (1923): 45–56; Arthur John Taylor, *Laissez-Faire and State Intervention in Nineteenth-Century Britain* (London: Macmillan, 1972); Oliver MacDonagh, "The Nineteenth-Century Revolution in Government: A Reappraisal," *Historical Journal* 1, no. 1 (1958): 52–67; John Dewey, *Liberalism and Social Action* (Amherst, NY: Prometheus Books, 2000).

19. In *Trustees of Dartmouth College v. Woodward* in 1818, the New Hampshire legislature sought to change Dartmouth College, a private corporation, into a state university. "The incorporating act neither gives nor prevents . . . [public] control." Trustees of Dartmouth College v. Woodward, 17 U.S. 518 (1818). From 1789 to 1865, the legislature of Connecticut, for example, passed more than three thousand special acts incorporating a wide range of social and economic organizations.

20. Progressive and New Deal reformers rejected the neoclassical assertion that firms are a "tool for individuals to achieve their personal goals," a "nexus of contracts" whose goals and powers simply reflect the goals and powers of the contracting parties." They argued that the political and economic power of corporations reinforce one another, threatening "the functioning of the free market economy," "the economic prosperity it can generate," and "democracy as well." Luigi Zingales, "Towards a Political Theory of the Firm," *Journal of Economic Perspectives* 31, no. 3 (2017): 114; Michael C. Jensen and William H. Meckling, "Theory of the Firm: Managerial Behavior, Agency Costs, and Ownership Structure," *Journal of Financial Economics* 3, no. 4 (1976): 305–60.

21. James Willard Hurst, *The Legitimacy of the Business Corporation in the Law of the United States, 1780–1970*, Page-Barbour Lectures, 1969 (Charlottesville: University Press of Virginia, 1970), 17; Lamoreaux and Novak, *Corporations and American Democracy*, chap. 4.

22. Lamoreaux and Novak, *Corporations and American Democracy*, 17; Rahman, "The New Utilities," 1630; Joseph D. Kearney and Thomas W. Merrill, "The Great Transformation of Regulated Industries Law," *Columbia Law Review* 98, no. 6 (1998): 1330–31.

23. Rahman, "The New Utilities," 1636; Kevin Werbach, "The Network Utility," *Duke Law Journal* 60, no. 8 (2011): 1761; Adam Thierer, "The Perils of Classifying Social Media Platforms as Public Utilities," *CommLaw Conspectus* 21, no. 2 (2013): 249; W. Kip Viscusi, Joseph Emmett Harrington, and John M. Vernon, eds., *Economics of Regulation and Antitrust* (Cambridge, MA: MIT Press, 1995), 323–25, 351–53.

24. Leverett S. Lyon, *Government and Economic Life* (Washington, DC: Brookings Institution, 1940), 616–17.

25. Horace M. Gray, "The Passing of the Public Utility Concept," *Journal of Land and Public Utility Economics* 16, no. 1 (1940): 9; Boyd, "Public Utility and the Low-Carbon Future," 1614; Lamoreaux and Novak, *Corporations and American Democracy*, 4; R. H. Coase, "The Federal Communications Commission," *Journal of Law and Economics* 2 (1959): 1–40; George J. Stigler and Claire Friedland, "What Can Regulators Regulate? The Case of Electricity," *Journal of Law and Economics* 5 (1962): 1–16; Harold Demsetz, "Why Regulate Utilities?," *Journal of Law and*

Economics 11, no. 1 (1968): 55–65; Richard A. Posner, "Taxation by Regulation," *Bell Journal of Economics* 2, no. 1 (1971): 22–50. Gary Becker's article in the first issue of the *Journal of Law and Economics* in 1958 is typical of the genre. "Does the existence of market imperfections justify government intervention?" "The answer would be 'no,'" Becker argued, "if the imperfections in government behavior were greater than those in the market. . . . It may be preferable not to regulate economic monopolists and to suffer their bad effects, rather than to regulate them and suffer the effects of political imperfections." Gary S. Becker, "Competition and Democracy," *Journal of Law and Economics* 1 (1958): 109.

26. Novak, "Law and the Social Control of American Capitalism," 144.

27. Novak, "The Public Utility Idea," 175.

28. John Maurice Clark, *Social Control of Business* (Chicago: University of Chicago Press, 1926), 4–5.

29. Boyd, "Public Utility and the Low-Carbon Future," 1619.

30. John B. Cheadle, "Government Control of Business," *Columbia Law Review* 20, no. 5 (1920): 585.

31. Nicholas Bagley, "Medicine as a Public Calling," *Michigan Law Review* 114, no. 1 (2015): 77; Novak, "The Public Utility Idea," 159.

32. Munn v. Illinois, 94 U.S. 113 (1877).

33. Walton H. Hamilton, "Affectation with Public Interest," *Yale Law Journal* 39 (1930): 1089–1112; Mcallister, "Lord Hale and Business Affected with a Public Interest"; Novak, "The Public Utility Idea," 170.

34. The Civil Rights Cases (U.S. 1883).

35. As Novak points out, in the first three chapters Wyman covers the legal duties of a vast range of corporations, including: ferries, bridges, bonded warehouses, tramways, railroads, transmission lines, lumber flumes, mining tunnels, sewerage, cemeteries, hospitals, turnpikes, street railways, subways, waterworks, natural gas, stockyards, docks, innkeepers, hackmen, messenger services, electric plants and power, refrigeration, railway terminals and bridges, signal services, telegraph lines, wireless, sarine cables, associated press, public stores, safe deposit vaults, marketplaces, and stock exchanges. Wyman, *The Special Law Governing Public Service Corporations*; Novak, "The Public Utility Idea," 142, 175.

36. Felix Frankfurter, *The Public and Its Government* (New Haven, CT: Yale University Press, 1930), 83, 31; Novak, "The Public Utility Idea," 142, 159.

37. Felix Frankfurter and Henry M. Hart, "Rate Regulation," in *Encyclopaedia of the Social Sciences*, vol. 11, edited by Edwin Robert Anderson Seligman and Alvin Saunders Johnson (New York: Macmillan, 1937), 104; Novak, "The Public Utility Idea," 174.

38. Rahman, "The New Utilities," 1681.

39. Ibid., 1691.

40. Roy A. Schotland, "A Sporting Proposition—SEC v. Chenery," in *Administrative Law Stories*, edited by Peter L. Strauss (New York: Foundation Press, 2006), 166; Lamoreaux and Novak, *Corporations and American Democracy*, 21–22.

41. Schotland, "A Sporting Proposition," 168; Lamoreaux and Novak, *Corporations and American Democracy*, 22.

42. Marco Iansiti and Karim R. Lakhani, *Competing in the Age of AI: Strategy and Leadership When Algorithms and Networks Run the World* (Boston: Harvard Business Review Press, 2020).

43. Jason Furman, *Unlocking Digital Competition: Report of the Digital Competition Expert Panel*, March 2019, 8, https://assets.publishing.service.gov.uk/government/uploads/system/uploads/attachment_data/file/785547/unlocking_digital_competition_furman_review_web.pdf.

44. Marco Iansiti and Karim Lakhani argue that, whereas the value that scale delivers in an industrial economy eventually tapers off, as costs increase and markets become saturated the digital operating model is effectively exponential. Iansiti and Lakhani, *Competing in the Age of AI*, chaps. 3, 4.

45. "The development of machine learning technologies and data analysis is a source of increasing returns to scale and scope that can contribute to digital market concentration." Stigler Committee on Digital Platforms, *Final Report*, George J. Stigler Center for the Study of the Economic and the State, Chicago Booth School, 2019, 37–39, https://www.chicagobooth.edu/-/media/research/stigler/pdfs/digital-platforms---committee-report---stigler-center.pdf; 360iResearch, "The Global Digital Advertising Platforms Market," *Valuates Reports*, August 2020, https://reports.valuates.com/market-reports/360I-Auto-7W134/the-global-digital-advertising-platforms; Azeem Azhar, "The Real Reason Tech Companies Want Regulation," *Exponential View*, January 26, 2020, https://www.exponentialview.co/p/-the-real-reason-tech-companies-want.

46. J. R. Raphael, "Facebook Overtakes MySpace in U.S.," *PCWorld*, June 16, 2009, https://www.pcworld.com/article/166794/Facebook_Overtakes_MySpace_in_US.html; Ami Sedghi, "Facebook: 10 Years of Social Networking, in Numbers," *Guardian*, February 4, 2014, http://www.theguardian.com/news/datablog/2014/feb/04/facebook-in-numbers-statistics.

47. Data are subject to economies of scope and scale, but in different ways from industrial economies of scope or scale because data are inexhaustible (data can be used repeatedly), iterative (the use of data creates new data), and nonrivalrous (data can be consumed by more than one party). Stigler Committee on Digital Platforms, *Final Report*, 34–37; Robert H. Frank and Philip J. Cook, "Winner-Take-All Markets," *Studies in Microeconomics* 1, no. 2 (2013): 131–54.

48. Alessandro Acquisti, Curtis Taylor, and Liad Wagman, "The Economics of Privacy," *Journal of Economic Literature* 54, no. 2 (2016): 444; Stigler Committee on Digital Platforms, *Final Report*, 48, 50–51; Alessandro Acquisti, Laura Brandimarte, and George Loewenstein, "Privacy and Human Behavior in the Age of Information," *Science* (American Association for the Advancement of Science) 347, no. 6221 (2015): 509–14.

49. Stigler Committee on Digital Platforms, *Final Report*, 30; Furman, "Unlocking Digital Competition."

50. Zephyr Teachout and K. Sabeel Rahman, "From Private Bads to Public Goods: Adapting Public Utility Regulation for Informational Infrastructure," Columbia University, Knight First Amendment Institute, February 4, 2020, https://knightcolumbia.org/content/from-private-bads-to-public-goods-adapting-public-utility-regulation-for-informational-infrastructure.

51. Brett M. Frischmann, *Infrastructure: The Social Value of Shared Resources* (New York: Oxford University Press, 2012), 334.

52. The public and social value of this infrastructure should not be overlooked simply because it is hard to measure. "In addition to the creation and sharing of various public goods, including speech and cultural content of all sorts, Facebook enables social interactions, the development of old and new relationships, and the strengthening of social ties (even ties that

are relatively weak). As a result of these social capabilities, it enables collective action and co-ordination . . . that would be incredibly difficult, and perhaps impossible in some cases, without the platform. The spillover effects offline are immense. Again, the wedge between private market value (value captured in market transactions) and social value is substantial. . . . Active, produc-tive users may become more aware, conscious of their (potential) role as listeners, voters, and speakers, but also as consumers and producers, as political, cultural, and social beings, and as members of communities." Ibid., 334, 336–37, 342–43.

53. Danah Boyd, "Facebook Is a Utility; Utilities Get Regulated," apophenia, May 15, 2010, https://www.zephoria.org/thoughts/archives/2010/05/15/facebook-is-a-utility-utilities-get -regulated.html. Zeynep Tufekci argued in 2010 that Facebook and Google are natural monopo-lies that underwrite the "corporatization of social commons" and the "privatization of our pub-lics." Zeynep Tufekci, "Google Buzz: The Corporatization of Social Commons,'" Technosociol-ogy, February 17, 2010, http://technosociology.org/?p=102.

54. Mark Zuckerberg, "Building Global Community," Facebook post, February 16, 2017, https://www.facebook.com/notes/mark-zuckerberg/building-global-community /10103508221158471/.

55. Thierer, "The Perils of Classifying Social Media Platforms as Public Utilities," 277.

56. FCC v. Pacifica Foundation, 438 U.S. 726 (1978); Napoli, *Social Media and the Public Inter-est*, 147.

57. The Court rejected the application of the pervasiveness rationale to the internet when striking down regulation in the Communications Decency Act (CDA) in 1996, which would have restricted the flow of pornography. Since the CDA would have restricted the flow of speech protected by the First Amendment, the Court ruled that there was "no basis" for "qualifying the level of First Amendment scrutiny that should be applied" to the internet. Reno v. American Civil Liberties Union, 521 U.S. 844 (1997). On the history of government regulation of broad-casting, see Red Lion Broadcasting Co., Inc., v. FCC, 395 U.S. 367 (1969). On the scarcity of frequencies at its inception, see Turner Broadcasting System, Inc., v. FCC, 512 U.S. 622 (1997). On its "invasive" nature, see Sable Communications of California v. FCC, 492 U.S. 115 (1989).

58. Napoli also argues that we should think of aggregations of user data as a kind of public resource that justifies the imposition of public interest regulatory obligations. "When large aggregations of user data become the lifeblood of a platform's business model, then this information-fiduciary status could expand into a broader set of social responsibilities." Napoli, *Social Media and the Public Interest*, 149–50.

59. The Supreme Court struck down a North Carolina law that prohibited registered sex of-fenders from accessing social media sites like Facebook as a violation of the First Amendment. In doing so, the Court may have also opened a legal window for the pervasiveness justification of public utility regulation of Facebook and Google. Justice Anthony Kennedy opinion, Packingham v. North Carolina, 582 U.S. (2017), citing Reno v. American Civil Liberties Union, 521 at 870.

60. It is not clear what regulatory implications courts or legislators will draw from the rec-ognition of Facebook's and Google's infrastructural power. For instance, *Packingham* was cited in President Trump's executive order that would have removed Section 230 liability for compa-nies like Facebook and Google under the CDA. "Executive Order on Preventing Online Cen-sorship," May 28, 2020, https://trumpwhitehouse.archives.gov/presidential-actions/executive -order-preventing-online-censorship/.

61. Stigler Committee on Digital Platforms, *Final Report*, 32.

62. Furman, "Unlocking Digital Competition," 41.

63. Stigler Committee on Digital Platforms, *Final Report*, 115.

64. David S. Bogen, "The Origins of Freedom of Speech and Press," *Maryland Law Review* 42, no. 3 (1983): 434; Postal Regulatory Commission, *Report on Universal Postal Service and the Postal Monopoly*, December 19, 2008, https://www.prc.gov/docs/61/61628/USO%20Report.pdf; Rahman and Teachout, "From Private Bads to Public Goods." In debating the act, Congressman Shearjashub Bourne of Massachusetts asserted that newspapers "ought to come to the subscribers in all parts of the Union on the same terms." Rep. Bourne, "Annals of Congress" (1791).

65. Western Union Tel. Co. v. Foster, 247 U.S. 105 (1918); Rahman and Teachout, "From Private Bads to Public Goods."

66. Genevieve Lakier, "The Limits of Antimonopoly Law as a Solution to the Problems of the Platform Public Sphere," Columbia University, Knight First Amendment Institute, March 30, 2020, https://knightcolumbia.org/content/the-limits-of-antimonopoly-as-a-solution-to-the-problems-of-the-platform-public-sphere.

67. Warren, "Here's How We Can Break up Big Tech"; Lakier, "The Limits of Antimonopoly Law"; Lina Khan, "Amazon's Antitrust Paradox," *Yale Law Journal* 126, no. 3 (January 2017): 710–805.

68. Lakier, "The Limits of Antimonopoly Law"; Kate Klonick, "The New Governors: The People, Rules, and Processes Governing Online Speech," *Harvard Law Review* 131, no. 6 (2018): 598–670.

69. Mark Andrejevic, "Public Service Media Utilities: Rethinking Search Engines and Social Networking as Public Goods," *Media International Australia Incorporating Culture and Policy*, no. 146 (2013): 129; Tim Wu, *The Master Switch: The Rise and Fall of Information Empires* (New York: Knopf, 2010); Tim Wu, *The Curse of Bigness: Antitrust in the New Gilded Age* (New York: Columbia Global Reports, 2018).

70. Benjamin R. Barber, "Calling All Liberals: It's Time to Fight," *The Nation*, October 19, 2011, https://www.thenation.com/article/archive/calling-all-liberals-its-time-fight/; Andrejevic, "Public Service Media Utilities," 124.

71. Miami Herald Publishing Co. v. Tornillo 418 U.S. 241 (1974).

72. Turner Broadcasting System, Inc., v. FCC, 520 at 197.

73. Lakier also notes that it would be even harder to make the bottleneck argument "if these companies get broken up." Lakier, "The Limits of Antimonopoly Law."

74. Marsh v. Alabama 326 U.S. 501 (1946).

75. Thierer, "The Perils of Classifying Social Media Platforms as Public Utilities," 274–75.

76. As Grimmelmann argues, this "centralized moderation offers a clear focal point for policy-making," because "centralized moderation offers the ability to stop unwanted content and participants by creating a single checkpoint through which all must pass. . . . But chokepoints are also single points of failure. . . . In comparison, distributed moderation offers more robustness and defense in depth. Centralized moderation offers a clear focal point for policy-making. If you don't like my post, you know where to complain." James Grimmelmann, "The Virtues of Moderation," *Yale Journal of Law and Technology* 17 (2015): 42–368.

77. Rahman, "The New Utilities," 1639; K. Sabeel Rahman, "Regulating Informational Infrastructure: Internet Platforms as the New Public Utilities," *Georgetown Law Technology Review* 2,

no. 2 (2018): 234; K. Sabeel Rahman, *Democracy against Domination* (Oxford: Oxford University Press, 2017).

78. Rahman, "The New Utilities," 1629; Ganesh Sitaraman, "Regulating Tech Platforms: A Blueprint for Reform," The Great Democracy Initiative, April 2018, https://greatdemocracy initiative.org/document/regulating-tech/.

79. Tristan Harris, "EU Should Regulate Facebook and Google as 'Attention Utilities,'" *Financial Times*, March 1, 2020, https://www.ft.com/content/abd80d98-595e-11ea-abe5 -8e03987b7b20; Ryan Grim, "Steve Bannon Wants Facebook and Google Regulated Like Utilities," *Intercept*, July 27, 2017, https://theintercept.com/2017/07/27/steve-bannon-wants -facebook-and-google-regulated-like-utilities/; Hamish McRae, "Facebook Is Destined to Become a Regulated Public Utility," *Independent*, March 21, 2018, https://www.independent.co.uk /voices/facebook-cambridge-analytica-regulation-regulated-public-utility-a8267226.html.

80. Jorge Valero, "Vestager: 'I'd Like a Facebook That I Pay, with Full Privacy,'" June 27, 2018, https://www.euractiv.com/section/competition/interview/vestager-id-like-a-facebook-that-i -pay-with-full-privacy/.

81. Harris, "EU Should Regulate Facebook and Google as 'Attention Utilities.'"

82. Tom Wheeler, Phil Verveer, and Gene Kimmelman, "New Digital Realities: New Oversight Solutions," Harvard Kennedy School, Shorenstein Center on Media, Politics, and Public Policy, August 20, 2020, 3, https://shorensteincenter.org/new-digital-realities-tom-wheeler-phil -verveer-gene-kimmelman/; Tom Wheeler, Gene Kimmelman, and Phil Verveer, "The Need for Regulation of Big Tech beyond Antitrust," Brookings TechTank, September 23, 2020, https:// www.brookings.edu/blog/techtank/2020/09/23/the-need-for-regulation-of-big-tech-beyond -antitrust/.

83. Susan Crawford, "Calling Facebook a Utility Would Only Make Things Worse," *Wired*, April 28, 2018, https://www.wired.com/story/calling-facebook-a-utility-would-only-make -things-worse/; David McCabe, "Why Regulating Google and Facebook Like Utilities Is a Long Shot," *Axios*, September 22, 2017, https://www.axios.com/why-regulating-google-and-facebook -like-utilities-is-a-long-shot-1513305664-9a388f01-f71a-4b45-8844-fec8b74d95d6.html.

84. Peter Swire, "Should the Leading Online Tech Companies Be Regulated as Public Utilities?," Lawfare, August 2, 2017, https://www.lawfareblog.com/should-leading-online-tech -companies-be-regulated-public-utilities.

85. Wheeler, Verveer, and Kimmelman, "New Digital Realities," 16–17.

86. Ibid., 10.

87. "The focus on competition and demonstrable harm to consumers is completely misguided. It distorts the debate dramatically and distracts participants from the more important, fundamental question, which is what type of internet environment our society demands." Frischmann, *Infrastructure*, 327; Antonio García Martínez, "How Trump Conquered Facebook without Russian Ads," *Wired*, February 23, 2018, https://www.wired.com/story/how-trump -conquered-facebookwithout-russian-ads/; Aaron Sankin, "How Activists of Color Lose Battles against Facebook's Moderator Army," *Reveal*, August 17, 2017, https://revealnews.org/article /how-activists-of-color-lose-battles-against-facebooks-moderator-army/; Rahman, "The New Utilities"; Jean-Christophe Plantin, Carl Lagoze, Paul N. Edwards, and Christian Sandvig, "Infrastructure Studies Meet Platform Studies in the Age of Google and Facebook," *New Media and Society* 20, no. 1 (2018): 293–310.

Chapter 8. Regulating for Democracy

1. Aristotle, *The Politics, and the Constitution of Athens*, bk. III.11.

2. Jean-Jacques Rousseau, *Letters Written from the Mountain* (Hanover, NH: University Press of New England, 2001), 292–93.

3. John Dewey, "Creative Democracy: The Task before Us" (1939), in *Classic American Philosophers*, edited by Max Harold Fisch (New York: Appleton-Century-Crofts, 1951), 394.

4. US Senate Committee on Commerce, Science, and Transportation, "Protecting Kids Online: Testimony from a Facebook Whistleblower," October 5, 2021, https://www.commerce.senate.gov/2021/10/protecting%20kids%20online:%20testimony%20from%20a%20facebook%20whistleblower; "Facebook Whistleblower Frances Haugen Opening Statement Transcript: Senate Hearing on Children & Social Media," October 5, 2021, https://www.rev.com/blog/transcripts/facebook-whistleblower-frances-haugen-opening-statement-transcript-senate-hearing-on-children-social-media.

5. Sandel, *The Tyranny of Merit*, 108–12. The "bright lines" of truth we draw can "prevent us from taking seriously the disagreements of others and from seeing why what looks so evident to us often looks like propaganda or ignorance to others," which "only polarizes us further." Danielle Allen and Justin Pottle, "Democratic Knowledge and the Problem of Faction," Knight Foundation, 2018, 4–5, https://kf-site-production.s3.amazonaws.com/media_elements/files/000/000/152/original/Topos_KF_White-Paper_Allen_V2.pdf; Onora O'Neill, "Trust and Accountability in a Digital Age," *Philosophy* (London) 95, no. 1 (2020): 3–17.

6. Daniela Cammack, "Deliberation in Ancient Greek Assemblies," *Classical Philology* 115, no. 3 (2020): 486–522; James Fredal, *Rhetorical Action in Ancient Athens: Persuasive Artistry from Solon to Demosthenes* (Carbondale: Southern Illinois University Press, 2006); Danielle S. Allen, "The Flux of Time in Ancient Greece," *Daedalus* 132, no. 2 (2003): 62–73.

7. David Watkin, *The Roman Forum* (London: Profile Books, 2011); Gregor Kalas, *The Restoration of the Roman Forum in Late Antiquity: Transforming Public Space* (Austin: University of Texas Press, 2015).

8. Jürgen Habermas, *The Structural Transformation of the Public Sphere: An Inquiry into a Category of Bourgeois Society* (Cambridge, MA: MIT Press, 1989); Dorinda Outram, *The Enlightenment* (Cambridge: Cambridge University Press, 2005), introduction; Mayor of London and London Assembly, "Public London Charter," October 8, 2021, https://www.london.gov.uk/publications/public-london-charter (accessed January 15, 2021).

9. Napoli, *Social Media and the Public Interest*, 23; Cass R. Sunstein, *#Republic: Divided Democracy in the Age of Social Media* (Princeton, NJ: Princeton University Press, 2017). One way to enforce these public interest obligations would be to make Section 230 conditional on "compliance with various public interest requirements drawn from media and telecommunications policy traditions." Stigler Committee on Digital Platforms, *Final Report*, 191.

10. Dewey, "Creative Democracy," 394; Richard J. Bernstein, *Philosophical Profiles: Essays in a Pragmatic Mode* (Philadelphia: University of Pennsylvania Press, 2015), 260.

11. Sunstein, *#Republic*.

12. Haan, "Profits v. Principles"; Barry Bozeman, *Public Values and Public Interest: Counterbalancing Economic Individualism* (Washington, DC: Georgetown University Press, 2007); Istvan Hont, "The Early Enlightenment Debate on Commerce and Luxury," in *The Cambridge*

History of Eighteenth-Century Political Thought (Cambridge: Cambridge University Press, 2006), 377–418; Cordelli, *The Privatized State.*

13. "Unlike the *Sun,* Google and Facebook have become essential infrastructure, unavoidable to anyone who wants to participate in modern markets and social life. . . . Platforms must be regulated through the family of structural antimonopoly tools. . . . Any response to the problems of private informational infrastructure must be structural: They must alter the fundamental business model and dynamics of the firms themselves." Rahman and Teachout, "From Private Bads to Public Goods."

14. William Boyd, "Just Price, Public Utility, and the Long History of Economic Regulation in America," *Yale Journal on Regulation* 35, no. 721 (2018), https://papers.ssrn.com/abstract =3176224. Rahman and Teachout, "From Private Bads to Public Goods"; Harris, "EU Should Regulate Facebook and Google as 'Attention Utilities.'"

15. The principles that guide how and where these structural firewalls are imposed could be developed from the Radio Act of 1927, which established an exclusionary licensing agreement on the condition that broadcasters recognize that their purpose is to serve "the public interest, convenience, and necessity." See, for example, FCC v. Pacifica Foundation, 438 U.S. 726 (1978). There are, of course, valid concerns about the effectiveness of these firewalls in the newspaper industry, but the industry's aspiration to separate its editorial and commercial aspects is what matters. Kathleen Chaykowski, "Facebook to Prioritize 'Trustworthy' Publishers in News Feed," *Forbes,* January 19, 2018, https://www.forbes.com/sites/kathleenchaykowski/2018/01/19 /facebook-to-prioritize-trustworthy-publishers-in-news-feed/.

16. Haan, "Profits v. Principles."

17. Wu, *The Master Switch,* 301–4.

18. Lina M. Khan, "The Separation of Platforms and Commerce," *Columbia Law Review* 119, no. 4 (2019): 973–1098.

19. A regulator, such as the AI Platforms Agency described in this chapter, would investigate exactly how and where structural firewalls should be imposed on democratic utilities. Jean Tirole, "Why Google and Facebook Can't Be Broken up Like a Utility," Columbia Business School, August 13, 2018, https://www8.gsb.columbia.edu/articles/chazen-global-insights/why -google-and-facebook-can-t-be-broken-utility; National Conference on Citizenship, "Civic Signals," https://ncoc.org/civic-signals/; Eli Pariser and Danielle Allen, "To Thrive, Our Democracy Needs Digital Public Infrastructure," *Politico,* January 5, 2021, https://www.politico .com/news/agenda/2021/01/05/to-thrive-our-democracy-needs-digital-public-infrastructure -455061; Ethan Zuckerman, "The Case for Digital Public Infrastructure," Columbia University, Knight First Amendment Institute, January 17, 2020, https://knightcolumbia.org/content/the -case-for-digital-public-infrastructure; Commission on the Practice of Democratic Citizenship, "Our Common Purpose: Reinventing American Democracy for the 21st Century" (Cambridge, MA: American Academy of Arts and Sciences, 2020), https://www.amacad.org/sites/default /files/publication/downloads/2020-Democratic-Citizenship_Our-Common-Purpose_0.pdf.

20. Sunstein, *#Republic,* 212, 213, 214.

21. Geographic concentration forestalls Madison's geographic solution to faction, in which geography disperses people of similar opinions across large areas and forces each representative to reckon with diverse and plural views within their constituency. Allen and Pottle, "Democratic Knowledge and the Problem of Faction," 5.

22. This is Geoffrey Fowler's idea about one way we could use "technology to break down walls during this particularly divided moment. With access to more information than ever online, how could other points of view be so alien?" Geoffrey A. Fowler, "What if Facebook Gave Us an Opposing-Viewpoints Button?," *Wall Street Journal*, May 18, 2016, https://www.wsj.com /articles/what-if-facebook-gave-us-an-opposing-viewpoints-button-1463573101.

23. Allen and Pottle, "Democratic Knowledge and the Problem of Faction," 31.

24. The Communications Act of 1934 established the Federal Communications Commission and gave it the power to grant, renew, and modify licenses to broadcasters as "public convenience, interest or necessity requires" and to create "such rules and regulations and prescribe such restrictions and conditions . . . as may be necessary to carry out the [act's] provisions." Communications Act, 48 § 1064 (1934); Federal Communications Commission, "Editorializing by Broadcast Licensees" June 8, 1949, https://www.fcc.gov/document /editorializing-broadcast-licensees; Federal Communications Commission, "Applicability of the Fairness Doctrine in the Handling of Controversial Issues of Public Importance: Public Notice of July 1, 1964," Regulation 10426; Kathleen Ann Ruane, "Fairness Doctrine: History and Constitutional Issues," report for Congress (Washington, DC: Congressional Research Service, July 13, 2011), 2.

25. This argument draws on the architectural view of the First Amendment, in which the First Amendment empowers government to pursue affirmative public ends through public ends, rather than simply protecting individual rights against government power. Red Lion Broadcasting Co., Inc., v. FCC, 395 U.S. 367 (1969); Owen M. Fiss, "Free Speech and Social Structure," *Iowa Law Review* 71, no. 5 (1986): 1405.

26. Despite insisting that they are not media, tech companies have increasingly moved into content production, such as with Apple TV. Philip Napoli and Robyn Caplan, "Why Media Companies Insist They're Not Media Companies, Why They're Wrong, and Why It Matters," *First Monday* 22, no. 5 (May 1, 2017): 26.

27. Jill Lepore, "The Hacking of America," *New York Times*, September 14, 2018, https://www .nytimes.com/2018/09/14/sunday-review/politics-disruption-media-technology.html. Facebook and Google relate to the internet a bit like cable TV networks relate to broadcasting, or radio networks relate to the radio. Just as the FCC extended its regulatory authority to cable TV and radio networks because they were deemed auxiliary to broadcasting and radio, Napoli argues, the FCC should extend its regulatory authority over ISPs to Facebook and Google. United States v. Southwestern Cable Co., 392 U.S. 197 (1968); Napoli and Caplan, "Why Media Companies Insist They're Not Media Companies." In *Red Lion Broadcasting v. FCC* (1969), which established the bottleneck concept, the Supreme Court upheld the fairness doctrine on public interest grounds. Red Lion Broadcasting Co., Inc., v. FCC, 395 at 390. The Court's rejection of *Red Lion* in *Reno v. ACLU*, based on the assertion that "the special factors recognized" as "justifying regulation of the broadcast media" were "not present in cyberspace," may not apply to Facebook and Google's ranking systems, which, by solving a problem of abundance, impose a kind of artificial scarcity on the content thrust into people's homes. Reno v. ACLU, 521 at 845. Samples and Matzko write, "If reformers can successfully assert that the internet falls under the public interest standard, Red Lion could be used to defend expansive internet speech regulations." Red Lion Broadcasting Co., Inc., v. FCC, 395 at 400; John Samples and Paul Matzko, "Social Media Regulation in the Public Interest: Some Lessons from History," Columbia Uni-

versity, Knight First Amendment Institute, May 4, 2020, https://knightcolumbia.org/content
/social-media-regulation-in-the-public-interest-some-lessons-from-history. As Lakier writes:
"The First Amendment—particularly as it is currently understood—makes regulating the platform public sphere more challenging, even when what those regulations seek to do is the same
thing the First Amendment is supposed to do." To the extent that there is a conflict between
First Amendment jurisprudence and regulating Facebook and Google to support the flourishing of democracy, she concludes, perhaps "it is First Amendment law that ultimately has to
change, and not our regulatory ambitions." Lakier, "The Limits of Antimonopoly Law."

28. Interestingly, these discussions often come at the end of the texts. Two examples are the
second two books of Hobbes's *Leviathan*, in which he gives an account of ecclesiastical power in
a commonwealth, and the second part of Rousseau's *Discourse on Inequality*, in which he explores
the role of family, education, and religion in a self-governing community. Thomas Hobbes, *Hobbes:
Leviathan*, edited by Richard Tuck (Cambridge: Cambridge University Press, 1996); Jean-Jacques
Rousseau, *The Social Contract and Other Later Political Writings* (Cambridge: Cambridge University Press, 1997); Christopher Brooke, "Nonintrinsic Egalitarianism, from Hobbes to Rousseau,"
Journal of Politics 82, no. 4 (2020): 1406–17; Dewey, *The Public and Its Problems*; John Dewey, *Democracy and Education: An Introduction to the Philosophy of Education* (London: Free Press, 1966).

29. Cass R. Sunstein, *Republic.Com 2.0* (Princeton, NJ: Princeton University Press, 2007),
143–44; Commission on the Practice of Democratic Citizenship, "Our Common Purpose";
Cass R. Sunstein and Edna Ullmann-Margalit, "Solidarity Goods," *Journal of Political Philosophy*
9, no. 2 (2001): 129–49.

30. For example, the Radio Commission created by the Radio Act of 1927 had two obligations: first, to regulate the airwaves in the "public interest, convenience, or necessity," and second, to prohibit censorship or any interference with "the right of free speech by means of radio
communications." Samples and Matzko, "Social Media Regulation in the Public Interest," 22.

31. Ibid., 26.

32. The Supreme Court has ruled that the US Constitution "does not disable the government
from taking steps to ensure that private interests not restrict, through physical control of a critical pathway of communication, the free flow of information and ideas." As Justice Stephen
Breyer wrote, policies that impose public interest obligations on corporations that exercise
bottleneck power over the flow of information and ideas "seek to facilitate the public discussion
and informed deliberation, which, as Justice Brandeis pointed out many years ago, democratic
government presupposes and the First Amendment seeks to achieve." Turner Broadcasting
System, Inc., v. FCC, 520 at 180, 227.

33. Furman, "Unlocking Digital Competition," 2.

34. Often the two arguments at play here simply talk past each other. Proponents of public
utility regulation argue that competition policy will be ineffective because Facebook and Google
are natural monopolies. Opponents like Jason Furman then respond that public utility regulation
would itself make Facebook and Google into monopolies by forestalling economic competition.
How we regulate Facebook and Google should not depend on these predictive judgments about
whether they are or are not natural monopolies, but on how best to ensure that the exercise of
their distinctive infrastructural power supports the flourishing of democracy. US House of Representatives Judiciary Committee, Subcommittee on Antitrust, Commercial, and Administrative
Law, *Investigation of Competition in Digital Markets: Majority Staff Report and Recommendations*,

2020, https://judiciary.house.gov/uploadedfiles/competition_in_digital_markets.pdf; US Department of Justice, "Complaint"; Federal Trade Commission, "Complaint for Injunctive and Other Equitable Relief," filed January 13, 2021, https://www.ftc.gov/system/files/documents/cases/051_2021.01.21_revised_partially_redacted_complaint.pdf; Furman, "Unlocking Digital Competition"; Competition and Markets Authority (CMA), *Online Platforms and Digital Advertising: Market Study Final Report*, July 1, 2020, https://assets.publishing.service.gov.uk/media/5efc57ed3a6f4023d242ed56/Final_report_1_July_2020_.pdf.

35. US Department of Justice, "Complaint"; Stigler Committee on Digital Platforms, *Final Report*; CMA, *Online Platforms and Digital Advertising*; House Subcommittee on Antitrust, Commercial, and Administrative Law, *Investigation of Competition in Digital Markets*; Doctorow, "How to Destroy 'Surveillance Capitalism.'"

36. I agree with Cory Doctorow that the "EU's new Directive on Copyright, Australia's new terror regulation, America's FOSTA/SESTA sex-trafficking law and more—are death warrants for small, upstart competitors . . . who lack the deep pockets of established incumbents to pay for all these automated systems." By focusing on specific legal duties to address specific kinds of content, instead of establishing structures of governance underpinned by broad principles, "these rules put a floor under how small we can hope to make Big Tech." Doctorow, "How to Destroy 'Surveillance Capitalism.'"

37. Competition and Markets Authority, "A New Pro-Competition Regime for Digital Markets: Advice of the Digital Markets Taskforce," December 2020, 5–6, https://assets.publishing.service.gov.uk/media/5fce7567e90e07562f98286c/Digital_Taskforce_-_Advice_--.pdf; Furman, "Unlocking Digital Competition," 9–10.

38. Harold Feld argues for sector-specific regulation instead of treating Facebook and Google as public utilities. The content of his argument closely mirrors my own:

> We therefore need not concern ourselves with whether specific digital platforms, or certain services such as search and social media, are "public utilities." Despite 15 years of argument over the status of broadband and net neutrality thoroughly confusing the matter, sector-specific regulation—including common carriage—does not need a finding that the service is a "public utility." It is enough to observe that digital platforms have clearly reached a level of prominence in our economy and in our lives to constitute a business "affected with the public interest." Taxi cabs are regulated as common carriers not because they are monopolies or public utilities, but because of their public character. . . . By the same token, digital platforms have become integral to our economy, with some becoming impossible to avoid in any realistic way. . . . By any criteria one uses to measure importance in our lives, digital platforms clearly meet them as a sector in need of oversight. No other sector of the economy, with the possible exception of the physical infrastructure through which digital platforms reach their users, has so much power to affect us in so many ways, yet remains subject to such little public oversight. If we are to remain a democratic society where citizens genuinely govern themselves, this needs to change. As was the case of the grain elevators in Munn v. Illinois, we have no difficulty concluding that digital platforms are "clothed in the public interest" and that sector-specific regulation is required to protect consumers, promote competition, and generally serve the public interest, convenience, and necessity.

Harold Feld, "The Case for the Digital Platform Act: Market Structure and Regulation of Digital Platforms," Roosevelt Institute, May 2019, 54, https://rooseveltinstitute.org/publications /the-case-for-the-digital-platform-act-market-structure-and-regulation-of-digital-platforms/.

39. The House Subcommittee on Antitrust, Commercial, and Administrative Law report quotes Supreme Court justice Louis Brandeis (although there is no evidence that Brandeis ever actually said this): "'We must make our choice. We may have democracy, or we may have wealth concentrated in the hands of a few, but we cannot have both.' Those words speak to us with great urgency today." House Subcommittee on Antitrust, Commercial, and Administrative Law, *Investigation of Competition in Digital Markets*, 7; Richard Hofstadter, "What Happened to the Antitrust Movement?," in Hofstadter, *The Paranoid Style in American Politics: And Other Essays* (New York: Knopf, 1965); Robert Pitofsky, "The Political Content of Antitrust," *University of Pennsylvania Law Review* 127, no. 4 (1979): 1051–75; Barak Orbach, "How Antitrust Lost Its Goal," *Fordham Law Review* 81, no. 5 (2013): 2253–77.

40. A range of technical methods have been developed to describe the inner logic of machine learning models. Riccardo Guidotti, Anna Monreale, Salvatore Ruggieri, Franco Turini, Fosca Giannotti, and Dino Pedreschi, "A Survey of Methods for Explaining Black Box Models," *ACM Computing Surveys* (CSUR) 51, no. 5 (2018): 1–42; Philip Adler, Casey Falk, Sorelle A. Friedler, Tionney Nix, Gabriel Rybeck, Carlos Scheidegger, Brandon Smith, and Suresh Venkatasubramanian, "Auditing Black-Box Models for Indirect Influence," *Knowledge and Information Systems* 54, no. 1 (2018): 95–122; Andrew Selbst and Solon Barocas, "The Intuitive Appeal of Explainable Machines," *Fordham Law Review* 87, no. 3 (2018): 1085; Zachary C. Lipton, "The Mythos of Model Interpretability," Workshop on Human Interpretability in Machine Learning, New York, 2016, arXiv:1606.03490v3 [cs.LG], March 6, 2017, https://sites.rutgers.edu/critical-ai/wp -content/uploads/sites/586/2022/02/Lipton_The-Mythos-of-Model-Interpretability.pdf; Joshua A. Kroll, Joanna Huey, Solon Barocas, Edward W. Felten, Joel R. Reidenberg, David G. Robinson, and Harlan Yu, "Accountable Algorithms," *University of Pennsylvania Law Review* 165, no. 3 (2017): 633–705; Jatinder Singh, Ian Walden, Jon Crowcroft, and Jean Bacon, "Responsibility and Machine Learning: Part of a Process," October 28, 2016, https://papers.ssrn.com/sol3 /papers.cfm?abstract_id=2860048; Marco Tulio Ribeiro, Sameer Singh, and Carlos Guestrin, "'Why Should I Trust You?': Explaining the Predictions of Any Classifier," arXiv:1602.04938v3 [cs.LG], February 16, 2016, revised August 3 and August 9, 2016, 1135–44, https://doi.org/10 .48550/arXiv.1602.04938; Tameru Hailesilassie, "Rule Extraction Algorithm for Deep Neural Networks: A Review," *International Journal of Computer Science and Information Security* 14, no. 7 (2016): 376–80.

41. Pasquale, *New Laws of Robotics*; Frank Pasquale, *The Black Box Society: The Secret Algorithms That Control Money and Information* (Cambridge, MA: Harvard University Press, 2015); Cynthia Rudin, "Stop Explaining Black Box Machine Learning Models for High Stakes Decisions and Use Interpretable Models Instead," *Nature Machine Intelligence* 1, no. 5 (2019): 206–15; Guidotti et al., "A Survey of Methods for Explaining Black Box Models." Some argue that the EU's General Data Protection Regulation (GDPR) addresses this issue by requiring individuals to be provided with "meaningful information about the logic involved" in an automated decision as part of the right to contest these decisions and to enforce other rights (see Articles 22, 13, 14, and 15). This is often called the "right to an explanation." Margot E. Kaminski, "The Right to Explanation, Explained," *Berkeley Technology Law Journal* 34, no. 1 (2019): 26; Isak Mendoza

and Lee A. Bygrave, "The Right Not to Be Subject to Automated Decisions Based on Profiling," in *EU Internet Law: Regulation and Enforcement*, edited by Tatiana-Eleni Synodinou, Philippe Jougleux, Christiana Markou, and Thalia Prastitou (Cham, Switzerland: Springer International, 2017); Bryce Goodman and Seth Flaxman, "European Union Regulations on Algorithmic Decision Making and a 'Right to Explanation,'" *AI Magazine* 38, no. 3 (2017): 50–57; Gianclaudio Malgieri and Giovanni Comandé, "Why a Right to Legibility of Automated Decision-Making Exists in the General Data Protection Regulation," *International Data Privacy Law* 7, no. 4 (2017): 243–65; Andrew D. Selbst and Julia Powles, "Meaningful Information and the Right to Explanation," *International Data Privacy Law* 7, no. 4 (2017): 233–42.

42. Kate Klonick, "Facebook Released Its Content Moderation Rules. Now What?," *New York Times*, April 26, 2018, https://www.nytimes.com/2018/04/26/opinion/facebook-content-moderation-rules.html; Jeremy Waldron, "Accountability: Fundamental to Democracy," New York University School of Law, Public Law Research Paper 14–13, April 1, 2014, http://dx.doi.org/10.2139/ssrn.2410812; Craig T. Borowiak, *Accountability and Democracy: The Pitfalls and Promise of Popular Control* (Oxford: Oxford University Press, 2011); Alexander H. Trechsel, "Reflexive Accountability and Direct Democracy," *West European Politics* 33, no. 5 (2010): 1050–64; Adam Przeworski, Susan Carol Stokes, and Bernard Manin, *Democracy, Accountability, and Representation* (Cambridge: Cambridge University Press, 1999); James D. Fearon, "Self-Enforcing Democracy," *Quarterly Journal of Economics* 126, no. 4 (2011): 1661–1708.

43. Cary Coglianese and David Lehr, "Regulating by Robot: Administrative Decision Making in the Machine-Learning Era," *Georgetown Law Journal* 105, no. 5 (2017): 1147–1223; Zemel et al., "Learning Fair Representations," 325–33.

44. Kaminski, "The Right to Explanation, Explained," 8; Margot E. Kaminski, "Binary Governance: Lessons from the GDPR's Approach to Algorithmic Accountability," March 12, 2019, DOI:10.2139/SSRN.3351404; Kroll et al., "Accountable Algorithms," 660; Selbst and Barocas, "The Intuitive Appeal of Explainable Machines," 1133.

45. An explanation that supports the form of justification required by accountability would answer the following questions: What are the goals of the decision-making procedure? What are the company policies that constrain or inform the decision-making procedure, including the role that machine learning plays within it? In machine learning specifically: How did the company define the outcomes of interest? How did the company select and construct its training data? How was the data labeled and by whom? Was the impact of using other training data considered? What features were included or excluded in the model? Does the decision-making procedure involve human discretion? How precisely do the automated and human elements of the decision-making procedure interact? Has the company considered how this interaction affects aggregate outcomes? Data protection impact assessments (DPIAs) could help elicit these justifications, as an "iterative process" for examining how decision-making procedures are designed and implemented. Bryan Casey, Ashkon Farhangi, and Roland Vogl, "Rethinking Explainable Machines: The GDPR's 'Right to Explanation' Debate and the Rise of Algorithmic Audits in Enterprise," *Berkeley Technology Law Journal* 34, no. 1 (January 1, 2019): 33; European Commission, "Newsroom: Guidelines on Automated Individual Decision-Making and Profiling for the Purposes of Regulation 2016/679," Article 29 Data Protection Working Party (A29WP), February 6, 2018, 29, https://ec.europa.eu/newsroom/article29/items/612053/en; Harris, "Data Protection Impact Assessments"; Lilian Edwards and Michael Veale, "Slave to the

Algorithm? Why a 'Right to an Explanation' Is Probably Not the Remedy You Are Looking For," *Duke Law and Technology Review* 16, no. 1 (2017): 18.

46. Demands for transparency tend to assume that if provided with the necessary information, people will take action against decisions they think are wrong. There are good reasons to be skeptical about this; many years of research have demonstrated that there is a significant gap between the promise of disclosure and its practical impacts. David E. Pozen, "Transparency's Ideological Drift," *Yale Law Journal* 128, no. 1 (2018); Lauren E. Willis, "The Consumer Financial Protection Bureau and the Quest for Consumer Comprehension," *RSF: Russell Sage Foundation Journal of the Social Sciences* 3, no. 1 (2017): 74–93; Omri Ben-Shahar, *More than You Wanted to Know: The Failure of Mandated Disclosure* (Princeton, NJ: Princeton University Press, 2014); Talia B. Gillis, "Putting Disclosure to the Test: Toward Better Evidence-Based Policy," *Consumer Law Review* 28, no. 1 (2015); Ryan Bubb, "TMI? Why the Optimal Architecture of Disclosure Remains TBD," *Michigan Law Review* 113, no. 6 (2015): 1021–42; Archon Fung, *Full Disclosure: The Perils and Promise of Transparency* (Cambridge: Cambridge University Press, 2007).

47. Mike Ananny and Kate Crawford, "Seeing without Knowing: Limitations of the Transparency Ideal and Its Application to Algorithmic Accountability," *New Media and Society* 20, no. 3 (2018): 973–89; Adrian Weller, "Challenges for Transparency," arXiv:1708.01870v1 [cs.CY], July 29, 2017, revised August 19, 2019, https://doi.org/10.48550/arXiv.1708.01870; Danielle Citron, "What to Do about the Emerging Threat of Censorship Creep on the Internet," Cato Institute, November 28, 2017; Tal Z. Zarsky, "Transparent Predictions," *University of Illinois Law Review* 2013, no. 4 (2013): 1503–69.

48. Edwards and Veale, "Slave to the Algorithm?"; David Brin, *The Transparent Society: Will Technology Force Us to Choose between Privacy and Freedom?* (Reading, MA: Addison-Wesley, 1998); Will Thomas Devries, "Protecting Privacy in the Digital Age," *Berkeley Technology Law Journal* 18, no. 1 (2003): 283–311; Joshua A. T. Fairfield and Christoph Engel, "Privacy as a Public Good," *Duke Law Journal* 65, no. 3 (2016): 385–457.

49. The GDPR's focus on individual rights, as well as its notice and consent framework, are characteristic of approaches to regulation focused on privacy. As Margot Kaminski puts it, "the strong system of individual rights" within the GDPR may come "at the cost of correcting systemic problems essential for achieving accountability in modern democracies." The GDPR itself is framed as a privacy law, even though its focus reaches far beyond the confines of privacy. Kaminski, "Binary Governance," 74; Lilian Edwards, "Privacy, Law, Code, and Social Networking Sites," in *Research Handbook on Governance of the Internet*, edited by Ian Brown (Cheltenham, UK: Edward Elgar Publishing, 2013); Elizabeth Denham, "Consent Is Not the 'Silver Bullet' for GDPR Compliance," WiredGov, Information Commissioner's Office, August 16, 2017, https://ico.org.uk/about-the-ico/news-and-events/blog-consent-is-not-the-silver-bullet-for-gdpr-compliance/.

50. Wheeler, Verveer, and Kimmelman, "New Digital Realities," 20; Competition and Markets Authority, "A New Pro-Competition Regime for Digital Markets"; Andrew Tutt, "An FDA for Algorithms," *Administrative Law Review* 69, no. 1 (2016): 83–123; Oren Bracha and Frank Pasquale, "Federal Search Commission? Access, Fairness, and Accountability in the Law of Search," *Cornell Law Review* 93, no. 6 (2008): 1149; Frank Pasquale, *New Laws of Robotics: Defending Human Expertise in the Age of AI* (Cambridge, MA: Belknap Press of Harvard University Press, 2020).

51. Commission on the Practice of Democratic Citizenship, "Our Common Purpose," 51; Rahman, *Democracy against Domination*; Borowiak, *Accountability and Democracy*, 179.

52. Archon Fung and Erik Olin Wright, "Deepening Democracy: Innovations in Empowered Participatory Governance," *Politics and Society* 29, no. 1 (2001): 5–41.

53. Jane Mansbridge, "Everyday Talk in the Deliberative System," in *Deliberative Politics: Essays on Democracy and Disagreement*, edited by Stephen Macedo (Oxford: Oxford University Press, 1999), 199; Jane Mansbridge, James Bohman, Simone Chambers, Thomas Christiano, Archon Fung, John Parkinson, Dennis F. Thompson, and Mark E. Warren, "A Systemic Approach to Deliberative Democracy," in *Deliberative Systems*, edited by John Parkinson and Jane Mansbridge (Cambridge: Cambridge University Press, 2012); Michael A. Neblo, Kevin M. Esterling, and David M. J. Lazer, *Politics with the People: Building a Directly Representative Democracy*, vol. 555, Cambridge Studies in Public Opinion and Political Psychology (Cambridge: Cambridge University Press, 2018); Hélène Landemore, *Democratic Reason: Politics, Collective Intelligence, and the Rule of the Many* (Princeton, NJ: Princeton University Press, 2013); Michael A. Neblo, *Deliberative Democracy between Theory and Practice* (New York: Cambridge University Press, 2015), 151; John Dryzek et al., "The Crisis of Democracy and the Science of Deliberation," *Science* 363 (March 15, 2019): 1144–46.

54. Douek, "Facebook's 'Oversight Board.'"

55. The United Kingdom has recently used citizen assemblies to develop policy to regulate machine learning models. Over five days, these eighteen-member panels learned about machine learning, considered how it is used in particular contexts, and then generated sound judgments— for instance, that explanations of the predictions of the machine learning models used in health care need not be provided where no comparable explanations would have been offered by humans. Center for New Democratic Processes, "Citizens Juries on Artificial Intelligence," Jefferson Center, https://www.jefferson-center.org/citizens-juries-artificial-intelligence/.

56. Michael Schudson, *The Good Citizen: A History of American Civic Life* (New York: Free Press, 1998), 310; Pettit, *On the People's Terms*, 225–26; Alfred James Moore, *Critical Elitism: Deliberation, Democracy, and the Problem of Expertise* (Cambridge: Cambridge University Press, 2017), 183; James S. Fishkin, *Democracy and Deliberation: New Directions for Democratic Reform* (New Haven, CT: Yale University Press, 1991); Shapiro, *Politics against Domination*; Shapiro, *The Real World of Democratic Theory*; Nadia Urbinati, *Representative Democracy: Principles and Genealogy* (Chicago: University of Chicago Press, 2006).

57. Jonathan Zittrain, "A Jury of Random People Can Do Wonders for Facebook," *Atlantic*, November 14, 2019, https://www.theatlantic.com/ideas/archive/2019/11/let-juries-review-facebook-ads/601996/; Robert E. Goodin, *An Epistemic Theory of Democracy* (Oxford: University Press, 2018), chap. 1.

58. Zittrain, "A Jury of Random People Can Do Wonders for Facebook"; Fung and Wright, "Deepening Democracy," 40; Rob D. Fish, Michael Winter, David M. Oliver, Dave Robert Chadwick, Chris J. Hodgson, and Ann Louise Heathwaite, "Employing the Citizens' Jury Technique to Elicit Reasoned Public Judgments about Environmental Risk: Insights from an Inquiry into the Governance of Microbial Water Pollution," *Journal of Environmental Planning and Management* 57, no. 2 (2014): 233–53; Walter F. Baber and Robert V. Bartlett, *Consensus and Global Environmental Governance: Deliberative Democracy in Nature's Regime* (Cambridge, MA: MIT Press, 2015).

59. Fung and Wright, "Deepening Democracy"; Dryzek et al., "The Crisis of Democracy and the Science of Deliberation"; Moore, *Critical Elitism*.

60. Ober, *Demopolis*, 119. "Athenian democratic institutions and practices . . . can be understood as a kind of machine whose design facilitated the aggregation of useful knowledge and produced benefits of routinization while maintaining a capacity for innovation. The machine of Athenian government was fuelled by incentives, oiled by low communication costs and efficient means of transfer, and regulated by formal and informal sanctions" (125).

Conclusion

1. Rousseau, *Letters Written from the Mountain*, 306.

2. Winston Churchill, address to the House of Commons, October 31, 1944.

3. "TrumpScript," DevPost, https://devpost.com/software/trumpscript (accessed February 12, 2021).

4. Surveys have found that one in four would be happy for AI to make policy rather than politicians. Oscar Jonsson and Carlos Luca de Tena, "European Tech Insights 2019," Center for the Governance of Change, 2019, https://docs.ie.edu/cgc/European-Tech-Insights-2019.pdf.

5. Brian Wheeler, "Nigel—the Robot That Could Tell You How to Vote," BBC News, September 17, 2017, https://www.bbc.com/news/uk-politics-40860937.

6. Ibid.; Thomas Frey, "Will Artificial Intelligence Improve Democracy or Destroy It?," Futurist Speaker, March 26, 2016, https://futuristspeaker.com/artificial-intelligence/will-artificial-intelligence-improve-democracy-or-destroy-it/.

7. Wheeler, "Nigel"; César Hidalgo, *A Bold Idea to Replace Politicians*, TED2018, June 2018, https://www.ted.com/talks/cesar_hidalgo_a_bold_idea_to_replace_politicians.

8. Madison continues: "Under such a regulation, it may well happen that the public voice pronounced by the representatives of the people, will be more consonant to the public good, than if pronounced by the people themselves." Alexander Hamilton and James Madison, *The Federalist* (Cambridge: Cambridge University Press, 2007), chap. 10; Ellen Meiksins Wood, "Demos versus "We, the People": Freedom and Democracy Ancient and Modern," in *Dēmokratia: A Conversation on Democracies, Ancient and Modern*, edited by Josiah Ober and Charles W. Hedrick (Princeton, NJ: Princeton University Press, 1996); Joseph A. Schumpeter, *Capitalism, Socialism, and Democracy* (New York: Harper & Row, 1975), 256; William J. Meyer, "Democracy: Needs over Wants," *Political Theory* 2, no. 2 (1974): 202; Christopher H. Achen, *Democracy for Realists: Why Elections Do Not Produce Responsive Government* (Princeton, NJ: Princeton University Press, 2016), 2; Guillermo A. O'Donnell and Philippe C. Schmitter, *Transitions from Authoritarian Rule: Tentative Conclusions about Uncertain Democracies* (Baltimore: Johns Hopkins University Press, 1986), 5.

9. Immanuel Kant, *Political Writings* (Cambridge: Cambridge University Press, 1991), 41. Kant was strongly influenced by David Hume, who had developed a complex theory of patterns, correlations, and causation. Ibid., 41; David Hume, *A Treatise on Human Nature: Being an Attempt to Introduce the Experimental Method of Reasoning into Moral Subjects and Dialogues Concerning Natural Religion* (London: Longmans, Green and Co., 1874). New theories of probability are encouraging philosophers to ask interesting new questions about freedom, causation, and the will. Ted Honderich, ed., *Essays on Freedom of Action* (London: Routledge and Kegan Paul,

1973); Thomas Nagel, *The View from Nowhere* (New York: Oxford University Press, 1986); Timothy O'Connor, "Probability and Freedom: A Reply to Vicens," *Res Philosophica* 93, no. 1 (2016): 289–93; Ned Hall, "Two Concepts of Causation," in *Causation and Counterfactuals*, edited by John Collins, Ned Hall, and Paul Laurie (Cambridge, MA: MIT Press, 2004), 225–76; Dawid, "On Individual Risk"; Dawid, Musio, and Murtas, "The Probability of Causation."

10. Evgeny Morozov, *To Save Everything, Click Here: The Folly of Technological Solutionism* (New York: Public Affairs, 2013); Bernard E. Harcourt, "The Systems Fallacy: A Genealogy and Critique of Public Policy and Cost-Benefit Analysis," *Journal of Legal Studies* 47, no. 2 (2018): 419–47; Kwangseon Hwang, "Cost-Benefit Analysis: Its Usage and Critiques," *Journal of Public Affairs* 16, no. 1 (2016): 75–80.

11. Stigler Committee on Digital Platforms, *Final Report*, 31; CMA, "Online Platforms and Digital Advertising," 322.

12. Hofstadter, "What Happened to the Antitrust Movement?," 125; Michael J. Sandel, *Democracy's Discontent: America in Search of a Public Philosophy* (Cambridge, MA: Belknap Press of Harvard University Press, 1996), 232.

13. Hans B. Thorelli, *The Federal Antitrust Policy: Origination of an American Tradition* (Stockholm: Akademisk Avhandling, 1954), 227; Sandel, *Democracy's Discontent*, 232.

14. Sandel, *Democracy's Discontent*, chap. 7; Wu, *The Curse of Bigness*; Orbach, "How Antitrust Lost Its Goal"; Harry First and Spencer Weber Waller, "Antitrust's Democracy Deficit," *Fordham Law Review* 81, no. 5 (2013): 2574; Daniel A. Crane, *The Institutional Structure of Antitrust Enforcement* (Oxford: Oxford University Press, 2011); Daniel Crane, "Technocracy and Antitrust," *Texas Law Review* 86, no. 6 (2008): 1159–1221; Richard Du Boff and Edward Herman, "Mergers, Concentration, and the Erosion of Democracy," *Monthly Review* 53, no. 1 (2001): 14–29; Dunn, *Democracy*; Paul Fawcett, Matthew Flinders, Colin Hay, and Matthew Wood, *Anti-Politics, Depoliticization, and Governance* (Oxford: Oxford University Press, 2017).

15. "Technicians, by virtue of their training, cultivate the illusion that it is possible to rationally and 'objectively' determine not merely the means but also the objectives of political action. A discourse as relevant today as ever before, and which should be read as favouring the dispossession of politics by economics and technology, is that which speculates on the 'complexity of technological society' in order to turn government into a mere form of administration." Alain de Benoist, *The Problem of Democracy* (London: Arktos, 2011), 39.

16. Shapiro, *Politics against Domination*, 75.

INDEX

abundance of information. *See* problem of abundance

accountability gaps, 2–3, 14, 115–16, 200–207

accuracy, machine learning's promise of, 26, 40

Achen, Christopher, 214

Adams, John, 134

Adams, Tina, 133–34

advertising: Facebook and, 58–60, 62–64, 67–70, 72–73, 81–82, 99–100, 135, 148–51, 188–89, 241n12; shared experience as principle informing, 193–96; as source of revenue for Facebook and Google, 188–90; surveillance capitalism and, 147–48. *See also* profit motive

Aesop, 48

affirmative action, 38, 73, 95–99, 255n34, 257n49

African Americans: and bank loans, 33; and child welfare provision, 1, 13–14, 20, 22–23, 28, 31; and criminal justice system, 23, 36–37, 42; machine learning screening of language of, 139; predictive policing and, 55–56; stereotypes of, 34–35; structural inequalities affecting, 47–48. *See also* discrimination; protected groups

AFST. *See* Allegheny Family Screening Tool

AI Equality Act (AIEA), 84, 102–3, 218, 258n60

AI Platforms Agency (APA), 185, 204, 207–10, 218–19

Ali, Kabir, 104–5, 107, 126, 129

Allegheny Family Screening Tool (AFST), 1–4, 6, 14, 19–20, 22–23, 25–31, 43, 49, 86, 92, 215, 216, 230n40, 232n55, 236n18

Allen, Danielle, 85, 91

Alphabet, 106

alternative employment practices, 245n31

Amazon, 106

American Civil Liberties Union, 209

American Library Association, 209

Ananny, Mike, 153

Anderson, Elizabeth, 88

anticlassification, 43–44, 63, 71–74, 76–79, 82, 83, 99

anticorruption, 186–90. *See also* corruption critique

antiracism, 87

antisubordination: anticlassification in tension with, 71–77, 83; and antidiscrimination, 71–77, 79; and political equality, 82–83. *See also* nondomination

antitrust law, 173–74, 196–99, 220

APA. *See* AI Platforms Agency

Apple, 106

Arendt, Hannah, 132

Aristotle, 37, 48–49, 51–53, 84, 88, 183

Arizona Educators United, 134

artificial general intelligence, 213

artificial intelligence (AI), 17, 213. *See also* machine learning

Ashurbanipal, 141

association, freedom of, 85

Athens, 186

attention utilities, 178

predictive policing, 55–56, 93, 100–101,
154–55, 216
predictive tools: accountability gaps with,
2–3; deployment of, 25–28; design process, 17–25; expanding use of, 2–3; experience gaps with, 2–3; human decision
making overshadowed by, 2, 27; human
element in design of, 17; language gaps
with, 2–3; political character of, 9, 10, 28;
in politics, 213–18; problems with, 2–3;
relationship of past and future in, 15,
34–35, 45, 56, 58–59, 74, 105, 215–17; social
inequalities amplified and entrenched
by, 36, 95; unintended consequences of,
37–38, 42, 44–45, 49–50; values and goals
built into, 59, 80. *See also* machine
learning
PredPol, 93
privacy, 7–8, 201, 204–7, 258n57
problem of abundance, 106, 129–31, 135, 140,
144, 146, 167, 172, 175, 189, 193, 195
profit motive: Facebook, 108, 134–35, 139,
145–51, 168, 188–89; Google, 135, 145–51,
168, 188–89
Progressive era, 158–60, 162–64, 180–81, 198,
274n20
Proposition 209 (California Civil Rights
Initiative), 94
ProPublica, 36, 38, 42, 46–47, 49
protected groups: demographic parity and,
44–45, 70; moral and political relevance of
characteristics of, 37, 44, 51, 56–58, 83, 87,
94–101; proxy variables associated with,
63–64; reasons for designating, 71–73,
87–88; redundant encoding and, 24, 44;
subgroup calibration and, 42–43; use of
information indicating status in, 24, 41.
See also African Americans; anticlassification; discrimination; gender; social
inequalities
p(share), 108
public interest obligations, 158, 161–65, 170,
178–80, 186, 188–90, 192–93, 195, 199, 201,
282n27, 283n32

public sphere: digital, 7, 135–40, 159, 174,
176–77, 186, 190–92, 198, 201, 208; erosion
of, by technology companies, 146–47;
Facebook as digital public square vs.,
135–40, 145–46; Facebook's and Google's
shaping of, 158, 170–73, 181, 186; Facebook's claim to protect, 128; financing of,
188, 190; machine learning's shaping of, 7,
9, 105, 126, 129–30; news organizations'
influence on, 138; organic development
of, 146; political deliberation needed on
values and regulation of, 7, 9, 105, 126,
129–30, 185, 187–99, 203, 207–11; political
economy linked to, 148–51; political significance of, 140, 146, 186
public utilities, 159–78; applying concept of,
167–78; concept of, 159–67; economic
(common) conception of, 162–63; Facebook and Google compared to, 167–73,
177–80, 196; monopoly power of, 158, 159,
162–64; origins of, 160–62; political conception of, 164–67; regulation of, 160–62,
164–66, 178–80. *See also* democratic
utilities
Public Utility Holding Company Act, 167

race: as cultural construction, 89; different
conceptions and uses of, 88; differential
treatment based on, 90, 94, 99; life
chances and circumstances related to,
28, 60, 63, 253n23; political equality and,
89–90
racial inequality. *See* social inequality
racism: Google's search engine and, 104–5;
institutional, 251n64
Rahman, Sabeel, 166, 177–78
RankBrain, 124
ranking signals, 109
ranking systems: anticorruption as principle informing, 188–90; composed of multiple machine learning models, 108; diversity as principle informing, 191–93;
Facebook and, 7–8, 106–12, 127–29, 135, 146,
148–50, 155–56, 158, 167–69, 172, 175–78,

A NOTE ON THE TYPE

This book has been composed in Arno, an Old-style serif typeface in the
classic Venetian tradition, designed by Robert Slimbach at Adobe.